Architecture of Migration

THEORY IN FORMS A series edited by Nancy Rose Hunt, Achille Mbembe, and Todd Meyers

Architecture of Migration

THE DADAAB REFUGEE CAMPS AND HUMANITARIAN SETTLEMENT

Anooradha Iyer Siddiqi

DUKE UNIVERSITY PRESS Durham and London 2024

Printed in the United States of America on acid-free paper ∞
Project Editor: Lisa Lawley
Designed by Aimee Harrison
Typeset in Portrait Text and Ogg by Westchester Publishing Services

Library of Congress Cataloging-in-Publication Data
Names: Siddiqi, Anooradha Iyer, author.
Title: Architecture of migration : the Dadaab refugee camps and humanitarian settlement / Anooradha Iyer Siddiqi.
Other titles: Dadaab refugee camps and humanitarian settlement | Theory in forms.
Description: Durham : Duke University Press, 2023. | Series: Theory in forms | Includes bibliographical references and index.
Identifiers: LCCN 2023013739 (print)
LCCN 2023013740 (ebook)
ISBN 9781478025245 (paperback)
ISBN 9781478020387 (hardcover)
ISBN 9781478027379 (ebook)
ISBN 9781478093701 (ebook other)
Subjects: LSCH: Dadaab Refugee Camp. | Architecture and society—Kenya—Dadaab. | Refugee camps—Kenya—Dadaab. | Refugee camps—Kenya—Dadaab—History. | Refugee camps—Kenya—Dadaab——Design and construction. | Architecture—Political aspects—Kenya—Dadaab. | Refugees—Housing—Kenya—Dadaab—History. | Dwellings—Kenya—Dadaab—History. | BISAC: HISTORY / Africa / East | ARCHITECTURE / History / General
Classification: LCC NA2543.S6 S575 2023 (print) | LCC NA2543.S6 (ebook) | DDC 720.96762/27—dc23/eng/20230728
LC record available at https://lccn.loc.gov/2023013739
LC ebook record available at https://lccn.loc.gov/2023013740

Cover art: Deqa Abshir, *Fragmented II*, 2015. Mixed media on canvas, 90cm × 120 cm. Courtesy of the artist.

Subventions for this book's color image program and open-access distribution were provided by the Graham Foundation for Advanced Studies in the Fine Arts, Columbia University Seminars, and Barnard College.

Walter Benjamin purchased an oil transfer monoprint with watercolor, *Angelus Novus* by Paul Klee, in Munich in 1921. In contemplating the work, he concluded that we need history, that struggle is nourished by the image of enslaved ancestors rather than freed descendants. He famously wrote of a strong wind forcing open the wings of the angel of history, driving the angel backward as he faced the past, suspended open-mouthed as the rubble of events piled sky-high at his feet. I have watched Sahil and Ruhi's grandparents, also windswept, yet treading into the future, uncaptivated by that rubble—facing forward.

For Shanta Raman, Dr. K. Venkata Raman,
Professor Najma Siddiqi, and Dr. Hafiz G. A. Siddiqi

As we stand in your giant footsteps

No one leaves home unless
home is the mouth of a shark.
—Warsan Shire

A migrant who chooses to
rewrite an inherited destiny
swims against the current and
faces the wrath of the gatekeepers
who shape that destiny.
—Shahidul Alam

At its best and most powerful,
the aesthetic is also ethical.
—Ngũgĩ wa Thiong'o

(*previous page*) A provisions shop near Ifo camp where people first encounter settlement at Dadaab.

Contents

Abbreviations (xiii)
Author's Note (xv)

Introduction (1)
Architecture and History in a Refugee Camp

1 From Partitions (51)
2 Land, Emergency, and Sedentarization in East Africa (99)
3 Shelter and Domesticity (141)
4 An Archive of Humanitarian Settlement (181)
5 Design as Infrastructure (249)

Afterword (305)
"Poetry Is a Weapon That We Use in Both War and Peace"

Acknowledgments (321)
Notes (329)
Primary Sources (363)
References (371)
Index (397)

Abbreviations

ICRC	International Committee of the Red Cross
IFRC	International Federation of Red Cross and Red Crescent Societies
IRC	International Rescue Committee
LWET	Lightweight emergency tent
MSF	Médecins Sans Frontières (Doctors Without Borders)
NFD	Northern Frontier District
NGO	Nongovernmental organization
NRC	Norwegian Refugee Council
OAU	Organisation of African Unity
UN	United Nations
UNHCR	United Nations High Commissioner for Refugees
UNICEF	United Nations Children's Fund
WRC	Women's Refugee Commission
WFP	World Food Programme

Author's Note

In this book, I write in collaboration with many cotheorists, named and unnamed. As with histories for which documentary evidence is scarce or provisional, this one relies extensively on unwritten sources and oral transfer of knowledge. I acknowledge the latter by either directly or anonymously citing interlocutors (according to individual wishes) in the primary sources of this book, where I also discuss the ethical complexities of doing so.

Ideas in this book have appeared in all works by the author listed in the references. The dialogue in chapter 1 is republished with minor text and image edits from Siddiqi and Osman, "Traversals." The epigraphs in the preceding pages refer to Shire, "Home," 24; *Shahidul Alam: Truth to Power*; and Thiong'o, "Abdilatif Abdalla and the Voice of Prophecy," 15. (See the references for full bibliographic citations.)

Terms and titles often abbreviated in humanitarian parlance are typically written out in full in this book. However, the list in the preceding pages provides readers with a brief introduction to the bureaucratic vocabulary of acronyms for agencies and organizations representing powers in the field of contemporary international migration: a veritable language that refugees must learn.

As a straightforward means to honor and archive the refugee settlements and their makers, this book's pages are filled with photographs from Dadaab. Yet, we know photography is an intrusion. While always made with the permission of those pictured or the family or community members responsible for their care, these photos have especially attended to people who were public figures already or otherwise explicitly comfortable with the frame of exposure a scholarly publication might produce. (Unattributed photographs are by the author in Dadaab in 2011 unless other details are provided.) As part of writing this book, I engaged people whose perspectives did not involve population management or migration control to imagine and produce artworks that renarrate and countermap the Dadaab refugee camps. These artists' works appear in dedicated exhibitions, beginning in collaboration with the GoDown Arts Centre in Nairobi, a home for the archive of materials the research for this book has produced.

Architectures of migration, humanitarian settlement, and the materialities of Dadaab form part of a common history and heritage, which I have tried to convey in language accessible to many, even if in a work of academic scholarship written in English. Somali and Kiswahili terms appear in frequently transcribed English forms. The name "Dadaab" may refer to the refugee camps and humanitarian complex together or to the adjacent Kenyan town. The word "architecture" is used metaphorically or with disciplinary specificity as called for in the context of an argument, and is often open to the reader's interpretation or investment. The term "refugee" appears in its ordinary usage as a person escaping harm and also in its precise technical usage by the United Nations in reference to those crossing an international border.

Rather than rehearsing bureaucratic definitions, with regard to legal terms such as "refugee," "asylum seeker," and so on, I ask the reader to consider how we default to received language and instead think about how these terms come to stand in for people's life experiences. While work has been done to acknowledge the power structures attending concepts such as "borderland," "the field," "clan," "community," or "care," the value such vocabulary provides as a shorthand normalizes forms of violence.

This book eschews bureaucratic terms and instead takes a cue from poetics. An aim of this book is to seek new languages and ways to speak of Dadaab, as well as other worlds belonging to migrants toward which Dadaab gestures. An architectural history centering the paradoxes of aesthetics and politics and the many timespaces of African modernity offers a step toward finding those languages.

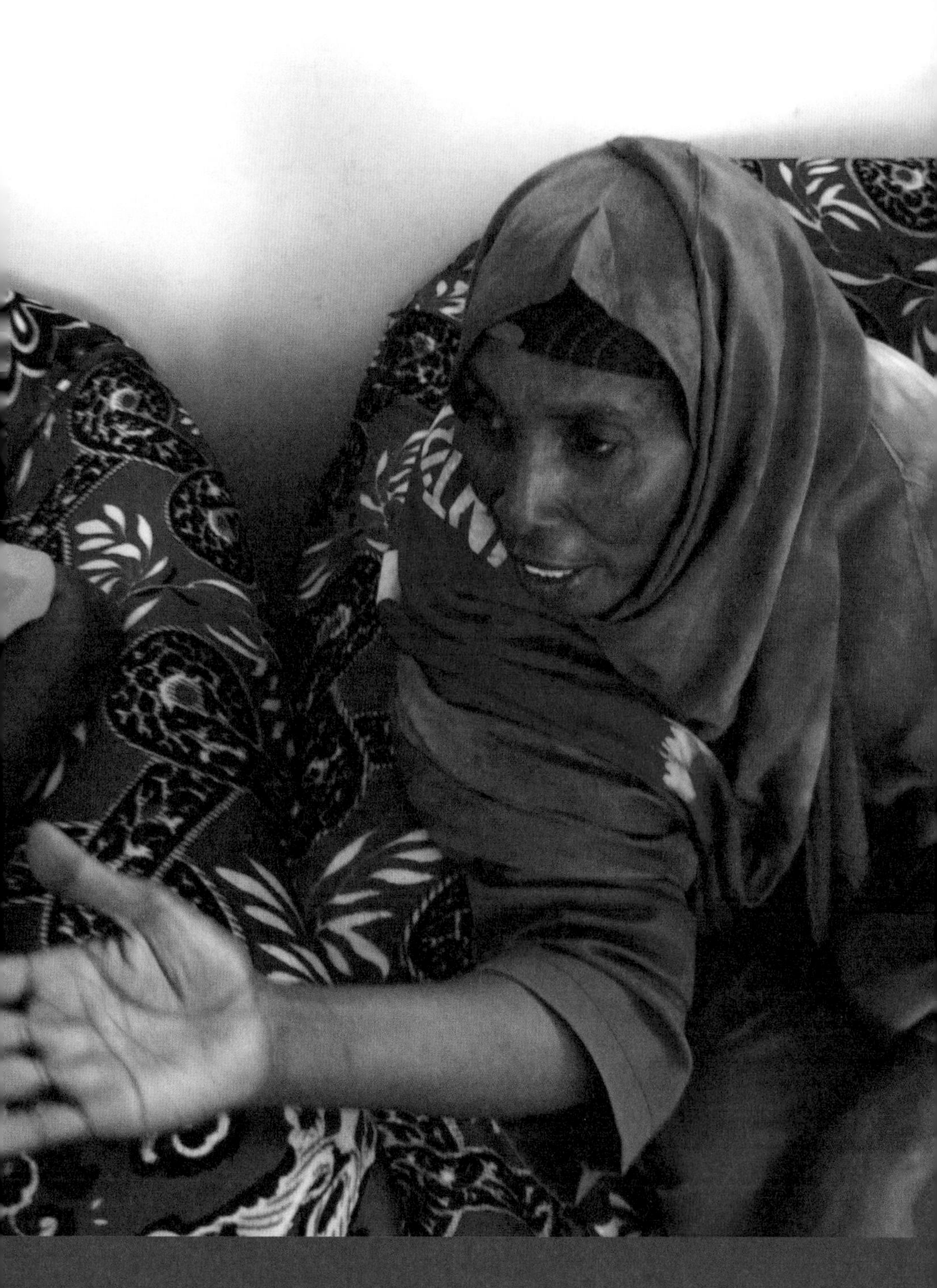

(*previous page*) Chairlady Isnina Ali Rage, Ifo camp.

Introduction

ARCHITECTURE AND HISTORY IN A REFUGEE CAMP

A refugee camp is not an object. It is one prolonged event in a history, marked through architecture. The migration occasioning this architecture results from disruption in state and civil order. This architecture extends emergency and gives it form through the materialization and visual rhetoric of precarity. As the architecture of emergency intervention reconfigures the state, international structures, and civil society, the ephemerality of the camp creates figurations of abjection, homelessness, and ahistoricity. This sleight of hand is performed in relation to predetermined frameworks for understanding forced migration only in its immediacy, and not as a factor within longer negotiated processes that slowly erode society and political and cultural imagination. These frameworks cast architecture only as an expression of fixity, establishment, and institution. They have yet to imagine an architecture of migration.

Preconceptions of violent migration and unsettlement circumscribe not only refugees' lives, but notions of home and history. These conditions consign the richer notions of domesticity to the provisionality of emergency shelter. They constrict histories to a limited scope of legitimacy, including only those framed by archives representing landed wealth and settlement. These circumscriptions would suggest that neither architecture nor history may be found in a refugee camp.

That this discourse falls into a racializing chassis may be too obvious to bear mention, as the question of whether or not something is architectural or historical has been inextricably bound up with questions of whether its proponents are fully human. Yet, centering such violence minimizes the more radical misdirection performed by this circumscription of architectures and histories. Such a limitation masks underlying migrations that form generative ways of life. These migratory worlds constitute alternate approaches to settlement, which resist colonization, fortification, and sedentarization. They propose architectural connections to the land other than those related to the political economy of resource extraction. Looking closely at the spatial and temporal paradoxes of a refugee camp brings into view how migration acts as a basis for people's lives, illuminating how historicity works, so that those lives are extended within landscapes of meaning and critical heritage.

What do we learn when we see a refugee camp? What lives and futures does its architecture trace? How does the space of emergency shape the experience of time? Can we imagine history and heritage in a humanitarian crisis? How does an architecture of migration build knowledge and consciousness for all? These are the questions that animate this book, as it brings into focus one set of refugee settlements as a basis for diverse explorations and concept histories. In 1991, near the village of Dadaab, Kenya, the United Nations High Commissioner for Refugees (UNHCR) initiated an emergency intervention that continues to the date of this writing, a relief operation spawning a temporary encampment into which three generations of people have been born. Dadaab is a Kenyan town whose English translation I have not found. The name also signifies a humanitarian complex of offices and staff residences opposite this town, across a highway, as well as camps to the north and south: Ifo; Dagahaley; Hagadera; Ifo 2; and, at one time, Kambioos. The Dadaab refugee complex began appearing on common maps with the advent of Google Earth in 2001, but for years it was the largest hosting operation ever undertaken by the UNHCR.[1] Its scale resulted from a policy instituted by the Kenyan government, which segregated and restricted the mobility of refugees. This form of apartheid impacted the education, labor, and migration of people. Dadaab has been called an "open-air prison," and in many ways it has been carceral.[2] Yet, it has cradled diverse experiences. In Dadaab, Isnina Ali Rage won an election. Alishine Osman joined the first cohort of refugee students passing through primary and secondary school. Maganai Saddiq Hassan designed and cultivated a farm. Shamso Abdullahi Farah built a home and a body of expertise. Sudanese and Somali women established a restaurant and founded construction workers' collectives. The experiences of these refugees underlie the making of this significant environment. This book sees them as architects and their work as an architecture of migration.

This book understands migration as its own form of knowledge. Through a refugee camp, I examine an architecture that has constricted movement and sedentarized people, yet nevertheless exposes longer migratory lifeways and traditions. While the category of refugee is a specific legal one, with political and social horizons different from those of the migrant, thinking with the Dadaab refugee camps allows us to place the refugee within the wider landscape of migration, regional and global, present and past.[3] People across statuses converge in Dadaab; all have migrated, and all have settled. I offer a concept history that uses the condition of migration as a method to study settlement.

A spatial politics of humanitarian settlement is the starting point for this book. The singularity and iconic role of the Dadaab refugee complex in the history of the international aid system provides a unique, urgent lens through which to investigate humanitarian settlement. More than any other documented emergency environment, Dadaab has functioned as a significant duty station for institutionally trained architects, arriving from around the world to work as physical planners and operations managers. The structure, infrastructure, and architecture of the complex of settlements iterate decades of emergency relief and physical planning expertise and have provided a test bed for design initiatives and spatial practice implemented worldwide. Dadaab has thus played an important part in a global history of architecture and an international field of humanitarian practice. From 1991 to the present day, Dadaab has been the site of many architectural and infrastructural projects, aggregating into a dense built environment. The refugee camps at Dadaab have housed temporarily displaced people and those joining a vast international diaspora, sustaining people's lives and the growth of communities. The camps have provided a workplace and residence for aid workers, officials in the international system, and architects and planners. If Dadaab has been a transitory space, it has also supported forms, spatial practices, and epistemologies of humanitarian settlement.

I argue for a knowledge gained through knowing Dadaab. Significant local and world histories converge in Dadaab, as explored in the chapters to follow, rendering it singular. Its architecture is not minor or unremarkable, but indeed historically and aesthetically distinct, authored, and monumental. Its epistemological richness provides the platform for diverse concept histories. The close examination of these problems is the aim of this book. Rather than allowing refugee camps to remain distant spaces formed from legal contracts, visible only in relation to the borders of the nation-state, these pages bring into full color the material practices and spaces generated by the forces of displacement and migration. In Dadaab, these practices and spaces are the results of design, construction, ecological and spatial imagination, and urbanism carried out by refugees as well as humanitarians. They scaffold forms of governance, political self-representation, and homemaking. I present Dadaab as a ground where people make worlds for themselves and where their worldmaking is conversant with global histories of abolition and humanitarianism. I show the vibrant empirical matter through which the Dadaab refugee camps offer a view into historicity and inhabitation, a springboard for theoretical conceptualization. Throughout, I follow individuals, in order to argue against monolithic understandings of refugee camps or humanitarian agencies and, instead, to make a place for a range of situated perspectives held by migrants, aid workers, architects, officials, and other figures. I trace the spatial complexity of the Dadaab refugee camps in the progression of this book as part of multiple histories within which they belong. At the levels of the camp and individual architectures, the camps serve at once as the culmination of a colonial territorial partition, a tool for land settlement, a testing ground for humanitarian shelter practices, and a significant iteration of the spatial languages of emergency relief. In these threads structuring the book's chapters, a seemingly irresolvable tension between the transience of the migrant and the anchoring of architecture imbricates migration and settlement.

This book pursues an architecture of migration that is full with epistemic possibilities. It eschews abstractions of refugee precarity, humanitarian emergency, or migration crisis, which collapse heterogeneous African and Muslim worlds into homogenous, othered zones. Instead, I make a space for diversity and polyvocality, inspired by pluralist and intersectional feminist thought: for example, legal scholar Sylvia Tamale's insistence on decolonizing master narratives that suppress multiplicity; law, development, and conflict studies scholar Radha D'Souza's complication of reductive "West versus Rest" critiques, through European underground and Third World intellectual perspectives; and anthropologist Saba Mahmood's assertions against universalizing epistemes, secular as well as religious, through the articulation of difference.[4] Building on these and other feminist framings, I suggest learning and imagining through the contours of the material and the sensible, through a historically specific architecture. If the term *architecture* implies an aesthetic approach that misunderstands or disregards political and humanitarian exigency, then this book begins with an argument for a different urgency, in which aesthetics and politics are inextricably entangled. Analyzing the architecture of a refugee camp through the affective, symbolic, and epistemic reverses the usual terms in which architecture is meant to represent a political framework. Through Dadaab, I argue instead that constructed environments and spatial practices inform political subjecthood and historical consciousness.

Dadaab lies at the core of an intellectual history. Rather than merely a flash point of crisis, the Dadaab refugee camps evince shades of meaning, whether seen as the artifact of institutions and the state or as the residue of people's lives and labor. The camps inscribe a condition in which the colonial has been immanent in the humanitarian, producing emergency and reproducing borders, but also entangling refugees and humanitarians in shared materialities and co-constructed territory. The ensuing architectural archive opens onto a people's history of land and migration. Much as architectural historian Esra Akcan has argued, in scholarship against borders, such aesthetic and historiographical openness creates an urgent generosity of theory that "has the strength of overcoming authority and chauvinism."[5] The following sections, which present, first, the social, historical, and environmental context of the Dadaab settlements "in situ" and, next, the epistemic possibility of a site "in theory," examine a politically complex and monumental architecture of migration.

Dadaab, in situ

To think with this architecture of migration first requires close looking, in order to see it in context and to see from its perspective. Dadaab is not merely an oppressed space and, indeed, has much to teach. Much in line with literary and media theorist Cajetan Iheka's vision, it presents an Africa of ecological degradation but also of generative accommodation.[6] Its discursive capacity is driven by its constitutive forms and environments, everyday landscapes that have been endowed with purpose by their designers and builders, similar to those built environment historian Sarah Lopez attributes to Mexican migrants who concretized "remitting as a way of life" by investing aspiration into seemingly ordinary architectures, either through individual acts of patronage or broader financial flows.[7] To understand such a capacity for architectural meaning, let us begin by hearing an inadvertent description of Dadaab's architecture by one of its elected leaders, pictured in the photo opening this chapter.

I met Isnina Ali Rage in 2011 while she served as Chairlady of Ifo camp, the first settlement to be established at Dadaab. Other refugees and aid workers spoke of her yearslong work on behalf of women in Ifo and her reputation as a leader able to resist the overwhelming temptations of power in Dadaab to persistently advocate for her constituents. I learned later from an aid worker that the Chairlady's unwillingness to compromise on principles put her life at risk, causing the UNHCR to resettle her to another country for her own safety. Our conversations focused on the election process and her advocacy work. I came to see her as a significant protagonist in Dadaab's history and also a custodian of its historical consciousness. Anthropologist Michel-Rolph Trouillot diagnosed the capacity of historical protagonists to become "aware of their vocality" and thus enact the subjectivity that "engages them simultaneously in the sociohistorical process and in narrative constructions about that process."[8] I did not discuss this theory with the Chairlady during the days we spent together in Dadaab, but her intellectual consciousness and political subjectivity were suggested in her comfortable movement between socially disparate communities and among leaders and officials, discussing women's advancement and representative self-governance in the camps. Her description of the process of refugee elections, in the following excerpt from one of our conversations, offers a glimpse into the formation of subjective narratives that arise from political self-realization and self-actualizing experiences.[9]

This conversation occurred during "country plan" meetings, moderated and recorded discussions between elected refugee representatives who met over the course of days to formulate a consensus contribution to Kenyan government policy. We talked outside the Ifo camp community center where the meetings were held, within the compound of the international organization CARE—one of the large World War II–era relief organizations that translated its postwar surplus resources and operations into international development aid—whose Kenya office managed the Dadaab refugee camps until 2006. As the Chairlady recounted her experience running for office, our colleague Hashim ("Abdullahi") Keinan, an interlocutor and interviewee in the research for this book, translated, interpreted, and occasionally intervened directly. A Kenyan raised in the Somali community in Dadaab, he worked in the camps after the refugees arrived as a staff member of the Norwegian Refugee Council (NRC), one of the twenty nongovernmental entities providing humanitarian aid and social services in Dadaab in 2011. As we conversed, it became difficult to distinguish story from setting; the twists in the Chairlady's narrative mapped directly onto the planned blocks and sections where they took place.

ANOORADHA IYER SIDDIQI: One of the things I'm studying is governance in the refugee camps. Can you talk more about your position?

ISNINA ALI RAGE: I'm the chairlady of Ifo camp. I was elected in 2008.

ANOORADHA IYER SIDDIQI: Tell me about the election.

ISNINA ALI RAGE: My election started at block level. In each block there are around three hundred people. They brought the ballot box.

In the block there was another lady, and she was fighting for the same position. From the male side, there were two who were fighting for the same position. Finally, it was me and a male counterpart who won the election.

The block that I was elected from is part of Section C. We have seven blocks. In that section, there were fifty-four community leaders who were elected. Twenty-seven of them were women, twenty-seven were men. The fifty-four community representatives elected me as their section leader.

In the camp, you have got 102 blocks. Within these blocks, 204 community representative leaders are elected, 102 of them being women and the other 102 men. There was another election within the representative leaders to elect the camp Chairlady and the camp Chairman. Of those who were vying, we were four female and six male candidates for the position of Chairlady and Chairman.

The campaign went on for five months! The election day was on the 20th of May, 2008.

HASHIM KEINAN [*for Isnina Ali Rage*]: On that night—the election was the following morning—she fell sick. She was pregnant, and she had a caesarean operation. From eight in the morning, the election started, while she was on the bed for a caesarean operation.

ISNINA ALI RAGE: I was told when I came from the theater: "You won the election."

The Chairlady's account teaches an important lesson. Her description resists the disempowering consignment, articulated by Black studies and feminist scholar Katherine McKittrick, that "the dispossessed black female body is often equated with the ungeographic, and black women's spatial knowledges are rendered either inadequate or impossible"—instead, confirming her proposal that "human geographies are unresolved and are being conceptualized beyond their present classificatory order."[10] The Chairlady's description of her experience of gendered agon provided a glimpse into the aspirations and politics a humanitarian enclosure produced. The contest, her investment, and its outcome were conditioned by the settlement and spatial organization of a refugee population. The drama she narrated, the seeding of a political world, was enabled by just enough architecture. Her meticulous description of representative governance brought into view the intricacies of a bureaucracy predicated on a refugee census. That census, in turn, was based on the spatial structure of blocks and sections in a humanitarian grid: a plan drawn by UNHCR technicians, implemented by aid workers, and built by refugees. From the level of the camp to that of the plots within which people housed themselves and created domesticities, this was an architecture impregnated with purpose. Further, the Chairlady's description illuminates precisely the possibility of subjectivity and narrative to be constructed within a sociohistorical process, to follow Trouillot's analysis, demanding that the architecture of a camp, which might be underestimated as merely utilitarian, be recognized not only as the setting but as wholly constitutive of the events of a refugee election, one laced with a suspenseful triumph during the mortal drama of childbirth. Following the Chairlady's account, I argue that the universalizing demonstration of participatory and putatively democratic governance in a camp—an example of the political and material structure imposed on and taken up by displaced people in emergency—reveals a practice of what I theorize as humanitarian settlement.

In Dadaab, representative governance within electoral districts of the refugee camps roots humanitarian settlement in a space external but parallel to the state, produced by emergency subjects. This space was provisioned in an overview plan drafted by a UNHCR technical unit and manifested in the fences, walls, and buildings refugees constructed on their plots. In this space, in standing for election, campaigning, and forging relations with or against the UNHCR, al-Shabaab, and a host of other entities, refugees employed a mechanism of democracy: the vote. However, it served an end other than sovereign governance. A body of leaders was elected to act as an organ for communication between refugee constituencies and the UNHCR and host state. What might be imputed to this labor and this form of representative governance? First, it put into effect the representation of a refugee body politic fully recognized within the nation-state system. Thus, it must be understood as political work. Second, this representative governance was ordered through designations of the built environment. Thus, it must also be understood as spatial practice. This emergent political work and spatial practice materialized a world, at the heart of which lies a practice of humanitarian settlement.

I follow the work and recountings of Isnina Ali Rage, Hashim Keinan, and other refugees and aid workers in the coming pages in order to theorize humanitarian settlement and, from it, an architecture of migration. They are among Dadaab's protagonists and often its archivists and theorists. However, the stories of Dadaab that begin with them open onto larger narratives of countries, institutions, organizations, fields, environments, and ecologies. Each chapter begins with localized narratives of particular individuals' experiences and structuring contexts, and then connects them to Dadaab's exceptional history of design intervention, construction, spatial imaging, urbanism, and beyond, to wider spheres of activity and thought. This is to say, each chapter draws a line from people's experiences of architecture to an intellectual history.[11] To better situate the architecture that provides this spine, a brief description of Dadaab's sociospatial and historical context follows, succeeded by suggestions for how to think with it.

SOCIOSPATIAL CONTEXT

Dadaab is located in Kenya's North Eastern Province, a territory sharing an international border with the Gedo and Lower Juba Regions of Somalia, once called the "Northern Frontier," a nomenclature stemming from a colonial imaginary of an unstable borderland. Long before the construction of this colony, people lived and moved across the region, watering goats and camels at "Hagar Dera," a lake appearing on British imperial military maps whose name fell to one of the camps, the Somali word for the tall *Commiphora africana*, or African myrrh tree, known for extensive medicinal benefits.[12] Dadaab, a town of 5,000 people, provided a hub for pastoralists before the refugee camps were built.[13] When the UNHCR planned the first refugee camp at Dadaab, the density of the surrounding region equaled fewer than five people per square kilometer.[14] In 1991 and 1992, the UNHCR planned and established three settlements, each for 30,000 inhabitants. Ifo was the first, initially self-settled by refugees who had been transported there from the border. Dagahaley and Hagadera were planned soon after, by European architects contracted by the UNHCR. After two decades, in response to the overwhelming of the physical facilities as more people settled around Dadaab, the UNHCR erected two other camps, Ifo 2 and Kambioos (later decommissioned). By late 2011, in settlements originally planned to accommodate 90,000 people, the UNHCR registered approximately 460,000 refugees at

I.1–I.5 (*overleaf*) The map and aerial photographs on the following pages, commissioned by the UNHCR, offer an instrumental record of the graphic coordinates, scale, and materiality of the refugee camps and Dadaab town, providing detail from the overhead perspective without engaging the people whose homes and bodies are captured.

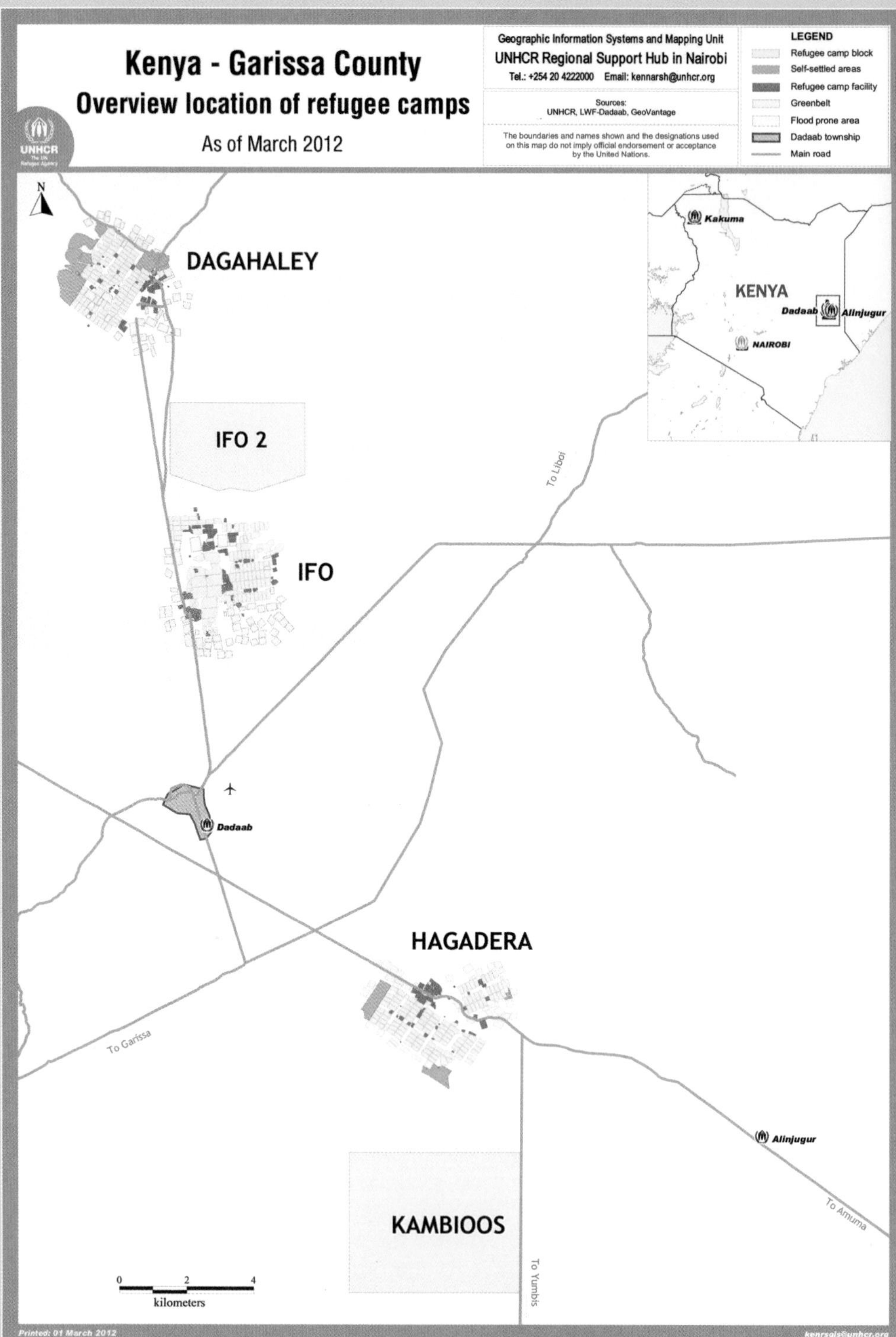

I.1. UNHCR overview map of Dadaab refugee camps, 2012.

I.2. UNHCR aerial view of Ifo camp, 2009.

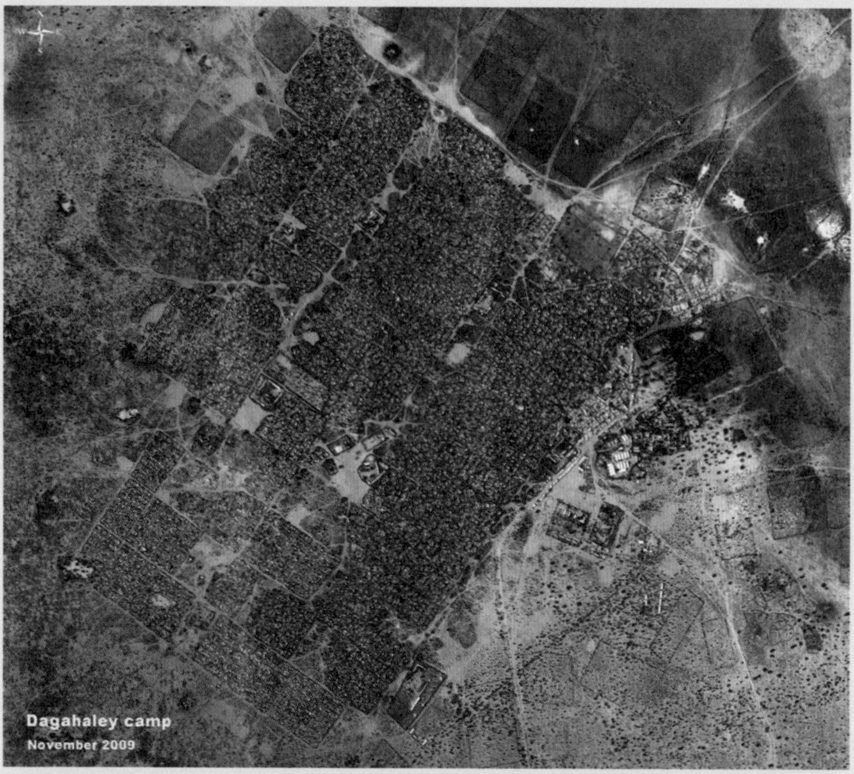

Dagahaley camp

November 2009

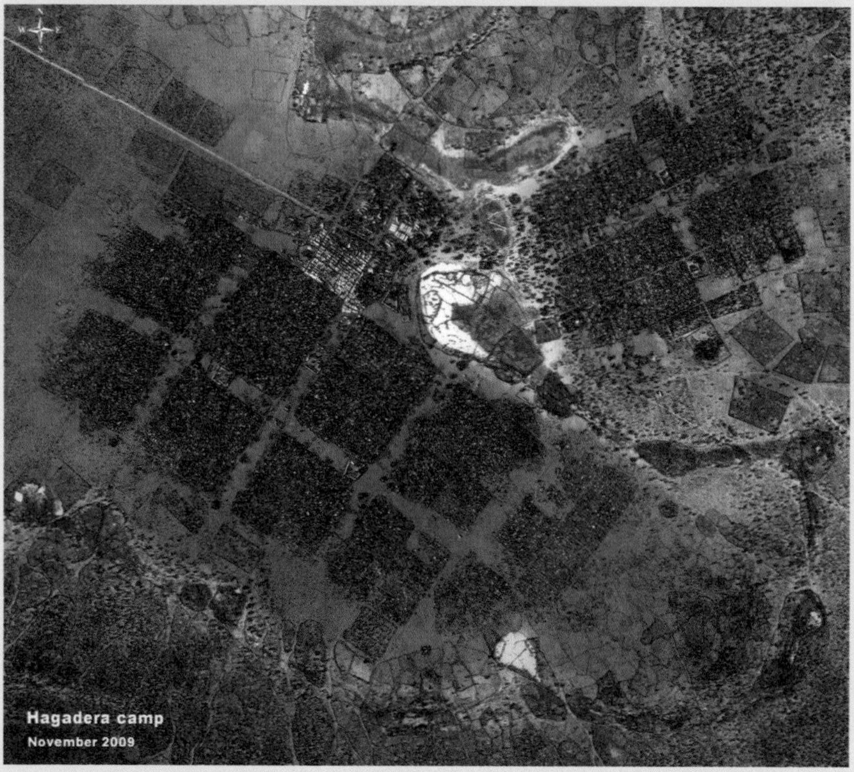

Hagadera camp

November 2009

I.3. (*opposite, top*) UNHCR aerial view of Dagahaley camp, 2009.
I.4. (*opposite, bottom*) UNHCR aerial view of Hagadera camp, 2009.
I.5. (*above*) UNHCR aerial view of Dadaab township, 2009.

Dadaab, with counts inclusive of unregistered migrants or asylum seekers reaching more than half a million.[15] Meanwhile, within a fifty-kilometer radius of the camps, the local population grew tenfold to more than 148,000 people between 1989 and 2010, well in excess of the rate in the rest of the North Eastern Province.[16] The astonishing population of the Dadaab camps, the third-largest grouping in Kenya after Nairobi and Mombasa, is often presented as the end of the matter, but behind this scale is the spatial confinement of people.

Several contradictions have manifested at Dadaab. Most important, as a humanitarian settlement intended to give succor to people displaced from home and execution of a rights framework to people displaced from citizenship, Dadaab has prolonged harm and grounded tensions. As the camp complex institutionalized, it acted as a provision of the security state to control the international border, allowing inequalities between refugees, neighboring host community members, and international aid providers to unfold without remit.[17] Although intended as a legal and political point of transit, Dadaab has provided an armature—an architecture—to suspend people in a prolonged liminal condition. Within it, abuses recorded from the establishment of humanitarian operations continue unabated.[18] Even as Kenya acceded without reservation to the 1951 United Nations (UN) Convention Relating to the Status of Refugees, the 1967 UN Protocol, and the 1969 Organisation of African Unity (OAU) Convention Governing the Specific Aspects of Refugee Problems in Africa (the continent's three primary instruments defining the refugee and determining her rights to legal protection), the country's government imposed restrictions, as did many others, on education, work, mobility, and migration.

Diverse groups have passed through Dadaab over the years. Without eliding the asymmetries of political status or citizenship, I note that the communities in Dadaab include not only refugees but also Kenyan migrants and international humanitarian workers. Together, they have bred a cultural imaginary of Dadaab within vibrant local, regional, and international diasporas and aid labor networks.

People from Somalia have comprised the majority in the settlements. However, Dadaab has housed refugees from many African countries, perhaps most famously children fleeing Sudan in the 1990s, known popularly as the Lost Boys, and Alice Lakwena (Auma) and her followers in the Lord's Resistance Army, the religious faction that escaped Uganda in the 1980s. Refugees were frequently housed in Dadaab temporarily while awaiting third-country resettlement, because the infrastructural capacity of the site lent itself to hosting people in the process of international transferal. For example, a Congolese refugee in a camp in western Tanzania might have been granted resettlement in North America, Western Europe, or Australia; prior to leaving Africa, she might have been transferred to Dadaab for a waiting period, in order to make place for others arriving at the Tanzanian camp. However, a great many people have also lived continuously in Dadaab since 1991, with children and grandchildren growing to adulthood knowing only the camps. These cohabitations have caused strange and sometimes sudden social reconfigurations and communities of belonging along lines of ethnicity, gender, class, kinship, nation, and more.

The government of Kenya granted refugees entry, but their welcome fell to a host community, ambivalent neighbors impacted by an international presence but ineligible for aid. Yet, members of this host community self-identify using many of the same markers as people living in the camps, shared with those across the border in Somalia: for example, speaking Somali, Boran, Kiswahili, and English; practicing Islam; sharing familial lineage; and adhering to communal economic approaches.[19] Some in Garissa County, where the camps are located, also share kinship affiliation with refugees. However, the complexity of the relationship between refugees and hosts lies in political status. The status of "refugee" has been shared, exchanged, and transferred over time. As an illustration, the first group of people to live in the refugee settlements at Dadaab totaled 4,057, but records showed that only 3,627 of them were transferred from the border.[20] The convoys knowingly or unwittingly incorporated Somali Kenyans, asylum seekers, and other migrants while in transit. By 2010, more than 40,000 people in the host community had come into possession of ration cards.[21] These instances point to complex relationships between hosts and refugees, intertwined communities that grew and changed together over time.

Aid workers, the humanitarian laborers who administer the provision of essential goods and services, form a third community in Dadaab. The UNHCR has contracted multiple nongovernmental organizations, or NGOs, to implement social services, physical planning, and the distribution of humanitarian aid and services, attracting and accommodating a diverse body of international and local employees who live on-site. Among aid workers, Dadaab has been a prestigious station for field duty.[22] The most prominent humanitarian organizations in the world have undertaken short-term relief and long-term aid in Dadaab.

The market is one of the spaces where these diverse groups and their things converge. While refugees have remained dependent on aid, the camp

I.6. A morning in Dagahaley camp market.

complex has supported a robust economy outside the financial instruments of the state, based on trade in humanitarian food and nonfood items and movement of goods between Dubai and Nairobi. This flow of capital, in combination with remittance funds and the activities of an international community of aid workers and officials, have formed a substrate of the local economy. By 2010, refugee-related operations accounted for $100 million in investment, with $25 million in trade moving through five thousand businesses, from petty traders to shopping malls, offering goods and services from the utilitarian to the luxury.[23] This can be explained by the creativity and imagination of Somali networks, their rapid movement of money, the commercial orientations of Kenya and East Africa, the optimal location of Dadaab on a highway between Nairobi and Mogadishu, and the direct interest of Northern aid economies—all forces catalyzing the growth of Dadaab into a "market town."[24] The "market" provides a rational language to describe the beating heart of a place that has matured into something analytically different from a camp.

The built environment at Dadaab has evolved according to its own political economic logics, while also occasioning a body of infrastructures. The long-range transportation and wireless communications technologies that enable humanitarian relief in "unmapped" terrains support operations in a former "frontier." They have produced artifacts: a small airstrip, telecom masts, fleets of ground vehicles adapted as mobile antennae, satellite hardware connecting field offices with headquarters in capitals worldwide, secondary schools and other educational infrastructure for people in the camps and Dadaab town.[25] Dadaab had full regional mobile phone coverage before much of the rest of Kenya.[26] These infrastructures are set within a specific ecology and have enabled settlement in an area little developed by the state.

These enabling infrastructures, emphasizing the extended political crisis around the relief site, tell of sudden development made possible by foreign largesse. However, Dadaab's bounty is not international aid but the continuous yield of the freshwater Merti aquifer. This relic of a Jurassic-era rift has made the duration of settlement possible, through a borewell system penetrating the Merti's sedimentary layers, consuming the freshwater confined between saltwater pockets beneath and at the perimeter. The hardware's pumping action and the intensity of inhabitation above have compromised the aquifer, breaching its envelope and introducing salinity into the groundwater at points, yet not risked its depletion.[27] Thus, though these refugee settlements are ever framed as resulting from protracted conflict, their growth and maintenance are also predicated on the aquifer's sustenance, reliable in a semiarid equatorial zone in spite of twice-annual seasonal flooding. The Merti aquifer has enabled the structure and institution of a massive built environment.

That built environment is composed of contradictions. Dadaab has signaled transience through spectacular visual frailty—dwellings clad in recovered textile and sheet-metal fragments, dusted red by the earth and wind. Yet, Dadaab's equally dazzling substance—an array of satellites and their dishes, aeronautic fleets resting on tarmac, all-terrain vehicular convoys, aluminum and polyvinyl chloride water storage towers, hydraulic extraction machinery, and the large settlements themselves—anchors hard infrastructures in the earth and sky. Many refugee camps leave a lighter infrastructural footprint. While durable masonry buildings constitute the central UNHCR compound where agency and organization staff members reside and work, the architecture of the refugee camps has been composed of lightweight, additive elements and

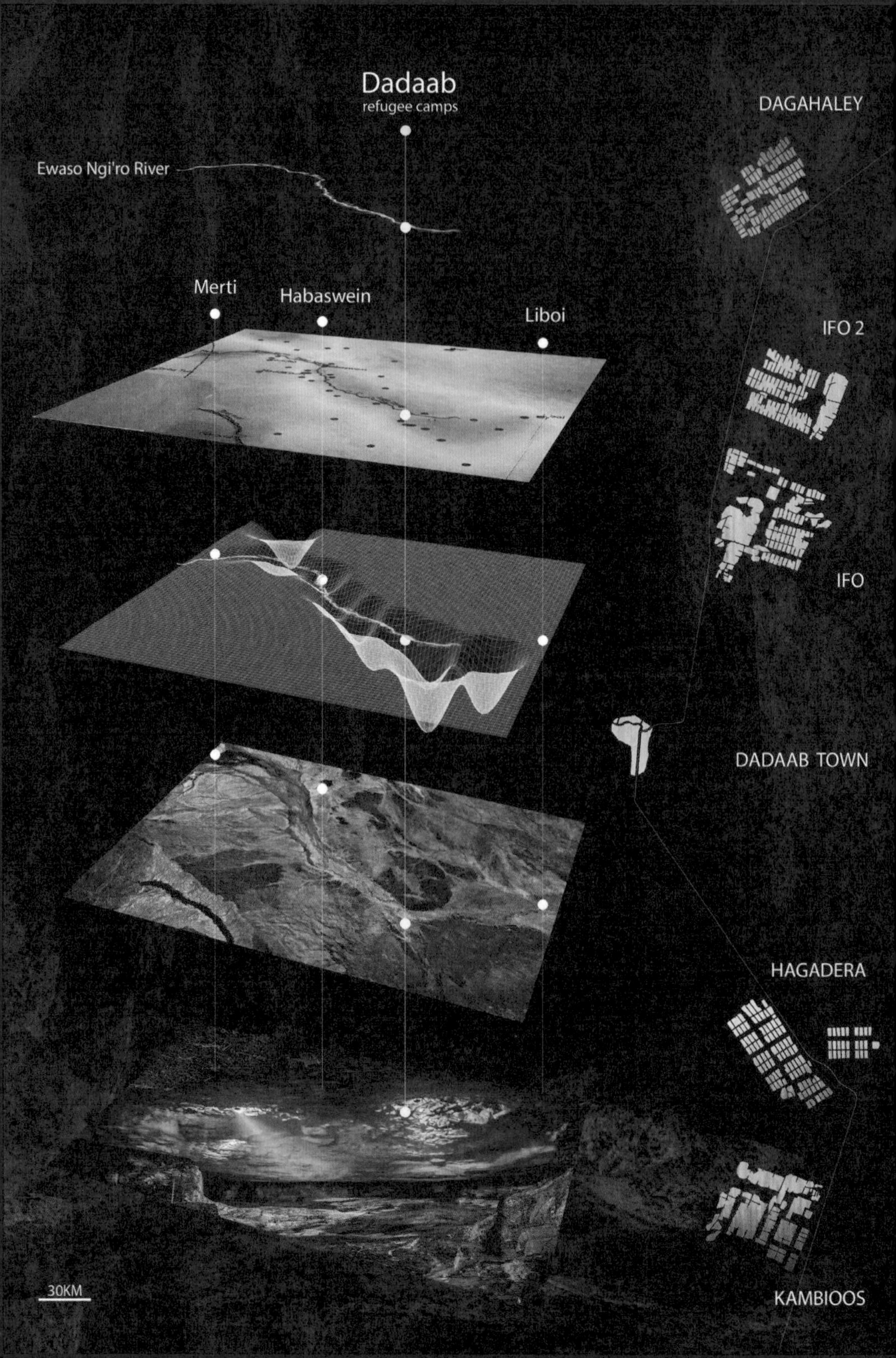

Dadaab
refugee camps

DAGAHALEY

Ewaso Ngi'ro River

Merti

Habaswein

Liboi

IFO 2

IFO

DADAAB TOWN

HAGADERA

30KM

KAMBIOOS

I.8. Tuqul dwellings surrounded by branches for protection against animals, Cawo Jube area of Ifo camp, photo by Bethany Young.

built of found, recycled, and remnant material. It is a landscape of vibrant modernity, composed of architectures that are difficult to read as stylistically modern. The aesthetics performs an act of cloaking, concealing cultural significance rather than making it legible. The architecture that constitutes Dadaab is rendered insubstantial, appearing as little more than shanties and huts in the bush.

The architectural form ubiquitous in Dadaab is the East African tuqul (or aqal, or waab in Somali), a dwelling constructed from green wood that has been bent, tied into a dome, and clad with woven mats or, in the refugee camps, with recovered textile fragments. Intended to be transported overland between grazing areas on the backs of camels, this mobile architecture

I.7. (*opposite*) Cave Bureau, architectural analytical construction of Merti aquifer geology, Dadaab town and refugee camps, and geographical and topographical setting, 2022. Exploded extract deducing lithography from heat maps, satellite imagery, and imagined subterranean hydrology. Ink on paper freehand sketch, digital linework in MicroStation, modeling in SketchUp, collage of textures in Photoshop.

remains stationary in Dadaab, populating the plots, blocks, and sectors of the camps. The tuqul is a recalcitrant object. On the one hand, it resists modernization, quite literally unable to accept mechanical connections to civil infrastructure. On the other, it resists its own history and architecture. The tuqul results from the long constancy of nomadic life, whose fullness is predicated on people's commitment to personal relationships, openness to the land, and free migration. Yet, the sedentary tuqul in the camps evokes an image of depletion of lives in the search for essentials, subject to the terms of vagrancy and representing an unwillingness to cooperate with the state. This tuqul is an architectural object that awakens distrust and the will to sedentarize the migrant. As art historian Allyson Purpura suggests, "ambivalence towards transience is . . . a cultural response, one shaped within a Western regime of value that, from the late eighteenth century onwards, extolled permanence as a virtue and preservation a right of sovereignty."[28] The normalization of fixity she identifies has been present in the European desire to control the unruly East African frontier and the British empire's extractive settler colonial project in the Kenyan highlands. The uncanny stasis of a dense field of tuquls encamped in Dadaab, as in figure 2.11, suggests a history of suppressed migration. The persistence of this recalcitrant architecture in an emergency context offers an architectural historical clue.[29] It calls for different traditions of apprehending architecture and, through them, new ways of knowing.

This knowing is held within an architecture of migration, a concrete and tenuous eco-materiality of myrrh; marabou storks; an aged aquifer; a town with shops and houses; camps and compounds with offices, residences, and restaurants; and worldwide infrastructures for communications, transportation, and storage. The market, infrastructure, ecology, and ways of knowing speak to urbanity and convivium—activity beyond the purely humanitarian—positing Dadaab as something other than a camp or city.[30] This thinking approaches Dadaab's constructed environment less through legal theory and social science than through aesthetic and historical analysis, building on understandings of subaltern and refugee urbanism.[31] Such theories posit the material and social complexity behind humanitarian settlement at Dadaab as driven not only by abstract forces of relief and development but indeed also by actual people.

It has been common to ascribe limits to Dadaab. For example, some have theorized the camps as an incipient but ultimately untenable urban or sociopolitical form, "an amputated town, bare by definition."[32] Such orientations offer little possibility for the larger historical and theoretical life of the Dadaab refugee camps or for the critical heritage it scaffolds, in both a tangible culture expressed in Dadaab's architecture and the intangible memories of people for whom it is home. Consigning Dadaab's constitutive political imagination to the margins forecloses the worlds that have been dreamed and created by Isnina Ali Rage and others who preceded and followed her. Archaeologist Sada Mire, who fled Somalia as a child, writes about learning to build a tuqul during summer holidays outside Mogadishu. The practice brought her closer to family as well as forms of knowledge and cultural heritage they valued. The practice also saved their lives. "In fact, we were supposed to learn how to build huts . . . when the war came, it was those skills that made us survive in those landscapes," she writes.[33] In that vein, moving beyond terms of scarcity and exceptionalism to describe Dadaab means refusing to relegate to the utilitarian a history and heritage of people, both African and foreign, whose lives, pasts, and futures have been defined by migration and this specific place and, instead, naming ways that Dadaab's architecture resolves in relation to the land where it sits.

In May 2016, following the horrors of the brutal takeover of Syria, the mass flight of people into neighboring countries, and the ensuing outpouring of international aid to Turkey to support humanitarian response, the Kenyan government announced it would close the Dadaab settlements before the end of the year.[34] In spite of passing an act of Parliament ten years earlier to ensure provision for refugees, the government dismantled the Department of Refugee Affairs, citing security threats and a lack of international support.[35] This closure was stayed by a ruling of Kenya's High Court in February 2017, yet produced significant political leverage within Kenya and internationally—especially in Europe, as states negotiated unprecedented asylum seeking. The Kenyan government's actions accentuate the paradox of permanent impermanence under which the Dadaab settlements have endured, fulfilling an existential *and* representational ephemerality. This architectural ephemerality deserves scrutiny so as not to be normalized in the negative terms of precarity. The following pages provide historical context that defamiliarizes this ephemerality and situates Dadaab not only as a product of space, but also of time: as a specific place at the intersection of histories, framing new concepts and theory.

HISTORICAL CONTEXT

To build this spatiotemporal framework, throughout this book, I contextualize humanitarian settlement at Dadaab as architecture with a history. This position counters reductive attempts to define refugee camps as characterized only by emergency, producing a flattened, textureless timespace of relentless urgency, and instead emphasizes their establishment and growth as events inhabiting longer historical processes. At Dadaab, a range of historical forces produced the intersecting forms of belonging, sedentarization, and underdevelopment to be explored in the following pages.

Processes of belonging, sedentarization, and underdevelopment intersect in the correspondence of architecture to land. The spatial and social belonging of people to land in Dadaab has not been through settlement—that is, settlement or cultivation in one fixed location. The erudition, cultures, and architectures of many East African communities were predicated on migrations, whether pastoralist or seafaring, orienting elsewhere.[36] A plurality of approaches to inhabitation have thus prefigured complex relations between architecture and land at Dadaab, an outcome not of emergency but of multiple forms of migrating and settling over generations.

The first refugee camps at Dadaab were planned to respond to emergency, meeting a putatively temporary need. Their prolongation as a humanitarian settlement was a result of war. Although humanitarian operations at Dadaab provided relief to refugees of wars in many locations, they have primarily responded to struggles within Somalia, or, as writer Rasna Warah trenchantly argues, struggles *with* Somalia, by international military actors.[37] The following historical contextualization of the architecture of migration at Dadaab necessarily begins by taking account of this militarism, especially as tied to the colonial territorialization that preceded it—both the settler colonialism of the empire and the interior colonization of the postcolonial state examined in the chapters of this book. Indigenous, anticapitalist, and feminist articulations of struggle crystallize the use of land for extraction and the criminalization of people whose relationship to land is not based on its circumscription into territory or property.[38] To understand the practice of humanitarian aid as it consolidated in the international system, East Africa, and the architecture of Dadaab requires this wider perspective on land. Belonging, sedentarization, and underdevelopment are forces that emerged from and shaped the ties between land and architecture, and ultimately undergirded architectures of migration and settlement.

Belonging

The violence and breakdown of centralized state structures of the Somali Democratic Republic, from 1988 to a saturation point in 1991, forced people to migrate en masse, precipitating significant territorial shifts, if part of a series of such shifts.[39] Political contestations and mobilities in East Africa across the contemporary countries of Somalia, Kenya, and Ethiopia stemmed from conflicting imaginaries of a land where people resisted settlement by others for a hundred years. Forces of colonization and development increasingly produced the justification and means to implement socially based divisions of land in Kenya during the long twentieth century. Expropriated or "grabbed" land and radical new divisions produced diverse territorial forms, such as urban peripheries around Nairobi and Mombasa; countrywide infrastructural transportation and agriculture pockets; and borderlands, reserves, and national parks.

These territorial constructions and divisions produced for the Somali-identifying majority in Kenya's northeast a tension around belonging.[40] While a tension around belonging was experienced differently by various communities coping with British cultural imperialism in Kenya, for people in the northeast, it was rooted in large part by conflicting approaches to territory and borders. Those approaches cast some communities in Kenya as indigenous and others as foreign in an oppositional vision of social, cultural, and political identity. Most people in the Dadaab camps have become familiar with conflations of pastoralist with migrant, misrepresentations exacerbating anxieties around border transgression. Nevertheless, orientations toward migration have defined life and politics in the Kenyan northeast. Explaining his migration from Somaliland to the Mediterranean Sea through the concept of the tahriib, "an Arabic word referring to a form of unregulated emigration," the writer Maxamed Xuseen Geeldoon notes, "the Somali people have a long history of migration. Historically, to go on migration has been a family livelihood strategy. It is one of the ways that Somali men from a pastoralist background have helped their families to survive during times of severe hardship."[41] The Somali, Boran, Samburu, Rendille, and other communities share agro-pastoral economies, political identities, and modernities, which provided unity across ethnic groups in discourses on a Greater Somalia, connecting people across a common, though not static or homogenous, identity forming one of the largest ethnocultural blocs in Africa.[42] The idea of a Somalia with land that did not resolve in borders animated nationalist formation during the independence movement, Africa's decolonization, and the years following. These citizens were to move freely across the Somali peninsula, known from colonial maps as the Horn of Africa (including present-day Somalia, Somaliland, Djibouti, Ethiopia, and Kenya). The borderlessness in this vision has produced a latent sense of apprehension toward refugees as well as Somali-identifying Kenyan citizens, translating for people from Dadaab and the northeast into an ambivalent sense of belonging within the nation.

In many parts of the world, negotiations over territory produced vexations for colonial authority as well as open questions in state formation after independence. In Kenya, the transhumance of pastoralists—the seasonal mobility based on economies, socialities, and lifeways of animal husbandry—increased the British colonial administration's ambivalence toward the northeast, unable to render within it a traceable population.[43] This ambivalence found territorial form in partitions and the construction of the "Northern Frontier."[44] The productivity of land determined its value to the modern empire: rendering the fertile highlands a heartland for settlers and the northeast a frontier. That frontier's fungibility was demonstrated by Great Britain partitioning the Jubaland in 1925, ceding its eastern region to Italy (which occupied adjacent Somalia) in return for support during World War I. The "NFD (Northern Frontier District) question" emerged most sharply on the eve of Kenya's independence. As in the example of Kashmir during the construction of an independent but partitioned South Asia, what would become a contested territory began with a "question" about the NFD that evolved into a "problem." In 1962, the people of the northeast voted in a plebiscite to join Somalia rather than Kenya after independence. This sense of self-determination was foreclosed as the British scuttled diplomatic resolution by evading it during their tenure and postponing the decision until after independence. The new government of Kenya declined implementation of the vote's outcome. Historian Keren Weitzberg has documented and argued that this encumbered the Somali sense of belonging in Kenya.[45] I argue that it also fueled the sentiment around northeast otherness that has supported a logic for encampment and persistence of a security regime around Dadaab. This bordering and containment of unfixed, or unfixable, populations echoes security practices performed in the postcolony worldwide to address vexing "problems" that persisted for states and international systems.

If the northeast has been marked by contestations and ambiguities related to the formation of political territory, its recent spatial politics has been actualized through the bordered, determined architecture of the refugee camps, shaped by deep geographical and geological relationships supporting agro-pastoral traditions over a long span of time. Pastoralists have lived with and benefited from the continuous water supply of the Merti aquifer, which has served animal husbandry while also sustaining refugees living in large camps whose sudden population density has pressured, but not compromised, the abundance and utility of this resource. To understand an architecture of migration is to accept sociocultural belonging as a condition that crosses borders and occupies wider ecologies such as these.

Historian Robyn d'Avignon tracks cavities under wide swaths of western African ground made sacred by orpailleurs—artisanal gold miners—building "subterranean knowledge," which would shape the discipline of geology, from the cosmologies, rituals, and territories that defined their belonging.[46] Art and architectural historian Ikem Stanley Okoye writes of the art and settlements of the great Niger River cultures as evidence of "enigmatic mobilities of ideas . . . certain kinds of spatial intensifications, whose pressures gave rise to new and emergent culture, such as might occur at river confluences, lakes and lesser or greater river bends, especially in the context of newly arrived peoples."[47] We might imagine the Merti aquifer producing such intensifications and subterranean knowledge. The belonging of people to this place has to do with the time and historicity embedded in that water and earth.

Sedentarization

The Dadaab refugee camps are a form of humanitarian settlement in which the practices of emergency relief have enacted people's sedentarization through encampment and the foreclosure of migration. This fraught outcome illuminates the relation between humanitarian and colonial practices. The Dadaab camps archive this relationship, providing a material record of past colonial practices that extend into present-day spatial practices. Three examples of colonial spatial practice follow.

The first centers on constructions of contingent territory. The refugee camps extend a form of colonial demarcation begun in the nineteenth century. The short-lived Imperial British East Africa Company, incorporated in 1888 by William Mackinnon, established operations in Mombasa to survey the territory, build a highway and railway to the interior, and develop agricultural land for European settlement, for which the Gĩkũyũ and Maasai highlands proved attractive. This venture did not succeed, and in 1895, the British Crown proclaimed a protectorate reaching to Buganda lands, with construction of the Kenya-Uganda railway the following year. This process produced the imperial territory of East Africa and the Kenya Colony's Northern Frontier. The highlands in the west were opened to white settlers from Europe through ordinances delineating "Crown Lands" and "Outlying Districts."[48] The imperial government controlled movement between districts through the use of kipande passes (implemented in colonial South Africa to regulate the mobility of racially identified groups), which are presently granted to citizens and denied to refugees in Kenya. Vis-à-vis this bordering, Dadaab's relationship to the former imperial territory is telling. While much of Garissa County falls within what was once the Northern Frontier, Dadaab and the camp complex do not. Dadaab occupies land that was external to the erstwhile Kenya Colony as well as its frontier, a *space* represented inaccurately on maps as a *line* dividing British Kenya and Italian Somaliland. It is a ghost space: contested territory in the present inhabiting unclaimed territory in the past. Fixing territory amid such embedded contingency prepares an environment for sedentarization.

The second colonial spatial practice marked in the Dadaab camps is the construction of enclosure. The camps parallel other settlement forms linked to principles of enclosing land as property—specifically, two conceptual precedents explored in these pages, religious missions and detention centers. Christian missions formed enclosures that directly connected nineteenth-century abolition and latter-day humanitarianism in Africa, for example, in the Rabai and Freretown settlements near Mombasa, established by the Church Mission Society in 1846 and 1875, respectively, which housed people who had escaped or been liberated from enslavement. Freretown was established explicitly with the social mission of rehabilitating newly freed people through practices of valorizing small-scale cultivation as a matter of *morality*, which engendered a cultural logic for land capitalization. Although preindustrial small-proprietor farming at Freretown differed greatly from the succeeding settler colonial schemes (which drew on African labor without supporting agrarian smallholders), it equated liberation with cultivation.[49] A variety of settlement forms stemmed from this philosophy of liberatory and rehabilitative land domestication, including, for example, "native reserves" established in ensuing years, which populated the landscape with an enclosure intended to confine the nomadic Maasai and others: the manyatta. This term is sometimes translated as "village"—poignantly, as the manyatta proliferated in "villagization" detention schemes the British adopted to repress the Land and Freedom struggle, or Mau Mau uprising. Villagization of rebels in manyattas—forced labor camps—across the Kenya Colony introduced a technique of enclosure that the Kenyan government adapted immediately following independence in the 1960s to contain pastoralist insurgents in the northeast. After declaring a state of emergency in the Northern Frontier District, the government ordered a police action in Garissa, confining people identified as shifta, or bandits, in fortified villages. Under a program of planning sites publicized as projects of modernization and development, the government ultimately sedentarized pastoralists.[50] The 1990s refugee encampment policy echoed the 1960s counterinsurgency strategy, as schemes for development and humanitarianism were conflated through a similar progressive rhetoric, ultimately effecting sedentarization. These colonial spatial practices of enclosure offer a trajectory of a history of capitalism, especially in consideration of the forced dependence of pastoralists on humanitarian aid as populations in the northeast were gradually settled—at the expense of a pastoral way of life, in its entirety. In many different contexts worldwide, such sedentarization practices enabled the criminalization of itinerancy and nomadism through forces as diverse as abolition, detention, and migration, linked unexpectedly to forms of land enclosure.

The third example of colonial spatial practice in Dadaab relates to building. The camps highlight the vexed relation of vernacular architectures to modernity as wholly contemporary settlements composed of traditional dwellings, and intervene in a spatial politics by architecturally representing indigeneity through domesticity in emergency and material expressions of a gendered social structure. Of particular note is the way that the camps contextualize the legitimacy or delegitimization of the "hut" in East Africa, historically based on its integration into or resistance to legal codes, in which the sedentary and taxable domicile articulated in British ordinances as the "makuti hut" stands in contradistinction to the mobile tuqul dwelling accompanying pastoralist ways of life across the region. The tuqul is a gendered architecture: a traditional house designed and built by women within specific rituals and ceremonies, and regularly also by women within contemporary contexts of duress in refugee camps across East Africa.[51] As a recalcitrant gendered architecture, as described earlier, the tuqul in the camps must also be understood as an object caught within forms of political violence, and thus subject to feminist questions of ambivalence on the ethical positions of women within militarized social contexts.[52] Moreover, the prevalence of the tuqul as a stationary architecture in the refugee camps at Dadaab suppresses its fullest actualization as an iteration of women's work, foregrounding the fraught gender politics of its ephemerality. Anthropologist Namita Dharia's meditation on the gendered ephemeral atmospheres of the building construction site in India—another migrant environment in which home and work are collapsed—gestures to qualities she reminds us to seek as we "look, smell, and listen for invisible durabilities within the ephemeral atmospheres of construction," and bears remembering in reading Dadaab, a putatively static landscape that cloaks the intimacies, socialities, anger, anxieties, and love in an environment built largely by women.[53] Architect and historian Mabel O. Wilson has articulated a "provisional demos" as the essential concept with which to interpret the spatial agency of a tent city built by African Americans for the temporary purpose of protest, an ephemeral form that marks a larger, more durable episteme of dissent inhabited by the Dadaab refugee camps.[54] Here, it is worth contemplating the well-known problem of the Palestinian refugee camp, whose historical particularities differ greatly from Dadaab's, yet whose centrality to the global historical conditions within which the Dadaab camps emerged demand parallel citation and consideration. Compared to a politics of ephemerality in Palestine, where a refugee camp's permanence plays a significant role in expressing the demand for the right of return to a land, in Dadaab, a humanitarian settlement's immobilization of constitutively mobile architectures does another kind of work. Rather than staking ground, fixed structures in Dadaab mask and transform their surroundings, changing people's relationships to the land in plain sight and through gendered precision. Dadaab's buildings erode openly migratory ways of being, through the perversion of the language of the "vernacular" dwelling.

These examinations of territory, enclosure, and building illuminate a complex process of sedentarization that the following chapters take up. They offer an interpretation of a regional history for which the Dadaab refugee camps capture a through line. However, the conditions behind the humanitarian intervention at Dadaab also bring together significant international dimensions with regional ones. They offer a model for reading other refugee camps in the past and present, suggesting that colonial practices of development and underdevelopment underlie any refugee context. Dadaab therefore acts as a powerful object lesson for understanding wider landscapes and architectures of migration.

Underdevelopment

Histories of Dadaab mark relations between three sets of pasts. One is of people belonging to the region for generations. Another is of contested land and architectures of sedentarization. The third is of the political-economic and social interaction between those people, that land, and the system of nations in the practice of underdevelopment. This latter condition has been realized in a late stage through the displacement of agentive community development in the contemporary international practice of humanitarian relief.

The international system in Dadaab operates in certain ways in concert with the exploitative relationship between development and underdevelopment that historian Walter Rodney painstakingly and dispassionately elucidated in *How Europe Underdeveloped Africa*.[55] His discursive recasting of the problem through the simplicity of a prefix suggests a method for rereading a refugee camp toward unfamiliar, liberatory ends. Framing the humanitarian system through the principle of underdevelopment disallows its normalization. Seeing from the perspective of Dadaab provincializes the humanitarian system and rejects the naturalization of development practice. This estrangement furthermore illuminates the work of refugees as significant contributions to Dadaab's constructed environment and situates the history of that constructed environment as central to a critical global history, in which the oppressions of underdevelopment impact refugees and humanitarians—rather, aid workers—together.

This is not to aggrandize the subject position of the international humanitarian system through continued critical focus. Rather, it is to estrange its subject position in order to disrupt its epistemic power. It is to acknowledge it as a structural force that defines everyday local life, yet also to read it as the foreign and contingent tool that it is. Cultural theorist Sylvia Wynter similarly defamiliarized and reversed the gaze, building on Black Arts and Black Aesthetics movement practitioner Amiri Baraka's "idea that Western thought might be exotic if viewed from another landscape," in her articulation of the liberal humanist circumscription of humanity in relation to the self-alienation and broader systems of alienation of Black people.[56] These inversions offer a strategy for analyzing and resisting the oppressions that play themselves out on macro and micro levels in the landscapes in and around Dadaab—"another landscape," in Baraka's terms. My first method in such an analysis and resistance is an estrangement of humanitarian environments, through visual, material, and conceptual means.

To make sense of this, it is important to first understand that international diplomacy frameworks and refugee law institutionalized after World War II brought into being transnational nongovernmental political structures and communities designated to focus on the relief of suffering.[57] On the one hand, they made spaces and networks for human rights and other advocacy movements to concretize. For example, from the early 1970s, marked by crises in (and media attention to) Bangladesh and Biafra, international activists in a range of professions, from medicine to journalism to urban planning, mobilized worldwide as part of designated state and nongovernmental relief and recovery networks. On the other hand, these structures and communities provided an apparatus for humanitarian action predicated on intervention by outsiders into sovereign territory. For example, by the 1990s, an international "humanitarian" military had intervened into the cities and countries that had constituted Yugoslavia. The justification of intervention into sovereign territory on the grounds of relieving suffering became a driving human rights principle in humanitarian culture. Moreover, this culture was predicated on an asymmetrical discourse locating subjecthood in the body of the individual rather than in political community. This paralleled broad privatization, emerging as an effect of structural adjustments as neoliberal economic approaches cemented themselves in formerly colonized and yet "developing" parts of the world. Social services that had once been the purview of states appeared in new private-sector humanitarian iterations.[58] Transnational nongovernmental activity replaced these social services and proliferated through increasingly individuated subjects and objects of humanitarian work during the rise of an international human rights culture. This activity displaced the making of political community with the relief of individual suffering—part of what has frequently been discussed as the "humanitarian alibi" or the "humanitarian paradox."[59] What has been less understood is the aesthetic construction of this relief of suffering, monumentalized in various ways through architecture, as in the complex of settlements at Dadaab.

Thus, the Dadaab refugee complex, with its unruly materiality and forms of settlement, has been rooted in a strict logic with more disciplined ends: the formalization of international humanitarian intervention. This process has systematized underdevelopment through the construction of a global industry refined to respond to emergency and relieve the suffering of individuals, rather than to support the construction of political community, or resource mutual aid. This practice of underdevelopment, a humanitarian displacement of politics by aesthetics, has been most palpable in the spatial practices of emergency relief. Therefore the structural embeddedness of one of the forces behind humanitarian settlement, what I term *humanitarian spatiality*, and the discourses behind it, deserve some explanation.

First, at the time that Dadaab was established, a humanitarian spatiality had begun to be defined by the intervention of architects and planners. I use the term to refer to already existing space as well as the bringing into being of spaces, spatial practice by humanitarian entities, and the social and cultural condition of making and inhabiting what has been widely understood as "humanitarian space," the conceptual location of humanitarian activity.[60] This humanitarian spatiality took shape through the combination of an international culture of sovereign intervention and the proliferation of nonstate actors privileging the rights of the individual, as noted earlier. As such, this spatiality was defined in alignment with the state, not within the state but in parallel to it, through the systematic production of architectures such as refugee camps, held legally and practically separate from adjacent environments. The material form-making of and in these spaces occurred through the engagement of both institutionally trained and emergent architects, humanitarians and refugees. The human rights movement held an urgent attraction for architects trained in institutions based mostly in the North, as they searched for a positivist potential during a precise convergence of the fall of the Soviet Union (as an actual government and the embodiment of an ideology) and the eclipse of the postmodern stylistic turn that dominated thinking in many architecture schools (reflecting economic globalization's coming into its own).[61] At the time, an international community concerned existentially with development and disasters—or, conceptually, with state-building and the environment—began to adopt systematized, technocratic means for realizing humanitarian space. With that, architects and planners began to find their way or be invited into international and nongovernmental spheres. By the 1990s, a rhetoric of moral and ethical consideration dominated international political discourse, and with it, architectural practice and humanitarian action came intentionally into concert.[62] Through these steps, spatial practices and practitioners facilitated liberal interventions into sovereign territory. They contributed to localized erosion of sovereign authority. Sometimes, this was achieved simply, if inadvertently, with the establishment of a border camp. This architecture, with the legitimacy it conferred on space, could help to realize an authoritative material infrastructure. Such outcomes—the construction of humanitarian space, the intervention into sovereign territory, the spatial practices of emergency relief, and the aesthetics of its form-making—accumulated into a humanitarian spatiality of which Dadaab remains a profound iteration.

Second, humanitarian spatiality in Dadaab must also be understood as culminating a trajectory of Cold War dynamics. While geopolitics has played only a partial role in long-contested "borderlands" such as that connecting the African "Horn" to the continental interior, the humanitarian intervention at Dadaab hinged on the shift away from a US-Soviet hegemony at the end of the twentieth century.[63] Many forces converged in the early 1990s, as the United States and the Soviet Union withdrew from proxy participation in wars around the world, removing protections and structural supports for civilians newly contending with markets flooding with small arms. Rapid urbanization—escalated by aggressive land speculation, rural people's migration toward resources, and dramatic climate impacts on new megacities, corridors, and other densely populated areas—produced profound food, water, and shelter insecurity. These convergences spurred forced migrations on scales and with suddenness never before experienced, at a moment when international relief networks began to bridge former political-geographic divisions and proliferate new nongovernmental donor structures. A field of emergency spatial operations growing out of years of practice began to systematize at that time, especially with the input of architectural and planning expertise.[64] While international political and financial support did not result in the production of more relief camps around the world at that time, it did result in the systematization of camp building and management as a global emergency relief strategy. As a ubiquitous set of architectures and iconographies—elements from tarps to tents to camps that formed landscapes—began to be perceived by a variety of publics and designated as specifically "humanitarian," the materiality of this humanitarianism impinged on the lives of more and more people in East Africa, and a growing number around the world, who increasingly confronted the security state through the border camps erected to stem their migration.

Third, as many people experienced all of these factors simultaneously and sought out established humanitarian operations for subsistence, emergency response as a practice began to be refined, formalized, and institutionalized as a system. This institutionalization was built in part on the overall systematization of spatial practice, anchored in prominent field sites. The refugee settlements at Dadaab became one such—if not *the*—prominent installation, as the UNHCR's largest operation for much of the period at hand and an architectural testing ground. The transformation from practice to system also carried with it certain forms of industry, such as an increasingly privatized, diversified, and competitive market of humanitarian provision of goods and services.[65] The consolidation of this diversity included the entrenchment of humanitarian spatiality through building programs, an architecture and planning culture, and an overall commodification of the designs and built forms of emergency response. The professionalization, privatization, standardization, scaling, and globalization of emergency response and aid delivery marked an overall growth of an international humanitarian industry, distinguished by refined spatial practices. From the architecture of the supply chain to the design of a humanitarian compound, a formalized and refined humanitarian spatiality inscribed an institutionalization of underdevelopment.

The capitalistic and industrial practices that characterized humanitarian settlement in the late twentieth century reproduced and enhanced the very forces of underdevelopment that Rodney exposed in 1972. Yet, ironically, they also marked an evolution of the universal liberal thought that constitutes the object of Wynter's critique. The conflicting and contradictory processes of underdevelopment, sedentarization, and belonging behind humanitarian settlement create unresolvable paradoxes for the liberal propositions of humanitarianism, through a variety of aesthetic, material, and spatial practices. To situate the historical context in this way is not to disregard or devalue the labors and desires of refugee migrants nor of aid workers. It is to study the past with open eyes and endow the present with realistic meaning, in order to creatively imagine the future. Locating the questions of an architecture of migration in a study of Dadaab in situ offers the empirical ground with which to theorize.

Dadaab, in Theory

This brief sociospatial and historical background of the Dadaab refugee settlements contextualizes the convergence of multiple architectures and historical threads, which the chapters of this book bring into greater focus. Throughout, I argue that architectures in the present provide a pathway to understanding the past and offer alternatives to received narratives. I also argue that the constructed environment at Dadaab provides a significant iteration of humanitarian spatiality and an object lesson on humanitarian settlement. As such, Dadaab offers a powerful basis for theory.

To elaborate, my experience as someone who approached Dadaab without a personal affiliation may demonstrate how its histories and possibilities extend far beyond the refugee camps themselves. I come to Dadaab as an art historian, inhabiting a field rife with the contradictions of empire and epistemic colonization, yet full with politically radical thinkers. As art and visual culture historian Kajri Jain notes, our disciplinary entanglement with capital and realpolitik puts us in "a position of strength to *resist* the discourse and practices of instrumentalization all the way up and down and right across our institutional structures. As artists and art historians, we know how to bite the hands that feed us."[66] Histories of aesthetic, material, and spatial practice and works have informed my methods over twelve years of scholarly intimacy with Dadaab. I draw from training in the architectural history of the global modern and the Islamic world as well as methods of ethnography, history, and media studies; capacity in multiple languages; ten years of work as an architect and planner, first in India and then in the United States; five years as a researcher for philanthropic and advocacy groups engaged with emergency relief and aid; and more than ten years of research into African history, with extensive study in urban areas and border camps in East Africa. My perspective from the humanities differs from that of most of the researchers who have studied refugee camps, usually through law, political science, social science, or technical specializations. My experiences have taught me to think of architecture in the broadest terms and in socially and politically engaged ways, and oriented me intellectually to East Africa, where the stakes of architectural history are high. This is made clear, for example, by archaeologist Sada Mire's recuperating and writing the archaeology of Somaliland and Somalia in a reclamation of heritage for societies still struggling with the cultural losses caused by war; Omar Deegan's architectural practice of recovering and documenting Mogadishu's designed and built environment in spite of its physical destruction and ruin; Delia Wendel's scholarly sifting through the material practices undertaken by the people and government of Rwanda to construct genocide memorials; or Dadaab's designers, builders, and thinkers making home and world.[67] Keeping those urgencies in mind, it is precisely my scholarly and impersonal relationship to Dadaab that has convinced me, over years, of its significance in unexpected architectural and historical registers.

In 2010, I began research in the UNHCR archives, which immediately turned my attention to Dadaab as a significant site of humanitarian operations. In order to focus on Dadaab and study the environments and architectures this book has ultimately examined, I sought a position as an intern at the Women's Refugee Commission, or WRC. As a research organization advocating for women and children, established by leaders of the International Rescue Committee, or IRC, it provided a supportive scaffold for a study of architecture and history in a refugee camp, and, in turn, I contributed my academic skills to its endeavors.[68] The organization commissions and publishes research on conditions impacting women and girls in displacement contexts, in order to advocate for refugees and support relief practitioners. It is able to conduct global-level research by working closely with organizations on the ground. I was skeptical of a US-based organization intervening in gender studies in heterogeneous Muslim, African, and Asian environments with which it lacks direct affiliation, and questioned how it worked in multiple global South contexts and managed relationships with local refugee aid practitioners and advocacy organizations. I also took note of its limited public criticism (despite the perspective its research might produce) of US policy on asylum, immigration, and borders, or the political responsibility the country holds for many displacements of people stemming from wars it has initiated, engaged, or escalated. Yet the actions of the WRC, as a small organization, offered a "light touch" (due to leanness in the organization's structure, shared by the IRC), and it was respected for the quality of its research, both in the fields of relief and advocacy within the countries in which it works as well as in the international humanitarian system. Working within the organization offered a remarkable vantage. In contrast to the methods of ethnographers whose long residency within or near refugee camps formed the core of their social science scholarship, my aim was to look closely at designed objects and built environments alongside institutions, which required examining the built environment from many perspectives: on the ground, in archives, and from elsewhere.[69] My position at the WRC provided a situated view of many environments where refugees and aid workers live and labor, and familiarized me with the internal operations of other organizations and agencies in the humanitarian system, notably offering me an "inside" view of the UNHCR without having to be embedded in that agency's bureaucracy, and also bringing me into close conversation with local entities serving displaced people, from the Refugee Consortium of Kenya to refugee construction collectives in Dadaab. Displaced people from diverse backgrounds and across the gender spectrum seemed to be comfortable with the organization, as evidenced by the sensitive material contained in its reports. I aimed to discuss objects, environments, and ecologies with women and people who did not identify as cis-male; around the world, they constitute the majority of people living in refugee camps, yet they are not always the people in refugee communities who venture forward to interact or work with researchers. The WRC and the organizations and people with which it collaborated enabled conversations with important interlocutors. In spite of the asymmetries that often exist between displaced people and the regime of humanitarian NGOs that can govern life in camps, the care and consideration behind these rare preexisting relationships enabled refugees to admit outsiders into the safe spaces and frameworks they coconstructed, and talk with ease. Refugees could also refuse to do so, and often did. The WRC makes clear that no remuneration, favors, or obligations accompany interviews. Ultimately, the organization's cultivated ability to move among all the constituencies constructing and inhabiting the architecture of camps, from the most vulnerable to the most powerful, provided a resource that deeply informed the scholarship in these pages.

On behalf of the WRC, I researched ways that various livelihoods exposed displaced people to gender-based violence or deepened their risk. I compiled the literature on gender violence prevention; conducted interviews with refugees, aid workers, and field specialists; and drafted a report for publication.[70] As I fulfilled my responsibilities, the WRC accommodated my scholarly research, providing me with logistical support during my international travel in return for my supervision of teams visiting camps and other sites. For example, I traveled with Columbia University School of International and Public Affairs student teams to refugee hosting sites in Ethiopia and Kenya, providing guidance and liaising with the WRC. One of the students who accompanied me to Dadaab, Bethany Young, contributed substantial significant photographic and interview material, as well as a special perspective as a Jamaican studying in the United States, and her work appears throughout this book. In 2010 and 2011, I visited several camps and other locations where refugees are hosted—for example, neighborhoods and apartment blocks in cities in Ethiopia, Kenya, and Bangladesh. Though I declined further travel with the organization, I prepared deep site-specific study for "missions," as the visits were called, to Uganda and Thailand, and further research in South Africa and India. The WRC permitted me to include oral historical questions related to my scholarly research in interviews conducted as part of its advocacy and policy research. Its teams conducted interviews in English and worked closely with interpreters sourced by the IRC and known within local communities.[71] Within refugee camps, the supportive labor of these interpreters involved far more than translation, often including deep bridging between the research teams and individuals and communities. Many of these interviews are included in digital collections the organization donated to the Duke University Human Rights Archive.

This work offered me the privilege of visiting Dadaab in person. To do so as a foreigner has never been a minor matter, and while the pages to follow will expound further, it is worth prefacing them by saying that my visits were chaperoned by the WRC, under the aegis of the IRC and in partnership with the UNHCR. It is common to travel to Dadaab from Nairobi by bus, from the predominantly Somali neighborhood of Eastleigh to the market in Ifo camp. Many do so in spite of having to cross multiple checkpoints and handling the burdens leading to and faced at each of these moments. My professional position required me to fly from the minor Wilson Airport in Nairobi on a World Food Programme (WFP)-chartered flight to the Dadaab airport; stay in the UNHCR compound with its international and domestic staff members and international staff members of all other agencies and organizations (except Médecins Sans Frontières, or MSF); adhere to curfews when visiting the camps; and travel within or between camps in the company of a police escort. These escorts were usually male; they were always armed with rifles, always remained within a line of sight and at a significant distance from the researchers, and never entered refugees' dwellings or shops in our presence. Security protocols varied per agency or organization—for example, MSF staff living in a compound in Dagahaley camp and UNHCR staff living in the segregated and fortified UNHCR compound away from the camps. Security protocols followed by the IRC, and in turn the WRC, represent a point on the spectrum between these. Dadaab was and is under the highest security restrictions and has been the target of both insurgency and counterinsurgency measures. I limited time spent directly in the camps, as the presence of non-residents drew from the pool of available resources (food, housing, and more) and had the potential to draw attention to interview participants beyond that for which they may have prepared. The risks I assumed, incommensurate to those faced by people living in the camps, stemmed from my visibility as both foreigner and female in a milieu in which unarmed aid workers had been kidnapped, raped, held for ransom, or killed—dangers indeed, although best framed in terms of the inequality of lives.[72] When my research could be undertaken remotely, in direct communication with refugees and aid workers in Dadaab, I elected this method. My decisions on how to conduct research raised sometimes unresolvable conceptual and methodological problems, and not a small degree of anxiety related to knowledge formation in military zones and in compliance with the police state, questions about the claims and distinctions of feminist theory and praxis, and concerns about how architecture and history collude with power and reinforce colonial practices. However, in the years since I began this work, the barriers between the worlds outside and inside the camps have been more frequently bridged by people who were raised in the camps. This has occurred through the mobility and migration of individuals, formal external initiatives (for example, education programs such as Borderless Higher Education for Refugees or Film Aid's journalism projects), and robust communications and remittance platforms.[73] This bridging and collaboration will work toward eroding the borders imposed on people in the Dadaab refugee camps.

Dadaab's significance has in great part to do with its place in a global history, however little known. Thus, to build on and contextualize primary research in Dadaab, during a period between 2010 and 2012, I consulted papers and interviewed people in unique institutions within the global field of humanitarian practice capable of archiving this significance. Among others, these included the Oxford Refugee Studies Centre and its papers in the University of Oxford Bodleian Social Science Library; Oxfam in Oxford; Shelter Centre and its curated library in Geneva; the International Committee of the Red Cross (ICRC) archives in Geneva; the UNHCR archives in Geneva, central offices in Nairobi, Bangkok, and Dhaka, and several regional suboffices, including in Dadaab; the UNHCR and International Federation of Red Cross and Red Crescent Societies (IFRC) shelter and settlements units in Geneva; the NRC in Nairobi; the Danish Refugee Council in Copenhagen; the IRC in Nairobi, Addis Ababa, and New York; and three MSF sections: the unit in Mérignac near Bordeaux, where I examined kits and mobile architectures designed and assembled for deployment in Africa and around the world (MSF

Logistique), the offices and library in Paris, where I studied the curated collection of books, papers, and manuals (MSF-France), and CRASH (Centre de Réflexion sur l'Action et les Savoirs Humanitaires), MSF's research and critical reflection unit.[74] Over the course of twelve years, I visited libraries and private collections in addition to those mentioned, across East Africa, South Asia, and Europe. I conducted individual and group interviews in person and remotely, involving approximately three hundred refugees, aid workers, architects, scholars, officials, and others. Because many people engaged openly in interviews, I often refer to them by name, as contributors to the oral historical record and protagonists in the history. Yet, because I cultivated discussions with so many people, and heard refrains emerge in multiple conversations, I also draw conclusions based on amalgams I have constructed, without citing any particular interviews. More than half of these interviews were based in Dadaab or involved people with intimate personal or professional connections to it. While the mobility to conduct a study with this range is a privilege, it was also an aspect of the methodology. It established a certain attentiveness and comparative knowledge in a study attuned to migration.[75] I conducted this work over a long span of time in order to enable research in many Souths as well as many Norths, and in spaces well beyond the capitals, centers, or humanitarian headquarters—including in many refugee camps.

Over time, I examined the files and libraries of several humanitarian organizations, interviewed architects in different parts of the world who had designed or managed camps, and talked with many refugees. I met with many refugee mothers who shared insights and travails. Part of my task in these pages is to build on their pedagogy by illuminating the place and significance of their work in broader histories common to all. Conversely, I believe they put faces and names into histories of modernity prone to abstraction. I present excerpts of some of our conversations in these pages. People placed faith in me to share this content, as well as images of themselves, their children, and the places where they live and work. I include photographs taken with the permission of those in the images, or their caregivers. (Please note that children in the photos are no longer recognizable due to the passage of time.) In all instances, I attempt to capture the context in which words and images emerged. My intention in deploying the words and images of others is to construct a fuller, affective picture of Dadaab, of humanitarian settlement, and of an architecture of migration. I also mobilize my own words in order to share the orientations, limits, aims, and imperfections of my questions and our dialogues, to build knowledge from embodied experience and relations with others, and to dismiss at the outset claims to anything other than a situated knowledge.[76] I insist that what I present here are *fragments*, from which fuller stories may emerge.[77] I invite readers to take this archive on its own terms and produce their own conclusions.

This pictorial writing and critical archiving strategy owes no small debt to John Berger's *A Seventh Man* and Edward Said's *After the Last Sky: Palestinian Lives*.[78] Each of these books was conceived as an entanglement of the text with photographs taken by photographer Jean Mohr, whose career included extensive reportage and image production for the UNHCR and the World Health Organization. They are iconic books not only for their style but for their pathos and their singular, sympathetic focus on migrants: the former on guest workers in Europe and the latter on refugees in Palestine. Read in the present day, they behave also as pictorial archives of the phenomena they discuss.

Much in the spirit of those two works, this book is predicated on an acknowledgment of the acute and profound practice of caregiving within which forced migrants labor. The intimate work of refugee mothers collaborating, crafting domesticities and worlds, and contending with emergency by making a built environment serves an end beyond survival. Indeed, by the time an asylum seeker reaches a space of refuge, she has already done more than survive. This intimacy labor conserves experience and memory and gathers energy toward life and futures beyond emergency. As such, it serves as a critical heritage practice. This intimate heritage work, embodied in architecture, its histories, and the possibilities it wages for the future, has shaped Dadaab, and carries impacts far beyond it.

AN ETHIC

To study architectural history in a refugee camp is to acknowledge a seeming epistemological precarity, underlying a moral one. The need to turn regularly to contingent primary sources begged the question of why secured repositories and official archives suggested a sense of fixity, and why the stories and things belonging to migrant people lacked this authority. Studying emergency environments, the international humanitarian system, and Dadaab regularly raised questions about the precarity of primary research sources, while also illuminating their inadequacy. Formal documentary archives alone were wholly unequal to the study of an emergency environment, that is, to building a conventional body of evidence for a history, or a credible one.[79] However, it became even more pressing to me to understand the intelligibility of an archive as both precarious and as inadequate.

As I collected a database of oral histories to counteract these problems, my own implication in the process of interviewing hundreds of people transformed my methods and my "authority." Officials, aid workers, and refugees alike, who seemed uninterested in what I had learned in archives, allowed me into their conversations after I notified them that I had visited Dadaab and several other refugee camps. As one young aid worker put it, in response to my questions about processes of establishing recognition and gaining the trust of both refugees and aid workers who would be the interlocutors for the research, "You've got to be in the field, you have to have done your time in the field, you have to have your battle scars from Somalia and Darfur . . . in order to establish yourself as a credible point person."[80] Moving beyond the colloquialisms of this speech, it was difficult not to notice the offhand militaristic language acknowledging the closed space of the refugee camp. What did it mean?

The central problem to writing a history of any emergency environment—humanitarian or other—is not the lack of an archive, but the absence of one. This epistemic vacuum seems to be a matter of politics well understood by those involved. Refugee camps are *not supposed to* leave a trace. They are intended to be fugitive spaces, sometimes obscured by the people sheltering, perhaps hiding, and sometimes by the activities of the people protecting them. Yet, many people in Dadaab sought to share their experiences and perspectives. Why? To resolve this question and recover the history in those absences, meanwhile, demands a risk of potential collusion with forms of carceral migration.[81] As quietly explained by Alishine Osman, a resident of Ifo camp in Dadaab for all of his childhood and youth, "When you live in a refugee camp for twenty-five years, you are not the same as others who have identity, education, and legal rights to move around the country or from one country to another."[82] Studying spaces steeped in the moral, practical, and discursive paradoxes of carceral migration is not a neutral task. It is a fraught one that demands an ethic.

In developing an ethic, I began with a close examination of research methodology. Ironically, Dadaab can be studied by conventional means, as the later chapters of this book show; that is, a narrative and an image—the basis of an architectural history—can be constructed wholly from outside of the camps. The settlements at Dadaab have been drafted and documented by many, which is not the case for many refugee environments.[83] Their planning, design, and construction exhibit the work of the state-sanctioned expert as well as the organic intellectual, offering a range of protagonists to follow.[84] Yet, a study of Dadaab raises problems well beyond scholarly methodological convention. While the present study aims to counter the epistemic violence of disappeared histories, it has also engaged forces responsible for other forms of spatial, environmental, and more directly encountered violence.[85] Perhaps more at Dadaab than at many other refugee camps, even those administered by the UNHCR, people have served with frequency as objects of research for academics, policy researchers, and practitioners operating from many institutional positions and in many disciplines.[86] To counter this problem demands rigors of a different kind.

Countering epistemic violence calls for methods tied scrupulously to an ethic. Mine revolved around a commitment to continuous negotiations in research and writing. Among the continuous negotiations were questions of how to research in ways that prioritized collaborative knowledge formation over colonial valuation practices and cultural imperialism, how to write in ways that would acknowledge historical difference reparatively and restoratively, and how to construct bridges to a shared narrative that might be common to many across asymmetries. My hope is that the historical constructions and methodology of this book bring Dadaab into the narrative such that those most intimate with it might comfortably and critically intervene over time if and as they see fit, and those most distant might comprehend the worth of an architecture of migration. Education scholar Linda Tuhiwai Smith (Ngāti Awa and Ngāti Porou, Māori), writing in favor of Indigenous agency in research, and more broadly on the researcher's being implicated in the research, warned protectively of this "research" that she called a "dirty word," in that "belief in the ideal that benefiting mankind is indeed a primary outcome of scientific research is as much a reflection of ideology as it is of academic training. It becomes so taken for granted that many researchers simply assume that they as individuals embody this ideal and are natural representatives of it when they work with other communities."[87] This book takes up her challenge to "question the assumed nature of those ideals and the practices that they generate."[88] I do so in considering the work of future readers and writers of a narrative of Dadaab and any architectures of migration it represents, and how the narrative constructed here might serve them. I propose that it does a form of bridge work, in addressing a partition at the conceptual and theoretical core of an architecture of migration—and of modern architectural history more generally, as it is broadly understood. The refugee camp, as an architectural end of humanitarian practice, *encourages* and certainly also *discourages* migration. This conundrum transforms the refugee camp from a site of aid for those in need—that is, a monument (if provisional) to the humanitarian ideal—to a site of concentration, which contours darker histories of detention. Just as modern architecture has been a partner to colonialism, the entanglement of migration and incarceration has been a common theme in its past, a ghost that inhabits its history.[89] This entanglement constitutes the implicit heritage of the refugee camp as a form of modern architecture, a legacy of the twinned condition of migration and incarceration, of modernity and colonial practices. Yet, this Janus-faced heritage also creates the discursive access point for the refugee camp, situating Dadaab as a locus for a critical history.[90] My aim is to negotiate an analysis and build critical understanding of this heritage, drawing on *an ethic as method* in order to make a historiographical bridge.

This book is a call for peace. It is a stand against militaristic knowledge formation. It grew out of a deep reflection on architecture as an instrument of power, informed by the quandaries of studying in war contexts in which people are denied freedom of migration. The oppressive scrutiny of people moving through the Dadaab refugee camps and the attendant production of a body of literature and imagery manufactured a viable object for historical study. Scholarship takes advantage of such enclosures and ought to assume equal burdens of intellectual and moral responsibility to understand them. That is especially so for scholarship produced in imperialist contexts—which describes all scholarship, like this book, produced in academic institutions of the United States. The relationship of scholarship to a militaristic framework is part of what this book aims to confront. These frameworks can be eroded through scholarly awareness and a commitment to an ethic. For me, this ethic has included taking seriously a suppressed architecture as a subject, listening to people directly involved in or impacted by its histories and ecologies, and mobilizing my own viewpoints as a situated and embodied scholar, in order to move toward a liberatory knowledge.

The ethical task demands the act of *writing with*, of researching and constructing narratives in critical sympathy and solidarity.[91] This has called for radical collaborations and the historiographical privileging, rather than effacement, of difference. In the words of feminist theorist Audre Lorde, "Only within that interdependency of different strengths, acknowledged and equal, can the power to seek new ways of being in the world generate, as well as the courage and sustenance to act where there are no charters."[92] As she argues elsewhere, exercises in privileged shame and distress over asymmetries must be superseded by action that takes difference in hand. As she writes, "Guilt is only another form of objectification."[93] In this book, I commit to many forms of difference, beginning with finding architecture and history in a refugee camp. This book is an attempt to learn from and write with the refugees at Dadaab and with others whose labor has contoured an architecture of migration. The intellectual work of these collaborators infuses this book. This acknowledgment is not to assert equivalences that diminish structural inequalities or suggest impossible commensurabilities, but hopefully to place value on the thinking, making, and knowing of interlocutors living their lives in state-administered camps or laboring in humanitarian regimes and to locate their work discursively within broader intellectual histories. It is also to acknowledge the epistemic and spatial violence that can go unstated in academic production.[94] Historiographic approaches can deny certain subjects access to discourse or, alternatively, radically bolster discursivity. In attempting the latter, I turn back to Trouillot: "Human beings participate in history both as actors and as narrators."[95] Following that kernel, this book intervenes first and foremost into the historical narrative, in a spirited, critical act of learning with its subjects.

Dadaab's discursive efficacy lies in the imaginations of its inhabitants and their transcendence of emergency subjecthood to do more than subsist. The text and images in these pages notate ways that, despite radical curtailments of agency, these figures have constructed lifeworlds and authority through architecture and the labor associated with it. Their words and faces as the architects and narrators of Dadaab infuse these pages. Writing with them shifts the narrative to new forms of authority. On this, it is important to note that, while I worked by listening to many people, I do not consider their words as testimony. My methods do not follow conventional ethnographic models, not even those that trace nonhuman subjects or, indeed, designed objects. While I acknowledge the inherently social life of my objects of concern, my precise aim is an analysis not of societies, but of an architecture of migration. Moreover, I do not believe that studying a built environment through ground-level approaches automatically equates to ethnography. Ethnography relies on an affective defamiliarization of a subject for the sake of its analysis. If anything, I have worked to develop an intimacy with the Dadaab complex of refugee camps—even to share with it a domesticity—with the aim of *writing it differently*. Working in Dadaab gave me the opportunity to observe an architecture in use and up close, and to meet people for whom this place and its history might have special meaning. Rather than studying people at a site, it was important to me to hear from people for whom Dadaab has been *home*, for whom my situating the camps as both *historical* and *architectural*—if we understand these markers as taking seriously the epistemic and heritage value of a place—would not occupy a theoretical realm alone. Rather than approaching Dadaab only as an unfamiliar, alien object of "research," this opened the potential for treating it instead as a sensible place, with its own history, origins, and forms of knowledge. This reasoning converges with Griselda Pollock's analysis that "all texts are structured by their own rhetorical figures," as she names another aim, that "the conscious awareness of 'narrative' when we write 'history' has special resonances for feminists in their desire not only to do history differently but to tell tales in such a way as to make a difference in the totality of the spaces we call knowledge."[96] This book's primary method has been to seek different subjects and objects, historical and political.

THEORETICAL POSSIBILITIES

This diversity emerges in the structure and arc of the book. Taking the Dadaab settlement as an analytic, the book's arguments unfold along a narrative path that reverses the typical structure of an ethnography or material study, either of which moves in the direction of observation and description to analysis and theorization. Instead, the chapters are arranged to present theoretical arguments at the outset, in chapters 1–3, in order to empower the reader to arrive with an expanded knowledge to the immediate history and ecology of the settlement in chapter 4, and to those of a global humanitarian material culture in chapter 5. Encountering a humanitarian environment without first implanting the conceptual premise of drawing theory from forms runs the risk of presenting a teleology, of naturalizing the foreign humanitarian camp rather than estranging it. Refugee camps are frequently rendered as objects of emergency, whose manufactured ahistoricity and abjection imply that people brought the camp, as an endpoint, upon themselves. Instead, Dadaab reveals long historical processes that could have come to other ends. It demonstrates material and epistemic richness in the present. The chapters of this book build, each on the last, to counter a teleology of a refugee camp and to show that it is *not* its own logical end. Rather than a tragedy of the refugee camp in general, and Dadaab in particular, this material and social trajectory is a profound site of theory. It is an architecture of migration.

The opening chapters reveal Dadaab slowly through three frames that build on one another, beginning with the vital conceptualization that undergirds the book: that when we see a refugee camp, what we encounter—what lies underneath—is a partition. That an architecture of migration comes *from partitions* is the first argument made in the book, in chapter 1, and is intended to immediately dispel conventional views of refugee camps by arguing that specific historical and rhetorical forces construct them as oppressed spaces. The first chapter argues that a camp is not an intact event but stems from partitions of land and self. Chapter 2 is intended to push the reader beyond the frame of emergency to see history in Dadaab, positing that the Dadaab camps emerged out of long and contradictory historical forces of sedentarization and not only a recent emergency. Chapter 3 leads the reader beyond the frame of shelter to intimacies and domesticities, illuminating Dadaab's located domesticities as part of broader, universal histories and global spatial practices of shelter. Having followed this path of eliminating preconceptions, the reader will be critically strengthened to arrive to the humanitarian camp in chapter 4 and humanitarian designs in chapter 5.

The chapters are organized along regimes of historicity: from the first, whose considerations inhabit a period of nearly three hundred years, to the fifth, which occupies a much shorter period during the first decades of the twenty-first century. They are also organized according to spatial registers, expanding or contracting with each chapter, from the single site to the spheres across which its subjects and objects migrate. In each chapter, a vignette brings into focus one aspect of the constructed environment in Dadaab. The vignette speaks to the empirical conditions that distinguish the Dadaab refugee camps, setting the stage for a global history and an intellectual history explored in each chapter. This structure is a strategy to demonstrate how Dadaab "in situ" can open onto Dadaab "in theory."

Chapter 1, "From Partitions," explores the argument foundational to the book, the question of what we learn through close looking at a refugee camp. Underlying a refugee camp is a partition. This chapter begins the book's study with two forms of partition central to understanding a history of the Dadaab refugee camps: the partition of land, a colonial practice that entrenches contestations over territory, and the partition of the self, a humanitarian one that stratifies the lives of persons. Beginning with a dialogue between myself and Alishine Osman, a former resident of the Dadaab refugee camps, the chapter uses the architectural and political divide created by the settlements as a lens on the long figuration and construction of a humanitarian borderland. It examines humanitarian settlement in the eighteenth and nineteenth centuries and the fraught partition of the Somali Jubaland in the twentieth century to study how emergency intervention entangled discourses on human rights with those of territory. Learning from the refugee camp in this way enables a conceptual reorientation toward it.

Chapter 2, "Land, Emergency, and Sedentarization in East Africa," uses the problem of enclosure—as legal strategy and empirical space—to argue that the refugee camp is prefigured by approaches to land that intertwine the construction of emergency territory with sedentarization. The chapter opens with a discussion of the yield of a farm, in the form of a kitchen garden designed by Maganai Saddiq Hassan on her assigned plot, which transformed the arid landscape of Dagahaley refugee camp into a lush, green cultivation. Her agricultural skill is the aftermath of a history of land contestations and practices of enslavement in the Jubaland and a longer path toward sedentarization enacted in a refugee camp. These threads are woven together, first, in an analysis of the construction of the marginal territory in which the Dadaab refugee camps were sited; second, in a prehistory for the refugee camps in the manyattas (the villages, or settlements) used for liberation or coercion in the nineteenth, twentieth, and twenty-first centuries; and third, in two building types, the makuti and the tuqul, which represent sedentarization and resistance to it. This chapter finds the justification for humanitarian settlement as well as the logic for settler colonialism in the abolitionist cultivation of land, a moral imperative that pathologized the nomad and instituted the drive to mass sedentarization, ultimately by carceral means.

Chapter 3, "Shelter and Domesticity," examines the architectural coordinates of shelter, so central to humanitarian practice and discourse, and the conceptual problem of domesticity, so crucial for refugee lives. The chapter theorizes the insurgent domesticities of Dadaab, to contextualize a shelter initiative led by Shamso Abdullahi Farah, a pregnant mother living in Ifo camp in the 2000s, and the NRC, an organization specializing in architectural design of shelters. The chapter sets this relief-cum-development work into a history of institutionalization of a global professional architectural and planning practice of emergency relief, beginning in the early 1950s and systematizing in the 1990s. Farah's authority emerges in the domesticities of emergency, in a context that reproduces the emergency homemaker as architect. The chapter explores this and other domesticities that extend the refugee camp well beyond the utilitarian practice and pragmatic discourse of shelter, while also reimagining the theory of shelter so deeply embedded in architectural history.

Chapter 4, "An Archive of Humanitarian Settlement," labors in the space of expanded knowledge built in the three preceding chapters, to present a history of the planning and settlement of Ifo, Dagahaley, and Hagadera camps. It moves through a carefully constructed archive and adopts the historical convention of periodization to produce a narrative of the Dadaab refugee camps from 1991 to 2011. These twenty years represent the time during which official archives of the Dadaab refugee camps remained classified and inaccessible to the public, and the growth, structure, and architecture of the settlements formed the primary record of life in the camps. This chapter begins with foreign architects—that is, *not* civil engineers, but professionals trained in spatial planning and aesthetics—working in Dadaab during the earliest phases of relief operations. It ends with Dadaab's architects, in a photo essay on Ifo camp's food and water distribution (the primary function and infrastructure of any refugee camp), which operates as an archive of humanitarian settlement.

Chapter 5, "Design as Infrastructure," zooms in on the Dadaab camps' component architectures, authored "works" by major relief organizations as well as refugees in Dadaab: that is, the tarps, tents, and other structures whose design histories chart the material intersections between the camp and the world. The chapter begins and ends with collectives of women whose labor, organization, design collaborations, and building have lent form to the site and created an infrastructure of people within an architecture of migration. Juxtaposing these spatial practices and mobile architectures gives a textured picture of Dadaab, in which *design*—as noun and verb—assumes the role of urgent, lifesaving infrastructure. Yet, ironically, the practices and forms that comprise this infrastructure evince authorship. This chapter examines humanitarian iconography, signature practices, and social lives of objects, putting refugees' localized work in Dadaab into conversation with the global work of humanitarian organizations. Together they create questions about the commodification of aid and paradoxical collaborations in the material practices of humanitarian relief, which underlie a contradictory liberal discourse.

The afterword, "Poetry Is a Weapon That We Use in Both War and Peace," closes on contemporary arts and architectural practices, highlighting work commissioned as part of the process of writing this book, to honor the landscape of pasts and futures a refugee camp opens onto and to test the arguments made in these pages. "Poetry is a weapon that we use in both war and peace," sings the Somali poet Hadraawi. Thinking with the aesthetic and oral traditions carried on by migrants, I argue that the same may be said of architecture. This book looks to the architecture and history of the Dadaab refugee camps for the poetic "weapon" of critical heritage, which endures through war or peace.

A set of critical knowledges comes from the terms set out in the first three chapters. A different ground then emerges in chapter 4, in which a humanitarian settlement represents not merely a zone of rupture and trauma but a historical place with recoverable architectural historical import. It then becomes possible to "see" architectures of emergency relief in chapter 5—the landscapes of tarps and tents—as part of an overall defamiliarization. This is the theoretical and discursive possibility offered by Dadaab.

At the heart of this book is an abolitionist feminist scholarly commitment. I undertake an exercise in close looking at a locus of forced migration as a setting for architecture and history, to clarify the growth and structure of a unique group of settlements; colonial forms and practices of underdevelopment, emergency, counterinsurgency, and sedentarization that prefigured those settlements; and the global histories of architects and architectures in which they played a part. This book is about Dadaab, but Dadaab provides a heuristic for many other pressing studies. I advocate for a nuanced understanding of Dadaab's specificity and significance, but also for the perception of its architecture as supporting diverse inquiry—theoretical, historical, political, and ethical—about the world. This existential as well as epistemic framing of Dadaab is intended to articulate a conceptual ecology through which to read the history of this site, and the wider histories onto which it opens. Architecture and history need not form a cage.

(*previous page*) The land across present-day Kenya, Somalia, and Ethiopia.

From Partitions 1

Keeping mouths, ears, and eyes shut,
parents had partitioned sorrow,
purchased even more silence,
and promised a "better future."
—Yvonne Adhiambo Owuor

Approaching Dadaab by air and seeing its landscape from a plane's window is a rare and privileged view. Divided land is framed as a spatial totality, one that a photograph might capture. The framing in this chapter's opening image makes a radical proposition. It whispers that the ground underneath the refugee camps is an undivided whole. To make an argument for that entirety, in which land is a commons, this chapter looks closely at partitions as the conceptual and material construct underlying the refugee camp. The text here offers a corrective to that ideology of partitions manifested in the architecture of the Dadaab refugee camps by setting it within a spatial and historical landscape of migrations.

Just as a refugee camp represents an afterlife of material and territorial partitions of land, it also partitions people and the individuated self. Legally and socially, the refugee camp severs groups of people within it from those outside it. In Dadaab, members of the same families or others who share forms of community or kinship live across such a divide. The refugee camp further segregates humanity according to who possesses the power to come into rights to receive care or be protected with dignity. Furthermore, the camp manifests conceptual and metaphysical partitions of personhood. The camp splits the modern subject, twinning this figure into itself and a double, the latter of which may be assigned race, gender, or other consequential designations. In refugee camps, people experience a radical partitioning of the self as they negotiate new forms of subjecthood in emergency. Like the material partitions of land that give rise to borders and the refugee camps that buttress them, these metaphysical varieties of partitioning reproduce what I call *partition thinking*.

I focus on two forms of partition in this chapter, both of which underpin a conceptual reorientation toward refugee camps and remain central to understanding Dadaab. Through the first, the partition of land, I substantively reframe the discourse on borders often used to theoretically situate the refugee camp. I turn instead to partitions as an analytic that imagines unbordered land. A rendering of land as territory, which a state can then rationalize as a divisible geometry, entrenches contestations and extends colonial practices into postcolonial time and space.[1] A refugee camp often establishes a latent form of division of a territory, as an architecture of emergency relief that responds to a pronounced geographical border that inscribes a partition. Most of the refugees in Dadaab migrated from Somalia, crossing a border reinforcing the British partition of the Jubaland in the 1920s. To counter the reproduction of this bordering in the architecture of the refugee camps demands a view of land as a continuous ground beneath one's feet, one that is part of older and longer histories. Territorial delineations of the nation-state do not map onto such definitions, as observed, for example, by pastoralists living in the vicinity of Dadaab. As such, the concept of territorial partition is one of the fallacies of the nation-state. In the end, land *cannot* be riven. While the nation-state has constructed borders throughout its history, this ultimate failure to reify them is the aporia that testifies to the concept of a continuous ground portrayed in this chapter's opening image. This chapter focuses on an analysis of partitions, via a refugee camp, which brings land and architecture into relation. To move beyond partition thinking, I center fuller depictions of the ecologies and materialities of the Dadaab refugee camps that acknowledge partitions and advocate for their traversals.

The second form of partition this chapter attends to is that of the self, a stratification of personhood, which underlies the divide between refugee and humanitarian defining life experience in a camp. The rationale behind the Western humanitarian impetus, rooted in liberal conceptualizations of rights that spring from the individual rather than the polity, is that a person's *humanity* entitles her to rescue and care. Yet, this humanity requires *recognition* by another. Herein lies a stunning paradox. Within the practical, legal apparatus of recognition in a refugee context, a critical bifurcation occurs, in that the self as experienced in emergency is increasingly differentiated from the self as recognized by others. This radical differentiation parallels the making of the racinated modern subject iconically identified in the psychiatric analyses that political philosopher Frantz Fanon forwarded as a deformed recognition of the colonized by the colonizer, a status obtained through deference and subterfuge rather than struggle, which was thus incomplete and insufficient; it results in a form of "underdevelopment" of the self, to return to historian Walter Rodney's key term, offered as a framing concept in this book's introduction.[2] This racialization and underdevelopment results in a doubling effect, a problem I examine in this chapter through theorizations by social historian W. E. B. Du Bois and others. A liberatory imaginary of an unpartitioned self counters this doubling condition and challenges the consignment of the refugee camp to limitations of form and theory. I work from the generous scaffold offered by Black and Brown consciousness theories to pursue this theoretical potential. Following Rodney, Du Bois, and others, I think on the Dadaab refugee camps within a global imaginary of Blackness and, in addition, within Afro-Asian and Indian Ocean consciousnesses.[3] Within these framings, a liberation from partition thinking, as it relates to selfhood, can be more generatively conceived.

Dadaab serves as an object lesson with which to think from partitions and move beyond partition thinking, by analyzing the partitions it embodies as an architecture of migration. I begin this work by introducing the reader to the vibrant environment of Dadaab at the outset, sharing my discussion with a former resident over photos that we each took within the refugee camps. Our discussion of the divides created by the camps and our traversals across them are captured below in a dialogue we coedited, followed by meditations on partitions of the land and the self.

Traversals

The following discussion of life in the refugee complex at Dadaab is an amalgam of exchanges between me and Alishine Hussein Osman from 2011 to 2017. We developed the text of this discussion together, for publication as "Traversals: In and Out of the Dadaab Refugee Camps," an article in the fiftieth issue of the Yale annual journal *Perspecta*.[4] Titled "Urban Divides," the issue was conceived by architects Meghan McCallister and Mahdi Sabbagh, whose committed intellectual interest in partitions in Ireland and Palestine buttressed our writing and editing process. Through our article, Osman and I refracted the most salient and urgent aspects of the partitions reinforced by the Dadaab refugee camps within a larger governed space. Although some of the conditions we discussed have changed since the time of this publication, presenting the previously published coedited dialogue in its narrative entirety achieves certain critical aims while introducing and contextualizing the architecture and landscapes of Dadaab in a way that informs the reading of the rest of this book. Namely, the coedited dialogue acknowledges the labor of collaborative knowledge production that is needed to study contested spaces and histories such as those Dadaab presents. As such, this dialogue remains true to the authorial and editorial contributions of its participants and retains the tone, and sometimes the ellipses, contradictions, and pivots, of conversation—all of which provide unexpected insights. It foregrounds spaces that, when theorized, have often been abstracted, rather than thought through the embodiment and aesthetics of actual lives that make the stakes of this theory palpable. Capturing this collaborative formation of knowledge and the aesthetic ecologies of Dadaab in our words and images underscores through a sensible, affective method the fundamental argument that follows in this chapter and throughout this book: that the refugee camp needs to be thought from partitions as well as their traversal.

As a child, Osman had traveled from Kismayo on the southern coast of Somalia to Dadaab, arriving to Ifo camp at age five in 1991 with the first group of refugees to be relocated in Dadaab. His education began in the primary school that was established by the UNHCR, and he was a member of the first cohort of refugee students to receive a high school diploma from Ifo Secondary School. He held multiple positions after completing this education, insofar as the humanitarian system enabled him to assume employment; he was a teacher for CARE, a firewood project monitor for GTZ (Deutsche Gesellschaft für Technische Zusammenarbeit, or German Agency for Technical Cooperation), a youth leader, an "informant" for an anthropological study by Cindy Horst, currently of the Peace Research Institute Oslo (PRIO), and a community organizer for the NRC, beginning in 2007—soon after which he was resettled in the United States, where he has since resided and become a citizen.[5] I met him in relation to his work with the NRC, discussed in detail in chapter 3. He was one of the organization's first "incentive" workers in Dadaab.

The humanitarian "incentive" scheme of employment bears attention because it offers a practical example of the partition thinking that governs life in refugee camps, and because "incentive" workers appear as foreground and background figures throughout this book, especially in chapters 3 and

5. Although international refugee law is intended to guarantee refugees the right to work and education, the government of Kenya took exception to those rights and enforced an encampment policy further curtailing them, as discussed in the introduction (a stance taken by many countries). In contexts in which legal employment is disallowed by host governments, "incentive" work enables NGOs to infuse cash and other resources into displaced communities and draw directly from their expertise. Many international organizations in Dadaab retained such a workforce in a mutual aid effort. These workers were paid "incentive" rather than full wages, due to government prohibitions on their salaried compensation—in spite of their qualifications and competence (and, often to their resentment, in spite of their need). On a practical level, however direct and useful in the short term, this system of indirect aid exacerbated asymmetries of labor and citizenship, producing ever greater power differentiations.[6] Conceptually, the system emphasized a partitioning between humanitarians and refugees, members of refugee and host communities, migrants with and without refugee status, people living inside and outside the camps, and people within different refugee communities. At the basis of these differentiations lay partitions of the self that many displaced people referred to in our conversations, and which Osman discusses later in this chapter, in a reflection on the chasm between his youth and the life he might have enjoyed outside of a refugee camp.

Dadaab illustrates a refugee territory divided from the political, social, and economic extents of a host nation. It is partitioned via a policed and surveilled breach between the space of the state and the parallel humanitarian environment. Yet, people and things regularly traverse that scission. Individuals and families formally registered with the government of Kenya or the UNHCR, unregistered asylum seekers, and migrants from within and outside the country cross that divide for goods, services, and opportunities. Other things cross it as well: for example, the mobile architectures that make up the settlements, from people's dwellings to humanitarian latrines, tents, and hospitals. Architecturally, areas of the camps, particularly the markets, share material and aesthetic characteristics with the Kenyan town of Dadaab. Social services related to health, education, physical planning, recreation, and administration, all implemented by NGOs in the settlements, parallel those of the state. Thus, the root partition is mirrored by its own impossibility, as the traversals of people and things reinscribe *and* contest the divide. This traversal of partitions lies at the core of the many paradoxes Osman and I theorize together.

ANOORADHA IYER SIDDIQI: Let's talk about how we each first entered the refugee settlements at Dadaab. It may begin to explain the spatial separation it presents.

As you know, I am a citizen of India by birth and became a US citizen at age sixteen. After working as an architect and in NGOs for many years, I entered doctoral study in architectural history. As part of my scholarly research, I worked with the WRC under the aegis of the IRC. To come to Dadaab, I traveled from the small Wilson Airport in Nairobi on the WFP plane chartered by the UNHCR. At the Dadaab airstrip, the IRC driver picked us up and took our group to stay in the humanitarian compound across the highway from Dadaab town.

ALISHINE HUSSEIN OSMAN: I first arrived in Ifo refugee camp with my family in 1991. After the civil war erupted in Somalia, my family had to flee the country. We arrived at the Kenya-Somalia border, where there were lots of other refugees. We were received by the UNHCR and screened. We entered Kenya by vehicle and were settled at Liboi. Because Liboi was close to Somalia, the UNHCR decided to relocate the refugees to Dadaab a few months later. We were transported by vehicles operated by the UNHCR, and moved to newly established blocks with empty tents, which would become our first home as refugees. That tent in Ifo camp became my home for the next seventeen years.

I graduated from high school in 2003 and worked in many jobs there, including in more than one NGO. I left the camp in 2007 for the United States. I got a bachelor's degree from Pennsylvania State University, and I also became a United States citizen.

It makes me emotional whenever I talk about this, particularly when I compare my seventeen years in Dadaab with my five years here, and think about the time that was lost. I first traveled back in 2009 and met some of my old friends, some of them my classmates in first and second grades. They still live in the refugee camp.

I have visited the camps three times since I moved away, to see my family and friends. During each visit, I was either a citizen or permanent resident of the United States. When traveling to the camp, I usually take the bus from Eastleigh in Nairobi, via Garissa, to the Dadaab camps; the bus station is in the central market in Ifo.[7] Occasionally I take a bus that terminates in Garissa, and catch another one to Dadaab. It is a long trip and sometimes I want to spend a night in Garissa to rest.

ANOORADHA IYER SIDDIQI: I have always been curious: When you applied to college, who wrote your recommendation letters?

ALISHINE HUSSEIN OSMAN: Nobody. I went to Harrisburg Area Community College in Pennsylvania, and took the assessment test for English and math. Based on the results, I was placed in classes in the community college, where I spent a couple of years. When I accumulated enough credits, I transferred to Penn State. The university requested a high school transcript, and they accepted the one issued by Ifo Secondary School. I now work in Harrisburg for a nonprofit social service organization.

When I think about where I grew up, I believe the Dadaab settlements are geographically and politically segregated from the rest of the world. Refugees do not have legal rights to move outside of the camp. Now when I travel there, I am aware that there are numerous checkpoints, in both directions. On the way back to Nairobi, there are many more checkpoints than on the way into the camps. The police check your bags, the photos on your phones, your calls. If you hold a foreign passport with a Kenyan visa, the police capture your biometrics. Even if the UNHCR gave identification cards to the refugees, they could not use them to travel to other parts of Kenya. They need to have an identity document that is called kipande, or kitambulisho.[8]

As time went on, things changed, but initially we lacked means of communication. We didn't have television or telephones. We could not go to Nairobi, or even Garissa. We could not go to Somalia because of the conflict there. We could not go to Ethiopia or other neighboring countries. After nearly seventeen years, I was among a tiny population of refugees offered a resettlement opportunity. When you live in a refugee camp for twenty-five years, you are not the same as others who have identity, education, and legal rights to move around the country or from one country to another, and so on.

ANOORADHA IYER SIDDIQI: Kipande divides people inside and outside the camps. It is a material object that makes spaces and borders. Can you describe it? Is it a piece of paper, or something else? Is it something that could fit in a wallet, like a ration card?

ALISHINE HUSSEIN OSMAN: It is a document, which looks almost like a driver's license that we have here in the United States. But to acquire one is not a simple process. You have to have at least one parent who is a Kenyan. So, how is a refugee going to get that document? A lot of my immediate family members, born in the refugee camp, cannot get Kenyan citizenship.

One of the functions of kipande, from a refugee's perspective, is that it enables travel around the country. In very limited situations, when a person needs medical attention, the UNHCR issues travel documents.

Some students are also issued travel documents so they can go to school for higher education. In 2006, the United Nations started giving an alien card. At the beginning, we refugees thought it would allow us travel privileges, but it did not. Kipande was what was required, which was issued to Kenyans only. Kenyans can travel, but the refugees cannot.

ANOORADHA IYER SIDDIQI: Can you describe how the government issues it?

ALISHINE HUSSEIN OSMAN: The Kenyan government and the UNHCR take biometrics—fingerprints and a photo—to capture the vital information of refugees over the age of eighteen. Once they capture that, they put it in a database. Persons in the database may not apply for Kenyan identification. People in the refugee camps in Kenya cannot acquire that identification and therefore cannot engage in business outside of the camps.

ANOORADHA IYER SIDDIQI: If you are born in the refugee camps, what country are you a citizen of?

ALISHINE HUSSEIN OSMAN: Somalia. Or Ethiopia. Wherever your parents are from.

1.1. UNHCR and Government of Kenya Department of Refugee Affairs movement pass, photo by Bethany Young.

DEPARTMENT OF REFUGEE AFFAIRS (DRA)
Ministry of State for Immigration and Registration of Persons
Box 42227, Nairobi
Kenya

UNHCR
United Nations High Commissioner for Refugees

UNHCR
Sub-Office, Dadaab
Box 43801, Nairobi
Kenya

REF: UNHCR/DDB/PROT/MP/

Date: 20 February 2011

RE:

MOVEMENT PASS

Name:
Nationality:
Case Or HH No:
Camp:
Ration/Token Card No:
DOB:
Garissa District, North Eastern, Kenya.

This is to certify that the above named person(s) is/are individual(s) of concern to the Government of Kenya and UNHCR, falling under the UNHCR's protection mandate.

Pursuant to Section 17(f) of the Refugee Act, 2006, the Refugee Camp Officer, Dadaab Refugee Camp, hereby authorizes the foregoing individual(s) to travel to Nairobi for the following reason: Care Procurement .

The authorities are kindly requested to allow him/her/them safe passage in accordance with this travel authorisation. This document expires on 31st December 2011 and should be surrendered to the Refugee Camp Officer upon return from travel.

Refugees who overstay the validity of the Movement Pass will be subject to sanctions in accordance to Section 25(f) of the Refugees Act, 2006.

H.C Komen
Refugee Camp Officer
Dadaab Camp

ANOORADHA IYER SIDDIQI: You are recognized as a Somali citizen if you were born to Somali parents in the camps in Kenya?

ALISHINE HUSSEIN OSMAN: Yes, the Somali government will not decline citizenship rights because of being born in the refugee camps; they acknowledge that the parents are Somalis.

ANOORADHA IYER SIDDIQI: So, people born in the camps are not actually stateless. If being born in the camps meant that a person did not have citizenship of any country at all, that would be one form of social and political separation from the general population, meaning that the population inside the camps exists outside national space. But to be born in the camps and to inherit the citizenship of your parents raises other questions. What if one of your parents is an Ethiopian refugee and another is a Somali refugee? It creates a different form of citizenship and social space.

ALISHINE HUSSEIN OSMAN: Well, let's say a child is born in the refugee camp, and one of the parents is a Kenyan citizen but the other parent is a Somali refugee. Logically, that child should be a Kenyan citizen.

ANOORADHA IYER SIDDIQI: If so, the Kenyan law could be seen as generous, in a sense.

ALISHINE HUSSEIN OSMAN: The problem is that this is not really something that can be implemented. If a Kenyan citizen marries someone of another nationality, then the spouse may become a Kenyan citizen through marriage. But that is just on paper. I know a Somali refugee who has applied for a Kenyan identification card several times, but was denied. The government has her fingerprints and photos; the system record shows that she is a refugee. This woman has one child, and has been married to a Kenyan citizen for over five years, and lives in Kenya with her husband, but she is still a refugee, and was never able to get a Kenyan citizenship.

ANOORADHA IYER SIDDIQI: On what grounds was she denied?

ALISHINE HUSSEIN OSMAN: It is not really clear on what grounds she was denied. Even though one can apply for citizenship through marriage under Kenyan law, the process typically ends when the authorities find out the applicant is a refugee. Rather than requesting further evidence of proof of relationship, such as a marriage certificate, to determine the eligibility of the claim, the government usually neglects to make the request.

ANOORADHA IYER SIDDIQI: Does she live in the camps?

ALISHINE HUSSEIN OSMAN: No, she lives in Garissa.

ANOORADHA IYER SIDDIQI: Does her child have a Kenyan birth certificate?

ALISHINE HUSSEIN OSMAN: Yes. At age eighteen, he will either register as a refugee, or apply for citizenship through his father. And let me explain the process of applying for identification cards, at least what I remember; things may have changed. First of all, the process doesn't happen every day. The opportunity comes along two to three times a year. There is a clerk from the central government who goes to one part of the city or to one village, with the biometrics equipment. That person waits for the elders to come. Then they gather the local government employees and people from the community. If I were the applicant, I would say: my name is so-and-so, and I am the son of so-and-so. Now, the community would have to say: Oh, we know him! They would have to identify me and verify whether I was the person I said I was. They would have to identify where I was born, and when I was born.

ANOORADHA IYER SIDDIQI: Is it done in a public place?

ALISHINE HUSSEIN OSMAN: They might do it in a school. And that's just the first part of it. These two or three government representatives collect all the biometric data, and they process it. After processing the application, if they find out that the applicant was once a refugee, it would likely be denied. If not, in about three to four months, the applicant would acquire kipande.

Now, the child I was talking about earlier is currently four years old. After he finishes high school, if he doesn't go through the refugee registration process, he should be able to apply for kipande, or kitambulisho, and would most likely have no problem acquiring it.

ANOORADHA IYER SIDDIQI: Why would he apply to be a refugee if he could become a citizen?

ALISHINE HUSSEIN OSMAN: Some people make a claim to refugee status to receive different forms of aid from the camps, including food. Some local citizens are able to register as refugees and come twice a month during the aid distributions to collect food, along with what the agencies call "nonfood items," like plastic sheeting and other materials. Relatives and friends update them with phone calls or text messages as goods become available.

ANOORADHA IYER SIDDIQI: At age eighteen, he could go through the process of registering as a refugee or a citizen. In your experience, is one more beneficial than the other?

ALISHINE HUSSEIN OSMAN: Not necessarily. But I never applied for kipande. Anyway, if I went to the committee, who would recognize me? It is unlikely that someone would apply without a strong case.

ANOORADHA IYER SIDDIQI: The processes that produce these divisions begin earlier than age eighteen. When did you get a refugee card?

ALISHINE HUSSEIN OSMAN: Age five or six.

ANOORADHA IYER SIDDIQI: Were you on your parents' card, or did you have your own?

ALISHINE HUSSEIN OSMAN: When we first came, we were head-counted. Our names were put in a book, and entered in a computer record later on. We were given a small card, for a family of one to twelve.

ANOORADHA IYER SIDDIQI: Were your parents with you?

ALISHINE HUSSEIN OSMAN: Yes, one of my parents was there. There were seven of us at the time, but they punched number six. When we went to the ration distribution center, we were given rations for six.

ANOORADHA IYER SIDDIQI: The cards are in categories, and one of the cards is for a family size of one to twelve. Is there a family size category larger than that?

ALISHINE HUSSEIN OSMAN: At the beginning, the maximum family size on the cards was twelve. Some families had two cards: one was punched for twelve and another for the remaining number. Today the ration cards can be punched for up to sixteen.

ANOORADHA IYER SIDDIQI: I suppose the number of dependents becomes crucial on distribution days, and even one extra ration can reverse a family's fortunes. When I visited the food distribution center in Ifo, I began to realize how it enacted power dynamics through architecture alone, by controlling the material flow of goods. There is a threshold that you can see in the photo, between the person receiving aid and the person placed in the position to distribute it. It represents boundaries between these two people and the agencies or donors as well. I remember the WFP officer describing a refugee dispute over

1.2. UNHCR ration card, photo provided by Alishine Osman.

1.3. People distributing and receiving the flour allotment at a dry rations station, Ifo camp food distribution point.

who was selected to distribute rations. It puts into play incredible power differences.

The donkey carts lined up outside the distribution point also suggested differentiated economic zones in the camp and a socioeconomic gradient from the camp interior to the perimeter. Aid recipients in Dadaab generally sell portions of their ration at the market just after distribution days. The donkey carts facilitate the sale of rations by people in the camp interior to people at the camp exterior. If you live close to the food distribution point, you can transport rations to your domicile without this additional expenditure. If you live outside the camp, you are likely an unregistered asylum seeker, do not receive rations, and have to buy food, or hire transport to move it from the center. The donkey carts suggest to me a disaggregation of the economy: there are wholesalers, delivery people, cart owners and renters, retailers, and consumers. Each occupies coordinates in space that can be mapped in relation to the distribution center. Here, the design of the camp matters, as does the allocation of plots, especially in terms of the proximity of all points to the aid distribution point.

I was also amazed by the markets; I saw everything being sold, from goat meat and camel's milk to construction supplies to bed frames and

1.4. People at Ifo camp market.

mattresses to televisions and mobile phones. The markets in the camps do not look different from the market in Dadaab town, but you could exchange hundreds of US dollars in the camps; you could not do that in town.

Also, the food distribution points and markets were not the only charged spaces. The water distribution points seemed even more volatile. This photo was taken at a tap stand that had been fenced off by one of the refugees.

ALISHINE HUSSEIN OSMAN: This photo looks like the tap stand where I used to live, in sector A in Ifo camp. Somebody built a fence around it. Twice a month, when we received the food ration, we would sell some flour and give that person a portion of our ration—equivalent to one dollar—to protect the water. This person protected the water. It was a mutual agreement; otherwise, people would misuse the water equipment, or even break the tap. Water usually runs from 7:30 a.m. to 11:30 a.m., and again after 2:00 p.m. This photo was probably taken at around 1:00 p.m. People bring water cans, and put them in line. They put them in order on a first-come, first-serve basis, and over time, they have worked out a particular order. That's the system, but sometimes people breach the system, and

1.5. People's jerry cans in a water tap stand queue between distributions, Ifo camp, photo by Bethany Young.

you'll find people fighting over this. Once we had to move from one block to another in Ifo because of water scarcity. Some blocks had more water than other blocks. There were no individual pipes or water storage systems for families. So if the water source equipment was broken or the pump was out of fuel then there would be no water for the families until it got fixed. We experienced this several times. This may be one of the biggest differences between life in the camps and in nearby towns like Dadaab or Garissa. The Kenyans have water running in their individual households or a system that reserves water in case of a shortage. That is not the case for the refugees.

ANOORADHA IYER SIDDIQI: It's very difficult. In addition to the harshness of this life, the problem is based on resource scarcity that Kenyans also feel. At this stage, the situation is also predicated on a politically awkward condition. After twenty-five years, with many refugees intermarried or in the same clan as members of the host community, divisions like these are in many ways only political—not social, or anything else.

I want to return to this question of how you were able to move around on a regular basis. Were you able to leave Ifo, other than in extreme circumstances?

ALISHINE HUSSEIN OSMAN: I could not leave permanently, but I could go to other camps temporarily.

ANOORADHA IYER SIDDIQI: What about when you were working for the NRC?

ALISHINE HUSSEIN OSMAN: Not unless I had a requirement for something official and had to travel for the organization, in which case I had to arrange for travel documents and paperwork. I couldn't just travel. But remember, this is Africa, there's a lot of corruption. If you have money, you can definitely travel.

ANOORADHA IYER SIDDIQI: As an employee of the NRC, could you go to its office in the UNHCR compound in Dadaab?

ALISHINE HUSSEIN OSMAN: Yes, but not beyond Dadaab.

ANOORADHA IYER SIDDIQI: Could you go to the central humanitarian compound before you started working for the NRC?

ALISHINE HUSSEIN OSMAN: Yes. Even as a regular refugee you could travel to the UNHCR compound in Dadaab. Beyond Dadaab is where the problem is.

ANOORADHA IYER SIDDIQI: If you lived in Ifo, how would you get to the other camps, Hagadera or Dagahaley, which are far away by foot? Would you take a vehicle, or would you walk? It's about thirteen kilometers, and took us a little over twenty minutes in a car. Do people take matatus?[9]

ALISHINE HUSSEIN OSMAN: There are not a lot of people taking matatus. You have to wait until enough people are on the matatu for it to go, and instead of waiting, people would walk. I would often walk to Dagahaley. I have walked so many times from Ifo to Dadaab to Hagadera.

ANOORADHA IYER SIDDIQI: The crossing between camps makes you aware of the great deal of space that a few kilometers can create. The landscape is harsh, with red dust and scrub as far as you can see, the occasional tree, and ominous marabou storks! The highways are unpaved. And when you leave a camp, there is no entry or exit; there are no gates. The boundary is existential: there is simply nowhere to go. Of course, you can see the edges and density of the built environment from above. But in the bush, on the road in areas where the acacia is tall, you could miss the camps entirely if you weren't directed to them.

As an international visitor, I traveled in all-terrain vehicles in the UN convoys at set times of day to move between camps. Every morning, we would leave the UNHCR compound and stop by the police station in Dadaab to pick up our police escort. I wasn't allowed to walk anywhere, because the agencies had to assume responsibility for me, and they wouldn't let me do my work unless I remained with the escort. It felt overblown, but I understand that the agencies have been reacting to regular threats against aid workers since the camps were established in 1991. After the kidnapping of the aid workers and the bombings in the camps in 2011, they stopped allowing visitors or nonessential personnel on site.[10] I had never worked in a context like that before, and often felt a combination of anxiety and shame. It showed how different my status was from that of the refugees, how my life was protected. I felt the contrast especially when I would watch women set out from the camps alone to collect firewood.

ALISHINE HUSSEIN OSMAN: That's true. The agencies are dealing with security on one level, but for the refugees, the security problem is very different. Walking outside the camps can be very risky. There are bandits. There are hyenas. I have seen a lot of people robbed. Some people would hide their money in their shoes. A lot of women are also raped, especially when collecting firewood for cooking fuel. Either bandits are trying to steal from them, or they are attacked because local people resent the refugees.

ANOORADHA IYER SIDDIQI: The lack of safety ties into the problem of work, because livelihoods create new power dynamics.[11] Through my research, I became very interested in the economies that structure life in the camps. Even in the safest of conditions, the architecture of the camp complex inscribes certain inequalities; for example, the distance of your dwelling from the food distribution center impacts your income, or the

1.6. Women collecting and transporting firewood by donkey cart at the periphery of Ifo camp.

distance of a dwelling from a school impacts whether children will be educated.

I studied the NRC's shelter initiative, as you know, which you worked on. It emerged from self-help development practices followed by architects and planners working with the UNHCR and the NRC.[12] In the pilot initiative in Ifo, the NRC provided materials for one-story mud brick shelters with tin roofs, and asked the beneficiaries to do the construction, so that they would take ownership of what they built, and not just trade the shelter materials. Certain refugees did that work and developed skills in masonry building, construction management, and design. Your role was different, though. Perhaps it was awkward as well; you were neither an NGO project manager nor an end user. You were employed by the NRC to organize refugees to receive and participate in this form of aid, as well as to direct construction on site. You probably did not receive the respect that a Kenyan or international aid worker would receive.

ALISHINE HUSSEIN OSMAN: That's right. There is this inequality in refugee employment. But think of the other end of the spectrum. Your photo of a tuqul explains it. When refugees come to the camps they usually have nothing, and cannot get immediate attention from the agencies. They have to find shelter. That's the initial stage that every refugee goes through. Most of us had to build a tuqul: a small dwelling made of sticks and pieces of cloth. I lived in one. We had to cut down trees and whatever branches we could find. Agencies give away extra materials, trying to provide shelter and satisfy secondary needs whenever they can. I think they do a great job, but the system has these inequalities built in. As a refugee, I might have a coworker who is a Kenyan citizen, doing the same job. I might have a high school diploma, and he might not. Even so, he might make five hundred dollars, and I might make one hundred dollars.

ANOORADHA IYER SIDDIQI: These jobs for refugees, which the agencies call "incentive" work, evolved because refugees could not be employed, and organizations were trying to legitimately hire and pay them, as well as help them build transferable skills. They are positions that would typically be salaried, but instead refugees are paid a small stipend; they are often trained and expected to take on responsibility. In addition to perpetuating inequality on a structural level, these jobs create frustration for the workers on both sides. Refugees do not stay in these positions because they cannot advance, and NGOs lose trained workers. At the time that the Kenyan government acceded to the Convention Relating to the Status of

Refugees, it took exceptions to the right to work so that the Kenyan citizen's ability to earn would not be diminished by the presence of refugees.[13] It was intended to discourage refugees from entering the labor market and capitalizing on the resources of the state from their position in the camps. A lot of countries did this, and the divisions created by the exceptions are in place in legal structures all over the world.

I am interested in the history behind this. There is a full generation raised from birth in Dadaab. It is important to start talking differently about this place, in terms of labor, land use, and settlement in Kenya, which has its own terribly violent colonial history and aftermath. It is also important to note the ways that Dadaab is and is not ephemeral. It is not temporary; it is forced to behave as temporary. Dadaab possesses potential that is not only economic but also political. I believe the government's announcement to close the camps has caused so much speculation, in part, because of this political potency.[14]

ALISHINE HUSSEIN OSMAN: Speaking of politics, why don't we talk about the elections? In my experience, at Dadaab, each of the camps—Ifo, Dagahaley, and Hagadera—had its own administration. In each camp, refugees elected one male and one female chairperson every two years. The camps were divided into sectors, designated as A, B, C, and so on, and chairpersons were elected by sector leaders. The sectors were divided into blocks, which were designated as A1, A2, A3, and so on, and sector leaders—again, one male and one female—were elected by the block leaders. Each family unit—about ninety to two hundred total—elected the two leaders of each block, one male and one female. Block leaders were elected by a process that varied across the camp and also changed over time. Sometimes block leaders were elected by direct vote, and sometimes they were appointed by a selected few. Many years ago, the position was simply held by volunteers, maybe because there was less incentive to become a block leader in the past.

ANOORADHA IYER SIDDIQI: These block and sector divisions are standard in UNHCR camps. Can you talk about who would vote? Was it only the head of household, or each family member?

ALISHINE HUSSEIN OSMAN: Anyone over the age of eighteen. And since I left, a lot of things have changed. In 2011, the refugee camps reached a population of one half million, and there were bomb explosions in the market that changed the security status and the political status of different leaders.

ANOORADHA IYER SIDDIQI: Can you describe the election process? Does everyone meet in one place? Does the UNHCR census and block and sector partitioning drive the voting?

ALISHINE HUSSEIN OSMAN: Well, during an election year, there is campaigning in the camps. There is a lot of corruption in the election of the sector leaders; again, they control voting for the chairpersons. There is influence over the process through the distribution of khat.[15] The election begins over the course of one day. People line up somewhere inside the block. The person who gets the longest line gets elected. If the lines are equal, they recount them.

ANOORADHA IYER SIDDIQI: Who does the counting?

ALISHINE HUSSEIN OSMAN: Members of the community, with members of the social service agencies involved. For example, CARE, one of the social service agencies, was involved. If the lines are equal—well, the lines are never equal!—but if the two lines are too close in length, they may recount.

ANOORADHA IYER SIDDIQI: This is a physical and spatial process. It also depends on the eyes of whoever is making the decision. In all ways, the human body is used as a measure.

ALISHINE HUSSEIN OSMAN: It's crazy, actually. There is no ballot, and everyone sees who you voted for.

ANOORADHA IYER SIDDIQI: So that is how the block leaders are elected. And later that day, do the block leaders elect a sector leader?

ALISHINE HUSSEIN OSMAN: Well, the sector leader can be someone already in office. Most of these things are predetermined. We know how many block leaders will run, and how many will run for the sector leader. Remember, the sector leader is not elected by the people; he is chosen by the block leaders. Often, he will buy them miraa; he may influence them that way.

ANOORADHA IYER SIDDIQI: At what time of day does all this happen?

ALISHINE HUSSEIN OSMAN: Most elections don't happen in one day, because there is a lack of infrastructure, transportation, and technology, and because of the process and number of agencies and people involved. The elections involve not only the refugees at the sector and block levels, but also local government officials and international agencies and organizations, such as the UNHCR and CARE, who keep the peace. So: block leaders are voted in one day, sector leaders the next. All of them are elected within a week or so.

ANOORADHA IYER SIDDIQI: That is a very exciting week! After all of this happens, what are they governing, exactly? I know that the leaders are representing the refugees to the national government and to the UNHCR, but what else are they doing?

ALISHINE HUSSEIN OSMAN: The refugees have a lot of issues! Say, they need bathrooms, and don't have materials. They contact the block leaders, who contact the social service agencies. They are facilitators; that's what they do.

ANOORADHA IYER SIDDIQI: What kind of power do they have after they have been elected? Can they affect who gets kipande or a travel permit? Do they control the flow of money or goods?

ALISHINE HUSSEIN OSMAN: I don't think they have power in those direct ways. They go to conferences. They go to the agencies and raise issues. They help families with their problems. But as you said, they do attend meetings with the Kenyan government and the UNHCR. And they do represent something bigger than just the day-to-day management of the camps.

ANOORADHA IYER SIDDIQI: Why would someone want to be elected?

ALISHINE HUSSEIN OSMAN: They are the first people to hear an issue in the community. They are representing many people; there is a sense of pride in that. Also, their election demonstrates clan support.[16] Winning is based on affiliations. A chairperson cannot become a chairperson unless he has the support of all those block leaders.

ANOORADHA IYER SIDDIQI: And so the social capital translates into the political. I think the emergent body politic and spatial politics are remarkably uncanny, especially because they have emerged in a closed space.[17] I think some of the social spaces in the camps bring this representative, political world into view, particularly now, under the threat of the camps being decommissioned. The documentation of this built environment has become even more important as an element of a disappearing heritage.

ALISHINE HUSSEIN OSMAN: Yes, for example, I took this photo when I went back to the refugee camp in 2009. I saw a lot of people turn out to watch this soccer match! An overwhelming number of people there were under the age of twenty-five, which is interesting, because this younger generation has access to the internet and television, and they are using this media to watch soccer! People would come out wearing jerseys from teams around the world: Arsenal, Brazil. . . . Even though this camp is a contained space, people have access to this information. A crowd like this wouldn't have appeared in 1994. This photo captures a big change in the social life of the camp over twenty years. Cellphones and Facebook have also had a significant influence in the refugee camps, just the same way they have had in developed countries.

ANOORADHA IYER SIDDIQI: Ifo cemetery captures another significant aspect of life in the camps, social as well as material. Dadaab has been dis-

1.7. Spectators at a soccer match, Ifo camp, photo by Alishine Osman.

1.8. Cemetery, Cawo Jube area of Ifo camp, photo by Alishine Osman.

cussed as approaching something urban, in terms of both social complexity and form. But I believe the cultural space and spatial designation for lives to end ceremoniously speaks most clearly to the ways in which this place is and is not urban, even as it is a home to many people. A burial ground in a refugee camp may not be unique to Ifo, but, in a context where the spatial separation for the living has been so acute, it represents a very different traversal out of the camps. The irony, especially if we think of the possibility of the Dadaab refugee camps being decommissioned, is that this way out of the camps is actually an anchor within them, and within the state as well.

Partitions of the Land

The reflections that Osman and I included in our dialogue center on Dadaab's spatial separations and other divides, as well as the architectures and objects that inhabit and traverse them. The marked grave or ration card, endowed with sacrality and authority in a refugee camp, illustrates points at which humanitarian territory falls into crisis, either of overdetermination (the food aid identity document exposing the camp's bureaucracy around life) or underdetermination (the handmade tomb exposing the camp's inadequacy around death). Each object, whether forming architectures of sustenance or memorial, works along the seams of physical and psychic partitions to constitute the camp environment. To contend with those seams, I next examine partitioning as the historical force underlying the refugee camp, with the partition of the Jubaland as a conceptual progenitor for the Dadaab refugee camps, and the continuous making and remaking of the settlements as a reproduction of partitions. I draw on significant "Partition" and borders scholarship, in particular, historically specific studies of the postcolony and the construction of borders in South Asia and Palestine.[18] I build on this scholarship to establish a principle of partitioning that undergirds the refugee camp, examining its expression in the architecture of Dadaab. Thinking with migration as a method, I then return to the burial place and the identity document to address partitions of the land.

Among the many territorial divisions produced in colonial East Africa, elaborated in chapter 2, the partition of the Jubaland in 1925 set the terms for the international border established in 1963 between Kenya and Somalia, as well as its ongoing contestations. The Dadaab refugee settlements reiterate the partition of the land situated around the Jubba River, contiguous with the Kenyan northeast. The banks of the Jubba were the subject of historical and political marginality for decades, as territorial frontiers that comprised the borderland between Britain's Kenya Colony and Italian Somalia. Attracting neither empire's commercial investment nor public works, the river acted as the barrier between them. Both banks became part of a fragmented hinterland, one side serving Italian ports and the other British. In 1925, the western bank was ceded from Britain to Italy as a concession for the latter's neutrality in World War I. It was divested during the economic depression and Fascist invasion of Ethiopia and later built up solely through smallholder agricultural projects, only to be de-developed after independence.[19] This land without "productive" purpose—disobedient land, however fertile—became an object for disciplining. The British exerted imperial control over territory of little service to the colonial enterprise *by partitioning it*: an act of abstraction that rendered the land universally fungible. Almost one hundred years later, the sequestering capacity of the Dadaab refugee camps, "geographically and politically segregated from the rest of the world," as Osman poignantly comments, acts out this territoriality through the reproduction of divisive practices.

This fungibility, marginality, and constructed devaluation of a fertile riverine region compounded a racial exclusion that offers historical context for some ethnic difference and tension in the camps. The riverine Jubaland was cultivated by Gosha communities. They formed significant minority communities among the Somali people who fled to Kenya from 1991 onward, particularly after the al-Shabaab takeover of southern Somalia in 2006. Gosha communities had been marginalized within Somali society historically, as race- and class-based minority communities considered to descend from enslaved people who were forced to migrate from southern Africa. The racial constructions of identity, community, and social structure in Somalia, particularly with regard to anthropologist Catherine Besteman's reflection on "how people construct themselves as cultural beings within fields of power shaped and directed mostly by others," offers some understanding of minority difference and exclusions in the Dadaab refugee camps.[20] With great respect for the multiplicities of identity and belonging in East African contexts, and not wishing to simplify the concept of bias in a refugee or emergency context, it is possible to note the ramifications for these southern Somali communities immediately identified as a vulnerable minority in the camps and processed for third-country resettlement, exacerbating hostilities against them.[21] In the camps, these agrarians lived among members of predominantly pastoralist communities. Some of these individual farmers who remained in Dadaab, such as Maganai Saddiq Hassan, interviewed in chapter 2, exerted a profound agricultural proficiency, which ensured the subsistence of their own families and also radically ameliorated the environment of the camps, turning the dusty landscape into a lush one, amid the scarcity of essential resources such as water. Her farm is among the latent forms that reproduced the power relations that haunted the partitioned Jubaland, extending them into the Dadaab refugee camps.

Thinking of the partition of the Jubaland as an event that behaves as an architectural progenitor to the construction of the Dadaab refugee camps builds on the implications of some critical "Partition" scholarship, which discovers the theoretical and historiographical silences around historically specific acts of partition and imagines their reproduction of conditions of incommensurability into the present day. Historian Vazira Zamindar remarks on 1947 for South Asia as a threshold, after which it is as though borders and histories of multiple nations "simply emerge fully formed."[22] In contrast, she provides histories of the politically and aesthetically messier textures of a long partition (for example, the demographic transformations of cities and urban cultures in Pakistan that followed the displacements and evacuations, or the persistent crafting and recrafting of the political category of Muslim in India), noting that the violence of a partition is not a vague consequence of border conflict but instead the direct result of bureaucratic shaping, as states attempt to resolve political uncertainty.[23] Historian Uditi Sen breaks with the European model of the refugee as the figure expelled from the nation-state and citizenship in order to demonstrate the refugee not as "the radical outsider" experiencing only loss, but as essential to the concept of the post-partition citizen in India, as one who could claim relief and rehabilitation from the state as a civil right.[24] While these historical circumstances vary substantially from those around partition and the refugee in East Africa, they offer imaginaries that extend foundational thinking on the refugee within the order of nation-states, posing her as the figure at the end of a partitioning process. The well-theorized refugee figure, whether viewed as the antidote to the impossibility of minority belonging ensuring the human right to have rights, following social theorist Hannah Arendt, or as a member of a coming political community devoid of political rights and existing at the bare limit of human life, as political theorist Giorgio Agamben argues, represents a dialectic of foreclosure, especially as consigned to the camp.[25] Through the insights of these thinkers, the camp has been named as a site of crises of the nation-state as well as the humanitarian promise to repair life and humanity. Such arguments are predicated on the central figuration of the refugee as someone who denotes lack, for whom the camp inscribes loss.[26] Building on these foundations, the imaginaries that scholars such as Zamindar and Sen propose complicate the horizon of the refugee, and thus her inhabitation of the camp.

Following and encouraging such complications, I note that a marked grave in a contested territory, for example, opens onto messier aesthetics, materialities, and histories. Osman and I tease out an understanding of Dadaab's architectures that acknowledges paradoxes: refugee promise as entangled with trauma and the camp's marginality with its fullness. The refugee and the camp become more textured and contradictory architects and architectures of migration through a root analysis that takes partitions of land as a fundamental concept.

This conceptualization is predicated on the principle of land as a shared whole, as alluded to in this chapter's opening photo, constituted by open migration as a historical form of inhabitation—one that does not presuppose borders. The architecture of a grave with a simple marker re-creates the uninterrupted land to which the body belongs: if not reversing the partition, then exposing its origins. Zamindar and I argue that as governments substitute shared land and space with partition, they set about fixing partition in place by producing and reproducing incommensurabilities in lives, through a *principle* of partitioning.[27] The Dadaab refugee camps reflect such a political process, in which the proliferation of territorial partitions assumes the form of a bordering architecture.

My posing of this problem intervenes into a discourse on borders by reframing it through the concept of *partitions*. Rather than focusing on the figuration of the border or the object of the wall—the architectural expression of nation-state crisis—I am concerned with the primacy and durability of the unpartitioned land beneath.[28] The theorization of the Dadaab refugee camps as an afterlife of partitions begins with the historical condition of their construction in the partitioned Jubaland. Yet, the partitioning process might be understood as the result of not only historically specific conditions, but also conceptual ones. That is, the historical partition behind a border camp might serve as a schema; for example, the Jubaland partition behind the historically specific example of Dadaab might echo or model partitions behind conceptually diverse refugee camps around the world. This theorization shares a foundation with (if a different emphasis from) aspects of the work of political theorist Sandro Mezzadra and cultural and social theorist Brett Nielsen, architect Eyal Weizman, and architectural theorist Irit Katz. For one, socioeconomic activity in Dadaab possesses characteristics similar to proliferating "border struggles" that Mezzadra and Nielsen identify as heterogeneous assemblages of power and law, which articulate the ever-infringing relation between capital and the state, activating the border through multiplications and diffractions of labor that both occupy the edge of the nation-state and transcend it.[29] Those transcendent economies and socialities of the border are, however, frequently absent in a UNHCR-administered camp, which is strictly and inextricably tethered to the nation-state. As robustly as the Dadaab camp markets encourage multiplicities of economic and social bordering in individual architectures (as I have argued elsewhere), their referent remains the bordered nation-state.[30] In addition, the modularity and extension of the Dadaab refugee camps—expanding from one settlement to three and later to five, ever subdividing within—reproduces partitions, recalling Weizman's argument on the plasticity of the frontier executed in the construction of a border wall that changed path, the disappearance of settlements and their reappearance elsewhere, and the proliferation and design of checkpoints, as Israel pressed into the Occupied Territories of Palestine.[31] "The camp," Katz furthermore argues, "which combines space and action, is an instrument inherently related to the frontier and the struggles within and over it, where temporality makes an inherent part of frantic spatial processes of construction and destruction as well as prolonged suspension and waiting."[32] However, the critical notion she forwards—that the border enacts its own shifts by reproducing itself architecturally through the camp—works differently in Dadaab, where the multiplication of refugee settlements and structures within do not derive from a formal program of expanding the frontier or an agenda directed by a single state. Dadaab's divides build on the principle of an originary partition of land, which reproduced itself in the borders of nation-states and continues to do so as space is shaped by governments, NGOs, aid workers, refugees, and other migrants in a refugee camp. That originary partitioning is *not* the historical partition of the Jubaland, but the conceptual precedents that established practices of territorial overdetermination. These produced a *partitioning principle,* which, much as philosopher Étienne Balibar writes of border creation, is "sanctioned, reduplicated and relativized by other geopolitical divisions, performing a "*world-configuring* function."[33] As the practice of partition brings new worlds into being, in each circumstance, it cements into place territorial asymmetries and thus incommensurabilities of lives. This reinscribing practice is based on the misconception that land can be divided.

I argue that Dadaab's constructed environment is marked with a knowledge of the land prior to the enactment of a partitioning principle. Here it is important to imagine, with architectural historian Hollyamber Kennedy, "the land as medium."[34] Thinking with cultural and media theorist Ariella Aïsha Azoulay, I argue for imagining land in a prepartitioned state of potentiality, "returning to the initial refusal of dispossession and the world out of which it emerged and bringing that moment into our present."[35] The architectures that re-create and reproduce partitions insert that potential into the refugee camps, as Osman and I sought to convey in describing movement between the three camps and the humanitarian compound. Street and compound edges in the Dadaab camps, fenced by growth or lashed-together vegetation, have made material the lines of the UNHCR plan and produced enclosure. Family plots thus designated carry claims to land, if not property. This production of space conflates the territory designated by the Kenyan government for use by the international community of states with a lived environment that has been built and rebuilt over three generations by people whose belonging has been tested over time and through immobilization. Such a landscape of soil and plants, constructions growing out of the ground, later entangled with corrugated aluminum gates and plastic sheeting arriving into the camps through regional and global supply chains, has been shaped in situ by activities of dwelling, trade, schooling, prayer, and cultivation. Every element in the landscape is a material resource; in this constructed environment, architecture enacts economics. Every element in the landscape inscribes territorial boundaries; in this constructed environment, architecture enacts politics. The cultural and sociomaterial freight of such a landscape is legible and felt, much as in other migrant environments impregnated with speculative cultural formations and capital, as built environment historians Kishwar Rizvi and Sarah Lopez explore in Pakistan and Mexico.[36] Moreover, as geographer Nida Rehman asserts, plants and soils behave and can be traced as historical actors, endowing the landscape with archival potential.[37] Here, the tangible environment articulates the durability of partitions of land. The economically, politically, and epistemically potent materiality of the constructed and cultivated environment reproduces the partitioning process as authorities and entities in the camps produce and reproduce territory. However, following Azoulay, the pregnant environment also produces and reproduces the possibility for traversals of those partitions, multiple potential futures that belong in the narrative.

Nowhere is this more acutely felt than in the architecture of a grave in Ifo cemetery, a construction that alludes to the stakes of a refugee's flight and the ground traversed. Osman indicated that while the cemetery held many who had died over the years, a significant number died in the first year after Ifo camp was established; they had been his neighbors. At that time, public hygiene was compromised and people risked exposure to waterborne diseases such as cholera and airborne viral outbreaks. The cemetery is near Cawo Jube, described by one journalist who reported on Dadaab for many years for Human Rights Watch as a "tough" neighborhood on the edge of Ifo camp.[38] As opposed to less volatile spaces in the interior, Cawo Jube is located in an area converging with the bush, where dwellings of newly arriving asylum seekers encroached on the perimeter of Ifo, the oldest refugee settlement in Dadaab, adjacent to its extension, Ifo 2. The cemetery thus inhabits a margin's edge. Burials there are not registered with the international authorities, as far as I could find. Therefore, in death, people in the refugee camps do not belong to the state. This suggests another form of traversal that the camp performs for the refugee, from a subject relationship with partitioned territory to one directly with the land.

The architecture of a grave is animated by the life that ends in it. Such architectures become "places of increase," in the words of cultural anthropologist Engseng Ho.[39] I did not ask Osman to whom the grave in the photograph belonged, out of respect for the privacy of the person buried there. Nevertheless, the particularities are less urgent here than the potentialities. While the marked grave in the cemetery in the refugee camp offers an immediate trace of a community's care or a life's worth, it also opens powerful theoretical possibilities through its uncommon and confounding sacrality.

The burial mound in the refugee camp, as a profoundly sacred subject, generates methodological speculations and frustrations. First, as the cemetery near Cawo Jube lies beyond the international order of the camp, its status within an official governmental archive is unreliable. Moreover, the security environment during the period of this research did not permit consultation of any mosque or church for records or even ascertaining that religious institutions in the camps retain written records or make them accessible to people outside of the community. As such, the grave forces one to grapple with "the limits of the sayable dictated by the archive," as literary scholar and cultural historian Saidiya Hartman articulates, with the impossibility of recovering histories of those consecrating the cemetery grounds remedied primarily by oral histories or critical narrative acts of fabulation.[40] Either of these strategies presents empirical challenges, and moreso, the risk of the representation of archival paucity, the penalty for which may be the affective reinscription of the foundational epistemic violence around the subject. Second, the marked grave unfixed by the archive or the nation-state teems with historical possibilities. It expresses one possible future in a partitioning of land, while providing the empirical bedrock to imagine others. This condition of archival proliferation opens onto multiple regimes of historicity—the need for narration of many potential futures, noted earlier. Third, the material precarity of the burial site manifests the crucial admission that to find the lives and deaths of refugees who made traversals in emergency is to invoke an archival torment. This fleeting encounter and embodied loss of knowledge recalls Hartman's lament, in seeking pasts of people sold into slavery, which would not come forward via conventional historical means, that "to read the archive is to enter a mortuary; it permits one final viewing and allows for a last glimpse of persons about to disappear."[41] These three scenes of archival paucity, proliferation, and tantalization describe the vexations of theory that might ensue from the material ecology at the edges of a refugee camp. However, such vexations produce powerful openings.

As the response, let us imagine the grave as not only the particular but also the universal artifact of lives lived in the traversal of partitions. This means imagining the land enveloping the fragile yet protected grave as a consistent datum that persists *with or without* the refugee camp. The vulnerable grave in Osman's photograph is hardly more than a mound of red dust, sure to be disturbed in the rainy season. The graveyard is ringed by the regionally ubiquitous *Commiphora* thorn bushes, grown into a fence by people trying to keep hyenas from unearthing the bodies of the community, of elders, of loved ones in the soil. That a life could end in earth marked so humbly, yet tended so carefully, emphasizes the potency and stakes of flight, the life to which one flees, and the life that has been lived. As the grave inters the bodies of migrating people into the land, the land inscribes people into archives and narratives that cross territories, writing them out of some histories and into others. The mound in Ifo cemetery is an architecture of migration that reminds us that land stages its own traversals.

Just as the grave speaks of life beyond, before, or without partitions, the axiom of the ration card or kipande, both identity documents with the power to segregate, makes vivid the principle of everyday partitions as they are lived and inhabited. The practices of territoriality ending in the public events described by Osman, of trial and recognition to determine refugeehood or citizenship, are not merely the outcome of a late twentieth century emergency. They are echoes of a long history of land division, devaluation, disuse, and evisceration at the levels of the locality and the state, which has translated to habits of stratification of lives. These practices inscribe multiple materialities: for example, a genre of paper documents that define refugee life and that speak to the deformed relation between territory and land.

Within this genre of essential paper infrastructures, two identity documents circumscribe the partitioned enclosure of the refugee camp. The interior of the camp is dominated by the ration card, a much-handled, worn piece of "currency," whose material vulnerability adds to its preciousness (figure 1.2), its fragility regularly demonstrated while bent between the thumb of the food distributor and a mechanical hole-punching tool (figure 4.29). The harsh grammar of the ration card lies in its dual role as lifesaving aid and arbiter of bureaucratic violence, reducing life to numericity. The squares lining its perimeter are punched during each semimonthly distribution cycle, the letters identify assigned nonfood-item package types, and the number stream in the center enumerates dependents.[42] Lost cards take time to replace, edges become frayed or torn, family sizes change over the duration allotted to one card. Meanwhile, these vital infrastructures are compromised, as Osman explained, when they are administered with inaccuracies. With one dependent erroneously omitted from the card, as Osman's family experienced, significant supplies or food can go missing from the family basket. This produces a politics of arithmetic at the scale of the wallet and of the camp.[43] Poignantly, these essential paper infrastructures remain ephemeral, replaced after thirty-four cycles (nowhere near the twenty-plus years, on average, during which a person remains displaced, according to UNHCR statistics that are themselves ever changing). Yet, in spite of their ephemerality, these papers commit a substantive act. They enact partition.

Another paper infrastructure linked to territory and the proliferation of partitions marks the exterior of the camp: the elusive kipande document that Osman and I discussed, without which mobility is profoundly restricted. Kipande, the word in Kiswahili for a fragment or a piece, was an artifact of the 1915 Native Registration Ordinance, which required that all African males age sixteen or older register with the colonial government, as a method of overseeing them and drawing them into the labor force. The registration papers, containing identifying information such as the wearer's ethnic group or comments on employment competency, were kept in a copper container worn on a chain around the neck commonly referred to as kipande. As journalist Juliet Atellah writes, people were forced to wear the kipande "like a dog collar" and were monitored by police who could order the wearers to display its contents on demand.[44] Even if the meaning of kipande has changed for the Kenyan citizen, the demand to produce papers is a similarly bitter experience for the contemporary refugee. Kipande—or kitambulisho, as the identity card is called in Kiswahili—behaves as a passport within the domestic space of the state, forming the paper infrastructure of a system that demands social commitment and enacts social spectacle, a national identity document that aligns conceptually with the international passport. It engages "material practices generated by state and non-state actors in their promotion and production of a certain politics of movement," as design anthropologist Mahmoud Keshavarz writes, in which "lack of a passport or its deprivation becomes a means of power imposition, discrimination, management, and control."[45] It is an object fundamental to mobility within the state and thus central to larger processes of migration, yet associated with a parcel of land, an entanglement of paper and earth.

While the kipande identity document is issued by the Kenyan state, the identity document that falls under the purview of the UNHCR operates based

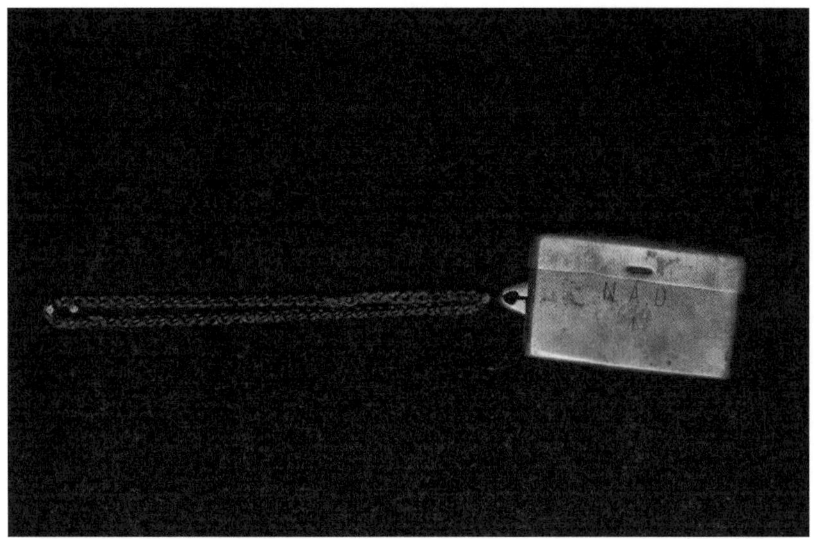

1.9. Brass kipande case and chain to hold an identity document, marked "N.A.D." ("Native Administration Document"), National Museums of Kenya, Google Arts & Culture.

on the agency's mandate in relation to refugee camps. At the request of the Kenyan state, soon after 1991, the UNHCR assumed authority over refugee status determination and began to recognize—that is, confer status on—refugees within a complex local and international refugee setting. In Kenya, the administration of refugees in camps was eventually limited to two locations where land was leased from the government: Dadaab in Garissa, in the northeast near the border with Somalia, and Kakuma in Turkana, in the north near the borders with Sudan and Ethiopia. When large numbers of people sought asylum in the country in 1991, they were cared for by the Kenyan Red Cross. Camp management in Dadaab shifted to CARE's purview after a year, an arrangement maintained for several years. Throughout, the UNHCR retained an unusual position. It was the body designated to protect the rights of refugees. It was the administrator in charge of overseeing organizations contracted to provide aid and social services and manage the camps. It was the primary contractor of the state police charged with keeping refugees from transgressing the boundaries of the leased land. As anthropologist Bram Jansen has described in relation to the Kakuma refugee complex, the UNHCR's position was critical to the means by which "refugee protection grew into a form of humanitarian government. . . . The result was that the camp became like a state within a state, where UNHCR was like a near-sovereign handing out something comparable to citizenship."[46] In Dadaab, the quasi-sovereignty of the UNHCR resulted from the recognition it was enabled to grant to refugees, which differed from that of the Kenyan state, as well as the UNHCR'S accompanying capacity to facilitate a refugee's movement throughout the country through the issuance of passes. The UNHCR determines refugee status according to multiple practices, often facilitating long interview processes in which individuals must demonstrate persecution, sometimes requiring multiple visits and interviews, or invasive medical examinations.[47] In times of emergency when people have crossed international borders in large numbers, the UNHCR has facilitated prima facie recognition, a process by which an individual is granted refugee status based on "the face" of things, usually because she belongs to a community known to be persecuted in a specific context (as asylum seekers had been in 1991 and 1992, in Somalia and Sudan). Sometimes these determinations have been made by UNHCR employees who themselves belonged to the communities of asylum seekers (for example, Somali-identifying citizens of Ethiopia or Kenya working in the border camps) and had to regularly negotiate their identities in relation to refugees as well as international agencies.[48] The UNHCR has also had the authority to directly confer refugee status on persons as a function of its mandate as a protection agency (that is, as an entity without the powers of being a signatory to the 1951 convention, in the manner of a state). As such, UNHCR "mandate refugees," as they are called, possess documents that differ from those issued by the Kenyan government. The legitimacy of these papers, based on varied registration processes, derives from the UNHCR's relation to the territory—the enclosure—of the camps.

Partitions have created and continue to create the enclosure of the Dadaab refugee camps. Thus, it is worth returning to the notion that into practices of partition are also built practices of traversal. The will to stand in long lines, to be counted, and to campaign in elections—as Osman illustrated earlier, or as Isnina Ali Rage did while pregnant, as discussed in the introduction—speaks to people's power and a political authority that is not unequal to the force of partitions. An architecture of participation, in terms of the totalizing experience of the Dadaab refugee camp elections, which persists in spite of corruption, injustice, and failure—even conscripting time as an accomplice, with voting unfolding over the course of many sunrises and sunsets—suggests the transcendence of a partitioning principle. The processes of recognition that Osman recalled in our dialogue, balancing forces of contestation and consensus building and involving not only refugees but also local officials, representatives of the state and international agencies, participants from nongovernmental organizations engaged in the care of the populace, and "clan" leaders hovering in the background, speaks to an architecture of the traversal of partitions.

The traversals examined in this section take migration as a form of knowledge in order to demonstrate that an architecture of partitions does not culminate only in rupture; it also participates in suture. As an architecture of the state responsive to borders, which acts as the shadow of migrations, the Dadaab refugee camps record a wound to the land and behave as the scab or scar to a territory formed from partitions. The architectures that ensue—a burial site, a system of paper documents—represent a set of traversals, which embody the potentialities that emerge from viewing land as an intact whole. The Dadaab refugee camps have cohered architectures that respond to the force of partitions with the force of traversals, equal to the ground covered.

Partitions of the Self

An election in the Dadaab refugee camps raises a critical problem in what it occasions; with it, refugees construct institutions, temporary and lasting, that further actualize the bifurcated context into which they have thrust themselves and been thrust by states, inscribing forms of recognition that reproduce partitions of the self. This logic of divisions builds on one that had been set into motion in Africa by colonial powers but extends colonial practices into the present. The practices of producing citizen and subject named by Osman recall political theorist Mahmood Mamdani's interrogation of these themes, particularly with regard to the institutional segregation that a refugee camp establishes. He discusses how tribal "customary" law responds to the conundrum of "the native question"—of how minority colonial powers ruled majority African populations unwilling to conform to centralized legal and social codes. Customary law enabled the production of "native" institutions that mirrored the multiplicity of groups to be administered, overseeing them while denying them franchise within the empire. While the refugee elections present an altogether different legal and historical context, it is difficult not to hear an echo of "native" institutions in the embodied practices that entrench the segregation of refugees from a larger body politic with which they otherwise traffic in a variety of social and cultural spaces. "The genius of British rule in Africa," Mamdani writes, "was in seeking to civilize Africans as communities, not as individuals."[49] The community unit of identity, that of the "tribe," produced a tenacious spatial logic to follow—a partitioning that was executed, for example, by the colonial kipande and its descendant documents. The ethnic community as the structural unit—at once providing the logic behind colonial "Native Reserves" and the Kenyan state census—had become a tool for partition thinking in Dadaab, as the UNHCR assigned individual and family plots and adjacencies based on ethnic affiliations. Social division based on community affiliation was the first of many forms of partition thinking in the camps impacting the bodies and psyches of individuals.

The partition of communities that separates people within camps in Dadaab elsewhere galvanizes the partition of the self, a psychic and social doubling that characterizes a refugee's life as she intersects with the modern state and the humanitarian regime. The need to tell certain stories about oneself in order to be recognized by authorities as a refugee is a problem that scholars have identified as the performance of suffering integral to the modern humanitarian moral economy.[50] Less attended to is the problem that this performance engenders an act of psychic partitioning, which in turn propels a process of racination. By this, I mean to take "race" as a social construction, not a reflection of biology or culture, as noted by historians Anupama Rao and Steven Pierce, an inherently unstable "position of privilege or disenfranchisement determined by one's relation to 'whiteness' as a phantasm."[51] That phantasm of power is conjured in the central experience that refugees undergo in the very public processes of requesting recognition: queuing outside the UNHCR offices to apply for refugee status or resettlement or, as Osman explained of a person born in the camps, seeking public witness from the community in order to obtain a national identity card. An element of this experience that he did not discuss is the partition thinking embedded in these processes, an inscription of racial thinking at the core of the production of subjecthood in emergency. Beyond declaring ethnic affiliation, a person must perform an act of self-racination or tell certain racialized stories about herself in order to be recognized as a refugee.[52] Race is created in these moments, when, as Fanon elucidated, an individual is required to be recognized by an authority in order to exist in the sociopolitical sphere, eliciting a psychic split. This partition of the self as part of systematic processes of recognition—on the one hand, being, and on the other hand, performing—places a person into a *racial architecture of doubling*. In a less metaphorical and more material sense, refugees become associated with certain racialized architectural forms—for example, in Kenya, the tuqul, which has retained its connotations as a recalcitrant structure, as discussed in the introduction, from the historical colonial context into the contemporary humanitarian one. "*They* live that way because they *wish* to," one aid worker remarked to me (emphasis added), referring to the provisional dwellings on the outskirts of Dagahaley camp built after a period of extreme food and water scarcity in Somalia that brought many new people to Dadaab.[53] I heard this statement in several Kenyan contexts, from the camps to the capital. "Look at the way they live," commented a colleague in an institutional context. "They are not forced to live this way. They choose this kind of house."[54] Whether in Dadaab or Nairobi, such statements were offered in many tones—with curiosity, as a practice of othering, out of outright contempt, or sometimes as a matter of fact—including by officials in humanitarian, governmental, arts, and cultural institutions.[55] The refrain might have escaped my notice if not for its suggestion that race might be directly apprehended in a form of contemporary architecture. Distinguishing racialization in architecture and architectural histories has formed a groundswell in recent critical scholarship, especially in the contribution of architect and historian Mabel O. Wilson, who writes of the inseparability of racial thought from the emergence of the modern discipline of architecture, one based on reason and abstraction distinct from the physical labor of construction and bodies of builders.[56] The racinating quality of partition thinking in the refugee camp parallels the inscription of racial thinking that she locates at the foundation of modern subjecthood, and that has been imposed within many specific historic contexts—especially in humanitarian contexts such as the Dadaab refugee camps—as well as within the self-construction of the modern subject, particularly in emergency.

In a refugee camp, the response to pressures to be recognized within the enclosure executes a profound partitioning of the self, among the severe, compounding ramifications of a racialized emergency architecture. On the twinning that race and racism carry out, philosopher Achille Mbembe points to the "fundamental characteristic of always inciting and engendering a double . . . substituting what *is* with something else, with another reality."[57] His analysis of an external perception echoes the internal problem of "double-consciousness" with which Du Bois grappled as he became sensible of his Blackness through its reflections in the behavior of others, developing acute awareness of his *soul* as it was measured "by the tape of a world that looks on in amused contempt and pity."[58] That framing, of pity entangled with contempt, cuts to the heart of recognition and recognizability in Dadaab, with "race making" an ever-present function governing those in the position to "recognize." This is not to flatten the nuances of multiple and intersectional identities in East Africa—which hew to markers far more complex than race or ethnicity, and where ethnicity alone represents diverse sociocultural assemblages from across Africa and the Indian Ocean—nor to suggest that whiteness or Blackness are the primary social or cultural signifiers in the refugee system, in Africa, or in Dadaab.[59] It is to analyze the creation of an "other" endemic to the racination immanent in the practice of partitioning, which emerges in the encounter between refugee and humanitarian and, more acutely, in the refugee's partitioning of the self.

Even if one does not differentiate oneself along the lines of race or other social constructs, the self as experienced and the self as recognized by others is ever bifurcated in a refugee context, a condition predicated on the intelligibility of one's status. The embodied citizenship process that Osman described—with elders, local government employees, and community members appearing in public to affirm an applicant and support her claim—gives some sense of the events behind official recognition of refugee status, the legal means by which a person is acknowledged by a specific nation-state or an international regime as eligible for protection. On multiple visits to the CARE compound in Ifo camp, I saw refugees waiting in crowds in the heat to appear before an officer, sometimes returning for a second, third, or fourth visit, to reach the front of the queue. Many had memorized details of their flight to repeat to the officer—the risks or losses that they contended with to travel to Ifo camp—as I learned from the interpreters and other colleagues I worked with, not wishing to disturb people in the queue at a time when they needed to rehearse in order to perform a narrative in a high-stakes interview, potentially resulting in the conferral of refugee status. The queue itself was a form of existential reckoning that might demonstrate authenticity of purpose through persistence. Certain details—even the decision to travel via certain routes rather than others—would serve as "proof" of a person's persecution, rendering her eligible for refugee status and aid. This "eligibility" depended on one's *intelligibility as a refugee*, how her life might be rendered as an object of persecution, entitled to protection, or one of suffering, deserving of aid. On what constitutes the legibility of a life as *grievable*, philosopher Judith Butler discusses a framework of "*apprehension*, understood as a mode of knowing that is not yet recognition," which remains different from "*intelligibility*, understood as the general historical schema or schemas that establish domains of the knowable. . . . Not all acts of knowing are acts of recognition . . . a life has to be intelligible *as a life*, has to conform to certain conceptions of what life is, in order to become recognizable."[60] A life in displacement, in that sense, remains divided, suspended between the apprehended and the intelligible, not yet able to be recognized without the performative act of narration. A person may know herself as displaced, yet, to achieve a status that can be leveraged for aid in emergency, she must be acknowledged within a grid of intelligibility endorsed by communities and states, reproducing partitions of the self. Beyond the immediate pressures that one faces in being forced to seek refugee status is the gnawing anxiety caused by a ceaseless doubling, a partitioning of a self potentially still to be unrecognized by others. This ever-othering, racializing practice of doubling forms the backdrop of psychic (and physical) risk and depletion against which the architectures of self-making by the people centered in this book may be felt.

Thinking from partitions in Dadaab illuminates not only architectures of self-making, but also forms of cohabitation in emergency. These cohabitations are forged in the immediacy of emergency and constituted of heterogeneous interrelations, intimacies, confrontations, and forms of difference.[61] They emerge particularly in the construction of domesticities in emergency, discussed in chapter 3, intertwining many forms of social difference and producing and traversing partitions in everyday lives. In Dadaab, these cohabitations do not always take architectural form in structuring a spatial order but impress themselves on the built environment in immaterial ways, through activities that are ephemeral, not buildings that are solid. Yet, this affective sensorium expresses the material and aesthetic entanglement of a shared space of profound difference. In these environmental cohabitations—not resolving difference, but enabling it—the Dadaab refugee camps have formed a structure in which people build solidarities and cope.

However heterogeneous within, as an architecture of the security state, the Dadaab refugee camps must articulate themselves according to sanctioned forms of difference within external frameworks, which view Muslim and Somali worlds through othering lenses and for which the settlements are coded as a rogue environment. To explain the architecture of sanctioned difference, I underscore, as I do throughout this study, that I can provide only a fragmented view, to which future scholars might add. Here I draw insight from a chance encounter that led to scheduled interviews with interlocutors who moved in spheres with which I did not expect to interact in Dadaab or in any of my research. At the end of one of my workdays with the WRC, I happened to be in the Pumzika café in Dadaab's central humanitarian compound—named for the Kiswahili word for "rest"—one of the only establishments operating into the late hours of the night, serving food and alcohol to aid workers coming off multiday shifts. A group of men entered the café and began talking with one another and the members of my team. I came to learn that they were part of a cadre at one time employed by the US military, now embedded in a humanitarian workforce, holding posts in UN agencies and international NGOs around the country and in the Kenya-Somalia "borderland." The group did not include any Africans, and their conversations reflected a deep familiarity with US military culture and Kenya-Somalia geopolitical relations. I think they spoke with us because they heard we were working with a US-based organization. As I heard many of them articulate in their conversations, the architectures of camps, compounds, bases, schools, and missions on the Kenyan and Ethiopian borders with Somalia were considered "essential" for the maintenance of order.[62] I came to understand that they viewed their work as establishing a sense of social and political "order," one that was liberal and multiracial, in contrast to an ethnoreligious "disorder" that they perceived in the region.[63] One or another of the individuals at the table frequently voiced distrust of the sense of self-determination held by people living in the camps, and the belief that they were not "ready" for political actualization and could not be trusted to treat minority populations fairly. Having not expected to come across these conversations in the Pumzika café, I declined to pursue further questions directly in that setting and followed up with certain individuals later, triangulating what I heard against interviews with aid workers and officials in other settings. In retrospect, I note that these discussions reproduced Dadaab as a crucial geopolitical architecture, which partitioned allowable diversity from disallowed difference.

Cultural studies scholar Neda Atanasoski is most uncompromising on this point of sanctioned difference, identifying a shift after the Cold War (a historical "postsocialist" timespace running concurrent with the structuring and growth of the Dadaab refugee camps). In it, the United States justified humanitarian intervention into sovereign territories by extending the platform for military humanitarianism through a framework of racial diversity (propounding a rhetoric of its own resolved racial difference and claiming to vanquish ethnonationalistic tyranny).[64] Her analysis closely matches what I heard in the Pumzika café. As I argued earlier and as Atanasoski claims, "race" encompasses other forms of difference—for example, religious or ideological—enabling new territorial deconstructions and reconstructions in order to claim larger spaces for a liberalism whose badge was the putative resolution of racial difference. Jasbir Puar forwards a not-unrelated argument for the cultural construction of certain communities as "terrorist," through the production of a liberal narrative of resolved difference (in this case, the mobilization of queer politics in the United States and its putative resolution

1.10. Pumzika café, UNHCR compound, Dadaab.

1.11. CARE compound gate and guardhouse, WFP sign listing international partners, on the main drive through humanitarian compound at Dadaab.

of sexual difference as part of that narrative).[65] In reflecting on my experience, more shocking than the common presence of American military and ex-military personnel laboring in various capacities on the border of Somalia was the delivery of such liberal values in the Kenyan-Somali "borderland" through manifold barbed-wire zones and other forms of architectural violence. The ways in which these landscapes segregated bodies and eventually divided selves, while accompanied by liberal promise and a capacious rhetoric of sanctioned difference, demonstrates how architectures of humanitarian intervention not only reflected but also enacted partition, creating and shaping it through such architectural clichés.

The construction of this zone of liberal diversity follows a theoretical tradition that situates the *individual* as the metric for human rights (worth understanding here in contrast to the partitioned self). This tradition valorizes transgressing sovereign territory to preserve the individual, tying together architectural and humanitarian intervention as the practical means of doing so. This individualistic orientation toward human rights has been enshrined in the Universal Declaration of Human Rights, although scholars have noted that rights-based antityrannical transgression of territory as the reason for humanitarian intervention is based not in legal theory, but in praxis.[66] Historian D. J. B. Trim argues that understandings of territorial sovereignty in the Peace of Westphalia in 1648, often taken as the starting point of the trajectory leading to the formation of the UN, never formed absolute legal conditions but instead established *practices* of morally driven interventions into other countries to combat tyranny (named in the *Vindiciae contra tyrannos*, published in Calvinist Basel in 1579).[67] Such an argument about praxis implies the significance of spatial practices, especially those that give material form to humanitarian interventions against the violation of the individual.

Practices of humanitarian spatial intervention have extended this individualism, while tying the construction of a *universal* individual to race-making partitions of the self and a racial architecture of doubling. These practices follow a humanitarian order predicated on the individual rather than a social community or polity, as anthropologist Miriam Ticktin argues.[68] The humanitarian order that came into being concurrently with the establishment of a "new world order" (famously proclaimed by leaders George H. W. Bush and Mikhail Gorbachev) was predicated on individual human rights, and in it, refugee camps—notably, those at Dadaab—inscribed an opposition between individual rights and sovereign authority into the sociopolitical realm through a material architecture. This opposition was enunciated in a 2001 report, *The Responsibility to Protect*, which advocated, in response to humanitarian violations, for the precedence of individual rights over sovereign integrity.[69] Philosopher Kelly Oliver outlines the debt of this discourse (based on the universal individual) to Kantian humanism—identifying the link of the first appearances of the term *humanitarian* in the eighteenth and nineteenth centuries with notions of Christ's individuation in the person of Jesus, his humanity superseding his divinity.[70] Historian Lynn Hunt emphasizes the emergence of the individual in European sociality after the fourteenth century, when individual self-containment displaced practices of commingling. "Defecation and urination in public became increasingly repellent. People began to use handkerchiefs rather than blowing their noses into their hands. Spitting, eating out of a common bowl, and sleeping in a bed with a stranger became disgusting."[71] This discursive trajectory, increasingly rationalizing the enclosure of the individual self, is difficult to read outside of the racializing encounter. The formation in early modern Europe of the individual and universal self, as outlined here, occurred just as Africans flowed into Iberia, auguring a tradition of individualism that would later trace itself into the partition of the Black self that Du Bois, Fanon, Mbembe, and others would analyze.[72] These epistemic and historical formations surfaced starkly in a discussion I had with one of my colleagues in Ifo camp, a former incentive worker describing the layers of racialization in his registration interview—as his performative self-categorizations met the scrutiny of his body by officers attempting to determine the veracity of his self-description.[73] He articulated the painful details of self-partitioning (a concrete consequence of refugeeness), which followed his pronounced individuation by authorities (a cornerstone in human rights and humanitarian logic). These paradoxes lie at the heart of a racinated partition.

How to think on the spatial and architectural ramifications of this? An illustration of modern planning coeval with emerging discourses of the individual and universal self provides a lesson. By the beginning of the sixteenth century, Africans in Lisbon, both free and enslaved people moving through Iberia, constituted one-tenth of the city's population. By 1755, during the decline of the Portuguese slave trade, Lisbon was among the wealthiest European cities and also a city of Africans.[74] After an earthquake struck on November 1, the aftershock of the tremors, the tsunami that drowned the urban center, and the six-day fire that leveled the city afterward resulted in nearly 100,000 dead in a city of 250,000. Tremors were felt from the Finnish to the West African coasts on that day and within the Iberian peninsula for another year, with tidal waves hitting shores as distant as Indonesia. Social and visual theorist Sharon Sliwinski details the response to the disaster in anachronistic terms as "one of the first great mass media events"; images circulated widely, forming a visual culture of engravings, wood-block prints, and other technologies preceding the advent of the daily newspaper.[75] From pamphlets of eyewitness accounts to renderings of imagined scenes, the reflection on the event sparked the production of ephemera, accessible across classes and around the world, remaining in circulation for a century and spawning a vast visual archive. These notated an architectural response to a humanitarian crisis. Architectural historian Spiro Kostof writes that the nobility among the homeless, not content to squat with the public in the urban squares or on church grounds, erected nine thousand temporary wooden structures within six months, many imported from Holland and some quite elaborate.[76] The city of Hamburg chartered four ships with construction materials, and Lisbon merchants offered to support reconstruction by paying the king a surcharge for imports from the colonies. The redesign by Eugénio dos Santos of the Baixa, the city's center, imposed on the ruin a grid of urban blocks made of prefabricated components assembled on-site among the fallen materials. These included ornamental frieze decorations; balcony sections; and the "Gaiola Pombalina," a wooden earthquake-resistant cage, or structural skeleton, designed to move independently of building walls (named for the royal overseer of Lisbon's redevelopment).[77] These effusive architectural responses proffered not only a global form but also a situated practice of disaster response. Yet, can these humanitarian scenes be imagined without the African subjects who co-constructed them? I argue that partitions of the self emerging in eighteenth-century African Lisbon mirrored its coeval formation elsewhere, shaping principles of partitioning and partition thinking, architectural methods not unfamiliar in Dadaab today.

Partition Thinking

When we look closely at a refugee camp, what do we see? I believe we see the afterlife of partitions. In humanitarian settlement at Dadaab, we find partitions of the self, partitions of the Black self, and the liberal tradition of partitions stemming from sanctioned difference and human rights rooted in individuation. Yet, these partitions of the self belie partitions of land. In the end, the complexity of a doubled self on riven land is an ontology that refugees at Dadaab have been forced to contend with, in a long history of migration, partition, and the architectures that have bridged their negotiation.

Yet, partition is ultimately a fallacy. It does not describe a true condition. It is a construction, a fiction brought into full narrative fruition through histories and through the authorized archives that undergird their dissemination. Even in acknowledging that a refugee camp comes from partitions, the histories in the following chapters propose very different terms. They propose knowledges that move away from partition thinking.

(*previous page*) Ifo camp, 1992, photo from slideshow provided by Per Iwansson.

Land, Emergency, and Sedentarization in East Africa 2

In addition to reproducing a territorial practice of partitioning, the architecture of the Dadaab refugee camps has systematized humanitarian settlement in emergency, as the people in this chapter's opening photo would learn in the months and years after it was taken. In 1992, the UNHCR contracted the person who took the photo, a Swedish architect by the name of Per Iwansson, to build on his previous experience planning a new town in Mozambique and draw up the plans for a refugee settlement in Kenya. He found a camp in place when he arrived. Ifo, pictured here in its earliest days, as well as Dagahaley and Hagadera to follow (the latter planned by Iwansson), instituted a spatial practice, exposed in this grainy photo, imposed on and engaged by refugees. People whose lives had been defined by migration were brought into contradictory processes of sedentary inhabitation and land cultivation as modes of living and thriving in Dadaab. These forms of settlement stemmed from lifesaving practices in emergency. Yet, they adhered to longer historical traditions of eroding and erasing the commons. Colonial approaches to the use and tenure of land in East Africa favored the sedentarization of laboring people, as discussed in this book's introduction, and all but criminalized nomadic and pastoral forms of living by integrating sedentarization into the built environment, to the present day. Following principles of partitioning, as discussed in chapter 1, I argue in this chapter that humanitarian settlement transforms common land into demarcated territory. The enclosure of common land, a legal practice inaugurated through parliamentary acts of private property creation in seventeenth-century England, has formed a logic of capitalism that the forces of itinerant mobility and collective inhabitation directly contradict. These forces have produced tensions between architectures of migration and sedentarization the world over. I argue that the Dadaab refugee camps, as a successor to these originary violations of land, form a thread with other forms of settlement and unsettlement in East Africa.

Emerging from this chapter's opening image of Ifo refugee camp is a story of land. Constructions to enclose land have cast settlement as stable and migration as transgressive. This tension engenders epistemic effects. It shapes normative scholarship by establishing landed archives as legitimate and those stemming from migration as illegitimate, conditioning the understanding of histories. Yet, migration is as important to history as sedentarism.

This chapter explores forms and forces of colonial settlement that eschewed free migration and produced a regime of sedentarization in response to emergency. To move away from partition thinking requires understanding a history of settler colonial as well as postcolonial policies, which accelerated the construction of what I term *emergency territory*. In the following pages, I examine settlement and unsettlement in East Africa through constructions of emergency territory in different moments by the colonial government, abolitionist missionaries, postcolonial authorities, and contemporary humanitarians and refugees. These examples are not intended to present a genealogical sequence or a set of similarities. Instead, each of the events and moments highlighted distinguishes itself from the others to build a narrative of architectures effecting sedentarization.

I open on a discussion with one refugee who transformed the arid landscape of Dagahaley refugee camp into a lush, green cultivation. The agricultural plot she tended offers an acute instance of sedentarization, through everyday subsistence labor, at the scale of a household. I argue that a refugee camp effects sedentarization through such individuated and everyday instantiations of land use. I follow the threads stemming from her story in the chapter's next three sections. The first analyzes the colonial construction of the contingent emergency territory in which the Dadaab refugee camps were sited. The second offers the establishment of liberatory and coercive forms of enclosure as a prehistory for the refugee camps. The third examines building types, which either cooperate with or resist settlement. Ultimately, this chapter examines a moral economy of migration, an approach to land that pathologizes the nomad and institutes the drive to sedentarization. I argue that this orientation to land has produced, in East Africa and beyond, not only the logic for settler colonialism but also the continuing justification for humanitarian settlement.

Living off the Land and Living on the Land

A discourse on humanitarian settlement concerning land must first acknowledge the contentious environmental problems accompanying the production of an architecture of camps in emergency. The unpartitioned land within the wider ecologies of a refugee camp is subject to the narrower concerns of authorities, namely, utilitarian effects rather than causes of settlement. Humanitarian attention to the environment in refugee camp contexts primarily focuses on deforestation. Sudden land clearance is part of the ecological impact of a new settlement, a recurring effect of the long-standing aid practice of supplying food without accompanying cooking fuel—dry foods being easier and cheaper to distribute and oil and gas expensive and scarce in regions where camps are established. To survive, refugees have often engaged in extreme foraging and denuding of vegetation in the vicinity of camps. The food distribution practice has been criticized by humanitarian professionals as increasing the risk of gender-based violence aganst those foraging for tinder, while creating calamitous environmental conditions—new flood plains, mosquito-breeding pits, and more. At Dadaab, uneven access to ecological resources has escalated tensions between communities of displaced people and their hosts, manufacturing a sense of lack, centered on land.

Land, in this all-too-common scenario, operates in instrumental terms and is narrated as a victim of illegitimate use, transgression, or spatial violence. This depiction obscures deeper ramifications of the relationship between architecture and land. It neglects the understanding of land as a medium for sedimenting forms of difference, as architectural historian Hollyamber Kennedy argues, on the one hand through territoriality and dispossession, infrastructures for the legitimation of state seizures and redistributions, and on the other as a palette for the entanglement of segregated enclosures that enact and obscure carcerality.[1] The authorized ejection of people from land has a long history, occurring with great frequency around the world, at the expense of citizens and subjects alike, in putatively normative contexts far from those fraught with emergency. The global history of settlement has shown that those who live and work the land and those who participate in private ownership of property, alike, have been threatened with removal, resettlement, expropriation, or devaluation. The production of new settlements has long provided the reason and urgency for state legitimation of radical changes in land tenure, use, or occupation.

A refugee camp is architecture without land.[2] This is a paradoxical condition, in which architecture is imposed, integrated, yet fundamentally separated from the cultural and social life, economies, politics, and material ecology of a place. Such a paradox, imposing a constructed environment on a place from which it is partitioned, results from recurring or protracted emergency. Yet, in spite of this partitioning and segregating principle, many refugees have cultivated land at Dadaab and have transformed the bush into a fecund interior with the potential to offer subsistence and autonomy to their families, ecological stability to the immediate and wider regional environment, and connections for all to the past. In short, the labor of a few to live *off the land*, but also to live *on the land* in a refugee camp, translates into a critical heritage for themselves and many others.

My conversation with Maganai Saddiq Hassan within the boundaries of her family plot in Dagahaley camp in 2011 conveyed how subsistence farming enacted ordinary reminders of home, archiving a recent migrant past as well as expertise forged over generations.[3] I met Hassan on one of two days when my research partner Bethany Young and I accompanied CARE Kenya aid worker Lucy Njenga and two "incentive" workers who worked as interpreters, Fardosa Abdullahi Mohamed and Mohamed Osman Mohamed, on visits to the large greenhouses in the camps and individual shambas, or farm plots, within designated spaces allotted to families. With a budget of 2.4 million Kenyan shillings (a little over $20,000), people in partnership with CARE operated two greenhouses each in Ifo, Dagahaley, and Hagadera camps and one in the town of Dadaab, while many individuals such as Hassan received seeds, soils, and other materials to grow what the NGOs referred to as "multistorey gardens." These activities demonstrate the intricate balance between development and relief, raised in the introduction and discussed in depth in chapter 4, maintained by organizations such as CARE in emergency contexts such as the Dadaab refugee camps. We interviewed several people, individually and in groups, on how the practice of farming increased their capacity for subsistence, impacted their quality of life, and connected them to the economy of the camp. Hassan's experience was not unique or remarkable, but I chose to draw from our exchange in the text that follows because her expertise stood out among the body of interviews our research team conducted, and her sense of relaxed confidence as a farmer attuned to her work and its accomplishments conveyed its affective qualities. Her tone emerges in the brief excerpt of the conversation included here, in which she explains her work, her background, and the ways her farm impacts her household. On the day we met, we were joined by Mohamed, CARE's "incentive" worker, who provided interpretation between English and Somali as we spoke. He referred to Hassan, as others did, as a "Somali Bantu." This ethnically and racially coded term was frequently used by aid workers to refer to a group of people from southern Somalia, discussed in chapter 1, who were recognized in the camps as socially different from the dominant Somali communities. Those differences were narrated by aid workers as the source of tensions behind their original flight, continued risk in the refugee camps, and need for third-country resettlement. Although Hassan lived among people of different ethnicities and she and the other farmers seemed to know one another and share materials and information, this distinction throws into relief the greater challenges she must have faced. Hassan came from a village along the Jubba River in Somalia. She welcomed me into the enclosure of her family plot and shared a sense of everyday life in Dagahaley for someone who knew how to grow food.

ANOORADHA IYER SIDDIQI: Mahadsanid [thank you]. Can you tell me about your garden, what are you growing?

MAGANAI SADDIQ HASSAN: Sukuma [collard greens], tomatoes, spinach, and okra.

ANOORADHA IYER SIDDIQI: And how long have you had this garden?

MAGANAI SADDIQ HASSAN: Nine months.

ANOORADHA IYER SIDDIQI: Is this the first time you've had a garden?

MAGANAI SADDIQ HASSAN: In Somalia, I used to be a farmer, but here, it is my first farm.

ANOORADHA IYER SIDDIQI: Did you have a big farm in Somalia?

MAGANAI SADDIQ HASSAN: Very big farm!

ANOORADHA IYER SIDDIQI: And did you work by yourself or were you working with your husband on the farm?

MAGANAI SADDIQ HASSAN: It's me and my husband. We used to work on the farm.

ANOORADHA IYER SIDDIQI: Is he here also?

MAGANAI SADDIQ HASSAN: He is around the house.

ANOORADHA IYER SIDDIQI: And he also helps you with this garden?

MAGANAI SADDIQ HASSAN: He helps.

ANOORADHA IYER SIDDIQI: How big is your family?

MOHAMED [*for Maganai Saddiq Hassan*]: She says seven children, her, plus the husband. That's nine members.

ANOORADHA IYER SIDDIQI: And do the children also work?

MAGANAI SADDIQ HASSAN: Most of them, they are students. During their free time, they help me, fetching water.

ANOORADHA IYER SIDDIQI: And does it produce enough food to feed your family?

MOHAMED: She says, what she is getting is enough for her family use.

ANOORADHA IYER SIDDIQI: So, what about your rations that you receive with your ration card? Do you still use that for food?

MAGANAI SADDIQ HASSAN: What we normally get, the food we get from the organization, we use here in the home.

ANOORADHA IYER SIDDIQI: So, you use the ration and the food from the garden.

MAGANAI SADDIQ HASSAN: Yeah.

ANOORADHA IYER SIDDIQI: Do you sell any of it?

MAGANAI SADDIQ HASSAN: I don't sell any of it. [*Laughing.*]

ANOORADHA IYER SIDDIQI: It's just enough?

MAGANAI SADDIQ HASSAN [*laughing*]: It's just enough.

ANOORADHA IYER SIDDIQI: Okay. Does your husband do any other work outside of the home?

MAGANAI SADDIQ HASSAN: He just does casual work. He may do construction, maybe today this family wants their house to be constructed, he goes there, he does the work, then he is paid some money. He is not an employee.

ANOORADHA IYER SIDDIQI: I understand. Like a day laborer. . . . When your husband earns income, how do you decide how to spend that money?

[*Laughing.*]

MAGANAI SADDIQ HASSAN: [We] spend that money to buy the type of the food that maybe we don't have. We use that money to buy milk, meat, sugar, those things which are not here [in the garden, and] we support it with the other food we have.

ANOORADHA IYER SIDDIQI: Do you both make decisions about what to buy together?

MAGANAI SADDIQ HASSAN: We sit and discuss together.

ANOORADHA IYER SIDDIQI: Can I take a picture of you inside the garden?

[*Laughs.*]

Hassan's understated account of daily subsistence in Dagahaley camp and the life she abandoned in Somalia crystallized in the lush, green landscape she designed outside her home. In an anomalous microenvironment created

2.1. Maganai Saddiq Hassan in the farm she designed and cultivated in Dagahaley camp.

in the dusty red clay of Dadaab, she satisfied the widely varying irrigation demands of spinach and okra together in a confined space, without access to sophisticated greenhousing. Although she grew vegetables in a plot at the scale of a kitchen garden (as I repeatedly and mistakenly referred to it), it was important to hear Hassan name this workspace as something else: a *farm*.

The pedagogy of Hassan's farm is manifold. On the one hand, her labor serves an immediate, qualitative need. Among the demoralizing factors in a life of subsistence in a refugee camp is the profound loss of appetite one feels, day in and day out. The bland diet of the dry food ration steals the sense of taste out of the mouth, draining the spirit and the will to joy. A vertical farm of tomatoes, eggplants, okra, and leafy vegetables has explosive ramifications for quality of life, offering a radiance among the monotonous diet of beans and pulses, and a massive boost for nutrition. Thus, Hassan's augmentation of her family's food basket with the vitamins and minerals she cultivated in diverse produce served an invaluable, immediate purpose.

Her architectural work added structure to this gesture, contributing to an environment that balanced the labor of a farmer with the development program of an NGO. The farm was constructed of several "sacks" of recycled plastic or canvas—fifty-kilogram cereal bags—provided by the WFP and placed adjacent to one another in the plot. The "multi-storey" elements of this architecture were the pyramids of empty oil cans, also provided by the WFP, stacked inside the tall sacks. Each can was filled with rocks and had holes drilled in the sides and bottom (except those forming the foundation). Hassan packed a blend of soil and compost around each of the oil cans, into the depth of each sack, planting the top layer with seeds. As she harvested early-growth seedlings from the top of the sack, they could be re-planted in holes in the sides of the bag, utilizing one sack for the preliminary life cycle of the farm. This method, implemented and tested widely in Dadaab by CARE and other organizations (and later imitated in settings in South Asia and elsewhere), enabled Hassan and others to grow a range of produce using a very limited amount of water (five liters, twice per day)—particularly gray water from rainwater collection or the household waste remaining after bathing or rinsing clothes. The gravity-driven drainage of water through the air pockets made by the cans and stones inside them enabled an even aeration and irrigation throughout the vertical farm. The leafy clusters of sacks in Hassan's family plot integrated her labor with CARE's in acts of cultivation. It is difficult not to read this humanitarian process as akin to the imperial technique of "turning the *pays* into a *paysage*," forwarded by visual historian and theorist Jill Casid, in which land is "emptied out and then repossessed by agricultural spectacle."[4] It is that spectacular architecture of cultivation that creates a paradox of land use in a refugee camp.

The pedagogy of this farm is one of living off the land and on the land at once. The WFP sack that separates agriculture from ground serves as a metaphor for the refugee camp in its entirety—demanding the work of cultivation and settlement yet reinforcing a partition that separates a farmer's yield from the land. Hassan's grounded practices of cultivation were conducted under emergency conditions, in a setting dangerous to her person that might force her one day to be resettled for her own safety. Her presence and labor in the refugee camp situated the knowledge of the riparian Jubba communities in a space crafted under conditions of emergency. Hers was among the paradoxical forms of ecological anchoring that refugees contributed to humanitarian settlement at Dadaab, achieved through provisional, putatively transitional means, through the imposition of emergency and responses to it. This production of emergency territory and iteration of humanitarian settlement is one instance in a long history of sedentarization in East Africa. Through the encampment of refugees, the architectures of the Dadaab camps have made visible a history of almost two centuries of fraught settlement—specifically, of attempts to arrest the migration of nomads, but also of complex incorporations of agrarian people—under conditions of emergency.

The constellation of territories, built environments, and spatial practices in the following three sections illuminate the materiality and aesthetics of emergency territory and the spatial practice of sedentarization. The following sections focus, first, on the construction of contingency through colonial territorialization; then, on instances of liberatory and coercive enclosures that set precedents for the Dadaab refugee camps; and finally, on building types that conform to or resist sedentarization. The Dadaab refugee camps are the successor to these instances of territorial construction, enclosure, and building in which land gives way to humanitarian settlement through the production of emergency territory.

Construction of a Contingent Territory

The incongruities of Hassan's farm stem from the stable agricultural architectures that she constructs in conditions of profound contingency, illustrating the paradoxical catalyst at the root of humanitarian settlement. Her lifesaving work and expertise contribute at once to her family's subsistence, while reproducing an underlying territorial instability. Her farm ironically actualizes the role of the Dadaab refugee camps in the construction of contingency and ultimate sedentarization of migrants, a spatial practice growing out of not only recent events, but also a colonial history and longer traditions of migration.

Occupying powers have treated with ambivalence not only the sovereignty of the territory where the Dadaab camps are located, but also the migratory ways of living on and off the land that people in the region have negotiated for hundreds of years. As discussed in chapter 1, the imperial government of Great Britain partitioned the region that is now Kenya's North Eastern Province, ceding the western bank of the Jubba to Italy after World War I. This partition of territory was reified in the international border between Somalia and Kenya adopted (even if contested) after independence. Maintaining the stability of that boundary has remained of governmental concern since, especially after the establishment of the refugee camps in Garissa County. As one of only two locations in the country where refugees were concentrated, this border has been rendered vulnerable to transgression, especially by migrants whose relation to the land lies outside the paradigm of the nation-state.

Over the course of years, as discussed in chapter 4, the Dadaab refugee camps have grown and become entrenched in an architectural form and structure that, while enabling stable humanitarian care and maintenance of refugees, has also produced a consistently unclear relationship to the land it occupied. In the language of aid agencies, the "care and maintenance" of people, a development term and concept, is a response to what are referred to as "complex emergencies," a compounding of events stemming from seemingly different sources, affecting large populations, and requiring humanitarian response. For example, in 2006, after an unprecedented number of people fled the forces of the militarized group al-Shabaab in southern Somalia and settled in the camps, severe rains and the flooding of Ifo forced people into a second displacement in the peripheries. As another example, in 2011, drought in Somalia exacerbated the food and water scarcity caused by the ongoing armed conflict. I argue that the establishment of the camps in 1991 and 1992 and their expansion, first in 2006 and then in 2011, have been understood through narratives of complex emergency, when instead the growth and evolution of the architecture of the refugee settlements iterated steps in a long trajectory of ambivalence and contestation over this territory and negotiations over this land. In short, the narrative succinctness of a "complex emergency" dominating the sociopolitics of a territory shrouds a far messier aporia of materialities and intimacies in which multiple subjects negotiate living on and off the land.

Writing the history of this architecture and the land to which it is tied is thus an equally complex endeavor. States and institutions assert themselves asymmetrically in parts of the world that fall between nation-states, resulting in uneven archiving of historical records and multiple competing claims to the historical record. This has certainly been so in East Africa, where human habitation, and thus society and politics, has further escaped view because of the prevalence of pastoralist lifestyles dominated by transhumance, leaving little material or aesthetic footprint to find. The problem of fugitive archives and the writing of "unofficial" spaces is compounded by competing narrative interests on both sides of borders, and with regard to the border itself. Land demarcation as a principle has been perceived radically differently in different parts of the region. The idea that the 1963–1964 OAU decision to adopt colonial boundaries at independence represented an accomplishment of European ordering is simplistic; rather, it drew on the marriage of these demarcations with preexisting African conceptual and practical forms of imagining territory.[5] Boundary-making in East Africa occurred through ground-level engagements. Therefore, prior to reading archives, the first notional stroke in an architectural history must be to deconstruct the making of territory and seek a material history of people's negotiations of the ground, the land.

Scholarship on the cross-border identification and politics of Somalia's unification, which characterized its relationship with its neighbors in the years preceding the civil war, helps to contextualize these land demarcation issues and Dadaab's underlying territorial (and thus historical) tensions. The pan-Somali nationalist imaginations of Soomaaliweyn, a Greater Somalia—intended to unite the Shanta Soomaaliyeed, the five Somalias partitioned into the territories of northeastern Kenya, Italian Somaliland, eastern Ethiopia (known as the Ogaden), British Somaliland, and French Somaliland—crystallized into a demand for unification after 1941. This followed the assumption of control by Britain of areas that had been colonized by Italy—the end of Italian colonialism in Africa—and the restoration of territories to Emperor Haile Selassie of Ethiopia. "More than simply a nationalist movement," writes historian Safia Aidid, "Greater Somalia was a structure of feeling," a political imaginary of possible futures based on territorial unification, conceived in reaction to a particular colonial present.[6] As she analyzes, this imaginary conflicted with agendas of the Ethiopian empire built over time, in which interventions or insurgencies by Somali-identifying people within or outside Ethiopia figured as "continuations of a perennial Somali problem that dated back to the 16th century conquest of Abyssinia," contributing in the twentieth century to tensions over the Ogaden in the east (territory that Ethiopia perceived as crucial to its statehood) and eventually to the Ogaden War of 1977 and 1978 (broadly understood as ending the political project of Greater Somalia).[7] Political scientist Christopher Clapham argues that "for most colonized African peoples, 'nationalism' involved a recognition of the common fate of those *within* a colonial frontier," but "for the Somalis it directly resulted from the resentments of those who had to move across such a frontier," and that Ethiopian representatives at the founding OAU summit in 1963 claimed "that the Somalis had never formed a united territorial state, as though that settled the matter."[8] For Somalis, a major aim was eradication of the contested colonial borders rather than their reification. Historian Lee Cassanelli explains the Somali phenomenon as a "unique case" of a state largely composed of members who claim one common ethnic identity, shared with people in three adjoining states—"in contrast to most of the rest of Africa, where independent states seek to forge a common national identity from a multiplicity of ethnic groups within their boundaries."[9] A famous adage emerged from the second OAU meeting in Cairo in 1964: "Wherever the camel goes, that is Somalia." Yet, the desire to open a territory does not necessarily paint a portrait of irredentism. This label promotes a deeper stigma and misconstrual of the imaginations and discourses that thrived in Kenya's northeast, as historian Keren Weitzberg argues, by privileging views from an international system over local, situated perspectives.[10] Sociologist Cawo Abdi, moreover, raises the peculiar transnational capacities of Somali networks as a mark of shared identity across vastly differing countries, regions, and social contexts.[11] I argue that the capacity by Somali-identifying people to construct a transnational space has been crucial to fueling materialities and architecture as well as imaginations and futurities in Dadaab.[12] In the imagined Somali nation and the territorial Somali state—together inhabiting a spectrum of nationalisms and globalisms—practices and histories of migrations as well as desires for borderlessness show that territory cannot be easily defined.

This returns us to the problem of a material negotiation over land, for which it is worth situating the pastoralist political imagination of Greater Somalia into the history of territorialization in East Africa. Approximately seventeen major boundaries were drawn in the regions between Sudan and Tanzania between 1891 and 1915, as a product of several treaties and agreements.[13] For pragmatic reasons, borders were explicitly softened in some of these agreements. The border demanded regular negotiation in the Northern

Frontier, an area that spanned half the Kenya colony, the easternmost region of which comprises the current Kenya-Somalia borderland. Its 1924–1925 demarcation by British and Italian authorities explicitly elicited frequent transactional negotiation around usage and passage. According to international relations scholar Gilbert M. Khadiagala, "if in certain areas specified in the treaty there existed a shortage of pasture for Somali clans, and if during rainy seasons the pasturage on the Kenya side exceeded local requirements, then those clans might be permitted to cross the boundary."[14] This recurring practice of compromise, creating occasions to yield or show generosity, sometimes enabling consolidations of resources and sometimes deepening antagonisms over often-performed tensions, has produced a highly complex set of politics and identifications.

These identity politics framed the nationalization and decolonization process in Kenya and, within it, the construction of a "frontier" as an emergency territory. This followed a set of events in the twilight of the British empire's reign over the Kenya Colony, which had profound ramifications. This was a period of diplomatic breakdown elsewhere in the region as Somalia and Ethiopia engaged in hostilities and halted diplomatic relations after the former rejected the 1897 boundary forged between eastern Ethiopia and British Somaliland, leaving no other boundary to the south between Ethiopia and the former Italian Somaliland. On the eve of Kenya's independence in 1962, as discussed in this book's introduction and in greater detail in the following section, the NFD of British East Africa participated in a plebiscite in which the people voted overwhelmingly in favor of a postcolonial union with Somalia, rather than Kenya. The subsequent retention of this land by the government of Kenya fueled an ongoing tension over "the NFD question" as the desire for a Greater Somalia began to be articulated through the plebiscite and its aftermath. Between 1963 and 1967, the Kenyan government went to war in the north against pastoralists perceived to be secessionist, implementing counterinsurgency tactics that included incarceration measures similar to those used to detain Kenyans in the anticolonial Land and Freedom struggle of the previous decade.[15] The "frontier" can be said to have been constructed within these events as much as within the colonial developments that preceded them, a process extending into the aggressions that followed, which interpolated Cold War geopolitics into Somalia's communist and Kenya's capitalist orientations. These events colored the region where the refugee camps lie today as a shadowy and interstitial rogue space, an emergency territory exceeding the contingent terms of its colonial production.

Along with the latency of these events and the narratives that followed them, the Northern Frontier was constructed through direct colonial territorial activities. The British Crown proclaimed a protectorate from the Mombasa coast to Lake Naivasha in 1895, began the construction of the Kenya-Uganda railway the following year, and in 1902 expanded its purview to include parts of present-day Uganda. Through ordinances that same year, the highlands were opened to white settlers for land capitalization, and imperial territories were designated through the delineation of Crown Lands and Outlying Districts. The Outlying Districts were "closed to all travellers" under the ordinance, meaning that entry was granted only to "natives of the district," public officers of the protectorate, and license holders, restricting the mobility of Africans between these "designated closed districts," as discussed in chapter 1.[16] A process of territorial designation in proclamations that built on this 1902 ordinance produced the Northern Frontier.

The contingency of the Dadaab site comes into view within this history of the negotiation of land and boundaries in East Africa, the vision of a Greater Somalia attempting to supersede them, and the construction of the frontier in the Kenyan northeast—forces mirroring others worldwide, shaping places that would come to be understood as "borderlands." This contingency here refers to a territorial construction as well as the challenge of writing "unofficial" space into history. Turning again to the direct spatial construction of territory by colonial powers, two proclamations are meaningful for the Dadaab site. The first, from 1902, declares a closed district south of the equator between the Nairobi, Tana, and Mackenzie Rivers, and another within a radius of thirty miles around the center of Mount Kenya. The second, from 1905, declares a closed district north of the equator and west of the 40th degree longitude. The 1938 War Office maps show a village adjacent to a small lake, with the name "Hagar Dera" printed next to it, as discussed in the introduction, placing this site as the earlier iteration of the refugee settlement Hagadera, on the main road between Garissa and the Kenya-Somaliland border, at the juncture of camel tracks running north and a proposed road running south, north of the zero parallel and between the 40th and 41st degrees longitude.[17] Its location, therefore, was external to the outlying district proclaimed on February 4, 1905, as "bounded on the North by the Equator."[18] In addition, the site fell outside the district proclaimed on April 26, 1905, as it sat to the east of the closed district named as lying to the "West of Longitude 40° E."[19] This detail relating to the history of the site of the refugee camps has become vitally important, as Kenya's Department of Refugee Affairs has at times been inaccessible to the public, impeding the capacity to construct a counterhistory. These military maps show Hagadera, the southernmost refugee settlement in the Dadaab complex—and by extension, the other camps—located outside the official boundaries of any named district in the British Empire, in a space unclaimed by any adjacent power. That is to say, the refugee camps inhabit territory that existed outside historic space proper, external even to the mapped frontier. Already, over the course of a century, the territorial margin where the camp complex would be sited was the object of a disfiguration of land and its transformation into vacuous space. This evacuated construction accommodated the figuration of *emergency territory*, creating and reproducing contingency and offering the destabilized grounds for a series of sedentarization practices to be examined in the next section, which prefigure humanitarian settlement.

Enclosures

Hassan's farm, located within her bounded family plot in Dagahaley, recalls other architectures of migration, precursors to the Dadaab refugee camps that appear in various forms of enclosure in Kenya in the twentieth century. In the following pages, I study two conceptual enclosures, the liberatory and the coercive settlement, through empirical forms: the abolitionist settlement at Freretown and the detention village incarcerating shifta. While the former was intended as a site of Christian humanitarian rescue and the latter a tool to force the settlement of migrants and pastoralists, both contributed to a regime of sedentarization. Each is a type of manyatta, a Maasai term used generically in contemporary parlance in Kenya, referring to specific historical forms of settlement that represent Indigenous practices of community-making, pastoralism, and land cultivation. For the Maasai, a manyatta was a compound composed of multiple structures, including a boma, the livestock enclosure, and multiple dwellings. The manyatta functioned as a seminomadic encampment associated with lineage, migration, warrior masculinities, fortification, and coming of age.[20] Nomadic Maasai men and youths would house themselves in manyatta established during ritual periods, and Maasai or Samburu extended families built them to tend herds before migrating with the grazing seasons.

"Manyatta" is often translated to "village," and although closer to the English language concept of "homestead," represents a bounded settlement form, a compound, a fortified village, or a temporary encampment. In different historical circumstances, it has acted as a liberating or coercive form, a conceptual object, and an epistemological source through sociospatial mark-making, aesthetics, and materiality. From 1916, when the imperial government established Native Reserves to confine pastoralist communities such as the Maasai, the manyatta began to be deployed as an architecture to contain, categorize, and discipline people.[21] Its meaning became perverted in the colonial context, as the settlement form increasingly carried conceptual connotations of violence against political and ethnic groups. Throughout the twentieth century in Kenya, the manyatta persisted as a form of coercive settlement in the counterinsurgency villages constructed to detain and rehabilitate anticolonial Mau Mau rebels, and later to suppress the postcolonial pastoralist insurgency in the NFD. In each moment, the manyatta was used to curtail or confine the mobility (and attendant culture and politics) of populations.

The manyatta provides a spatial and material basis for a concept history of settlement and unsettlement in which the Dadaab refugee camps act as successors to distinct forms and practices that produced the logics for enclosure. The following examples emerged in historically different contexts in Kenya. Some equated liberation with sedentary forms of land use, such as the first missionary compound in present-day Kenya (established in the 1840s) and the first constructed specifically to shelter formerly enslaved people (established in the 1870s). Some equated development with coercive architectures of settlement, such as the counterinsurgency villagization rehabilitation strategy implemented by the Kenyan state during the antipastoralist wars beginning in the 1960s (based on the same spatial technology deployed by the British Empire during the anti-imperial revolutionary uprisings in the 1950s). Each type serves as a prelude to the international humanitarian encampment of the late twentieth and early twenty-first centuries. These iterations of enclosure show how an opposition to pastoralism was inscribed over and again, through architectures of abolition and humanitarian intervention.

LIBERATORY SETTLEMENT

The mission in Freretown, Kenya, a fraught architecture of migration established near Mombasa Island in 1875 for the rehabilitation of newly freed people, acts as a predecessor for the contemporary humanitarian settlement. In its aggressive equation of liberation with plot cultivation, the mission prefaced land capitalization in Kenya. Through smallholder agriculture, the practices at Freretown commingled spiritual and material concerns in instigating extractive relationships between people and the land. As a social environment of encounter between diverse people from across Africa, South

Asia, and Europe, Freretown associated cultural capital with the cultivation of land. While operating with a different agenda and at a radically different scale than the settler enclosures that would later dominate the highlands, the transformations of land at Freretown produced the cultural logics and terms for political economies implemented at a much larger scale by the settler colonial empire. Though Freretown is not connected genealogically with the Dadaab refugee camps, the cohabitation of rescued and rescuer in the abolitionist settlement is mirrored in the blocks and sectors of Dagahaley camp, where refugees such as Hassan make new lives alongside humanitarians. Paradoxically, one end for both enclosures is the practice of land cultivation in small plots, such that the sukuma (collard greens), tomatoes, spinach, and okra that Hassan grew with CARE in Dagahaley might well have been grown by the Church Missionary Society in Freretown.

Freretown's practices of lifesaving culminating in land settlement offer a theory of enclosure. Rescuing survivors of the slave trade, Freretown was the first settlement in East Africa to produce material relationships between a liberation ideology and the land.[22] Freretown offered what historian Frederick Cooper calls a nineteenth-century "language of shared humanity and the rights of man," humanitarian principles of abolition, which were "used first to expunge an evil from European empires and the Atlantic system and, from the 1870s onwards, to save Africans from their alleged tyranny towards each other."[23] In 1846, well before establishing its settlement at Freretown, the Church Missionary Society, with newly converted Mijikenda people from coastal villages and Reverend Johann Ludwig Krapf, established the first church in East Africa, the Rabai mission twenty-five kilometers inland from the coast.[24] It was a site of modern learning for Africans, and the Rabai institution of the National Museums of Kenya holds the 1850 Kiswahili dictionary written by Krapf and his uncredited interlocutors, illustrating the depth and complexity of the intellectual relationships that the rescuers and rescued forged in a crucible on the Swahili coast.

Rabai became the base for expeditions to the continental interior. These exploratory journeys (along Kamba commercial routes later traveled by Swahili and Arab caravans, including those trading enslaved people) expanded the missionary network.[25] They produced a scientific and cultural imagination of empire, initiating the travels, routes, and experiential mapmaking processes behind modern cartographic visualizations of Africa. Church Missionary Society representatives Johannes Rebmann and Johann Ludwig Krapf were celebrated as the first Europeans to sight Mount Kilimanjaro (in 1848) and Mount Kenya (in 1849), with maps from Rebmann's expeditions to Lake

2.2. A group discussing the journals, maps, and plans the late Dr. David Livingstone worked with others to make, consisting of (*from left to right*): Agnes Livingstone (daughter), Thomas S. Livingstone (son), Abdullah Susi, James Chuma, and Reverend Horace Waller (the compiler of M.S.S. [manuscripts]), Newstead Abbey, Nottingham, United Kingdom, 1874, photo in "Bombay Africans 1850–1910," Royal Geographical Society exhibition, National Museums of Kenya–Rabai, by R. Allen & Sons (Nottingham) / © Royal Geographical Society S0010346.

Nyasa stimulating European interest in the Nile River system. Along with these German men, African men such as Abdullah Susi and James Chuma would lead the later European expeditions, including those that brought David Livingstone across the continent and traversed back to deliver his corpse to British authorities in Bagamoyo, on the Swahili coast. Both missions thus occupy a utopian imaginary of modernity in which the cohabitations of humanitarians and refugees were productive in diverse ways, as they structured forms of humanitarian settlement.

Just as Hassan brought an expertise and worldview into Dagahaley camp, I argue that Susi, Chuma, and others migrated with the same to

Freretown. They belonged to a community of people who made global historical contributions of social justice, humanitarian practice, scientific understanding, and empire building, which, in turn, presented complex histories, social constructions, and moral and ethical questions. Members of this community played a decisive role in exploration, abolition, and the erudition and cultural life of the Rabai and Freretown missions, the latter established with explicit humanitarian purpose to deliver aid and provisions to African refugees from the Indian Ocean system of human trafficking. The cultural and social template for the Freretown settlement lay in the history of this community, referred to in Royal Geographical Society literature as the "Bombay Africans."[26] During the first half of the nineteenth century, when treaties between the British Navy, Omani and Somali chiefs, and other negotiating authorities up the Swahili coast to the Persian Gulf restricted Indian Ocean enslavement practices, liberated African men, women, and children were placed with families or housed in missionary shelters on or near the coast of Bombay, where the British Navy's antislavery operations were headquartered.[27] Missions were established in Nasik, Poona, and Bandora (present-day Bandra). In them, newly liberated persons, including women and children, learned English, Hindi, and a variety of technical skills, and developed themselves as a community.[28] Hundreds were repatriated to Africa in the second half of the nineteenth century, especially following the 1873 treaty to end the East African slave trade, signed by Sultan Bargash of Zanzibar and Governor Sir Henry Bartle Frere of the Bombay Presidency, who was also president of the Royal Geographical Society. Frere recommended the employment of freed Africans educated in India for work in expeditions and missions in Africa, linking the antislavery movement with imperial expansion. Along with Susi and Chuma, Mark Wellington and Cephas, two men from the Nasik missions, performed notable work in both areas, as did others. These figures imagined and drafted the African continent, establishing the cultural and social frameworks for abolitionist settlements, especially the mission established expressly for this purpose at Freretown.

Such practices of visualization and activism entangled multiple figures in an enclosure on the East African coast, linking the antislavery movement with imperial expansion through humanitarian settlement. Experiments in human rights seeded in the social crucible of Freretown lay the foundational logic for settler colonial agricultural transformations of Kenya. As historian Bronwen Everill notes, three settlements established to house formerly enslaved people—Freetown in Sierra Leone, the Kat River Settlement in South Africa, and Freretown in Kenya—"helped to form British thinking about human rights, refugees, governance and forms of humanitarian state-building."[29] Freretown's establishment owed a debt to the discourse on the role of Christian settlements in West Africa in abolishing trade based on enslavement. A statement by the Bishop of Ripon in 1874 advocating for ending the East African trade urged the British government beyond the abolitionist mission toward a civilizing one, which would "afford opportunities to those who were earnestly bent upon it of promoting their welfare, of instructing them in agriculture, general education and in religion."[30] The positive perception of work in Freetown by freed, Christian-converted Africans as well as the potential for contributions to new missionary societies in Africa by communities of Africans on India's Arabian Sea coast together posed an argument for investment in an East African abolitionist settlement. It would fall under the responsibility of the Church Missionary Society, whose presence had been established in Rabai, and be named for the signatory to the abolitionist treaty, Governor Bartle Frere. The Church Missionary Society established Freretown near Mombasa in 1875. Fifteen years later, the construction of the Mackinnon Road began at that port, setting the path for the Uganda Railway originating six years later from the same point, which in turn lay the ground for the territorialization of British East Africa.[31] As diverse people established this technology and assumed custodianship of the land, the vision for the liberation of bodies and souls in the enclosure of Freretown generated the moral economy for the domestication of East Africa, providing an architecture of migration that effected humanitarian settlement.

The Freretown settlement produced a model for its residents to cultivate the land while adopting a range of habits associated with a Christian life. According to historian Robert Strayer, Freretown was "a well-planned settlement complete with church, schools, cricket field, prison, cemetery and mission shambas (farm plots) as well as individual gardens for married couples."[32] The central church still stands, around which Africans and Europeans lived in dormitories. The worldly Africans and Europeans in this site of encounter had traveled great distances, spoke multiple languages, and absorbed the violence and loss of slavery, some directly in confrontation, some indirectly through dehumanization. Together, they negotiated the

2.3. (*opposite, top*) "Frere Town," National Museums of Kenya–Nairobi, Sibbie (née Bazett) Burns Photograph Album, Album II, c. 1892–late 1890s.
2.4. (*opposite, bottom*) "Outside Emmanuel Church, Frere Town," National Museums of Kenya Nairobi, Sibbie (née Bazett) Burns Photograph Album, Album II, c. 1892–late 1890s.

2.5. Freretown church interior, Mombasa, Kenya, 2016.

complex roles of rescuer and refugee. For its first quarter century, the Freretown settlement staged interaction between Africans and Europeans in the region, forging a cosmopolitan, laboring society of more than nine hundred men and women by the early 1890s, impacted by exposure to the proximate centuries-ingrained, urbane population in Mombasa, including elite traders and inland agriculturalists.[33] Freretown's development equates in certain ways to "quilombo urbanism," as architectural historian Ana G. Ozaki terms the postabolition, "historically Black, egalitarian, and emancipatory sociospace" in Pequena África, Rio de Janeiro, the port of disembarkation for the largest concentration in the world of African diasporic forced migrants, even if Freretown did not house the "fugitive communities" of Ozaki's quilombos and lacked the "true emancipation, hospitality, and Black sovereignty" of those spaces.[34] More likely, Freretown embodied a post in the liberal modern empire that created a seedbed of the emergent intimacies literary scholar Lisa Lowe theorizes as the "dangerous ... sexual, laboring, and intellectual contacts" between socially disparate enslaved and indentured people: highly controlled by the mission, in order to quell those dangerous intimacies, as abolition subjects on the Kenyan coast transitioned to colonial subjecthood.[35] Freretown's exercise in settlement equated African liberation with a colonial pedagogy entangling the building of survival and social skills, technical instruction in agriculture, and the development of Christian morality with the deepening of epistemic, discursive, and material capacities for land capitalization. Its inhabitants lived off the land well beyond subsistence; they produced surpluses, engendering a logic of extraction. Their work situated Freretown as a socially and politically critical site of incipient colonization, just as the territorializations accompanying the railway, beginning at the coast and reaching across East Africa, augured a radical transformation of the land.

Among these forces, allegedly liberated people found their bodies enclosed and their mobility restricted, as Freretown assumed aspects of what became—learning from this settlement's mirroring in Dadaab—an emergency territory. In their new land, repatriated Africans were caught in an irony stemming from the problem that the mission and the colonial state worked in opposition: necessitating their protection and precipitating their confinement. While the Church Missionary Society provided humanitarian food and shelter to the newly freed, the Imperial British East Africa Company deepened trade on the Swahili coast with Omani Arab and Swahili farmers running small plantations using the labor of enslaved people (long after the ratification of abolition laws, according to Cooper).[36] The risks to the new residents of the Freretown settlement and the practicalities of their sustenance raise questions concerning the negotiations between the Church Missionary Society and the Imperial British East Africa Company as the former sought funds and the latter moral authority, both maintaining responsibility for a community of displaced people whose status remained marginal, however privileged.[37] As such, Freretown reflected all the complexity of power relations in East Africa in the late nineteenth century, prefiguring the refugee architectures that occasioned similar negotiations a century later. These articulations of humanitarian settlement and its mirror, humanitarian encampment, animated a long process of sedentarization.

COERCIVE SETTLEMENT

The paradox of an indirect rationale of encampment in the nineteenth-century missions contrasts with the explicit aims of the twentieth-century villagization schemes in Kenya. Used as an instrument of detention by the Kenyan government against pastoralists, just as the British military had implemented them against the Mau Mau, these manyattas were rationalized by the state and the press as tools of rehabilitation and developmentalism.[38] They thus share conceptual affinities with "multi-storey" gardens in the shambas of Dagahaley camp, as development projects that yet obfuscate forms of confinement and sedentarization. Just as the settlement of Freretown offers a prelude to a moral economy, power differentials, and cultural difference within the Dadaab refugee camps, the construction of fortified villages to detain separatists in the NFD presages the policing, surveillance, and securitization that has restricted the migrations and inhabitations of refugees in Dadaab under the rubric of humanitarianism and development.[39] Where the example of Freretown offers a conceptual precedent for the Dadaab refugee camps, the villagizations in the northeast provide the political prehistory. In Dadaab, I heard a refrain articulated by several people: that their families had fled the northeast to escape villagization, only to return as refugees into a state of encampment.[40] Examining liberatory and coercive humanitarian settlement is not to reinforce an opposition between two types of enclosure, but to exhibit the spectrum under which a range of manyattas have worked. Through that paradoxical spectrum from missions to detention centers, I argue that the rhetorics around the Dadaab refugee camps not only echo past discourses, but also animate an artificial tension between liberatory and coercive settlement, conditions of enclosure that instead coexist comfortably.

The spatial politics of the Dadaab refugee camps can be traced to the declaration of a state of emergency and decades of war the government waged

2.6. Fortified manyatta where people were detained behind barbed-wire-and-sharpened-stake fencing during the Mau Mau uprising, National Archives (UK), "Kikuyu village," ref. CO1066/9.

against people in the northeast. This spatial history extended the counterinsurgency techniques the British military used as measures against rebels in the anticolonial Land and Freedom (Mau Mau) movement. I limit the discussion of the Mau Mau here, as it is a comparatively better known and debated history with prominent scholarship, except to say that the historical connections between this and the shifta struggle, and the empirical ties between actual participants in each, present an urgent matter for scholars as people in these generations age and pass on.[41] That the shifta conflict extended well into the years immediately prior to the humanitarian intervention at Dadaab in 1991, as the now well-publicized Wagalla Massacre of 1984 demonstrates, reinforces the implication that political ends were served in the production of the humanitarian enclosure in the 1990s, and, conversely, that humanitarian activities obscured practices of sedentarization.

The architectures that instituted measures of sedentarization targeted people whom the Kenyan government identified as shifta. The name, from the Amharic word sheftenat, which means "bandit," denied their participation in a dissenting body politic and voluntary insurgency. Instead, adopted as a pejorative by the Kenyan government, which undermined the pastoralist in general and the Somali in particular, as historian Hannah Whittaker argues, the term conflated militant secessionism with mere criminality.[42] Derived from the root shaffata, meaning "to rebel," the label shifta was reclaimed defiantly by insurgents in the war and has been reappropriated with pride by later generations identifying with the separatist movement in the NFD, where the architectural strategy of villagization was deployed as a counterinsurgency measure.

The movement for secession grew out of the discourses concerning a Greater Somalia discussed earlier and followed the debates over Kenya's legal and territorial constitution, part of a contentious drafting process that preceded independence in 1963. Decolonization was to follow the 1962 appointment of a Northern Frontier District Commission to tour and report on the desires of that constituency, with the British government agreeing to uphold the decision of the people.[43] The commission reported the plebiscite's polarizing results—the desire of the majority to unite with Somalia rather than Kenya—but, ultimately, the British government disregarded the findings and postponed the "NFD question" as a matter to be handled by the postcolonial state.[44] Multiple competing nationalisms led to the outcome of the 1962 referendum. The discourse was impacted by dominant international rhetorics of self-determination and pan-Africanism, as well as diverse positions on the nationalist movement for a Greater Somalia, which sought to claim the NFD as one of its five partitioned territories. Weitzberg and anthropologist Catherine Bestemann identify particularities of the nationalist and separatist visions during the iconic independence moment, related to the racial self-identification and social history of Somalis in Kenya; the complex demographic composition of the NFD, including Somali, Boran, Samburu, Rendille, Gelubba, Maa, Sakuye, and others uniting to varying degrees through pastoralist ways of life; and the ambivalent relationship of the northern populations, particularly Somalis, to structures of power.[45] The question of the NFD reflected the awkward condition of state sovereignty and territorial integrity acting paradoxically in opposition to self-determination of certain populations. Such social fragmentation in the drive toward the nation-state has been an iconic challenge vexing nation-state configuration and national identity formation throughout the twentieth century, particularly in the construction of minorities, whether resulting in the splintering process of manufacturing "outcasts" of the nation, as political theorist Partha

Chatterjee argues, or the reclamation of a stigmatized identity and its reconstruction in a confrontational subjecthood, as historian Anupama Rao theorizes.[46] Weitzberg notes that, at the moment of independence and since, subordinated nationalist conflicts in Kenya have been reductively portrayed as "clan" or ethnic rivalries, arguing instead that they "reflected tensions inherent to the liberal nation-state, which has historically fostered anxiety among groups who perceive their demographic predominance to be waning."[47] Precisely these forms of insecurity around constructions of territory, belonging, and power appear in a handing-over report written by a British district officer in 1962 in the northern capital of Isiolo, in which he records one Somali leader's blunt question: "Why should we be ruled by Kikuyu? [*sic*]."[48] These forces of fragmentation ironically multiplied within a context of East African anticolonial debate in favor of unbordered identities and pan-Somali and pan-African approaches to territory, which sought neither to reinscribe European borders nor reify European approaches to space, but instead to privilege philosophies and forms of unity.

These constructions of territory gave way to spatiotemporal strategies in which colonial practices turned into military techniques. As reported on the front page of the *Daily Nation* on New Year's Day, 1964, not a month after independence, the Kenyan government endorsed a state of emergency in the NFD. Proclaimed via unanimous parliamentary declaration the week prior, this decision averted constitutional crisis and sent security forces within the week to "round up shifta" in Garissa (not far from the present location of the Dadaab refugee camps).[49] The villagization policy was declared two years later. The rationale behind these coercive settlements surfaces in a speech by Mr. G. G. Kariuki on the floor of the National Assembly on June 4, 1965. In his call for detention, he argued that "this problem of *Shifta* will never be defeated until Somalis are villagized in order to enable our security forces to deal with them effectively. . . . Let them be put in a camp where we can scrutinize them."[50] In implementing a severe state of emergency, the government borrowed counterinsurgency techniques used by the British against the Mau Mau guerrillas of the Kenya Land and Freedom Army (whom Kariuki had invoked in his speech), which included town curfews, martial law, detention without trial, random searches and confiscations of property, and an automatic death penalty for unauthorized possession of firearms.[51] Derek Franklin, an officer in the British Imperial Special Branch forces, writes in his memoir of leading "pseudo gang operations," first, against Mau Mau insurgents and, later, after being seconded as a special operative to the Kenyan government, against shifta.[52] By the late 1960s, the new state government reproduced the carceral architectures that had been used across the Kenya Colony in the counterinsurgency camps for the detention, rehabilitation, and forced labor of those who had taken the Mau Mau oath.[53] However, following a late colonial policy and an incipient international discourse, they linked these settlements to models for enclosure and development.

The terms and tools of enclosure and development dominated the governmental discourse and approach to settlement in Northern Kenya, where pastoralist territory had yet to be fixed and stabilized at the time of independence. Practices in Northern Kenya built on colonial policies stemming from the 1954 report by Department of Agriculture official Roger Swynnerton, which recommended land enclosures and consolidations to promote smallholder production of cash crops and indebtedness; the Swynnerton Plan generated a propertyless majority and provoked a profound landlessness, notably, separating commoners in Gĩkũyũ country from their ancestral lands and intensifying calls to join the Mau Mau uprising.[54] During the early period of the shifta conflict, the translation of practices of enclosing and "grabbing" land from colonial to postcolonial contexts dovetailed with international actions and rhetoric across the ideological spectrum, especially following Julius Nyerere's 1967 Arusha Declaration, which led to the Ujamaa villagization schemes for cooperative agricultural production in Tanzania, justifying some of the most significant mass displacements in the world.[55] In Northern Kenya, implementation of villagization was driven by thinking that radically prioritized sedentarized agricultural production over pastoral subsistence. Officials argued for wholesale changes in way of life. On November 4, 1966, a motion was forwarded by Mr. Oduya, leading to spirited debate in the National Assembly "to initiate talks with the Shifta leaders, Somali elders, M.P.s and other leading personalities of the Somali tribe, with a purpose of ending this dirty war which is costing the country large sums of money and many lives and . . . to introduce economic projects, education and social revolution in the Somali area immediately."[56] The government executed planning and provision for twenty-eight villages, each including administrative offices, housing, police headquarters, a store, and a tax clerk. The six nearest the present location of the Dadaab refugee camps—Balambala, Bura, Ijara, Madogashe, Masalani, and the county center Garissa—still function as towns, with schools and other infrastructure.[57] That the area has been otherwise little developed calls into question the rhetorics of improvement behind the creation of settlements unsupported by civil and regional infrastructures. While not enclosures legally enacted to privatize property for development, their contribution to the underdevelopment of the region, recalling historian

Walter Rodney's analysis, underscores the argument that notwithstanding the possibility of "economic projects, education, and social revolution," their intention lay in mandatory settlement, ultimately effecting sedentarization.

Finding architectural evidence of this sedentarization principle is challenging, as the architectural history of the shifta villages is spectral. To piece it together is to work without design or construction drawings or photographs, with only rare written documents and interviews; to read governmental reports and National Assembly debates against the grain; and to think critically with the recent past, with the ways that the Dadaab camps behave inadvertently as a site of underdevelopment—that refugees such as Hassan, ironically, perform the work of settlement.[58] As architectural historian Samia Henni demonstrates, in reading the French military archives of the occupation of Algeria, the critical distrust of archives is the first step in a methodology that understands the central role the built environment plays within military histories.[59] As author Ngũgĩ wa Thiong'o remembers, Kenya's architectural history is one in which people were not only resettled, but ancestral villages were razed as part of the colonial practice of dislocation.[60] Against this backdrop of spatial violence, marked by the production of emergency territory as postcolonial policy extending colonial practices, I argue that it is worth interpreting with irony the emphasis government leaders placed on education and self-help as progressive prongs of development, especially as they did so through agricultural reform, achievable through land consolidation, irrigation, and settlement schemes.[61] In the first National Development Plan, reorganization of the agricultural sector was allotted almost one third of the total expenditure—accounting for the occupations of 90 percent of the Kenyan population.[62] Policies around land use set into motion countrywide distrust of governments well after independence.[63] Of the immediate effects in the late 1960s, Hannah Whittaker writes: "Under the guise of 'development' and 'social progress', villagization facilitated the application of punitive measures against those considered subversive, both civilian and shifta, at the same time as rehabilitating the 'criminal' nomad to a settled life."[64] That people were forced to register in new villages sited in locations less than optimal for development underscored the schemes' ambivalence of purpose.[65] The formal structure, spatial organization, and architecture of the villages suggested detention and corrections. They were ringed by eight-foot-wide by twelve-foot-deep perimeter trenches surrounded by barbed wire, with two gates opposite each other manned by armed police personnel, and housing in rows with clear lines of sight, likely modeled after specific British detention centers in Kenya.[66] In hyena country, barbed fencing is not uncommon; in

Dadaab, refugees construct it with thorny acacia bushes, and humanitarians with sheets of chain-linked metal. However, District Reports from Garissa, Wajir, Marsabit, and Isiolo show that patrols monitored movement within the villages; passes were required to move through the gates to the exterior; and residents could leave the premises only to water animals within a five-mile external perimeter, accompanied by armed escorts.[67] Policing was more ambiguous, as both local people and visitors were deputized. The former were employed by regional administrative authorities, and the latter by the Kenyan army and state police.[68] In 1962, the Northern Frontier District Commission had counted a population of two hundred thousand. By 1967, only half that number had acceded to villagization.[69] The shifta conflict is broadly understood to have ended by 1968. Yet, the silences around it and the elusiveness of its documentation persisted well into the twenty-first century.

I argue that the struggle over Kenya's northeast from the 1960s to the 1980s culminated in a spatial strategy in Dadaab in the 1990s, resulting in sedentarization within a context of emergency. In this, Daniel Arap Moi's experience as home minister in the 1960s translated into concrete forms during his presidency in the 1990s, as earlier policies to confine pastoralists within enclosures led to later practices of establishing encampments for people from the same or related communities. The latter imposition, reinforced by refugees' material dependency on aid, was supported with the implicit and explicit partnership of the international community through the production of a humanitarian enclosure in the North Eastern Province. First under the national apparatus of development, and then under the international rubric of humanitarianism, each moment resulted in the mass sedentarization of people and foreclosure of migration.

The links between the architectures of counterinsurgency and humanitarianism trouble narrations of the nation-state that deny fluidities in the identities of people living in areas marked as "borderlands." "Somali Kenyans" in Kenya's northeast and people who form the majority population in the camps—that is, citizens and refugees alike—share a heritage beyond pastoralist or Muslim self-identification and together complicate narratives of ethnic identities and minority positions that reinforce border hegemonies.[70] The divides between those who are internal and those who are external to the nation-state are specious at best and reproduce partitions, as described in chapter 1. Along these lines, the suspicion of nomads by the imperial and postcolonial state together speaks of past and present distrust of migrants, exposing a practice of incarceration in the contemporary humanitarian settlements that parallels earlier colonial and development-based detention, which ultimately reinforces borders through the sedentarization of migrating people. In thinking on Dadaab, it is worth remembering the extreme measures taken against not only migrating people, but nonhuman life as well.[71] Social anthropologist Alex de Waal asserts that "a military onslaught on the entire pastoral way of life" defined the 1960s in the NFD. "Vast numbers of animals were confiscated or slaughtered, partly in order to deny transport to the guerrillas," he writes, "and much of the population was confined to a few population centres, where an underclass of destitutes developed."[72] While the history of the shifta war presents interrelations between pastoral communities with competing visions and articulations of political self-actualization more complex than this quotation allows, the destitution and dependence on humanitarian aid in the refugee camps demonstrates an erasure of economies and societies based in migration. The formation of such enclosures culminates the underlying territorial contingency of the camps discussed earlier, enabling the reification of sedentarism in emergency.

This historical interpretation is vital to shifting an understanding of what architecture demonstrates and how it interacts with land and territory. However, reconstructing an architectural history for forms of community that circumvent state borders and challenge conventional notions of sovereignty is no small task.[73] In many of my interviews with refugees in Dadaab, the plebiscite, the war, and its costs for Somalis came up. The war impacted some families obliquely and others directly. As discussed earlier, some migrated to Somalia to avoid the ramifications of villagization, only to return as refugees in the 1990s into a state of encampment.[74] That images of the detention centers have been kept out of public archives begs looking closely at the refugee camps themselves as a form of evidence for silent histories. Indeed, they serve as more than mere shelter. They operate discursively and epistemologically as the trace of foreclosed migration, realized through a form of enclosure that enacts humanitarian settlement.

The forms of enclosure discussed here, established with intentions either liberatory or coercive, make the argument that migratory ways of life have been systematically degenerated in favor of the fixing of people and borders. That this foreclosure of open migration and enabling of forced migration has dovetailed with capitalistic practices and settler colonial approaches to the land is a familiar story. That it has created farms in a refugee camp—as I infer that it did in the precedents of abolitionist settlements and detention villages—poses a thornier problem, intertwining liberatory and coercive settlement together in one built environment and bringing the practices of land privatization into emergency territory. As I argue in the next section, these paradoxes of sedentarization, emergency, and land also iterate themselves architecturally, at the scale of the building unit.

Building Types

Beyond the construction of the contingent territory and the enclosures delineated earlier, architectural forms and building types play political and social roles in histories of land, emergency, and sedentarization. Central to these histories of power are the architectural discipline's own discourses on the role of vernacular buildings in constructions of autochthony.[75] This section focuses on two building types in particular, the makuti and the tuqul discussed

2.7. Makuti-style dwelling and shop, Ifo camp.

in the introduction, each a gendered and ethnicized object. Together, they provide a background for thinking about the paradoxical materialities in the Dadaab refugee camps and their relationship to land. The typologies of makuti and tuqul also offer a theorization, which builds on the sedentarization processes discussed earlier, at the level of territory and settlement; they construct contingency on the one hand and enclosure on the other, at the level of architecture.

The makuti appeared in the landscape of colonial law in Kenya in 1901, in the language of the Native Hut Tax, a South African legal model dispersed throughout the British empire (a tax from which Somalis in Nairobi were eventually exempted).[76] According to the language of the imperial government, the makuti is an architecture of mud, or wattle and daub, suggesting construction of vertical walls built from the compressive force of clay stacked and shaped with relatively even thickness from a wall's base to its top, on which the roof structure rests. This definition matches that of Gĩkũyũ village structures, the homes of Mijikenda on the Kenyan coast, and the dwellings built by Sambaa farther south.[77] Nevertheless, the makuti designation refers to a roof, specifically one made of grass thatch, the "native" building technology at the core of the Native Hut Tax (appropriated by postcolonial governments elsewhere for its cultural value).[78] In a Kenya National Assembly debate on lending schemes on November 13, 1991, one of the members, Mr. Mahihu, argued that the government should "encourage lenders to loan out money even to people who want to use makuti on their houses. After all, we inherited the habit of thatching houses with makuti from our forefathers."[79] Multiple makuti building materials are harvested inland and in the coastal areas of Kenya, including tall grasses found in marshes and along rivers, which may be bundled or braided together, or wilting coconut palm fronds that are picked and then plaited, in order to dry in place. The makuti thatching process was traditionally a collective and communal one. The coastal makuti that His Majesty's Commissioner signed into law in 1901, in the vicinity of Mombasa, would have been built by an entire village, with twenty or thirty women wielding pangas (machetes) and entering the riverbed at dawn to cut tall grasses—a measure to find green plants that do not dry too fast—tying them together with ropes or twine, and carrying the bundles back to the village in time for a morning meal. The entire population of the village worked together on the construction of each makuti dwelling for a family, or set of dwellings for a joint family within a manyatta.

The architects of the tuqul, typically, have been women. The construction process of the mobile dome dwelling is tied into coming-of-age rituals

2.8. Tuqul clad with animal skins, harar (woven grass mats), and textiles, pictured here with the designer/builder and her children, Kebribeyah, Ethiopia, 2011.

2.9. Tuqul structure, Ifo camp periphery.

in Somali communities and others in East Africa.[80] For example, in an examination of the work of women in the Somali pastoral economy, Rhoda M. Ibrahim discusses their pragmatic and symbolic role in the construction of the dwelling.[81] Women are responsible for all aspects of the process of gathering materials, fabrication of the various construction elements, and erecting the structure. These skills are built on years of practice, beginning in puberty and culminating in building a first tuqul after marriage.[82] This gendered responsibility has continued in postconflict contexts, in Dadaab and other

2.10. Child beside his family's tuqul of recovered textile, foam, and paper, Dagahaley camp, photo by Bethany Young.

East African refugee camps, in which scarcity of materials takes on symbolic and material urgency. One agency staff member remarked on the increase in domestic violence against women in Afar, in Ethiopia, as a consequence of a windy season when several tuquls blew away.[83] The labor intensity of the tuqul construction process is also notable, as bound up as it is with gender identity. The object was crafted for mobility, intended to be mounted on camels' backs for travel in caravans or transportation between water and grazing lands. The structure is typically constructed and reconstructed with regularity. It is built out of harar (woven grass mats) and bent green wood branches. Primary structural elements, from the horizontal roots of the galool tree (an acacia), are cut from green wood, with both ends inserted into the ground until they dry in the shape of an arch, forming elements of a strong frame. Eight to twelve of these structural members are bent into crescents over several days, arranged in a circular plan with branch ends meeting in the middle at the top. Fifteen to twenty-five longer, elastic branches are stretched perpendicularly around them and tied at joints. These are covered with a woven harar mat, animal skins, or other found textiles.[84] In contemporary refugee contexts, these coverings are substituted with foraged elements: plastic sheeting, discarded fabric, and remnants of other nonfood aid materials, emblazoning people's homes with donor or agency names and logos, such as "USA" or "UNHCR." This remaking of forms in new materials offers an understanding of humanitarian architecture as a spatial practice conjoint with economies of ragpicking and recycling.

The historical behavior of these building types and their suppressed behavior in the built environment at Dadaab, I argue, are archives of a form of resistance to sedentarization. The Native Hut Tax named the makuti's legal coding, a means to draw natives into a modern labor economy. The makuti was also forced to engage with modernity architecturally, through its thick, upright walls. Whether circular in plan as in the Sambaa dwelling, or rectilinear as in the Mijikenda dwelling, makuti walls could engage with modernization through the civil infrastructure of plumbing or electrical wiring connected to a territorial grid. These details and forms for interaction with the colonial and postcolonial state align with the long processes of sedentarization discussed earlier. The tuqul, on the other hand, a modern architecture populating the Dadaab refugee camps, would have posed legal and aesthetic challenges to a Hut Tax. As opposed to the makuti, it was not a building that could accept a plumbing branch pipe, nor did it provide the physical stabilities required for enumeration and taxation. This East African mobile dwelling form resists modernity and modernization.

As the first shelter form in the first refugee camp established at Dadaab, the tuqul building materials have been included in the nonfood aid packages distributed in all of the camps in Kenya and Ethiopia established along the border with Somalia.[85] The tuqul occasionally housed aid workers along with refugees.[86] It has become a predominant architectural form in the morphology of the settlement, used even by refugees fleeing from urban contexts or from other parts of Africa. In many ways, it is the architectural symbol of the Dadaab refugee camps. Thus, photographs that show dozens of tuquls populating the refugee camps, clustering in stationary groups, fix in place an impossibility. They imagine sedentarization, through a spatial arrangement that forecloses a pastoral economy and activates a gendered spatial politics. Yet, this architecture was not meant to relate to the land in this way. The tuqul made dystopically stationary in the camps is a modern and vernacular architecture that upsets expectations for each. For generations, its design, made for mobility, has resisted extractive and capitalistic approaches to the land within the colonial and postcolonial state and humanitarian regimes. Even as the tuqul produces a visual representation of emergency, it lends

2.11. Dagahaley camp periphery, October 2011, Brendan Bannon/IOM/UNHCR, © Brendan Bannon 2011.

form and architectural continuity to that resistance over time. While there is no simple argument to be made of the agency of a refugee architecture against the forces of settlement, the image of the tuqul, even fixed in place, provides a compelling visual rhetoric of a heritage form, a feminist construction, and a recalcitrant architecture of migration. It is toward this imagination that a history of architecture and land, contingency and enclosure, and emergency and sedentarization might gravitate.

Beyond Emergency, toward Migration

These many episodes, at the scale of region, settlement, and building, record a recurring will to sedentarization that has inscribed emergency territory into past enclosures and the Dadaab refugee camps today. Yet, thinking with Dadaab beyond the frameworks of emergency means thinking beyond a constricted temporality to meaningful historicity and materiality. It means thinking beyond space to land. Through these imaginative leaps, I argue for reading a refugee camp in resistance to a politics of occlusion, in favor of the possibility of seeing different pasts and thus different futures. This epistemic possibility is one of the reasons to study with Dadaab. Studying with a contested architecture or territory, as an object whose story extends over a much longer period than expected, produces historiographical methods that may profitably disrupt expected chronologies, regimes of historicity, geographies, and other analytics. Rather than privileging the lens of the territorial archive and its history, which fix the refugee camp as a subjugated space rather than an object of enclosure of land and bodies, I advocate instead for an intimacy with longer, open histories of a refugee camp. These provide "critical closeness" rather than critical distance, as historian of architecture Jay Cephas theorizes, enabling alternate imaginations of its pasts and potentials.[87] Yet, to come to this, as chapter 3 does, it is worth unsettling core discourses that have arrested any imagination of inhabitation beyond the ramifications of emergency. This liberating strategy enables us to see in an image such as that opening this chapter profound iterations of intimacy and domesticity in emergency: if enclosures for sedentarization, then also architectures of migration.

(*previous page*) Store and shelters designed and built by Shamso Abdullahi Farah, Ifo camp.

Shelter and Domesticity

3

The conceptual and material unit of shelter has been closely identified with modern architectures of emergency relief. As yet undertheorized are the ways that shelter has enacted domesticity and how that domesticity has formed a basis for knowledge. To build this theory, I draw on foundational arguments presented in the two previous chapters, that a refugee camp emerges from partitions and that its logics are predicated on the production of emergency territory and paradoxes of humanitarian settlement. Partitions are manifested in the architecture of shelters and their relation to the land a camp occupies, but architecture does not merely resolve in the state constructs used to delimit migration, such as camps or shelters. Rather, architecture undergirds migratory domesticities and ways of life. In this chapter, I confront shelter as a schema, material form, historically specific spatial practice, and empirically precise means to arrive at a theory of domesticity.

Shelter is one of the significant conceptual, material, and aesthetic forms in a camp, an elemental practice of humanitarian spatiality and an architecture integral to humanitarian settlement. Shelter's aim—domesticity—is critical to understanding an architecture of migration. I am concerned with the difference between shelter and domesticity in global history as well as histories local to the emergency contexts of the Dadaab refugee camps. I argue that shelter forms a methodology for domesticity in emergency, while acts of domesticity in Dadaab contribute to a global knowledge. In this chapter, I theorize insurgent domesticities of Dadaab and closely examine one episode of building a shelter in relation to the construction of international architecture and planning expertise on shelter. I conclude with an examination of emergency, land, and labor to produce a critical theory situating domesticity within the materiality, sociality, and design of shelter, and also extending it well beyond, as a form of knowledge.

From Shelter to Domesticity

A history of emergency in which architecture serves as the primary referent has a special part to play in reimagining and rewriting domesticity. The work of a refugee mother in Dadaab, as builder and provider, extends beyond the expediencies of shelter or even the critical act of dwelling, toward the expansive aim of domesticity. Her home is her economy and her imaginary, her children's bounded world, her refuge in which to domesticate emergency and from which to peer into a life beyond it. Her homemaking is performed under duress, an act of building the provisional dwelling as well as crafting the timespace of domestic interiority. Her activity mitigates emergency and constitutively marshals time, space, material, and labor toward the radical creation of an interior.

Within broader studies of architectures of migration, scholars have begun to analyze the emergency domesticity at the basis of this radical worldmaking.[1] Some argue that making home and being displaced need not be understood as oppositional to one another, and eschew "not only overtly romanticising the homeplace (especially, as a rooted and immobile state of affairs and things), but also demonizing displacement."[2] Others target the politics of inhabitation, "the question of power inherent in the control, demarcation, and formation of architectural space," arguing for the "deconstruction of the techno-material foundations of architectural production by positing it as a mode of subject position *in* and *of* space," in which "alternate modalities of architecture are produced, authorship falls in the hands of the many (beyond technocrats and the state), and thus inhabitation acts as a mediation between conditions of dis-placement and place-making from below."[3] The discursive shift called for by the critical term *inhabitation* draws attention to thinking on housing: a classed, raced, gendered, nationalized, and largely European theoretical tradition stemming from a dialectic of improvement and accompanying legislation, which "regulated the extent to which government and its local representatives could intervene in the lives and property of individuals in order to ameliorate public health and moral character," and "has remained a means for ordering and policing the lives of the poor."[4] Taking in hand these various discourses, my scholarship and collaborative work theorize the politics of home "within the present worldwide protectionist climate, in which 'home' is still a fiercely pursued, maintained, and guarded space."[5] I privilege "the more processual aspects of domesticity," from which "histories of solidarity, disobedience, stealth, and militancy" provide a fine grain for understanding paradoxical and sometimes contradictory insurgencies "from the scale of the clothesline to that of the state."[6] I build on all of these interventions to situate a history of shelter and domesticity in emergency.

My questions on shelter and domesticity are equally informed by thinking that critically distinguishes the timespace of migration, particularly in emergency. "The refugee camp fundamentally brings time and space into a new collusion," architectural historian Somayeh Chitchian and I argue, as the "pushing of time into space fundamentally characterizes life in emergency, providing the irreducible conceptual unit that denotes a camp as such."[7] Recalling that behind this collusion, the figure of the refugee—"as the name for one who flees (*fugere*)"—conceptually invokes not only the migrant but the fugitive, literary theorist Angela Naimou argues: "Refugee timespaces are generated in the emplacing, displacing, replacing, and misplacing of life and borders and rights."[8] Domesticity based on this migrancy and fugitivity is a space of yearning and becoming; its present is tethered to the memory of an immediate past, but also immediately and urgently contingent on a dream of a potential future. The timespace of emergency shelter and domesticity fits within planetary and ecological frameworks that occupy larger expanses of historicity and knowledge. I build on an eco-planetary scope in studying how migration frames histories and critical theory, rather than being framed by them as in conventional narratives of modernity. These wider, plural views encourage multiple temporalities to emerge, and urgently engage the human and nonhuman collaboration and cohabitation inherent to migration. Anthropologist Anna Tsing has offered a parallel glimpse of "other temporal patterns" that grow out of "multiple time-making projects, as organisms enlist each other and coordinate in making landscapes," in her analysis of the ruins of capitalist development around the world seen from the perspective of the cultivation and growth of fungi.[9] The Dadaab refugee camps inhabit similar ruins, not only of capitalism, but of the liberal state, in which such acts of enlisting and making proliferate. Like Tsing, by watching "unruly edges," I seek to "put unpredictable encounters at the center of things," namely, those constituting the timespaces of humanitarian settlement at Dadaab, which, I argue, resolve into domesticities.[10] Naimou notes that the temporal landscapes of refugee life "shuttle between the material present and the remembered past" as they "collide or collapse into each other across space to generate new possibilities for recognition and critique."[11] Such openings make a space for eco-critical feminist understandings of the Dadaab refugee camps, locating their domesticities in an expanded political field of time and space. These understandings recall anthropologist Elizabeth Povinelli's formulations concerning the earth's ecologies and atmosphere, situating human experience and social chronologies within long geological spans and the proposition of "an anthropology of the otherwise," of forms of life contrary to dominant modes of social being.[12] The history of the Dadaab refugee camps and its shelters and domesticities are histories of a biodiverse environment—a life-sustaining aquifer and people and animals migrating together on the land across it, long before that land's partitioning or those people's encampment. The timespace of emergency and the domesticities forged within it share an affinity and intimacy with the historicity of that larger ecology.

I build this argument and related ones in this chapter on the premise that shelter occupies the threshold of critical theory, and domesticity forms the knowledge that erupts forth. For the domesticities in this chapter, I diverge from the framings of many critical studies of humanitarianism, which are structured by theorist Michel Foucault's work on biopower.[13] Those that analyze humanitarian materialities and infrastructures think further with his articulation of the *dispositif*, referring to the apparatus around an activity—for example, institutional, regulatory, discursive, epistemological, and aesthetic, or, in other words, architectural.[14] Scholars have drawn on this *architectural* authority in critical examinations of humanitarian environments; for example, philosopher Adi Ophir posited a "structured assemblage" by which humanitarians enact a paradigm of biopolitical control that can transform the sovereign condition itself, by spatial and other means.[15] For work on domesticity, I learn from meditations on two specific aspects of Foucault's work: the first, Povinelli's articulation of the limits of Foucault's biopolitical theories describing contemporary systems of power and the governance of life, and the second, her extension of his analysis of the insurrection of subjugated knowledges as a process of being or becoming "ethically otherwise."[16] I pair this thinking with the constructive insistence of bell hooks on the ethical and political purpose of the desubjugation of knowledge.[17] First, if theorizations of biopolitics are insufficient for imagining a timespace governed by the inhabitants of the line between life and nonlife, then domesticity in emergency—people's critical constructions of migratory ways of life—also speaks to this limitation. Theorization of these capacious lifeways, evidenced in an architecture of migration, benefits from articulations of "an otherwise" and imaginations of life structures that are animated by wider ecological cohabitations.[18] Second, I argue that the domesticities to be examined in the following pages are the material and conceptual iteration of an insurgency of subjugated knowledges. I sympathize with attempts to extend critical theory beyond Foucault's articulations of biopower not because I disagree with his arguments, but because they have been so readily and exhaustively applied to theorizing the spaces and subjecthood of people who have become refugees without prioritizing rigorous intimate or embodied understanding of these people's experiences. According to Foucault, knowledges have been subjugated for historical reasons (subsumed into governmental systems) or conceptual reasons (perceived as incoherent by the scientific apparatus). I see a need to disrupt the dominant framings of the refugee camp that follow both of these modes: relegating it to an architecture for population management and also deeming it nonconceptual. My disruption upends existing knowledges by extending a theory in which *migration* marks space and time, rather than the action happening in the other direction. This countering of the putatively normative framings and interruption of the dominant episteme is part of a critical pedagogy, within which hooks has much to teach, especially on the matter that "a radical cultural politics . . . must offer theoretical paradigms in a manner that connects them to contextualized political strategies."[19] If I join her promotion of the "insurrection of subjugated knowledge" as an agenda to "enable colonized folks to decolonize their minds and actions," I do so with the additional aim of pushing critical theory on shelter beyond its present limits.[20] Those limits halt the discussion of emergency migration at the boundaries of shelter, rather than treating shelter as a gateway into broader understandings of domesticity. This expanded theory drives the questions architectural historian Rachel Lee and I chart, for example, in research on "feminist architectural histories of migration," in which "the dynamic of a situated and re-situated perspective" forms the basis of approaches that "destabilize presumptions of historical fixity."[21] These questions support our theorization of constructed environments and designed forms as articulated within margins and collaborations—drawing again from hooks—rather than within putatively stable and singly situated objects and narratives, producing a multiplicity of perspectives in which a field of inquiry on the architectures of shelter and domesticity may be grounded.[22] The scholarship in this chapter builds on all of this theoretical work with an aim toward radical, nonhierarchical equality and a political commitment to alterity. This lies behind the construction of ecofeminist architectural histories of migration through attention to the insurgencies of domesticities. For this, again, I name shelter as a threshold rather than an endpoint, and domesticity as the further unbounding of knowledge construction and consciousness formation.

Though named "shelter" by humanitarians, domesticity is the endgame for intervention into emergency relief by professional spatial practitioners. This is so whether or not these practitioners have an awareness of domesticity; indeed, perhaps they work in a way that is "detached from the inhabitant . . . and, as a result, inhabitation," as architects and historians Shahd Seethaler-Wari, Somayeh Chitchian, and Maja Momić argue.[23] Yet, shelters in Dadaab were planned, designed, and constructed by trained architects as well as unlicensed builders, figures who have constructed emergency shelter environments powered by insurgent domesticities. The insurrectionary quality of those domesticities stems, in part, from the work of emergency homemakers to extract intimacies and comforts from a system that impedes critical forms of inhabitation, one that narrates privacy and interiority as luxuries rather than necessities and does not imagine such luxuries for such homemakers. Domesticity offers a theory that moves beyond consigning displacement to the domain of lack. As an affective element in the life and vitality of migrating people, the basis for a politics in Dadaab, and a driving force in humanitarian settlement, domesticity constitutes a core spatial strategy and material practice used by people who have been displaced.

Domesticity as such, even if gendered, sexualized, raced, and ethnicized, is an affective, poetic, existential form of expertise. This complicated and troubled expertise informs competence on shelter, including professional competence. To examine the nuances and complexity of domesticity, a history of interventions into the field of humanitarian relief by architecture professionals helps to clarify the construction of knowledge on refugee camps and emergency spatial practice. This history marks the difference between shelter, on the one hand, and domesticity, on the other, emphasizing the profound intellectual and material labor they demand in contexts of forced migration and displacement.

This extreme element of emergency domesticity—the "work" of housework in contexts of displacement—is most worth attention. The existential pressure of this labor pits it in stark contrast to placid understandings that have long driven discourses on dwelling and shelter.[24] These limiting discourses assume structural fixities in environments, governments, and knowledge formations. Theorizing sheltering in migration instead demands a paradigm shift, toward new feminist and architectural languages of *an ecology of domesticity*, into which refugees in Dadaab have opened a portal, to borrow writer Arundhati Roy's prescient concept for the world's collective entry into a new timespace and consciousness wrought by a bioplanetary event.[25] I argue that people in Dadaab made this shift as architects: evidenced by the complex built environment produced by their individual labors, dependent on emergent acts of domesticity.

Insurgent Domesticities

To tie the expertise of the architect to the labors of homemaking in emergency, I draw from a theory of insurgent domesticities informed by paradoxical, contradictory, and collaborative forms of solidarity, stealth, and disobedience in Dadaab.[26] To explain, let us turn to a photograph taken in 2011 in a built environment that is by now altered. It is from Ifo 2, a settlement inhabited and operating as a humanitarian relief site as of this writing, but no longer existing as this image depicts. The shelters in this photograph speak to competing narratives. On the one hand, they represent an international humanitarian initiative to expand a refugee settlement, artifacts of a regime of development and rights gesturing toward the horizon of the nation. On the other, as argued in chapter 2, they mark the afterlife of the extractive capitalist settler state, holding and retaining obscured histories. As I learned, these structures whispered of illegitimate spaces, queer shelter and caring, and clandestine ways of living that carry meaning for feminists.

In the emergency of 1991 and 1992, people had hurriedly self-settled Ifo camp, constructing shelters in allocated low-lying areas adjacent to the highway. Dadaab was intensively restricted, with contracts forged between the UNHCR and the Kenyan police force. Women and children formed the majority living in the camps (as is so in camps throughout the world), making for a deeply gendered social context for this policing. Compelled to live within strict confines, they extracted what they could from the surrounding environment. Season after season, women mined soil to build and buttress the walls of shelters, deepening the depression in which their plots were situated. Depending on food aid packages that did not include fuel, mothers denuded its slopes over several years, clearing vegetation to gather tinder for cooking fires. These slow and disastrous pressures curtailed the biodiversity and material texture of the environment, increasingly shaping the ground occupied by their dwellings into a basin. In 2006, heavy rains flooded it. Residents found themselves doubly displaced after winds blew the roofs off of their shelters, destroying homes and unsettling an already precarious habitat. The Ifo 2 extension was immediately planned to solve the crisis, expanding

Ifo to the north in a settlement for eighty thousand inhabitants, which would address the growing number of people temporarily stationing themselves in the peripheries of the three camps, Ifo, Dagahaley, and Hagadera. By 2010, the UNHCR and NGO partners began construction of Ifo 2, establishing plots and designing and building prototype shelters. Ifo 2 was produced in the tradition of model Siedlungen—settlements—a development strategy for testing and showcasing experiments in construction and a significant practice in the history of architecture and design in the twentieth century. Several humanitarian NGOs forwarded bids to provide shelters across the new camp.

However, the Kenyan government resisted, raising concerns that a sign of permanence for refugees would create security threats. The government refused to grant possession of the land to its international humanitarian partners, interrupting Ifo 2's commissioning and eventually halting construction altogether, forcing the three camps to densify rather than allowing people to move into the new settlement. Its well-ordered site plan, generously defined

3.1. Shelter prototypes by Danish Refugee Council, Ifo 2 camp.

green space, civil and sanitation infrastructure, schools, police barracks, and rows of tidy mud-brick homes with ample perimeter grounds for cultivation and animal husbandry constituted a built environment whose architectural design and construction far surpassed any other in the region. The construction impasse caused a ready environment to remain unoccupied for over a year, even while, by March 2011, thousands of refugees arrived in Dadaab on a weekly and occasionally daily basis.

However, before the camp was officially populated, the prototype dwellings and other structures were unofficially inhabited by women forming contingent kinships with one another and with police officers. According to interviews I conducted, the income generation and housing stability enabled by the transactional sexual labor of these secret families enabled their clandestine dwelling and informed the domestic fabric of the interim camp. Yet, this cloistered and liminal life was short-lived, as Ifo 2 was fully commissioned and officially opened to refugees in 2012.

The ephemeral insurgent domesticities narrated here constituted the social life and built environment of the largest designated refugee camp at that time. Quotidian intimacies of coercion and collaboration contributed to many forms of slow violence in this significant built environment, not only direct sexual oppression. However, if the transactional nature of this space curtailed or conditioned forms of consent, joy, healing, possibility, and pleasure, it also created paradoxically emancipatory opportunities for some women.[27] Some women spoke of friendships forged in a context that sheltered them from other harshnesses of the camps, as they generated collaborative domesticities in complex forms of homemaking. These were not necessarily centered on a trade in sexuality, a condition which itself could not be subject to any single interpretation. "Marriage," in this context—to police officers, to registered refugees, to wealthy or privileged asylum seekers—held many possibilities and protections, to be understood along with their constrictions and threats. Thus, how we understand a complex homemaking of coercion and collaboration—how we think with the paradoxes of insurgent domesticities—presents a critical theory, extending shelter beyond a static and confined meaning. Because of these complexities in emergency, domesticities constitutive of the practice of sheltering frame radical knowledges and consciousness.

With this historical backdrop in mind, I return to the position that the insurgent domesticities of the Dadaab refugee camps form an expertise. This expertise is tied to the multifarious labors of homemaking in emergency, which take place in the margins and as part of collaborations, yet comprise the vivid material fabric of the built environment.[28] I argue that this expertise is an architectural one. To develop this claim, the following sections set the work of a refugee mother and a nongovernmental organization into a longer historical trajectory of the construction of humanitarian spatial expertise.

Building a Shelter

The historical episode to follow extends better known narratives of expertise in international development into an embodied example of how humanitarian knowledge is constructed and contributes to an epistemic foundation. The built environment of the camp serves as the material palette for this knowledge construction, with refugees as its theorists and makers, and the coercions and collaborations described earlier as its social fabric. To examine homemaking in emergency, I spoke with Shamso Abdullahi Farah, a refugee mother who was among the first participants in a shelter program initiated by the NRC in Ifo camp.[29] Through her work with the NRC, Farah built two dwellings and a small shop from which she could run a business while minding her children.

The narrative of Farah's work that follows in this section draws from her own account in 2011 of a shelter initiative in which she had participated in the preceding years. It also draws on interviews with other refugees, aid workers, officials, and professionals in Dadaab and elsewhere who could contextualize this work. I limited the scope of my interviews with Farah and focused on her intellectual and physical labor in helping to seed an initiative with historically significant ties to discourses and practices of dweller-controlled housing. These processes have fueled political economic adjustments made by the international system of states and wealthy nations throughout the twentieth century. As remnants of those structural adjustments, these emergency practices are at once entangled with the geopolitics of nation-states and the political status of individuals. Nevertheless, such practices are rarely recounted through their materiality or the labor of people involved. The following dialogue is excerpted from a discussion during which Farah and I walked around her two assigned plots in Ifo camp and examined the buildings she and her family built, accompanied by Columbia University School of International and Public Affairs student Bethany Young and NRC staff member Abdullahi Keinan.[30] During our discussion, Keinan translated and interpreted in real time, from English to Somali and Somali to English. As he did in the interview with Isnina Ali Rage

3.2. Shamso Abdullahi Farah in her shop, Ifo camp.

reproduced in this book's introduction, Keinan occasionally participated directly in the conversation.

ANOORADHA IYER SIDDIQI: How long have you been living here?

SHAMSO ABDULLAHI FARAH: Eight years.

ANOORADHA IYER SIDDIQI: And you came from where?

SHAMSO ABDULLAHI FARAH: Somalia. Buuloxaawo, near the Mandera border.

ANOORADHA IYER SIDDIQI: I see that you have two houses and you have a shop. Is it all in one plot?

SHAMSO ABDULLAHI FARAH: Two plots . . . Normally, a family size of eight and above are given two plots because it is an extended family. . . . A plot is fifteen by thirteen [meters], so it cannot be used by more than five people.

ABDULLAHI KEINAN [*for Shamso Abdullahi Farah*]: She says although her family size is [officially] eight, there are two other dependents with her, so the family size is [actually] ten. The ration card number is ten. She requested from UNHCR two houses because her family is extended. She participated in the construction. . . . It was only the building material and technical [advice] that was given.

SHAMSO ABDULLAHI FARAH: Did any of your children also participate in the construction?

KEINAN [*for Shamso Abdullahi Farah*]: She says her whole family took part in the construction, including her husband.

ANOORADHA IYER SIDDIQI: And when did you open the shop?

ABDULLAHI KEINAN [*for Shamso Abdullahi Farah*]: She recently opened the shop. She got a credit facility. . . . It [has been] one month.

ANOORADHA IYER SIDDIQI: And also, you got some credit from an NGO, or from . . . ?

SHAMSO ABDULLAHI FARAH: From individual shop owners in the market.

ANOORADHA IYER SIDDIQI: Is that a common practice?

3.3. NRC shelter designed and built by Shamso Abdullahi Farah, Ifo camp.

3.4. NRC shelter (*foreground, left*) and shop (*background, right*) designed and built by Shamso Abdullahi Farah with members of her family (pictured here), Ifo camp.

SHAMSO ABDULLAHI FARAH: This depends on whether the person is your relative or you have known him for quite some time. . . . It is [because of] that trust, somebody gives you the material.

You bring the goods here to sell, and then return the money back to him and get your profits out of it. So the person has to trust you, has to be somebody you have known for quite some time. [Otherwise] they can't just give credit like that.

ANOORADHA IYER SIDDIQI: The person who you got credit from is someone you know?

ABDULLAHI KEINAN [*for Shamso Abdullahi Farah*]: It's somebody she has known for quite some time, and who trusted her.

ANOORADHA IYER SIDDIQI: Did you and your husband make a decision together to go and obtain credit?

ABDULLAHI KEINAN [*for Shamso Abdullahi Farah*]: She says the decision of household labor . . . was done with her husband, but her husband doesn't know these people. [She] went to the market, approached these people, and [got] these things. . . . He was for the idea, but he did not go and get the money.

ANOORADHA IYER SIDDIQI: Did you also obtain the animals here?

ABDULLAHI KEINAN [*for Shamso Abdullahi Farah*]: She bought [them] from the market here. She did not come with [them] from Somalia.

ANOORADHA IYER SIDDIQI: Are there any people who are able to bring animals from Somalia?

SHAMSO ABDULLAHI FARAH: Very few. Very few families.

ANOORADHA IYER SIDDIQI: Can we walk around and look?

SHAMSO ABDULLAHI FARAH: [*Nods yes.*]

ANOORADHA IYER SIDDIQI: When are you due?

ABDULLAHI KEINAN [*for Shamso Abdullahi Farah*]: This is her seventh month.

ANOORADHA IYER SIDDIQI: It's a hot season to be [pregnant] like this!

SHAMSO ABDULLAHI FARAH: [*Laughs.*]

ABDULLAHI KEINAN [*for Shamso Abdullahi Farah*]: She was plastering the house. See the mud, now. . . . Remember she was washing her hands? She wanted to plaster . . . [to] keep on maintaining. We [the NRC] advise them, if they continue plastering the house, it will last longer.

ANOORADHA IYER SIDDIQI [*to Abdullahi*]: And you know her very well?

ABDULLAHI KEINAN: Yes. She told me, although I didn't know her name, "you are familiar."

ANOORADHA IYER SIDDIQI: How did they decide to open a shop? Is there a need for a shop in this area?

ABDULLAHI KEINAN [*for Shamso Abdullahi Farah*]: There are lots of things missing from the food basket [in the aid package]. The only way to get some of the missing items is to sell some of these vegetables and get money to buy meat and sugar.

ANOORADHA IYER SIDDIQI: And where do these vegetables come from?

SHAMSO ABDULLAHI FARAH: From Garissa.

ANOORADHA IYER SIDDIQI: What about the other things you're selling? Where do they come from?

SHAMSO ABDULLAHI FARAH: Some come from other parts of Kenya, others Somalia.

ANOORADHA IYER SIDDIQI: And do you have relations there, or does someone from this household have to go and get them?

SHAMSO ABDULLAHI FARAH: From Somalia, the items go direct to the market. . . . It is the business community who have connections in Somalia [who are] getting the material.

ANOORADHA IYER SIDDIQI: And did you have connections with the business community there [in Somalia]?

SHAMSO ABDULLAHI FARAH: [*shakes her head no.*] Only with those who are in the camp.

Shamso Abdullahi Farah arrived in Kenya with her extended family in 2003, twelve years after the establishment of Ifo camp in 1991. A milieu of acute emergency dominated her earliest years in the camp. People were as much in need of shelter as food and water. Between 2003 and 2006, shelter aid assumed paramount importance in humanitarian relief. Farah participated in an initiative by the NRC to address this urgency. While this initiative was intended to provide shelter, I argue that her contribution was to produce domesticity. She did so within the enclosure of her dwellings, the architectures on her plot, and the relationships she formed in their making.

Refugees in Ifo did not trust the shelter programs previously instituted by CARE, the international relief and development organization that had been managing aid distribution and social services since assuming responsibility for the Dadaab camps in 1992.[31] CARE had constructed shelters that proved deadly after heavy winds blew the roofs off of several structures. To respond to this local crisis and others elsewhere, the UNHCR initiated a program of shelter research and prototype development (at its headquarters in Geneva, discussed in chapter 5) and contracted the NRC to provide expertise in shelter design, production, and distribution.[32] The NRC was to provide shelters in Dadaab and intended to produce these with community support.

The NRC managed emergency sites around the world and maintained a roster of experts available to be deployed within seventy-two hours to assist in any emergency, providing capacity to humanitarian ground teams or being seconded to agencies and organizations in need of specialized knowledge, such as specialized UN units.[33] The NRC had integrated into its staff specialists in the spatialization of humanitarian operations. The organization had led training workshops on camp management since 2005. In 2008, it produced a state-of-the-art field guide, *The Camp Management Toolkit*.[34] Through these practices and formats, the NRC formed a body of expertise in shelter construction and management of settlements, building these core competencies in line with sweeping international and interagency reforms in the late 1990s, one outcome of which was to encourage international humanitarian organizations to hone professional specializations.

From 2006, when it commenced work in Kenya, the NRC employed several project managers trained in architecture, many holding degrees from European architecture schools, and others with training in allied fields such as construction.[35] In the Dadaab settlements, the organization built 3,000 shelters in 2007 and 3,500 in 2009, considered a high volume of production for shelter aid.[36] In Ifo camp, the NRC had to respond to a complex humanitarian context, with several competing concerns arising out of the organization's specific orientations.

These concerns centered on the NRC's preference for architecture as a category of knowledge. The organization favored and indeed relied on architectural expertise. Its approaches to shelter valued the discipline's concerns. For example, the NRC was extraordinarily attentive to design details, the craft of building, and a rational process of construction in the units it made, in spite of the well-established principle in the international field of humanitarian shelter relief that dwelling units were among the costliest commodities for the aid provider. To achieve a high production volume of shelters attentive to architectural quality, in a milieu of international competition for funding for humanitarian work, the NRC circumvented the rationale of the global market through the largesse of the Norwegian government.

With this financial sponsorship, the NRC produced a strange, carefully detailed, and well-made object. Under its mud plaster protective exterior, the walls of the dwelling incorporated squared, wire-cut, kiln-fired, cement-stabilized soil blocks, a modern technology surpassing technical and aesthetic standards elsewhere in the refugee settlements and surrounding towns. This technology offered possibilities for prefabrication and mass fabrication. Humanitarian engineers designed the walls to be supported by foundations set ten bricks deep into the ground, within a one-meter foundation dug by a specially trained NRC team. These measures were intended for durability and longevity, to combat flooding, to secure the vertical structure for roof support, and ultimately to produce high value for the user.

The process of making this object was central to the initiative conceived by NRC staff members. In short, to receive the aid package, refugees were expected to participate in the design and construction of shelters. The NRC's commitment to durable, well-crafted architecture was to work doubly in refugee settings as a form of community mobilization and construction training. Staff in Dadaab approached the craftsmanship and subsequently the labor for shelters with the intention of establishing a sense of ownership and empowerment in refugee communities by instituting livelihoods and skills training, physical protection, and community building as multiple derivatives of the shelter aid package.

Alishine Osman (an interlocutor in the research for this book, and co-editor of the dialogue in chapter 1) was employed as a team leader and community mobilizer by the NRC, joining the organization in 2007 as one of its first "incentive" workers.[37] Employed at seventy-five dollars a month, Osman underwent construction training required for NRC team leaders to learn the proper use of tools, techniques for mud-brick construction, and the organization's unique requirements for setting a foundation. Having lived in Ifo for seventeen years, enduring multiple relocations with his family as homes flooded, roofs scattered during windstorms, and shelters proved deadly, Osman recalled people's mistrust of the competence, and indeed the motives, of most NGOs engaged in shelter aid. He remarked on the NRC's "fascinating" and "completely different" architectural detailing and building practice. He found that the "very strong" houses he was involved in building in 2007 remained in unusually good condition during a return visit he made to Ifo in 2009. According to Osman, the architectural design and construction methods took into account Dadaab's extreme environmental factors. The design precluded the problems that had led to previous unrest in the camps.

In spite of the dissatisfaction with previous shelter solutions and the existence of few other options, refugees in Ifo camp vehemently resisted the NRC's shelter initiative. It demanded work beyond that of other shelter programs, drained family resources, and exacted labor that might be applied more productively elsewhere. Refugees were forbidden from subcontracting the construction because they were encouraged to participate in the skill- and ownership-building construction process. They were discouraged from trading shelter materials, even those that could provide higher value as commodities, as those materials were integral to the design. Meanwhile, the housing quality produced in the shelters surpassed that of other housing in the camps and the region, exacerbating hostilities and misgivings felt by the host community and aggravating local and geopolitical tensions by expressing refugee permanence, while perhaps producing construction of a grade that far exceeded any family's needs. Donors viewed the high unit costs as inappropriately luxurious and chafed as potential beneficiaries in the refugee camps criticized the program's ideals as well as the shelters themselves for these excesses.

NRC staff members raised concerns as well. NRC shelter adviser Jake Zarins discussed the politics of the beneficiary selection and bidding and contracting process.[38] Block leaders directed the subcontract awards, in part to exercise power and in part out of dependence on a share of the aid package for their own income. In a setting in which no legal forms of employment existed, he noted, this tension lay at the very crux of refugees' forced dependence on aid. NRC shelter project manager Unni Lange described the strain between refugees and host communities over soil removal around the Dadaab settlements.[39] Refugees removed soil surrounding the camps to acquire material not only to make bricks for NRC shelters, but also to build commercial buildings in the camps or fencing to secure their plots. Lange discussed the central conflict of constraining this form of resource extraction while requiring that refugees use the material at the basis of these disputes to build shelters. Aid workers were in the position of demanding that refugees produce humanitarian space to standards they had not self-determined, while working toward an ideal against their real interests. Meanwhile, the production of this humanitarian space intervened in the land value and political economy of the region, impacting local and international relations.

Against this complex backdrop, Farah found a utility in the NRC's aid package. She was among the first to participate in the NRC's pilot shelter initiative in 2007, in which refugees were provided construction materials and required to perform all construction labor. In Ifo camp, this form of participation was negotiated within a space in which residents were not citizens, land users could not legally own property, and the state denied refugees the right to waged compensation for labor. Yet, this asymmetrical process was nevertheless transactional. In return for her participation, Farah was granted materials and trained in design and construction. She executed the project by working from specifications provided by NRC engineers. During construction, she directed a team of skilled and unskilled workers. This group included her children and spouse. Because the project allowed modifications, she requested additional materials to build a small shop. The shop, as she described in our dialogue, enabled her to establish a trade of goods that she acquired from selling portions of her family's ration. Thus, she built not only the material interiority and enclosures for her family's private domestic life, but also relational economic networks and architectures at the basis of the domestic enclosure of Ifo camp at large.

Farah's domesticity—homemaking, in all senses—was her expertise. Her homemaking was not an uncommon form of gendered labor in humanitarian environments, yet the precise form of her labor—directing a construction project, no less—perhaps confounded the gender expectations of aid workers. As I have written elsewhere, Farah leveraged her domesticity and the work of homemaking into a form of economic and sociopolitical actualization.[40] She created a shelter unit whose material form was at once part of Kenyan state territory, Somali material culture, the political space of the international order, and the social world of the community of refugees and the stateless, inserting latent representations of Norway into Ifo's aesthetic, political, socioeconomic, and ideological fabric. In the following sections, I situate Farah's sheltering and homemaking within the coercive and collaborative emergency environment of Ifo camp as forms of expertise, and her domesticity as constitutive of an epistemic foundation.

Humanitarian Expertise

Farah's labor in the NRC shelter initiative in Ifo culminated in vivid visual forms, but its complexity and depth as a form of knowledge is harder to see. She constructed humanitarian expertise centered on domesticity in emergency. She worked, first, to shelter the activities of domesticity; second, to produce shelter in order to enact domesticity; and third, to engage in design and building work that demonstrated the difference between shelter and domesticity. Here, practical aims achieved the scope of the epistemic, framing domesticity as a form of knowledge. This articulation draws on a conceptual analysis by literary scholar and feminist theorist Susan Fraiman, who categorizes domesticity in extremis into acts of privacy, storage, adornment, routine, intimacy, and kinship.[41] Aspirations and realizations of these categories might be identified in many architectures and spatial practices in Dadaab, certainly in those that Farah developed. She created privacy in the enclosure of her two dwellings. Her shop manifested storage in its arrangement of inventory. She achieved adornment in the shop's distinct roofline and the construction detailing and other design elements of the buildings. Her routine appeared in her habits of trading and stocking vegetables in exchange for meat and sugar. She expressed intimacy in her home maintenance practice of plastering walls during the latter stages of her pregnancy. Kinship was exhibited in her family's joint construction practice. These aspects of Farah's work demonstrate the complexity, effects, and affect of domestic work in emergency. They illuminate the multiple valences and meanings behind practical and intimate activities. Most urgently, her work in the realm of the practical and the intimate should be understood as constituting bodies of expertise and traditions of knowledge.

Farah's project, rooted in so-called participatory practices, grew out of what are referred to as "self-help" development models emerging from planning discourses in the 1960s and 1970s, in which dwellers were to control the use of land (if not its tenure) as well as the design and construction of their own homes, after being granted a parcel within a power and water grid (known as "sites-and-services" infrastructures) on which to build.[42] Self-help housing has long animated development discourses led by modern architects, perhaps most famously by the UN Housing, Town and Country Planning unit led by Ernest Weissmann; by John F. C. Turner in Peru; and by international planning figures such as Catherine Bauer, Jacqueline Tyrwhitt, Otto Koenigsberger, and Constantinos Doxiadis.[43] Realization of self-help principles in the latter-day construction of refugee camps at Dadaab demonstrates how they have functioned at once within two sorts of international structures, on the one hand, as a tenet of humanitarian emergency relief and, on the other, as a cornerstone of political-economic development.

Self-help housing has been predicated on the notion of a dweller-driven practice. International humanitarian networks had standardized and disseminated so-called best practices for enabling dweller-driven housing in UNHCR-administered refugee camps by the time Farah began work with the NRC in 2007, outlining participatory practices in the construction of shelter in humanitarian environments in common guides such as *The UNHCR Tool for Participatory Assessment in Operations*.[44] However, in Dadaab, not only did the use of land not translate into squatters' rights as it might in some development contexts, but participation was negotiated within conditions of emergency. This perpetuated an extreme version of what architectural historian Ijlal Muzaffar has described as one of the "key fictions of the development discourse . . . the idea of a participating and consensual clientele."[45] "Participants" have been subject to disaster capitalist strategies, following social activist Naomi Klein's argument, in which profound structural changes have been enacted while these participants endured the shock of humanitarian crisis or were displaced because of it.[46] In Dadaab, self-help development has been intertwined with the shock of emergency, which has suspended people in an equivocal status, neither citizen nor guest, as the state has denied them the legal ability to seek a better life within its borders.

In humanitarian discourses, "shelter" often serves as a practical end distinct from wider concerns with domesticity, reducing the act of sheltering to the production of shelter. Thus, humanitarian pursuits in the architectural and planning disciplines have focused on technical problem-solving, rather than an experiential or embodied understanding of emergency homemaking. They have not systematized as a form of knowledge the labor, self-care, and mutual aid to be found in the extreme domesticities and profoundly gendered contexts of displacement, nor problematized the equation of housing to the provision of nuanced material intimacies, comforts, and settings for caregiving—that is, understanding that people may yet be unsheltered even if housed. Moreover, a narrow focus on "shelter," which informed the planning and structuring of settlements at Dadaab, has absorbed, yet effaced, the work of the individual emergency subject.[47] This paradoxical problem has stemmed from state and nongovernmental techno-scientific concerns with development as a problem-solving exercise. The problem lies close to Muzaffar's articulation of self-help interventions that have facilitated the development subject's "incorporation into circuits of global finance through land reform, property tenure, and loan mechanisms," in which the space between her social life and economic activity constitutes a differential between development and underdevelopment, as argued in this book's introduction.[48] Naming this erasure of human agency and political power is perhaps the most ready critique of an overwhelming humanitarian positivism that eases flows of capital through architectural and spatial practices dedicated to designing and providing shelter. However, it would be reductive to understand Farah's activity in simple transactional financial terms. To assess her shop as only a site of petty trade—even if it moves the economy of Dadaab through spaces of microcredit, occupying a program line item for the NRC within the UNHCR's large budget for contracting refugee operations in Kenya—would be to misunderstand her full labor. These conditions may define the event of shelter production, but capturing the labor of a mother and emergency subject as a product of effacements produced by neoliberal global economies, even as an expression of a dialectic between structure and agency, is a limiting interpretation. Much more is at stake in the construction of domesticity at the basis of Farah's work. Yet, to see it demands setting the housing unit at the center of her time and labor into a historical genealogy related to emergency shelter. Here, shelter plays a vital role in domesticity, perhaps even in a new formulation of it, but just as significantly, shelter captures the heterogeneous formation of a body of development-related expertise.

If such a body of expertise might be identified, its backdrop would be entropic humanitarian knowledge formation. The diffusive nature of the practices underlying emergency and humanitarian response, the proliferation of smaller centers and organizations as part of an overall neoliberal rise of nongovernmental culture, and the larger geopolitical geographical divisions that produced institutional archival silos during the Cold War caused a dispersion of knowledge bases and repositories, ultimately splintering rather than cohering humanitarian expertise. Nevertheless, by the 1980s, knowledge and academic study related to the conditions experienced by refugees appeared to consolidate. The international institutionalization of the refugee studies field began in university initiatives in the 1980s, such as the Oxford Refugee Studies Programme (later the Refugee Studies Centre) established in 1982 by anthropologist Barbara Harrell-Bond; the Centre for Refugee Studies at Moi University in Eldoret, Kenya, established in 1991, concurrent with the settlement of Ifo camp at Dadaab; and others established in the following decade at the University of the Witwatersrand in Johannesburg, Makerere University in Kampala, and the American University in Cairo.[49] Early academic research from the spatial disciplines on emergency, shelter, and settlement was housed in architecture schools, most prominently the Special Interest

Group in Urban Settlements (SIGUS, established in 1984 from the Urban Settlement Design Program founded by architects John F. C. Turner, Horacio Caminos, and others at the Massachusetts Institute of Technology [MIT]) and the Centre for Development and Environmental Planning (CENDEP, established in 1985 by architect Ian Davis and others at Oxford Polytechnic). As I have written elsewhere, these consolidations grew out of Cold War–era interventions by members of the spatial disciplines focused on humanitarian shelter and settlement and disaster relief and planning, intervening on the ground into postcolonial environments and at the global level into international agencies concerned broadly with human rights, structural adjustment, and development.[50] From the early 1950s through the end of the 1990s, two humanitarian agencies, the UNHCR and the United Nations Disaster Relief Office (UNDRO), occasionally yet consistently sought shelter expertise from the formal professions of architecture and planning, just as architects and planners concertedly engaged in humanitarian relief projects, bringing their training to bear on emergency settings.

The outstanding careers in this history constructed a field of expertise on emergency shelter, a body of knowledge joined by the work of Farah and other displaced people in Dadaab and elsewhere. German architect Otto Koenigsberger, known for designing and planning in the postcolonial world while working with the UN and as the head of the Tropical Architecture School (at the Architectural Association and later at the Development Planning Unit at University College London), built on his experiences provisioning refugees with prefabricated dwellings while he served as India's first director of housing, and, prior to that, developing accommodations for workers in planning industrialist J. R. D. Tata's complex in Jamshedpur (the first workers' housing plan on the subcontinent) while he served as chief architect of the Princely State of Mysore.[51] Koenigsberger's student, English architect Ian Davis, specialized in disaster relief and development during the 1970s and 1980s, working internationally in the design and construction of shelter and developing significant research for UNDRO based on his PhD dissertation research.[52] American planner Frederick C. Cuny, founder of the firm Intertect with partner and fellow Texan Jean "Jinx" Parker, provided disaster relief, reconstruction, and planning in direct consultancy with the UNHCR, UNDRO, and nearly all other agencies in the international humanitarian system, infusing them with his ground-level experience from every notable complex emergency in the world between 1968 and 1995.[53] Davis and Cuny collaborated together over decades, individually and together consolidating a body of humanitarian knowledge through a constellation of distinct events and publications. In 1978 (two years

3.5. Attendees of the First International Workshop on Improved Shelter Response and Environment for Refugees, Geneva, 1993, from Zimba, "Summary of Proceedings."

after the landmark UN "Habitat" conference in Vancouver), they participated in a symposium of architecture and planning professionals, "Disasters and the Small Dwelling," producing state-of-the-art research and a professional network. In 1982, they published two critical documents, UNDRO's *Shelter after Disaster: Guidelines for Assistance*, which built on Davis's PhD dissertation and drew from Davis and Cuny's joint fieldwork, and the UNHCR's *Handbook for Emergencies*, which included Intertect's recommendations for best practices in relief and planning.[54] Both texts had far-reaching impacts as the emergency relief and humanitarian aid industry professionalized, standardized, and globalized. Not least, the emphasis Davis and Cuny placed on privileging local and Indigenous knowledge and people and enabling dweller control of the housing process—all owing a debt to self-help urbanization discourses—found their way directly into Dadaab, as Farah's work demonstrates.

Building on these constructions of expertise, the UNHCR's efforts in the 1990s provide the most solid evidence of nascent consolidations of a field of emergency shelter or humanitarian architecture and planning.[55] Beyond the physical planning of large-scale refugee settlements, especially at Dadaab, where ninety thousand people were sheltered in 1991 and 1992, the UNHCR appointed the first professional architect at its Geneva headquarters, Wolfgang Neumann from Germany, the senior physical planner/architect in the Programme and Technical Support Section. In 1993, the First International Workshop on Improved Shelter Response and Environment for Refugees convened architecture and planning professionals and building tradespeople from nineteen nations, including, to name a few, Malawi, Australia, Pakistan, the United States, Norway, and the former Yugoslavia.[56] The workshop was organized in part by Sabine Wähning, an architect in Neumann's unit who had been involved in the site selection and initial physical planning of the Dadaab refugee camps. Participants from two architecture and development think tanks concerned with disaster management and urban settlement were engaged to lead the workshop on operative and theoretical issues: Nabeel Hamdi from CENDEP at Oxford Brookes University (formerly Oxford Polytechnic) and Reinhard Goethert from SIGUS at MIT. They commissioned a state-of-the-art overview paper from Hamdi's colleague and codirector Roger Zetter, who had founded the *Journal of Refugee Studies* five years earlier and later became the director of the Oxford Refugee Studies Centre.[57] In total, sixty invited architects, logisticians, manufacturers, and diplomats attended, including the anthropologist Barbara Harrell-Bond, the founder and then head of the Oxford Refugee Studies Centre, whose scholarship offered a scathing criticism of encampment as a practical, ontological, and ethical problem wrought by refugee policy.[58] This "first" event in Geneva was never followed by a second, but in theory, it promised to build professional momentum and community, linking academics, practitioners, and vendors in the building trades (who exhibited shelter products and prototypes on the lawn outside the meeting area). Teams in working sessions were tasked with developing an emergency shelter concept, a policy framework, and a means for implementation that would consider emergency response protocols, standards, and technology and establish a standing forum for the dissemination of information and knowledge.[59] Inasmuch as the attendees shared an interest in the capacity of architecture and planning to intervene in matters of politics, society, and human need, this workshop held in the Château de Penthes in Geneva, just a short distance across the park from the Palais des Nations, evoked the origins of the CIAM (Congrès Internationale d'Architecture Moderne) at another château sixty-five summers earlier in nearby La Sarraz, convening on social problems that modern architects might solve.[60] Although, in practice, the UNHCR workshop may have resembled less a systematic consolidation of technical expertise than a gathering of multiple and sometimes competing interests, it nevertheless contributed to an institutionalization and epistemic foundation of humanitarian knowledge.

This point is notable because casting humanitarian knowledge as an ad hoc formation of uncredited labors risks omitting the contribution of refugees such as Farah and Osman. Whether or not the First International Workshop on Improved Shelter Response and Environment for Refugees represented an act of systematization, many oral histories I collected suggest that no comprehensive knowledge base on architecture and planning in emergencies had been developed or codified before 1993. In spite of the dissemination of the *Handbook for Emergencies* and the technical and professional workshops on operational themes held by the UNHCR Programme and Technical Support Section (and the Engineering and Environmental Services Section that grew out of it), the agency's internal research on shelter and camps had been limited and rarely brought together built environment professionals.[61] Interagency institutional knowledge seemed to be stunted by the frequency of what were newly referred to as "complex" emergencies. Taxing multiple governmental and nongovernmental systems, perhaps in various stages of decolonizing, they hindered the memorialization of staff experience. Institutional knowledge also seemed to be impeded by a lack of programs or technologies for archiving knowledge across the humanitarian field, across the UN system, or even across a single agency's headquarters and field stations. Expertise in emergency settlement planning and shelter design, such as it was, lay largely in the academy and private sector, the research of UNDRO and the UNHCR field guide discussed earlier, and humanitarian organizations with a public health and hygiene specialty, such as MSF and Oxfam. The latter organizations had been able to remain active in regions where Cold War politics limited access for the UN agencies, and they had gathered field knowledge and even provisionally codified it.[62] Outside of the minor repositories these created, professional architects and planners appeared to be the custodians of this expertise.[63] As the examples of Cuny and Davis show, the entry of these professionals into the international humanitarian agencies brought into those bureaucratic yet urgent landscapes not only technical concerns, but also humanistic and aesthetic orientations.

The First International Workshop on Improved Shelter Response and Environment for Refugees offers a meaningful punctuation mark in a half-century of humanitarian and architectural discourse. In the workshop, the thinking and a professional culture coalesced, immediately prior to unprecedented crises in Bosnia and Rwanda, auguring new scales of emergency for which systematized architecture and planning solutions would be implemented, and producing a watershed in humanitarian self-reflection that resulted in significant reforms in professional practice, such as the formation of the Sphere Project consortium in 1996, "the first attempt to produce globally applicable minimum standards for humanitarian response services," part of an international initiative on the part of agencies and organizations to establish norms, hone core professional competencies, and codify expertise.[64] This initiative included work in areas of spatial practice such as "camp management" and "shelter"; the same year, the research group shelterproject began developing a field manual for transitional shelter and settlement of refugees, an exercise out of which the Shelter Centre emerged, in a coach house behind the Department of Architecture building at the University of Cambridge.[65] Many credit the Shelter Centre's director, Tom Corsellis, with forging the contours of a contemporary field through the organization's unmatched technical proficiency, resource database, and professional network.[66] The review process for the field manual initiated the biannual Shelter Meeting in 2004.[67] As a highly systematized avatar of the First International Workshop on Improved Shelter Response and Environment for Refugees, the Shelter Meeting integrated and institutionalized expertise within the international humanitarian system. That the discourse on disaster and development culminated in the iteration of *shelter* speaks to the act of figuration by the architects at the center of this history.

My aim in setting Farah's work into conversation with that of these figures and the events in this historical thread is to think critically about how humanitarian expertise is constructed. The mythology around these humanitarians has been as significant in a construction of expertise as the empirical knowledge they each developed (a matter of aura, which I attend to in chapter 5). For this reason, it is worth heeding the cautions of feminist architectural historians Rachel Lee and Elis Mendoza, who help to visualize the hidden figures and migrant networks that supported the reception of Koenigsberger and Cuny, respectively.[68] Setting Farah's work into conversation with that of well-known humanitarian figures is intended to mitigate the extolling of patriarchal genius in recalling a humanitarian history, which, as Mendoza notes, "is not the only one to canonize and aggrandize male figures and use them as anchors in its construction."[69] However, equally important is critical theorist Emily Bauman's argument situating the narration of exceptionalism as a conceit peculiar to contemporary humanitarianism, which I argue contributes to its formation of knowledges. The proliferating stories around protagonists in the relief efforts associated with noted crises, the passionate memoirs of aid workers in extreme circumstances, and the life writing Bauman studies—populated with characters whose actions and approaches are the product of both naïveté and genius—are, as she asserts, "much-needed by an industry reliant on public donations and on the perception of its status as a player outside the systems of state sovereignty and global capital . . . just as humanitarianism has become more professionalised."[70] They provide assurance "that the face of this global multi-billion dollar industry is still predicated on the spontaneous ingenuousness and ingenuity of the rogue actor bucking the system in order to effect social change."[71] While empirical evidence suggests that Farah's building experiments and work as an emergency homemaker contributed to a broader shelter expertise, I characterize her as a protagonist in a humanitarian history to deconstruct the auratic figuration of its experts and demystify and concretize the processes of emergency sheltering and domesticity. Such tangible processes are often abstracted within global humanitarian knowledge and exempted from histories that rely exclusively on official archives and organized documentary collections rather than drawing from the positions and experiences of the people who participated in the events occasioning the knowledge.

Having said this, my discussions with Farah, Osman, and others in these pages who experienced forced displacement firsthand specifically avoided highly personal questions. Their relationships with NGOS and participation in initiatives rendered them as semi-public figures in the camps, which I took into account in the decision to include their photographs in these pages. Nevertheless, in speaking with Farah, I especially elided any query related to the flight or refuge she and her family were forced to undertake. If such details were to provide context for the events she described, they would have done so invasively and at the expense of her privacy. I elected instead a form of historiographical attentiveness that respected those boundaries while centering the forms of domesticity she was able to generate through the exercise of her own faculties, agency, and valuation of her diverse resources. By contextualizing her work in this way, I hope to highlight a form of fullness in her practice that other modes and metrics of documentation tend to miss. Indeed, even with these self-imposed limitations, I was able to surmise a great deal from interviews with Farah, her coworkers, and others in related positions in Dadaab and elsewhere. I noted that Farah did not come to the NRC project with formal education or training in design or construction. The NRC did not select her for participation due to any preexisting expertise, as defined by the organization. Farah, like many displaced women in Dadaab, had a large family with many children. She was pregnant at the time of the interview. To have obtained refugee status in the first place, and to become a visible prospect to the NRC to the extent that it became possible for her to participate in an inaugural shelter initiative in Ifo camp, she would have had to have had community support and, most likely, political support from parties with diverse interests. Other questions—about her present circumstances, her position in the community, her relation to al-Shabaab, the status of her family, her understanding of the social organization of the camp or the place from which she fled, any particular skills or knowledge she exhibited or gained vis-à-vis the NRC that provided a form of social or political capital, or even her personal growth and evolution—went purposely, and purposefully, unanswered.

Key to the historical episode related earlier is that Farah played a critical and instrumental role in the NRC's first shelter initiative in Dadaab, providing intellectual and material labor that would cement the expertise and global reputation of the NRC in the financially speculative and existentially high-risk field of humanitarian relief. Her project inaugurated a large-scale emergency shelter initiative punctuating one strand in a history of modern design and building in regions once identified as "the tropics" and later as "the global South": a history of construction led by dwellers, ostensibly contributing to ecological and social sustainability. Her central role in the project positions her as a meaningful protagonist in a global history, one centered on domesticity in emergency. Farah's position and knowledge center her not only as an actor in a history, but as an expert—one who is embodied and can be named—in an emergent epistemic field of humanitarian knowledge.

Refugees who participated in constructing this expertise negotiated asymmetries and their own implication within them. Farah found a transactional utility in the NRC's aid package, leveraging a type of work that she would have performed in a nondisplacement context—that is, the construction and maintenance of the home, as in the tuqul for which women from East African pastoralist communities are often responsible (as discussed in chapter 2 and later in this chapter)—into a form of economic and sociopolitical actualization. Similarly, Osman negotiated consensus across dynamic inequalities, utilizing his unique experience and responsibility as a community mobilizer:

> We set goals. This week we built ten. Next week we're going to make our goal twenty. . . . Most of [the participants] will make their bricks themselves. . . . They have to make sure they bring five or six people who will work with them to start the foundation. . . . [The NRC has] three or

> four people also, or at least one or two engineers. . . . When everything is complete they will put [up] the roof. . . . My role as a mobilizer was to inform people [of] the benefits of building this thing. . . . But along the line, I really gained a lot.[72]

Although Osman worked on a project whose inception occurred outside the community, it followed in the tradition of community-rooted development practices. His acknowledgment of the technical and leadership skills he gained from the project stemmed in part from reflecting on his limited term of work, as he was resettled within the United States within the year after he joined the NRC. This outcome demonstrates how the institutional processes that Osman and Farah helped to develop in Ifo reconstituted their own social mobility, even if the trajectory was different for a multilingual English-speaking Somali man with a high school diploma than for a Somali-speaking woman pregnant with her seventh child. I argue that these institutional processes established each of them as an expert, whether or not understood or acknowledged as such by the organization that benefited from their labor.

That expertise carries new formations of subjectivity and historical ramifications, rooted in homemaking. One might argue that the valorization of Farah's or Osman's experiences offers an alibi for oppressive development practices. Yet, in this episode, an architecture of shelter produced forms of legitimacy and authority independent of the development apparatus. Shelter as a concept (a home) and shelter as a specific built object (a spatial commodity) cohered relief with aesthetics, redirected material flows, signified the nation-state within a refugee camp (Kenya and Norway in particular, and the international system more broadly), and institutionalized a team of designers through a practice of making architecture. This architecture and the spatial practices associated with it suspended the liminality of the two refugees named here and other unnamed actors in this narrative. Their interaction with a paternalistic and transnational political, economic, and social system produced a situated expertise, power, and mobility through an embodied practice of designing and building domestic space, which led to other forms of power, vulnerability, and difference. In this setting, the architectural work of producing emergency domesticity rendered banal matters such as professional licensing, as refugees engaged deeply with humanitarians, institutions, and the state, in spite of profound asymmetries. Understanding this work and social transformation in this way has epistemic ramifications. It conditions the way a history might be understood or written and what we name as knowledge as stemming from the making of home, of domestic life.

3.6. Shamso Abdullahi Farah in her shop, Ifo camp.

Domesticity

To bring together a final set of considerations on domesticity and shelter, this section focuses on two scales of space, that of the built shelter defined by the refugee's labor and that of the state in terms of the camp's relation to the land.[73] A theory of domesticity is needed to understand the architecture of the shelter as well as the camp. Within the camp, the labor of making domesticities inscribes practices onto the land, and neither the land nor the labor of domesticity is necessarily coterminous with the nation-state. The domesticities that architecture enables in emergency enact the deeper practice of inhabitation.

Many forms of domesticity have produced an architecture of migration in Dadaab. At the level of individual households, domesticity takes form in shelters. At the level of the settlement, space is domesticated in the structuring of housing plots. At the level of the state, the domestic interior provides the territory for refugee space. As discussed earlier, these multiple scales of architecture concentrate domesticities within spaces of coercion, collaboration, and conjunctions of both.

These coercions and collaborations demand labors that both divide the camp from the land and dedicate it within the environment, producing extreme intimacies across partitions. For example, the photograph of a tended grave in Ifo camp in chapter 1 points to quotidian mortalities that form part of daily domestic life in Dadaab, implying the intimacies of home in forced migration settings, when people live and labor in the proximity of their departed. In a camp, dying is thus yoked to homemaking. However, in contrast to the notion that the home—specifically, the dwelling—might be formally, aesthetically, and epistemologically *connected* to the environment within which it has been constructed (the concept of the traditional dwelling, the architectural vernacular), the architecture of the refugee camp is *delinked* from the land: legally, figuratively, symbolically, and often practically. The camp has been partitioned from the space and territory with which it is contiguous, and people have traversed its boundaries by taking great pains. This traversal into and out of the domestic interior of the camp imagines the acts of coercion and collaboration that form its boundary.

Notwithstanding this domestic boundary, as a destination for forced migrants and a site of forced settlement, Dadaab must be understood through a different domesticity—namely, as iterative of a long history of migratory living. Many of the camps' inhabitants come from communities in East Africa for which an intimate relation to the land is not lived through partition or demarcated according to conventional capitalistic principles. For generations, people have migrated across the region for trade, animal husbandry, and other forms of subsistence, documented and undocumented, bringing into being strong material iterations in the form of provisional, but nonetheless structuring, architectures. The tent has not signified emergency or destitution, but instead has contoured and symbolized a direct habitation of the land for generations.[74] This has been so even during the period marked by modernity. Indeed, ephemeral and migratory domestic architectures have offered a rejoinder to modernization by not complying with its infrastructures. They have behaved recalcitrantly, as argued in the introduction, and thus been cast as an immanently fugitive architecture, an architecture of displacement. Such connotations must be read into domesticity in Dadaab.

Two mobile architectures have made legible the complex condition of migratory living, corresponding to two analytical problems. The first is the installed imported structure, which, analytically, creates a territorial problem. The UNHCR single-family shelter (discussed in chapter 5) and the large WFP food storage unit are tensile architectures with a fabric skin, which can be flat-packed, warehoused, and deployed throughout a global supply chain. These objects and their mobilities conform to the political economies of actual states, but not to the land the camp occupies. Architecture, as it is designed and built, often takes form in relationship to a state economy or territory that adheres to geopolitical boundaries. The refugee camp and its architectures cannot follow this logic in quite the same way; in other words, the Dadaab settlements are in Kenya but not of Kenya; Farah's shelter is of Norway but not in Norway. While planners defined the spatial implementation of humanitarian operations at Dadaab, the settlement complex evolved and grew not in response to *planning*, but in response to multiple forces of *domestic structuring*. The domestic space of the state has defined the domesticity of the refugee camp, but not constituted it. The planners and designers of the architecture of Dadaab (such as Farah and Osman, Neumann and Wähning, or the architects discussed in chapter 4) are not architects without a country. Yet, the refugee settlements and the shelters within do not correspond to any single national or political entity. These paradoxes of domesticity ensue from the camp as well as the mobile architectures that make it material.

The second mobile architecture is a very different set of portable architectures, which, analytically, present a problem of materiality. The tuqul dwellings in which many refugees live for years are built from plant materials such as the *Commiphora* (myrrh) bushes that grow in the Jubaland region, along with recycled building elements such as UNHCR tarps, WFP grain sacks, or

3.7. WFP food storage unit, Ifo camp.

3.8. Tuqul constructed from recovered textiles (location undisclosed to retain privacy).

scrap textile sheets. These dwellings do not map directly onto any national political economies, but instead concretely onto the land. Even if the refugee camps were plotted by planners, the structures within them grow from the land beneath; each plot is bordered by live fencing, the walls of each individual compound growing from the ground. Thus, the structures, composed of the very soil and earth, correspond to the uses of the land, as well as the politics of this use. In Dadaab, the hegemony of the horticultural border and its power to effect zoning appears in a variety of instabilities embodied in the materiality of that border and its ordering capacity, resulting in risks ranging from hyena attacks to sexual violence for those transgressing the demarcated perimeter of the camps—for example, for women seeking food, water, or cooking fuel. According to one aid worker, as a group of mothers excavated the clay soil around the perimeter of the camps to make bricks for shelters, the large pits left behind brimmed with water during the rainy season, quickly transforming into mosquito breeding grounds. This stirred a public health crisis. An otherwise divided population of "refugees" and their "hosts" within the domestic interior of the state became united under the coherence of disease. The affected populations included, on the one hand, refugees cared for by foreign doctors and, on the other, citizens overseen by domestic health care workers. The brick production by women maintaining their homes to care for their children inaugurated a battle over the building trade and construction contracts, producing bizarre entanglements between domestic economic interests and international refugee law and policy. In such scenarios, abstractions are untenable, whether of a refugee camp or the nation-state. Both become concrete through forms of domesticity, at the scale of the shelter and of the state. In such a scenario, meaning and potency are embodied within architecture directly, rather than architecture symbolizing power located elsewhere or laboring on behalf of a referent. The refugee camp may be disconnected from the territory of the land—that is, the camp may disallow the land as a referent for its architecture—but it cannot be disconnected from the materiality of the land. In Dadaab, land elements literally constitute forms of domesticity.

In addition to these deliberations on land, the domesticity at issue here requires considerations of labor. The matter of labor is central to the architecture resulting from Farah's work as it exceeded requirements for shelter meeting the most basic needs for survival. Indeed, the constructed form represented the result of an involved, scientific process. It offered a technical, professionally engineered solution for mitigating the extreme environmental challenges of the region. The design and implementation process produced evidence-based data that broadened the NRC's platform of technical expertise. This furthered the organization's social construction of expert status. These practices at Dadaab cemented the organization's empirical knowledge base, while also building its international profile, as professional staff members disseminated findings from this high-profile site of humanitarian operations in conferences and other circuits. This construction of institutional reputation drew from the physical and intellectual labor of refugees, especially that of Farah and including many others. Labor's multiple valences in this process—intellectual or manual, performed by refugee, citizen, or other—constituted the potency and the stakes of Farah's work. This was a labor based in domesticity.

Here, architecture produced various forms of legitimacy predicated on the labor of creating domesticity in emergency. Architecture cohered relief with a legible aesthetic regime, even a roofline that recalled Norwegian design in Somali Kenya. It redirected material flows, from the soil and cement of the brick walls to an NGO's laboring bodies. Architecture signified actual states as well as the international refugee framework. Farah was institutionalized as an "architect" in charge of the programming, design, construction, and use of a set of buildings—indeed, of an expanded domestic space. While formally certified architects, refugees, and unregistered others have been jointly responsible for the mass construction and architectural grain of the Dadaab settlements, Farah's architectural work—her *homemaking*, writ large—rendered irrelevant matters such as professional licensing, because of the emergency context in which she labored. She engaged intensely with humanitarians and institutions, in spite of an asymmetry between herself and the state. Farah, the NRC, and the UNHCR together ordered a sphere of sociality, politics, and aesthetic and cultural work, disrupting the normative order of the nation-state and even Farah's liminal status as a refugee. Rather than the political sphere producing built form, architectural forms of domesticity effected Farah's political subjecthood. Moreover, they rendered her a subject of emergency as much as of any state or international order. The subjecthood set by these conditions of emergency, as well as her embodied practice of designing, building, and intersecting with a transnational political, economic, and social system, produced alternate forms of authority in the camp. For her, they enacted situated expertise, power, and mobility. Her homemaking, in the emergency context, was a form of worldmaking.

How might this world be understood, in which domesticity is rooted in emergency and provisionality is expressed in bricks and mortar? How do we understand Farah's domesticity, in terms of building a shelter, housing her family, and becoming a technical expert and social organizer through homemaking, when homemaking is based on the paradox of a shelter—and, beyond it, a camp—that can be provided only on the condition of its ultimate ephemerality? Finally, taking such a paradox in hand, how is such homemaking and worldmaking to be brought into scholarly view, when conventions of the state break down, causing archives to do so as well?

Farah's domesticity asks whether shelter is inalienable from the nation-state and how it exerts state and nongovernmental dynamics. A history of her work suggests that the limit concept for the refugee camp was not necessarily the nation-state, its territory, and its borders, but more materially, her labor and the land, and the use, negotiations, and transgressions of each. Farah was not a wage worker whose labor was fixed within the political economy of a nation, and yet, she was a modern subject—one who was not a subject of the state, nor a subject in training, but sovereign in ways that lie outside the nation-state construct. Her sovereignty was tied to the land, rather than to extraction from it, and to her own labor, instead of to its quantification. She lived on the land, rather than off it. Her work created domesticity, instead of a domesticity framing her work. This element of extreme domesticity—the work—is worth a great deal of attention, as a feminist, environmental, and architectural problematic that moves our understanding and theory beyond the irresolvable tension in the concept of shelter as the architectural articulation of humanitarian aid. Shelter, as an aesthetic outcome, is conceptually distinct from the lifeworlds that emerge from it or arise because of it. This is perhaps what Cuny and others experienced in their work, and intimated in their writings and the discussion and architecture culture they supported, and what is embodied in Farah's individual and collaborative labor. The histories that cast shelter as an expedient, contingent, modular house form—an architecture of emergency or displacement—fail to enable its comprehension within longer, deeper histories of migration. Such histories give shelter a larger life, an insurgent notion of domesticity and inhabitation. In them, domesticity forms an expertise and makes the built environment into an epistemic foundation. Such a foundation allows for the methodological approaches in the next chapter, which builds on the understanding of the Dadaab refugee camps as an architectural expression of domesticity to write a history of refugee and humanitarian settlement. In it, I approach this architecture of domesticity as a basis for knowledge, possessing the capacity of an archive to speak beyond the nation-state toward something less determined, which assumes the characteristics of settlement.

FAX CABLE

[illegible]/HCR/0451 KEN/NYC/HCR/0312 KEN/USA/HCR/0319 KEN/GBR/HCR/0320

KEN/ETH/HCR/0321 (INFO NYC, USA, GBR, ETH)

[illegible]

[illegible] 2374 - 07/[illegible]

[illegible] GENERAL SITUATION

[illegible]

'91 V -8 14:46

UNHCR TELECOMMUNICATIONS UNIT RECEIVED

AFØ4

(*previous page*) UNHCR Sitrep No. 7. For a full transcript of the cable, see pages 182–85.

4

An Archive of Humanitarian Settlement

> I was determined to fill in the blank spaces of the historical record and to represent the lives of those deemed unworthy of remembering, but how does one write a story about an encounter with nothing?
>
> —**Saidiya Hartman**

The archive of humanitarian settlement that follows aims to reorient understandings of the refugee camp, estranging the emergency environment and refusing the abjection usually accorded to it. This archive builds on principles in the previous chapters: that people in Dadaab have lived across partitions of land and self; that the camps occupy a territory made contingent through emergency construction of enclosures and people's sedentarization; and that people in Dadaab have crafted insurgent domesticities while sheltering in place, shaping environments of intimacy and epistemic import. These theoretical and historical positions set the stage for narrating architecture and history in a refugee camp, interpreting Dadaab's planning and design as an iteration of humanitarian spatiality that continues to reproduce it as an emergency territory. However, I show emergency as processual and historical, reversing paradigms of urgency. I confront the precariousness of the war

Sitrep No. 7, Fax Cable Issued by UNHCR Nairobi Branch Office, May 8, 1991

Page 1

Incoming fax cable

KEN/HCR/0451, KEN/NYC/HCR/0318, KEN/USA/HCR/0319, KEN/GBR/HCR/0320, KEN/ETH/HCR/0321 (info NYC, USA, GBR, ETH)

Sitrep No. 7

Period covered: 23/4–07/5 [April 23–May 7]

AAA General Situation:

Reverses in civil war in south of Somalia (Fall of Kismayu to USC [United Somali Congress]) resulting in new influx of reportedly tens of thousands to SOM-KEN [Somalia-Kenya] border. GOK [Government of Kenya] has not yet advised HCR [UNHCR] if refugees in quote no mans land unquote will be granted asylum in Kenya and if UNHCR will be requested to provide assistance. Some one thousand refugees have reached Liboi and GOK has agreed to their registration. BO [Branch Office] arranging provide food and shelter. Joint HCR/GOK /NGO assessment mission left for Liboi area (Garissa District) on 7/5 [May 7] morning and scheduled return Nairobi 9/5 [May 9] evening. Meanwhile BO has decided to stockpile at Garissa shelter materials, food and medicine for an initial 10,000 additional caseload and depending on further developments, for a further 10,000 at later date.

BBB Refugee Statistics and Registration:

Mombasa: 10,999 as of 26/4 [April 26]

Liboi/Hulugo: 6,320

Marsabit: 2,989

Note:

I) Mombasa statistics reflect registration, not actual camp population. Re-registration is in progress.

Page 2

II) Following re-registration in Liboi, camp population figure declined to one-third, but expected to increase again with new arrivals.

CCC Protection:

Refugees were faced with number of protection problems as described below.

Mombasa:

I) Another ship, MV Kwanda, with 850 persons on board awaiting GOK decision to disembark. Vessel chartered by

Italian govt to carry relief material to Somalia was commandered by armed men. BO has requested GOK to allow access to assess if persons on board are of concern. BO preparing shelter of refuge component at Utange camp. Representative currently on mission to Mombasa.

II) Entire population at Mombasa showgrounds camp transferred to new camp at Utange end April. Manner of transfer was very controversial. Although not forced, number of incidents of high-handedness by certain police officials were reported. In any event, move not in line with plan agreed earlier with district officials. Consequently, it was chaotic and caused

Page 3

needless hardship to refugees. BO has expressed grave concern to GOK. Minor incidents of violence among refugees at new site not uncommon at present, refugee __ [illegible, looks like 2 vertical lines, like "II"or "II" but grammar doesn't make sense—should read "refugees" or "refugee movement" or "refugees' movement"] unrestricted but GOK indicated movement will be restricted soon.

Garissa:

BO awaiting return of assessment mission. Telephone report: No serious problem.

Marsabit:

During last week April, several incidents of violence between Sudanese, Somali and Ethiopian refugees. On 30 April, serious violence among refugees resulting in police intervention and use of force. Some 40–50 wounded, urgent mission from Nairobi comprising BO staff, Kenya Red Cross staff and Moha official was despatched.

DDD Food:

Mombasa: Basic rations being provided. Actual distribution (based on registration) in excess of estimated camp population, will be adjusted when re-registration completed. Local charities occasionally provide cooked food. Egerton University students made small distribution by skipping lunch, emulating example of Princess Anne. UNHCR thanked faculty members and students for kind gesture and assured it will be conveyed to HQS. BO London may wish to mention to SCF-UK [Save the Children Fund, UK].

Page 4

Garissa: Food supply to Liboi camp just adequate but none could be delivered to Hulugo camp for last three weeks as road cut-off. Two attempts to reach failed and trucks got stuck. GOK being requested to airlift food to Hulugo, or provide 4WD [four-wheel drive] trucks.

Marsabit: No improvement in sight until camp relocated. Supplementary feeding programme could not be launched due to Red Cross could not transport food supplies from NBI [Nairobi]. Disturbances mentioned CCC above also hampered progress as nutrionist [*sic*] (temporarily seconded by SCF-UK) spent time on dealing with volatile situation.

EEE Shelter:

Mombasa: Chaotic transfer from showgrounds to Utange end-April resulted in majority of refugees with absolutely no shelter. Construction of shelter and distribution of plastic sheets during last week has eased situation but still not fully satisfactory. Intermittent heavy rains further aggravated condition.

Garissa: Gradual improvement but expected to worsen if new arrivals along border are transferred to Liboi camp. Tents and plastic being sent in anticipation.

Marsabit: No change.

Page 5

FFF Health:

Mombasa: Rudimentary health service at showgrounds suspended upon transfer of population to Utange where new clinic under construction and will be operational this week. Meanwhile, no implementing agency in place to provide service. Urgent cases receiving treatment from local health facilities.

Garissa: Camp clinic operational.

Marsabit: Upgrading of camp clinic at hand.

GGG Water and Sanitation:

Mombasa: Periodic shortage of water in camp in particular and area in general. In case of acute shortage, water trucked to camp. Occasional fights over water. Sanitation most unsatisfactory. Only 39 pit latrines operational. Crash completion of other units in progress. Drainage problem further aggravated by rains. GOK public health officials working on solving latter problem.

Garissa: Second pump and generator purchased by ___ [illegible first character of three, "_HI"—looks like "PHI"] in Nairboi and on way to Liboi camp.

Marsabit: Problem somewhat relieved on completion pipeline to camp but general water shortage plagues whole of Marsabit District.

HHH Implementation:

Signing of sub-agreements with implementing agencies awaiting HQS approval of revised 91/EF/KEN/EM/140.

Page 6

Preparation of sub-agreements in progress. ___ [illegible, same acronym "_HI"—could be "FHI"] is operational. Discussions ongoing with CARE. Red Cross performance has yet to reach satisfactory level. In short, BO is still compelled to undertake most assistance activities with very limited manpower and supporting resources.

III External Affairs/Coordination:

I) US consul in Mombasa, Swiss ambassador, WFP rep and UNICEF [United Nations Children's Fund] rep and team visited Mombasa camps.

II) GOK convened another meeting with NGO and selected UN agencies and again appealed for increased assistance to meet urgent needs.

III) LRCS has issued appeal based on budget indications from KRCS.

IV) UNHCR representative and UNDP [United Nations Development Programme] res. rep. Kenya will hold briefing for diplomatic missions on 10/5 [May 10].

JJJ Actions Required from HQS.

I) Approval of revised budget for EM/140 including authorisation to proceed with signing letters of intent with implementing partners to enable initial advance instalments.

Page 7

II) Approval of staffing requirements and urgent deployment of permanent international staff.

III) Decision on formal establishment of field offices in Mombasa, Garissa and Marsabit.

KKK Acknowledgments.

BO appreciates despatching of physical planner at short notice. She is currently in Mombasa and will go to Marsabit on 9/5 [May 9].

(UNHCR Nairobi)

Drafted by: K. Zaman [with signature]
Date: 08/5/91 File:

Authorized by: S. Awuye [with signature]
Date: 08/5/91

archive by archiving a refugee camp, assembling diverse primary sources, one of which is the UNHCR communication whose first page opens this chapter and whose full contents are transcribed within these pages.

The image opening this chapter is a photograph of that document, a "sitrep" (military terminology for a "situation report"). This is the first page of Sitrep No. 7, a cable that the UNHCR branch office in Nairobi issued on May 8, 1991, to announce the arrival of tens of thousands of people in Somalia to its border with Kenya, a place described in the document as a "quote no mans land unquote." The document, eventually filed and held in the archives of the UNHCR Geneva headquarters, was declassified in 2011. In 1991, many offices used thermal printing processes in telecommunications, which meant that when a digital message arrived, a facsimile of an image or text was printed on a fine, coated paper as it spooled off a roll and passed over a heated printer head. This paper was impregnated with a mixture of dye and chemical matrix. As the paper heated to a temperature exceeding the melting point of the matrix, its coating turned to black, in the trace of the word or picture that had been digitally communicated to the printer head. This thermochromatic technology did not use ink, but the coating was vulnerable to a process of decomposing, as it almost has here, making the text illegible to the human eye. The central archives section of the UNHCR in Geneva often filed photocopies of such fax documents, early in their lives, destroying originals that had little material durability. It did not do so in this case. This page, printed in 1991 and photographed in 2011, represents a precise historical intersection, in which the humanitarian intervention at Dadaab, Kenya, and a prevalent communications technology that produced vulnerable artifacts came into confrontation with a UNHCR protocol: a twenty-year period of document classification. The intention behind classifying records for twenty years was to protect persons fleeing political persecution for a significant length of time, a period beyond which the imminent danger might not last; in practice, the duration spanned a person's life, covering the course of more than one generation.

This protective protocol, paradoxically, endangered the historical record. Of course, this instance of archival fragility may seem negligible in a struggle for survival, in war, or in comparison to other very real perils that render documents precarious in a refugee camp—from environmental degradation to the mortal risk that their custodians may face. The insecure archive is a minor concern among these urgencies. Yet, it effects erasures and occlusions with staggering ramifications for the otherwise profound endurance that histories and records provide. That an enduring architecture can result from emergency is alone a matter of historical record and critical heritage. The Dadaab settlements are of concern as a basis for people's histories or an architecture of the commons, in opposition to an architecture based in private property or land-based capital. Although over the years the site may have been visible and knowable to those living in the immediate vicinity or possessing a targeted interest, it has been obscured to those without specific points of access. Despite its astounding footprint, the site barely registered in conventional historical scholarship during the years of its radical transformation in scale, social complexity, and phenomenological affect—hardly a camp anymore, yet an urban form without legal incorporation, not a city and thus not documented as such. Therefore, the documents that do exist set into motion radical potentials. *If the Dadaab refugee complex were a town, its founding document would be Sitrep No. 7*. It is in this imaginary of an architecture of migration—a humanitarian settlement—that this chapter's stakes lie.

Those stakes demand framing a refugee camp as a site of critical heritage, finding its urgency not in the war around it but in its own architecture and history. Sitrep No. 7 is critical to this framing. When I first confronted this document in 2012, I read the words on its pages by holding them up to a desk lamp in the UNHCR archives, studying the impressions of the letters stamped on the page—silhouettes that may no longer be legible for others to cross-reference.[1] My findings included a surprising revelation in the final paragraph. "BO [branch office] appreciates dispatching of physical planner at short notice. She is currently in Mombasa and will go to Marsabit on 9/5 [May 9]." This all but lost document revealed that, as it happened, during the very first phases of this emergency, the expert the UNHCR deployed to the site was none other than an *architect*. The UNHCR's engagement of a professional in the position of physical planner whose training and concerns cast well beyond essential matters of food and water distribution, public health, and hygiene—beyond civil engineering—raised questions around architecture and the archive.[2] The presence of this figure argued for the radical prioritization of the architectural study of Dadaab, as a method for examining core aspects of Dadaab's fraught history and, indeed, its precarious archive. This epistemic reorientation situates the refugee camp as a critical heritage form in world history.

An architectural study of the humanitarian archive directly confronts contingency as an epistemic principle. A study of built environments and spatial practices illuminates modes of "seeing" and "drawing" the camp, enabling the interrogation of the putative precarity of primary research sources and the very notion of archival "lack." Approaching the growth, structuring, and morphology of the Dadaab refugee settlements with an architectural view contributes to a complex landscape of historical evidence, consisting of the work of institutionally trained architects and autodidactic designers and builders of the environment together.

Putting aside for a moment the work of these laborers responsible for the design and construction of the Dadaab refugee camps, it is worth speaking to the "official" archive of Dadaab, that is, the public record maintained by the agency responsible for the camps' administration. During the years when the settlement complex at Dadaab evolved to become the largest under the purview of the UNHCR, it was not possible to cross-reference the physical evolution of the site with the activity of refugee protection and population management documented by the agency. The year 2012 altered that evidentiary conundrum. Following institutional protocols to grant public access to sensitive materials only after twenty years had passed since the initiation of humanitarian operations, the UNHCR declassified documents from 1991 in the year 2012.[3] The dates 1991–2011 thus bracket a period within the UNHCR documentary record in which the history of Dadaab that could be recuperated depended on examining materials that had not been classified. These materials included technical reports. Some were written by architects. Reports on the site selection and spatial and material aspects of planning and design richly and affectively described the camps. That they did not demand classification is ironic, as these documents demonstrating great sensitivity, in one sense, were, in another, not deemed sensitive. The UNHCR papers were of course not the only documentary record, nor the only archive, and I eventually gathered and compiled a database including interviews with refugees and architects, gray literature by NGOs, journalistic and photographic records, academic white papers and other reports, video and audio by refugees and aid workers, and myriad other materials that I have named "the migrant archive."[4] In addition, reading the architecture and design of the camps produced its own form of knowledge. This is to say, I assembled primary sources on the humanitarian intervention, studied the camp architecture, and notated my observations on the ground and in the writing of others. Given this strategic possibility, the limitations of the "official" archive then beg other questions.

This crisis in the official record isolates a moment when the powers of humanitarian epistemology wane. If the classification practices of one influential agency—the UNHCR—circumscribed the "disappearance" of a documentary archive from public records for twenty years, such a resource must be recognized as already invisible to many, accessible only to researchers privileged with sociospatial mobility and other rights of access. Indeed, this acknowledgment of gaps in the archive illuminates the contrivance, even the impossibility, of the universal analytical frameworks that institutional and nation-state histories purport to tender. In response to such defects of universalism in what are ultimately colonial practices in postcolonial contexts, I have adopted the model of the situated and embodied narrative promoted by thinkers such as bell hooks, Maria Puig de la Bellacasa, and Donna Haraway, whose differing but explicitly ethical practices demand a "ground view."[5] I foreground a multiplicity of characters and perspectives and refuse to understand any context or institution as monolithic. Refugees and aid workers designed and constructed Dadaab. My historiographical labor consists of finding them as figures on the ground and in archives. I approach the archival landscape of Dadaab through a "resistance from within," which architectural historian and theorist Isabelle Doucet imagines as an approach rooted in *practice*—not merely rehearsing critical theoretical oppositions or presenting value-neutral landscapes, but finding transformative effects within the wide "tangle of actors, including not just users, designers, builders, and decision-makers but also materials, ideologies, construction techniques, aesthetics, activism, technology, and so on."[6] In thinking with such a plentiful epistemic landscape, my aim differs slightly in that I seek to write an emergency environment into coherent narratives, while retaining respect for the fragmentary character of situated and embodied knowledge. I use the migrant archive that I have painstakingly gathered to explicitly reverse humanitarian epistemology, writing from the generative position of the incompleteness of all archives, rather than lamenting or critiquing the fugitive or broken archive. I insist on writing in a conventional historical format, placing the subject within the threads of history rather than outside of history—rejecting the consignment of a refugee camp to abjection. To effect this reversal of terms, I co-opt common historiographical conventions in this chapter, including the linear arrangement and periodization of diachronic events, comparative analysis of synchronous events, overviews of the physical and social development of a site, collection of visual images from authorities and unofficial sources, and, not least, the organization of a narrative thrust. This approach borrows a strategy from architectural historian Suzanne Blier's exegesis of Battammaliba architecture—while not honing in on an "anatomy" of architecture as hers does, the analysis here offers an anatomy of a history, and, more conceptually, of humanitarian settlement as a process.[7] The narrative itself reproduces an archive of humanitarian settlement—for example, in the full transcript of Sitrep No. 7 earlier in this chapter and the photo essay of Ifo's food distribution system at the end.[8] This is speculative work, performing a critical act of solidarity with those for whom Dadaab is a place of heritage.

This categorically provisional history of Dadaab aims to expose the fissures in conventional institutional histories predicated on claims to fixity. It throws into relief the reality that refugees confined in these settlements have made the architecture of their lives by marking time and creating spatial and historical perspectives that do not follow the "universal" terms generated by "productive" activity, signaled by things that life in the Dadaab refugee camps does not provide—for example, universal institutional systems of education, wage and market economies formalized by nation-states, broadly accepted cultural preservation initiatives, political independence, and open migration. With this foundation, I aim to respectfully and generatively think openly with the Dadaab refugee camps and to institute a critical archiving and heritage practice intended for the commons.

1991–1993: Establishment of Emergency Territory

GENERAL SITUATION:

Reverses in civil war in south of Somalia (Fall of Kismayu to USC [United Somali Congress]) resulting in new influx of reportedly tens of thousands to SOM-KEN [Somalia-Kenya] border. GOK [Government of Kenya] has not yet advised HCR [UNHCR] if refugees in quote no mans land unquote will be granted asylum in Kenya and if UNHCR will be requested to provide assistance. Some one thousand refugees have reached Liboi and GOK has agreed to their registration. BO [branch office] arranging provide food and shelter. Joint HCR/GOK/NGO assessment mission left for Liboi area (Garissa District) on 7/5 [May 7] morning and scheduled return Nairobi 9/5 [May 9] evening. Meanwhile BO has decided to stockpile at Garissa shelter materials, food and medicine for an initial 10,000 additional caseload and depending on further developments, for a further 10,000 at later date.
—Sitrep No. 7, cable issued by UNHCR Nairobi, May 8, 1991

Physical planning in emergency is an incipient practice of humanitarian settlement. The employment or contracting of professional architects by the UNHCR in 1991 and 1992 set into motion short- and long-term aesthetic practices as a function of humanitarian response. The construction of camps at Dadaab, unfolding from the events described in Sitrep No. 7 that catalyzed the UNHCR intervention, established an emergency territory that culminated in refugee encampment in Kenya, laying the ground for humanitarian settlement in Dadaab.

Long before refugee camps were established in Kenya, the UNHCR and international NGO emergency response mechanism was triggered. Prior to these events, the Kenyan government's policy toward registered refugees did not restrict people to encampments. The international response to war in Somalia and longer historical forces discussed in previous chapters brought about this restrictive measure.

After independence in 1963, Kenya became a party to the primary international instruments relating to refugees, as mentioned in the introduction: those of the UNHCR and the OAU. The first, the 1951 UN Convention Relating to the Status of Refugees, with the 1967 Protocol, which followed the mass displacements, expulsions, and exiles taking place before and during World War II, defined the refugee as a person fleeing outside the country of citizenship due to a "well-founded fear of being persecuted." The second, the 1969 OAU Convention Governing the Specific Aspects of Refugee Problems in Africa, defined the refugee as the UN did, with additional language concerning persons compelled to flee a country of origin due to "external aggression, occupation, foreign domination or events seriously disturbing public order," broadening the grounds for seeking refugee status beyond armed conflict, for example, to environmental or food insecurity.[9] I heard two common perspectives on these legal instruments in Africa and elsewhere from people working in the humanitarian system, articulated by directors at the WRC and the MSF research unit, CRASH. First, during the early years of independence in Africa, refugees were viewed sympathetically as "freedom fighters" and leaders in pan-African anticolonial struggles.[10] Second, during the concurrent Cold War, refugee policy reflected an international rhetoric of solidarity, as asylum seekers were positively perceived within capitalist regimes as "voting with their feet" against communism.[11] Over time, public and political sentiment shifted from these perspectives. Groups of people arriving at borders began to be described by governments as "influxes" (as in the excerpt of Sitrep No. 7 presented earlier), denoting mass displacements of people in languages of border fragility rather than political solidarity. This shift was entrenched with the fall of the Soviet state and associated realignments, along with the rise of the security state, accompanying an absence of expected international burden-sharing in human rights protection. The international response to multiple emergencies, discussed by anthropologists Didier Fassin and Mariella Pandolfi and sociologist Craig Calhoun as "cycles," were tied to the rhythms of financial flows of relief aid.[12] The "fatigue" experienced by aid donor nations and publics in response to this cyclical process delinked understandings of the concept of "emergency" from the breakdown of governmental structures to which it referred and associated it more strongly with nongovernmental activities of humanitarian relief. The emergency in Somalia in 1991 has been understood as a watershed in this global shift in understanding.[13] Nevertheless, events in Somalia unfolded in concert with other factors that led to the construction of settlements at Dadaab.

Transitional settlements for refugees were established after the breakdown in governmental structures in Somalia caused enormous displacements: an estimated 1.7 million people, or a third of the population in the southern region, were internally displaced before they crossed the international border into Kenya. The effects of the civil war were compounded by food insecurity in rural areas in different regions, with drought and famine pushing a quarter of a million people into emergency relief camps in Mogadishu.[14] Four hundred thousand people from Somalia arrived in Kenya, those with resources settling in Nairobi or sailing to Mombasa from southern seaports such as Kismayo, in order to shelter with relatives or contacts while waiting out the war.[15] During the same year that these events occurred, several young Sudanese men—known commonly as "the lost boys"—entered Kenya on foot from camps in Ethiopia, arriving in the Turkana region in the Northwest. The government of Kenya sought assistance from the UNHCR in registering these many refugees and began designating land for refugee encampments.[16] Refugee camps served as an efficient point for the distribution of material aid and social services. Large settlements, moreover, attracted financial assistance as they could be comprehended spatially and imaged visually in the request for relief donations.

In May 1991, the UNHCR dispatched to Mombasa an architect, Sabine Wähning, referred to at the end of Sitrep No. 7, to begin the process of planning transitional settlements in several regions.[17] She worked with the senior physical planner in Geneva, Wolfgang Neumann, in a unit created to build technical support for UNHCR programs in fields such as education, health, and physical planning (discussed in chapter 3).[18] She was a member of a ground team that overlapped with and immediately succeeded the emergency coordination unit led by Maureen Connelly (discussed in chapter 5). Wähning was dispatched to Kenya as part of a "mission"—a military term, perhaps not to be divorced from its Christian connotations, used by international humanitarian organizations to describe short field visits made by headquarters staff. Wähning joined a water development expert and a public health officer to

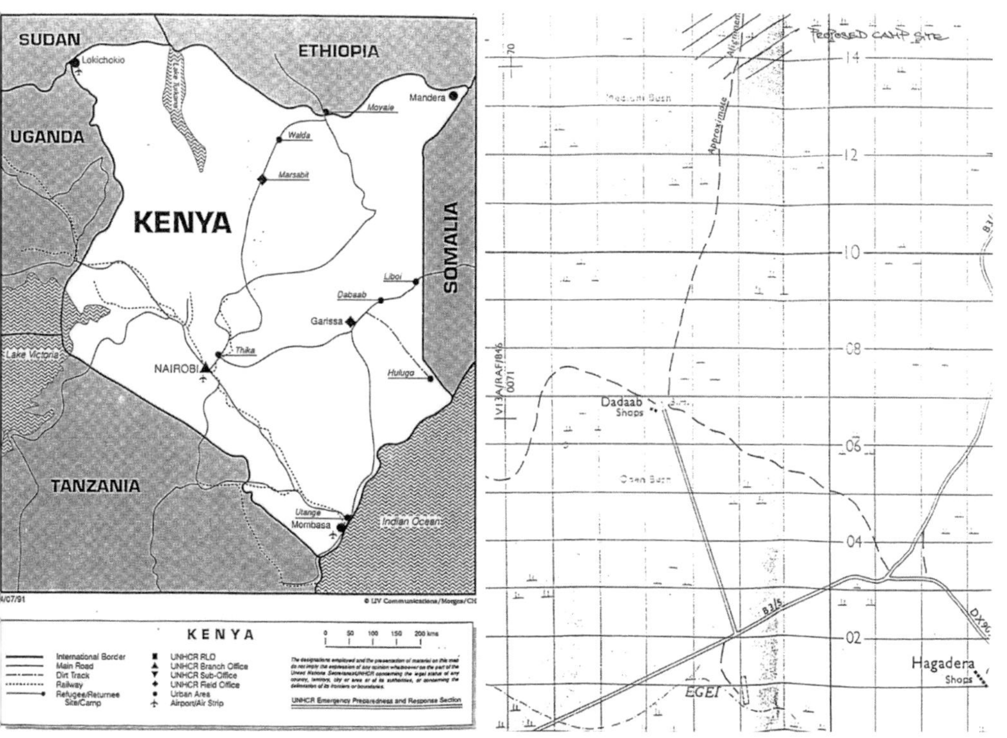

4.1 and 4.2. The UNHCR spatial archive of the Dadaab refugee camps originated with maps proposing a location for Ifo camp in 1991, from Dualeh, UNHCR Programme and Technical Support Section Mission Report 91/14.

undertake site selection and planning for facilities around the country to accommodate the nearly fifty thousand refugees who had registered in Kenya since the end of 1990.

The first sites planned by the UNHCR included a refugee reception center and ad hoc settlement in the North Eastern Province near the border village of Liboi. The mission report noted their limited or poor quality water supply, sanitary facilities, and shelter, along with the concern that "the staff presently prefers to sleep in the open."[19] To respond to these conditions and mitigate instabilities that would be exacerbated by leaving the refugees in proximity to the conflict they fled, the government of Kenya resettled them to a location 680 kilometers from the border, a "reasonable distance from the frontier of their country of origin," following a provision articulated by the OAU to uphold the integrity of border regions in countries of asylum.[20] The new settlement, called Ifo, was 6 kilometers north of Dadaab, a village between Liboi to the east and the provincial capital Garissa to the west, on the unpaved highway that connected Nairobi with Mogadishu.[21] Dadaab was a pastoralist village of five thousand inhabitants, not yet electrified when the UNHCR established its field office.[22] Refugees and humanitarians erected tuquls in which to live and work during the first weeks, as mentioned in chapter 2.[23] One might imagine that aid workers learned a great deal from the people they served in those first weeks, while sleeping "in the open" in country sensationalized by stories of shifta, discussed in chapter 2, as well as the hyenas and marabou storks that continue to loom around the camps.

The state did not make public its criteria for selecting this particular site. While locating the refugees in a long-contested territory—a constructed *emergency territory*, as I have argued in chapter 2—enabled certain authoritarian measures to be taken, such siting was not unusual, as states providing asylum in response to neighboring conflict often located refugee camps in border areas. Resident host community members and aid workers suggested that Garissa's local and regional politics played a part in the decision, as the international presence brought with it economic growth, including lucrative construction contracts.[24] By the early 1990s, international humanitarian aid proliferated, lessening the impetus and incentive for a country to integrate refugees into its economy or social structure.[25] A settlement strategy was decided on for Dadaab.

The planning process from the outset indicated that the settlements would be anything but temporary, incorporating principles of modularity and scalability that facilitated expansion and social control, and activating a global machinery of design and construction. In June 1991, in its infrastructure and shelter recommendations, the UNHCR articulated uncertainty around the long-term political situation in Somalia. The UNHCR technical mission for site selection and planning recommended drilling operations for four new wells around an existing borehole, to accommodate a large population in Ifo camp to the south.[26] The mission proposed a modular shelter design, able to adjust for possible increases in population while also offering a means to adapt the spatial configurations of settlements to separate conflicting communities as necessary.[27] This measure of social control followed instances of extreme tension recorded from the first months of emergency in 1991, with acts of violence committed between different communities of refugees and against refugees by authorities or host community members. In May 1991, the moment described in Sitrep No. 7, the UNHCR articulated concerns around a "manner of transfer [that] was very controversial" and a "number of incidents of high-handedness by certain police officials."[28] The planning of the camps enabled discipline and control of people, including the very people to be served by this architecture.[29] The alacrity of the design and construction, while based on lifesaving need, drew on the resources and privileged the priorities of the international system so exclusively that it eclipsed local concerns. The site selection and planning mission urged that "some of the basic construction activities be undertaken before the onset of the next rainy season, which is expected by late September," and recommended the immediate contracting of local firms for technical services, including geophysical and topographical survey, planning, architecture, and construction.[30] Although this recommendation was not implemented, construction began in October 1991, at which time the UNHCR decommissioned three refugee camps in Kenya and moved 4,585 Somali and Ethiopian refugees to Ifo camp.[31] They settled the area west of the highway that connected the district capital, Wajir, to the north and the town of Dadaab to the south, clustering in three types of dwellings: standard-issue canvas tents fabricated in Pakistan and sourced from UNHCR stockpiles, A-frame timber shelters covered with plastic sheeting, and tuquls crafted from green wood and repurposed textiles.[32] Meanwhile, the UNHCR contracted the Nairobi firm International Technical Advisers, Ltd., to plan and build a settlement for thirty thousand people east of the same road. By then, a camp manager and nutritionist had been deployed to the site, several international organizations were distributing food and providing medical services, a school had been instituted with approximately one hundred pupils attending, a site had been selected for afforestation, four borewells had been drilled, one elevated water tank had been erected, and a police force had been established.[33] By summer 1992, the UNHCR contracted a local safari company to conduct topographic surveys of the area, and the Nairobi-based Swedish firm Skanska began earthworks and general contracting.[34] The UNHCR also contracted two consultants to plan additional settlements. Werner Schellenberg, a German architect, planned the Dagahaley settlement north of Ifo, and Per Iwansson, a Swedish architect, planned the Hagadera settlement around a small body of water south of the town of Dadaab.[35] The robust international presence, the rapid facilitation of the encampment policy, the urgent implementation of physical planning contracts and dispatch of technical support from UNHCR headquarters—all discussed in multiple reports—amount to a great deal of evidence suggesting that the UNHCR, and, by extension, the governments it coalesced, prioritized building for longevity at Dadaab while in the throes of emergency response.

The curious entanglement of aesthetics and politics in the humanitarian archive adds a layer to this history. While UNHCR field operations have often followed military models and, at Dadaab, have been led by former officers (as

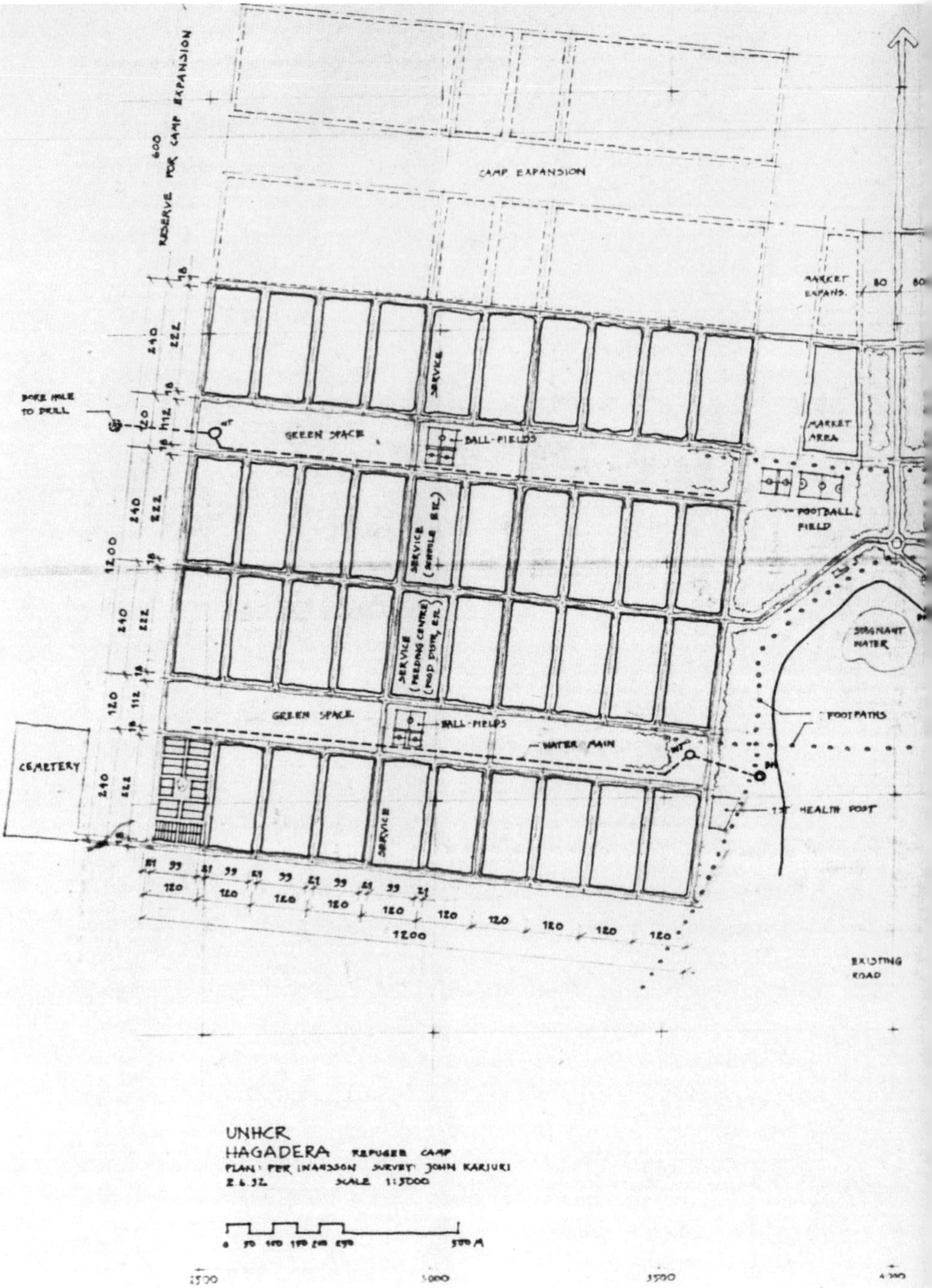

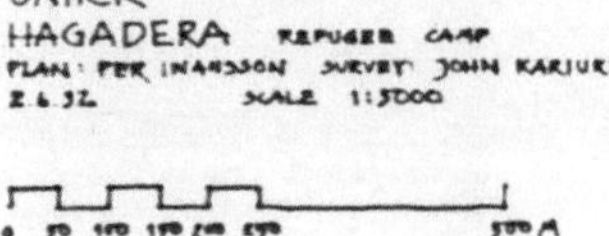
UNHCR
HAGADERA REFUGEE CAMP
PLAN: PER IVARSSON SURVEY: JOHN KARIUKI
2.6.92 SCALE 1:5000
0 50 100 150 200 250 500 M
RESERVE FOR CAMP EXPANSION
CAMP EXPANSION
MARKET EXPANS.
BORE HOLE TO DRILL
GREEN SPACE
SERVICE
BALL-FIELDS
MARKET AREA
FOOTBALL FIELD
SERVICE (MOBILE ETC.)
SERVICE (FEEDING CENTRE) (FOOD DISTR. ETC.)
STAGNANT WATER
FOOTPATHS
WATER MAIN
CEMETERY
1ST HEALTH POST
EXISTING ROAD
2500
3000
3500

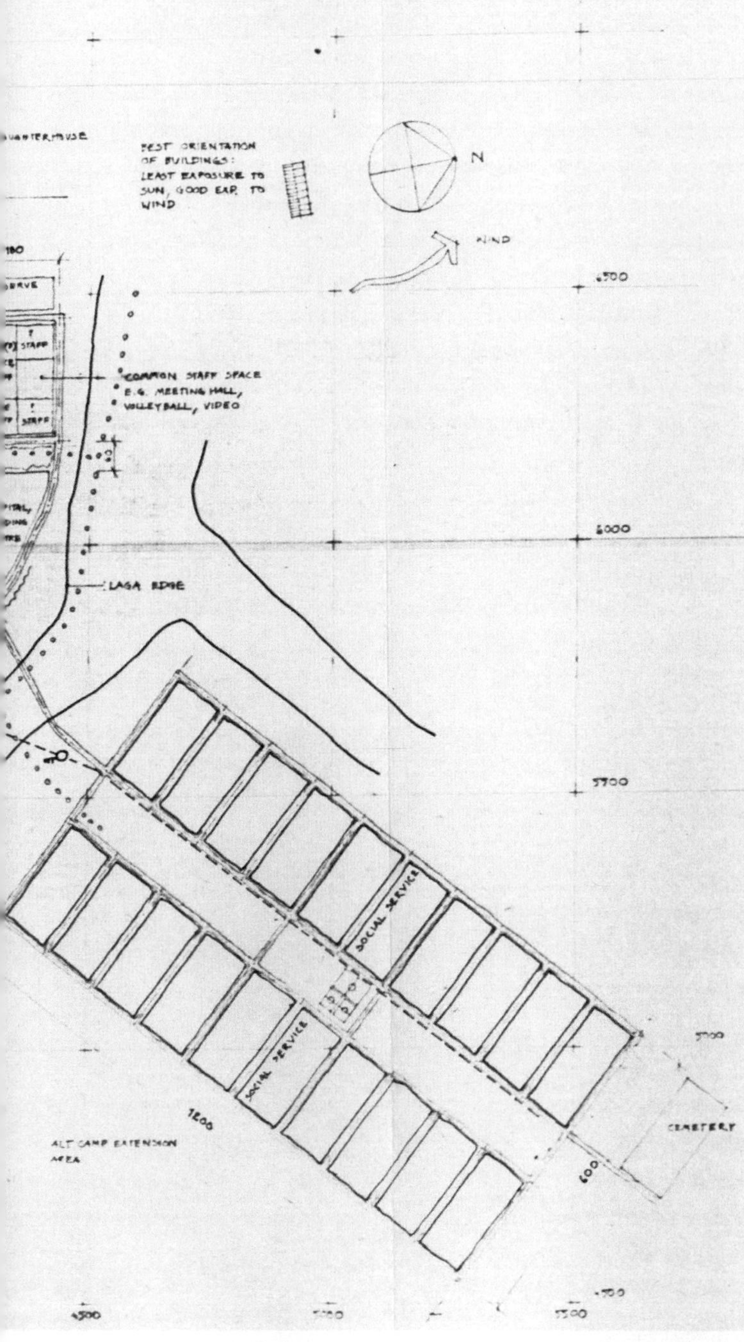

4.3. Per Iwansson, plan of Hagadera camp, 1992, from Iwansson, UNHCR Programme and Technical Support Section Mission Report 92/44.

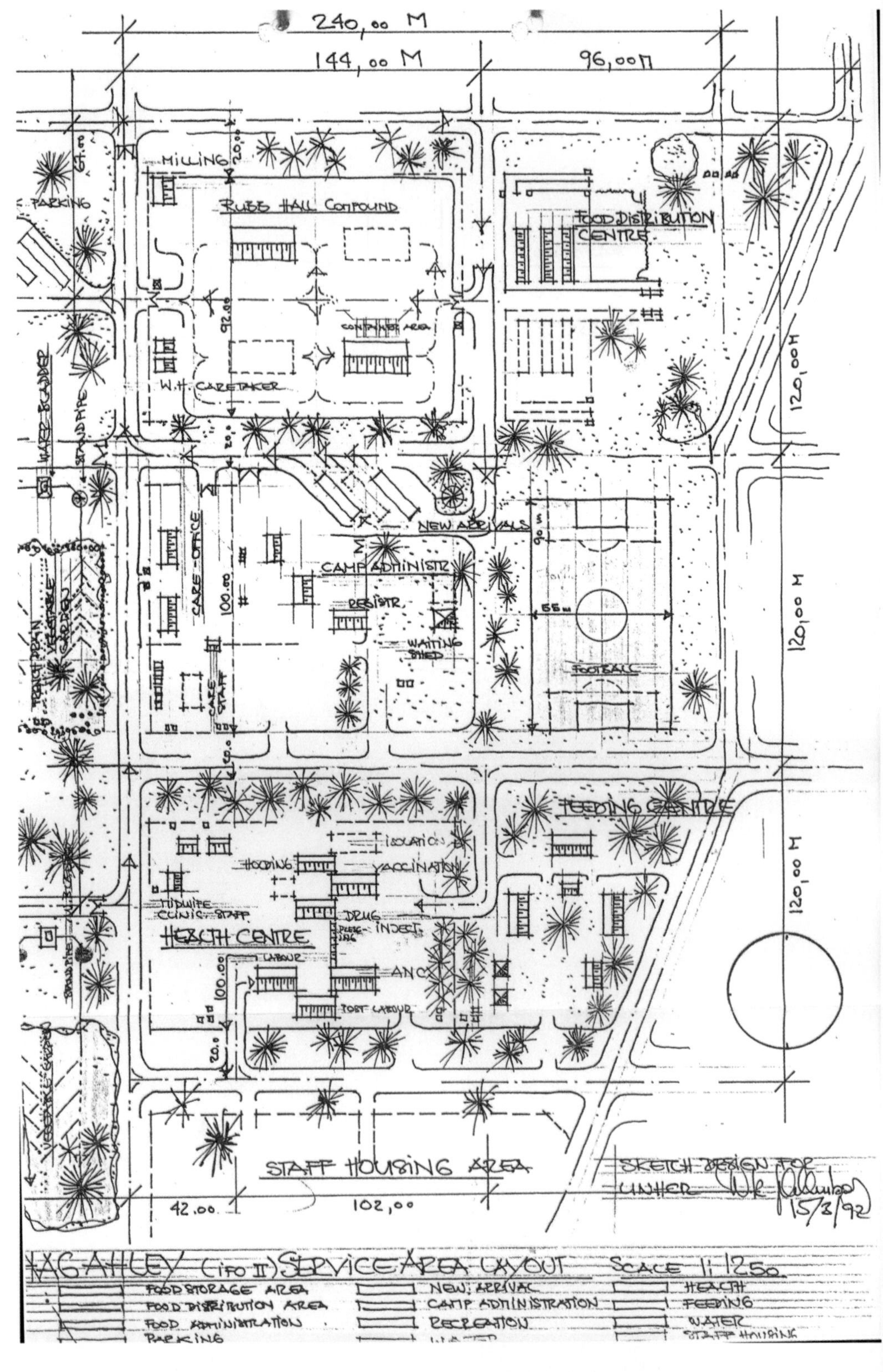

240,00 M
144,00 M
96,00 M
MILLING
PARKING
RUBB HALL COMPOUND
FOOD DISTRIBUTION CENTRE
CONTAINER AREA
W.H. CARETAKER
STANDPIPE
CARE OFFICE
NEW ARRIVALS
CAMP ADMINISTR
REGISTR.
WAITING SHED
90 m
55 m
FOOTBALL
120,00 M
120,00 M
120,00 M
FEEDING CENTRE
ISOLATION
VACCINATION
HOLDING
MIDWIFE CLINIC STAFF
DRUG INJECT.
HEALTH CENTRE
LABOUR
ANC
POST LABOUR
STAFF HOUSING AREA
SKETCH DESIGN FOR UNHCR
15/3/92
42.00
102,00
SERVICE AREA LAYOUT
SCALE 1:1250
FOOD STORAGE AREA
FOOD DISTRIBUTION AREA
FOOD ADMINISTRATION
PARKING
NEW ARRIVAL
CAMP ADMINISTRATION
RECREATION
HEALTH
FEEDING
WATER
STAFF HOUSING

discussed in chapter 1), the mechanical drawings of architects rather than engineers emerge as the notable documents in UNHCR archives. Drawings by four architects show the attentive linework taught in academies and polytechnic schools of architecture, demonstrating training in draftsmanship, design for minimal dwellings, and town planning following modernist models for standardization and flexibility implemented in European and African cities (notably, Nairobi). Neumann developed standardized services and details, including a water tap stand detail for all UNHCR sites. Wähning designed an ideal residential planning module, with a standard minimum area allotment for sixty persons, clustering twelve households per block to support communal activities. Iwansson defined a sector module in the plan for Hagadera, establishing a grid using the recommended water-ration supply-line length, subdivided to take advantage of high ground and slopes for runoff and laid out radially around central food distribution and market areas; the camp was populated by a kit of parts including Oxfam's prefabricated water tanks (discussed in chapter 5). Schellenberg laid out Dagahaley's spaces for food distribution, health services, education, and recreation.

What to make of community planning and design detailing in the bush? How to interpret an emergency relief operation by international actors creating a parallel system in a country? These events demonstrated the expectation for settlement growth and longevity, reflecting a decision made to destroy and reshape the environment and erect permanent infrastructure, rather than reuse existing architecture, despite an encampment policy predicated on a *temporary* refugee presence. Spatial planning at the scale of towns, intended to facilitate rapid aid distribution, bears evidence of a technology and industry that, by 1991, had incorporated a diverse array of disciplines in locations that were neither "remote" nor lacking resources. The UNHCR ideal planning module and plans for Dagahaley and Hagadera show settlements designed for urban sociability, even though in 1992 there should have been little expectation that three generations of refugees would spend their lives in them. While humanitarian spatiality at Dadaab has prolonged the existence of a political space evacuated of civic belonging, producing permanent ephemerality, more momentous than the political crisis is the array of aesthetic workings that brought this form of settlement into being in the

4.4. (*opposite*) Werner Schellenberg, plan of Dagahaley camp, 1992, from Iwansson, UNHCR Programme and Technical Support Section Mission Report 92/44.

first place. To see evidence of architects at all during urgent phases of relief demonstrates the normalization of war and a broader cultural response to it.

1993–2006: Permanent Ephemerality

> With the current situation in Somalia changing from day to day, it is difficult to predict what will happen to the refugee camps, or when the refugees can return home. Adjacent to those areas of Somalia where it is safe to return, some camps have already closed, and refugees have returned. For those areas of Somalia where security is still uncertain, the camps across the border in Kenya remain. CARE is committed to remaining in the camps until their closure. It has retooled its programme to begin assisting refugees in preparing for their eventual return. It will continue its flexible approach to programming in response to the changing needs of the refugee community. CARE-Kenya's wish is that the refugees eventually return to their country, and return with a sense that they have been well served in their time of need in Kenya, and have been well prepared to face the realities of the New Somalia.
> —Redding et al., *Refugee Assistance Project of* CARE*-Kenya*, 1994

> We are attempting development approaches mid way through a programme that has been profoundly non developmental. Social Services has been treated much like food and logistics. Logistics even permeated the way we did things. We built the schools. We assumed what type of education was required. We built community centres and ran around like headless chickens trying to force people to use them. They were used. Their use coincided precisely and uniquely with the arrival of senior staff from Nairobi. The tone of CARE's operations was one of food. We gave and they took. We didn't like them, the refugees, very much. We believed they had to be controlled, made to understand. They were not to be consulted lest they took advantage of the situation. The context was one of mutual dislike and suspicion. No one thought about this because it was an emergency situation.
> —CARE internal memo on camp management, October 29, 1993

To further examine humanitarian settlement, this section illuminates tensions between emergency and development, demonstrating how each thrust reinforced the other, entrenching encampment in Dadaab between 1993 and 2006. These excerpts from two documents illustrate these tensions. One public and one internal, each was issued by the Kenya office of CARE, the international development organization contracted by the UNHCR, as mentioned in previous chapters, which provided aid to refugees and primary management of the camps for the first fifteen years of official refugee hosting at Dadaab. Over the thirteen years that followed the circulation of the documents excerpted above, CARE remained responsible for social services and camp management at the Ifo, Dagahaley, and Hagadera settlements. During these years, as the settlements grew and "camp management" solidified as a sector of global professional humanitarian work, the management of the refugee camps evolved as a form of governance. The transformation of the settlements into an enduring architecture accompanied a remarkable process of imaging—an act of surveillance resulting in an inadvertent and prolific visual archive for a refugee camp. From 1993 to 2006, a period in Dadaab during which operations could no longer be described only in terms of emergency, the settlement process shifted from a transitional to a protracted condition.

Humanitarian agencies and NGOs effected the permanent ephemerality of the settlements through development techniques rooted in architecture, planning, and design, and also based in practices of enumeration—for example, recording population growth in the camps, from 90,000 in 1992 to, twenty years later, more than 300,000 registered refugees and approximately 500,000 people total. The aggregation of numbers in the humanitarian record is a red flag. Such numbers provide clues about the construction of camps, as population management metrics translate into justifications for funding. Humanitarian data provides not only the empirical evidence justifying relief activity, but also the rhetorical stagecraft behind planning and settlement.[36] Spatial practices based in development—the methods preferred by CARE—privileged quantitative data.

During this period of growth, CARE managed the Dadaab camps, first from its Kenya offices and later from its headquarters in Canada, overseeing unprecedented operations, both in terms of the scale of a single site and its management by a single NGO. To address the logistical and administrative challenges posed by the arrangement, the UNHCR eventually divided the responsibility of the overall management of the Dadaab camps and provision of aid and services among twenty agencies and organizations.[37] In 2006, the UNHCR directly contracted the majority of organizations working in Dadaab as "implementing partners." Other "operating partners," working independently in parallel and coordinating with but not reporting to the UNHCR, included grassroots and mutual aid groups and MSF.[38] CARE-Kenya's records show a significant expansion of prior operations, which had been dispersed around the country, from mid-July 1991, when the organization was contracted by the UNHCR to manage emergency assistance for refugees in Garissa District, to the middle of the next year. The organization provided food at the two border stations established by the UNHCR to receive refugees from Somalia, accommodating approximately 21,000 people in the middle of 1991 and, by late 1992, more than 400,000 people from Somalia, Ethiopia, and Sudan in eighteen camps across Kenya.[39] CARE-Kenya eventually provided food at fourteen sites, as well as social services, education, and water and sanitation at seven of them.[40] The number of refugees in Kenya dropped in 1993, after the deployment of the UN Operation in Somalia (UNOSOM), one of a series of militarized interventions in the 1990s under the framework of humanitarian peacekeeping.[41] By 1994, CARE-Kenya's Refugee Assistance Project recorded 200,000 cases.[42] These numbers account only for those who registered with authorities in Kenya, not an overall count of people displaced in the region by ongoing conflict and international intervention. Such enumerations in the humanitarian record give the first hint of a spatial logics predicated on *development* and not only *relief*: the first steps in humanitarian settlement.

Tensions between emergency relief and development operations took hold in the earliest phases of humanitarian intervention in Dadaab, which reveal the process of making a camp from the perspective of the camp managers, different from the view of a single shelter's construction as discussed in chapter 3 or the materiality of dwellings discussed in chapter 2. These varied works show how the Dadaab refugee camps evolved both within institutional planning practices and also as institutionally resistant forms of making, processes unfolding amid unpredictability of conflicts in neighboring countries and an understanding that refugees might be repatriated at any time. A devastating drought in 1992 and 1993 fueled regional food and water insecurity, compounding the civil emergencies and precipitating displacements above those the civil war had caused in 1991, and catalyzing and consolidating efforts to obtain funding for drought relief and recovery, refugee aid and repatriation, and cross-border operations—amounting to $156.6 million raised for Kenyan humanitarian operations in 1992.[43] Ultimately, these complex, inconsistent conditions made the argument for development approaches, to produce an infrastructure parallel to that of the state.[44] The pivot toward "development" in Dadaab also stemmed from the UNHCR's eventual ambivalence about designating it an "emergency" site. After 1992, the UNHCR left unoccupied the crucial position of emergency coordinator (previously held by Maureen Connelly, discussed in chapter 5, whose storied work in Tanzania in 1994 to respond to the Rwandan emergency built on the spatial practices she developed during two prior missions to Dadaab in 1992).[45] On October 15, 1992, Jeff Drumtra of the United States Committee for Refugees noted "complaints that Geneva has not yet seen this as an emergency for the fast track," demonstrated by the UNHCR having filled only ten of its fifteen positions, unlike other fully staffed agencies and organizations such as UNICEF, MSF, and CARE.[46] CARE program managers cited unreasonable expectations from donors, particularly its largest, the UNHCR. An internal memo among camp managers argued that "they seek to judge us by development standards and criticise us when we don't meet them," while also being "anxious that nothing we do should encourage the refugees to stay."[47] Following criticisms from their senior staff, CARE program managers identified an exclusive focus on "physical" results: "How many trees, how many girls in school, how many beans."[48] These reflections demonstrated a shift from emergency aid practice to an emphasis on development achievement metrics, which the program managers saw as the UNHCR's default orientation. This turn from fostering a strong climate of relief to introducing development measures was reinforced in the establishment and institutionalization of the physical environment. The making of the camp grew out of the need to demonstrate architectural results.

The making of the camp architecture resulted from a divided spatial approach. As indicated in the internal memo excerpted at the beginning of this section, camp managers named myriad problems resulting from instituting development models of care for refugees while still implementing strategies of emergency response. They noted that this divided approach disabled CARE from being able to sufficiently staff programs and properly train its teams, raising the expectations of aid recipients beyond the organization's capacity to deliver on promises and thus weakening efforts by CARE to build relationships with the communities it served. The camp managers offered a number of criticisms, illustrating these problems as well as their subjectivities within them. They criticized the ways their working methods exacerbated social disparities between those distributing aid and those receiving it (however little acknowledging the political status and legal rights conditioning the relationship between the two). They lodged complaints about the consistent waste of resources, assessing as a problem that refugees trained by the organization would attempt to leave as soon as they gained skills. They criticized the immobilization of people, naming the futility of promoting income generation programs within a population whose only market economy stemmed from aid commodities and where even "the most basic infrastructure . . . is likely to be a target for theft."[49] These complaints regularly took shape against a backdrop of contradictions posed by the UNHCR and other donors. "We are criticised for not producing enough mats to sell, yet we must not allow refugees to become in any way financially independent lest that encourages them to stay in the camp."[50] The paradoxical tensions articulated by the camp managers stemmed from practical matters. On the one hand, groups of refugees entered the country over the course of three decades as part of mass displacements, which occurred such that one neighborhood or another in the camps had to suddenly accommodate new refugees, reproducing a state of emergency continuously over time, which demanded infrastructural and architectural development. On the other hand, because donations tied to humanitarian relief became more readily available than structural aid for development, the camp managers often had to articulate goals and budgets reacting to shorter humanitarian funding cycles. Moreover, forms of professionalization of the field of humanitarian aid within a neoliberal economy, in which global budgets for relief aid increased radically and suddenly, produced a system with many more donors, both private and public, who expected material outcomes as part of the performance of this relief aid; this process further introduced the conflicting missions of physical planning and architectural development into the context of settlements originally established as a temporary means to mitigate emergencies. These persistences of the emergency relief effort along with forces of material development ultimately supported the architectural entrenchment of the Dadaab refugee camps. Thinking with Rafico Ruiz, I understand such architectural and material entrenchment effecting a "disturbance" of the landscape, through slow and persistent concretizations of colonizing infrastructures: a veritable medium of infrastructure (of various kinds—religious, medical, governmental, architectural) inscribing the colonial into the ground.[51] In Dadaab, refugees and humanitarians reproducing emergency alongside development have effected a similar architectural disturbance of the land. The entanglement of these contradictory approaches and their material entrenchment reveal a hidden process of humanitarian settlement.

The transformation of emergency contexts using development methods amounted to a spatial practice that established in Dadaab an enduring architecture. As the following sections examine, this architecture fixed asymmetries in space through encampment and also fixed encampment in time by bringing forth multiple architectures and material cultural elements and enabling a range of practices of seeing and surveilling Dadaab. These have, in turn, produced a material and visual record of the camps. The following analysis of humanitarian artifacts records the durability of the relief-to-development exercise as a practice of fixing an architecture of migration in space and time.

ENCAMPMENT: FIXING ASYMMETRY IN SPACE

The architecture of the Dadaab refugee camps was shaped through a localized imposition of difference. In the early 1990s, when several refugee hosting sites around the country were decommissioned, anyone not repatriated to home countries was resettled within encampments at Kakuma, on the border of Sudan and Ethiopia, and Dadaab.[52] In Dadaab, the CARE camp managers described the implementation of a tight geography of extreme social, political, and cultural heterogeneity. They called it "artificial," a space that grouped "nomads, pastoralists, [and] sophisticated urbanites together," where those "who control the camp may place little importance on traditional divisions within the family and between tribes, clans and sub clans."[53] As refugee hosting sites were decommissioned across Kenya, the continued resettlement of people in Dadaab further aggravated localized asymmetries and conflicts in the camps.

These sociospatial tensions stemmed from the historical complexities argued in the previous chapters as well as the immediate context of displacements from Somalia and the arbitrariness of policies of protection and control. The conflicts caused by the presence of encampments in Kenya's Coast Province provide context for the will to concentrate and confine people. People fleeing Somalia began arriving to the Coast Province by boat, attempting to disembark in Mombasa in January 1991. Many were Bajuni community members who lived in fishing villages on the coral islands and the facing mainland agricultural settlements stretching north to south from Kismayo in Somalia to Pate Island in Kenya, and whose presence for centuries left its mark in hand-carved wooden doors in Lamu and elsewhere, contributing to the famed architectural heritage of the Swahili coast.[54] Pushed violently out of these homelands in 1991 after the overthrow of President Mohamed Siad Barre on the mainland, many fled in sea vessels inhabited sometimes by 850 people, which docked or ran aground in Mombasa. Many passengers died in these crowded conditions, initially denied permission to disembark, spurring the UNHCR to negotiate with Kenyan authorities to open the border at Mombasa.[55] The government agreed in July 1992, opening the Jomo Kenyatta showgrounds in Mombasa to 10,000 refugees, "without any proper amenities," according to UNHCR protection officer S. Kimbimbi, establishing "Mogadishu camp," a fifteen-acre site in Utange intended for 8,000 refugees, in spite of offering only one hundred and fifty-nine shelters, with one out of three public tap stands in working order.[56] Legal scholar Giulielmo Verdirame argues that the location of these transitional settlements allowed many refugees to benefit from urban trade that, by UNHCR regulation, "was not subject to taxation," and to establish businesses that "were highly visible in the main market in Mombasa."[57] Resentful Kenyan business owners lobbied the government to close the camps and relocate the refugees.[58] In 1994, President Daniel Arap Moi ordered 100,000 refugees hosted in the Coast Province to leave. In December 1998, as refugees left Jomvu camp, the last to be decommissioned, they were given the choice to repatriate to Somalia with a thirty-dollar remittance or move to Dadaab or Kakuma, then the only remaining options for refugees in Kenya. Convoys organized by the UNHCR transported some to Kakuma, but many, particularly Bajuni, chose to return to their homes in Kismayo. Conditions in Somalia later became so unsafe for them that many returned to the border of Kenya's North Eastern Province as refugees and ultimately found their way to Dadaab.[59] Such experiences of double and triple displacement were not uncommon. Many people moved to Dadaab carrying with them such layers of recent conflict, rooted in irresolvabilities of social difference.

Those forms of social difference inscribed themselves in the architecture of Dadaab for fifteen years after its establishment, a period of contrasting thrusts of emergency and development, as several social and political groups demarcated living and cultural spaces in the camps. Sometimes the humanitarian layout drove this territorial delimitation, as Ifo camp's morphology demonstrates, with nonorthogonally clustered sections to the west by the highway (Sections A and D) settled by refugees from Somalia prior to the establishment of a water distribution grid, and gridded sections to the east settled by refugees from Sudan and Ethiopia who arrived after the initial blocks and plots had been planned. Sometimes people's own building practices produced territory, as they used the building materials they foraged or were given to make living spaces in the blocks and sections. In either instance, the architectural expression of living spaces emerged from the immediate juxtaposition of socially different groups and the identity formation that ensued.

A body of ethnographic scholarship teases apart problems of social difference and identity formation in ways that are helpful to understanding the construction of built environments by refugees and humanitarians and their coproduction of humanitarian spatiality and emergency territory.[60] Anthropologist Liisa Malkki's study of refugee camps for Burundian Hutu people in Tanzania concludes that distinct displacement-based identities emerge differently in camps than in towns in which refugees might integrate into a national context.[61] In the same camps, anthropologist Marnie Thomson notates and theorizes distinctions between several forms of sovereignty born of displacement.[62] Sociologist Fred Ikanda's study of the Dadaab camps in relation to the surrounding host communities concludes that divisions between the refugees and host community stem from "the insecurity associated with the refugees, the general poverty of the locals that makes them perceive refugees as leading better social lives, and the protracted refugee situation" as well as the "perception that refugees are better off economically than their hosts."[63] I build on these studies of displacement-induced identity within confinement contexts in considering the architectural shaping of Ifo, Dagahaley, and Hagadera during the long entrenchment of emergency-to-development shifts in practice and thinking. Two studies enable me to analyze an architecture that emerged in the refugee camps; I revisit these studies to augment Dadaab's archive, as they provide clues behind the built environment at specific moments in time.

The first study, in 1999, by anthropologist Cindy Horst, helps to understand the material cultures of members of the Somali majority community in the camps. Through it, we can make sense of a transition that occurred in the built environment, marking the flow of remittances through transnational networks connecting the North American and northern European diaspora with Dadaab. Horst writes of a time when shopkeepers introduced the taar, a telegram or cable, which facilitated communication and financial transfer through the xawilaad system, an aspect of Somali social networks that both formalizes and strengthens community ties, undergirding the social safety net of many in the Dadaab settlements.[64] The taar was not licensed by Kenya's telecommunications authority and was maintained illegally through a system of police bribes.[65] In a time prior to the advent of the camp-wide information infrastructure of the internet, or state- or private-based communications systems such as Radio Gargaar, this support allowed for three conditions: a flow of information about the war, the transmission of resources to survive it, and an increased standard of living in the majority communities of the settlements.[66] Architecturally, solar panels began to materialize above the roof tarps of the markets as some taar owners invested in hardware enabling them to regularly recharge their radio sets.[67] As I conclude from my more recent analysis of the built environment in Dadaab, the "skyline" soon became dotted with satellite dishes. Certain blocks were suddenly ameliorated with gated entries to family plots, durable shelters built from brick, or the proliferation of shops built using pristine corrugated aluminum or unblemished plastic sheeting. These new landscape elements made visible the transmission and entrenchment of wealth, knowledge, and status.

The second study, in 2000, by anthropologist Michel Agier, helps to understand the inscription of sociocultural difference in the architecture of multiple communities. Through it, we can understand identity formations expressed in the architecture of Dadaab. He notes that a southern Sudanese block in Dagahaley camp documents "the patching together of new identities, the strengthening of particularisms, as well as anti-ethnic behaviour and inter-ethnic exchange":[68]

> They constructed an unusual space, different from that of the Somalian refugees, but also from that of the Sudanese in the other two camps. The habitat was organized in lines of small mud-brick houses, well aligned on either side of a completely straight main road some 50 metres long, at the end of which a mud-brick church had also been built, with a sure sense of perspective. A day nursery, a line of shower and toilet facilities and a little volleyball pitch end up forming what looks like a modern southern Sudanese village, or more certainly a neighbourhood of a miniature town. The whole is surrounded by a fence of thorn-bush and barbed wire, where a dozen men take turns each night, three at a time, at guarding the bloc's perimeter. As in the other blocs, the entrance gate is closed for the whole night at 6 p.m. . . . The words "Equatoria Gate" are inscribed in recycled metal on the gateway, as a reminder of the department of southern Sudan from which the refugees here fled in 1994–5.[69]

He described the Somali sections of Ifo as "a scattered habitat with family enclosures roughly demarcated by a few low thorn-bushes . . . frequently overflowing the marked-out blocs," and found in the two contiguous Ethiopian blocks "a high density of habitation, narrow lanes, high fences and the presence of a number of shops—coffee shops, video shops, hair salons, photo studios—summarily erected under cloth sheeting, and the huts are made out of wooden planks, cardboard or metal."[70] Such illustrations of material configurations deliver a detailed image of the camps, while not limited to the social scientific models of description and metrics of enumeration that the CARE camp managers criticized and engaged, years earlier.

These descriptions by Horst and Agier offer a primary source of knowledge for the Dadaab refugee camps. They comprise part of a provisional archive for

Dadaab, offering crucial glimpses into the social makeup of the camps over time. Through these documentations of Dadaab's materiality, the broader social landscape of difference in Dadaab may be imagined. Several communities fleeing wars and varied pasts appeared in Dadaab and co-constructed the refugee settlements—from the coastal Bajuni and riparian Gosha of Somalia to the former members of the Lord's Resistance Army in Uganda and the Lost Boys of Sudan—representing the political, social, and economic diversity encompassed in the process of humanitarian settlement at Dadaab, the conflicts that ensued, and their resolution in an architecture. The inscription of their differences in the Dadaab refugee camps promises an archive in the codings of a built environment.

SEEING DADAAB: FIXING ENCAMPMENT IN TIME

The frequent visual capture of the Dadaab refugee camps during the period at hand is exceptional. Few UNHCR-administered refugee camps can claim a graphic record, and even fewer can claim one containing the projections and abstractions of architectural parametric drawings. During several years when the Dadaab refugee camps did not appear on commonly accessible maps, they were sketched, mechanically drawn, photographed, charted, and visually analyzed—on foot, from the air, and by satellite.[71] While some of these documentary materials are classified or held in private collections, limiting or restricting public access, the imagery and spatial data that have been widely accessible—for example, in official documents, gray literature, the media, and miscellaneous specialized studies—demonstrate an engaged, selective focus on the Dadaab refugee camps since their establishment. This eclectic but concerted gaze has produced a body of spatial documentation that fixes a visual record, notably, of a site that was intended to be provisional. Such attention furthermore realizes sophisticated forms of surveillance. An end result of this material is that it constitutes an archive for an ephemeral, politically charged space. My historiographical labor and critical heritage practice of assembling documents for an architectural study of Dadaab is thus a distinctive element of my study, and I provide a review of the recovered materials in this section. My hope is that this conceptually *archaeological* endeavor will allow researchers with an interest in the Dadaab refugee camps to pursue these primary sources and that others with broader architectural, spatial, or geographical historical interests will consider this methodology of archival assemblage in relation to their own practices. Of course, many aural, material, and other nonvisual forms of recording a built environment exist, but I focus here on a conventional practice of "seeing" through visual materials that have not before been presented as a coherent archival corpus.

One body of sensible material from the years prior to 2006, the moment when Dadaab began to be widely captured on the internet, consists of photos, sketches, and films of the camp complex by refugees, aid workers, researchers, and visitors. Many refugees and aid workers retain material in their private holdings, and much is held in the collections of the UNHCR, CARE, MSF, and other humanitarian agencies and organizations. International and local photos and reports by members of the press followed each drought, flood, conflict, or other "disaster" affecting the camps, supported by the hospitality unit of the UNHCR suboffice at Dadaab (which facilitated my stay, under the aegis of the WRC). International organizations such as Film Aid promoted the work of residents of Dadaab to self-narrate in a range of visual media. Many people and organizations have "imaged" Dadaab's daily life.

The earliest sketches of Dadaab in the public record were prepared for the establishment of Ifo camp and appear in a UNHCR mission report produced in June 1991 by Public Health Officer M. Dualeh, Water Development Expert D. Mora-Castro, and Associate Architect S. Wähning.[72] These consist of maps and drawings with little detail and generic elements that were not specific to this site. Further documentation, again with no site-specific detail, followed in November 1991 in a status report by the NGO Lutheran World Federation.[73] The first representative plan of Ifo camp was made by Per Iwansson, an architect contracted by the UNHCR for a brief mission in 1992 to develop a plan for Hagadera camp. At the time, vehicles could not be readily accessed by a consultant, and gaining an aerial view of Ifo camp would have been possible only by climbing a water tower.[74] Iwansson recalled walking the perimeter of the site, using his stride as a measure to make a plan sketch drawing—following a common architectural disciplinary practice to engage the body as a tool for measuring and scaling. With few material supplies provided in Dadaab, he drafted his sketch on a roll of transparent architectural trace paper that he had brought from Sweden. As he sat under the sun in an open field, with falling beads of perspiration threatening to ruin his work, he requested that UNHCR Associate Architect Wähning bring a more durable vellum paper on her next mission to Dadaab, and he made multiple photocopies of the sketch of Ifo on his next visit to Nairobi.[75] In his UNHCR mission report, he recommended for any future site planner "a minimum of working resources," including "a drawing table and tools."[76] While in Dadaab, Iwansson made other pertinent drawings also contained in the mission report, primarily producing plans for Hagadera. Werner Schellenberg, another architect contracted by the UNHCR in 1992, produced plans for Dagahaley during this time. The availability of this pool of technical professionals suggests that the UNHCR made parallel deployments elsewhere in the world, meeting similar technical standards. This body of work (figures 4.1–4.6) and experiences constitute the earliest architectural records of the Dadaab refugee camps.

The photographic record of the camps is substantial, and both aerial and satellite photography constitute significant genres of the humanitarian depiction of Dadaab.[77] The technology of aerial photography had been available for decades, but only when host governments commissioned it would refugee camps be mapped in this way. As an example, the Ethiopian government commissioned aerial maps of the UNHCR camps hosting Somali refugees in Kebribeyah and Jigjiga.[78] The UNHCR began mobilizing the technology to map sites under its purview in the late 1990s. In 1996, the UNHCR commissioned the French research organization Institut de Recherche pour le Développement (IRD) to study the environment and demographics of the Dadaab and Kakuma refugee settlements in Kenya, a less frequently occurring partnership, as described by IRD at the time, than the ones it had with other UN agencies or humanitarian NGOs.[79] The researchers produced comprehensive overlays of demographic information over geographic representations, showing by block and sector the overall population and specific categories: women, men, children, families of various sizes, district of origin, ethnicity, and so on. This exercise spatially contextualized previously unrecorded population data, which enabled aid workers to modify programs to target areas of need, while also introducing an unprecedented level of surveillance of the site, providing high-resolution imagery of every built structure and all vegetation and other environmental conditions. The IRD's work included analysis and development of state-of-the-art methods for this type of image acquisition. The second volume of the report provides a detailed explanation of implementation and a technical guideline, including "the preparation of a flight for images acquisition and the integration of the aerial mosaic in a geographical information system," focusing "on the refugee camps of Kenya, in which this method of acquiring images has been used to come up with a precise cartography of the camps."[80] The use of the camp for the testing and innovation of such technology does not register in the report. No such comprehensive cartographic survey of Dadaab was produced after this 1999 report, but aerial photographs were produced periodically, every year or two after these. The UNHCR later established a sophisticated in-house mapping unit that evolved into a humanitarian satellite geospatial information systems unit.

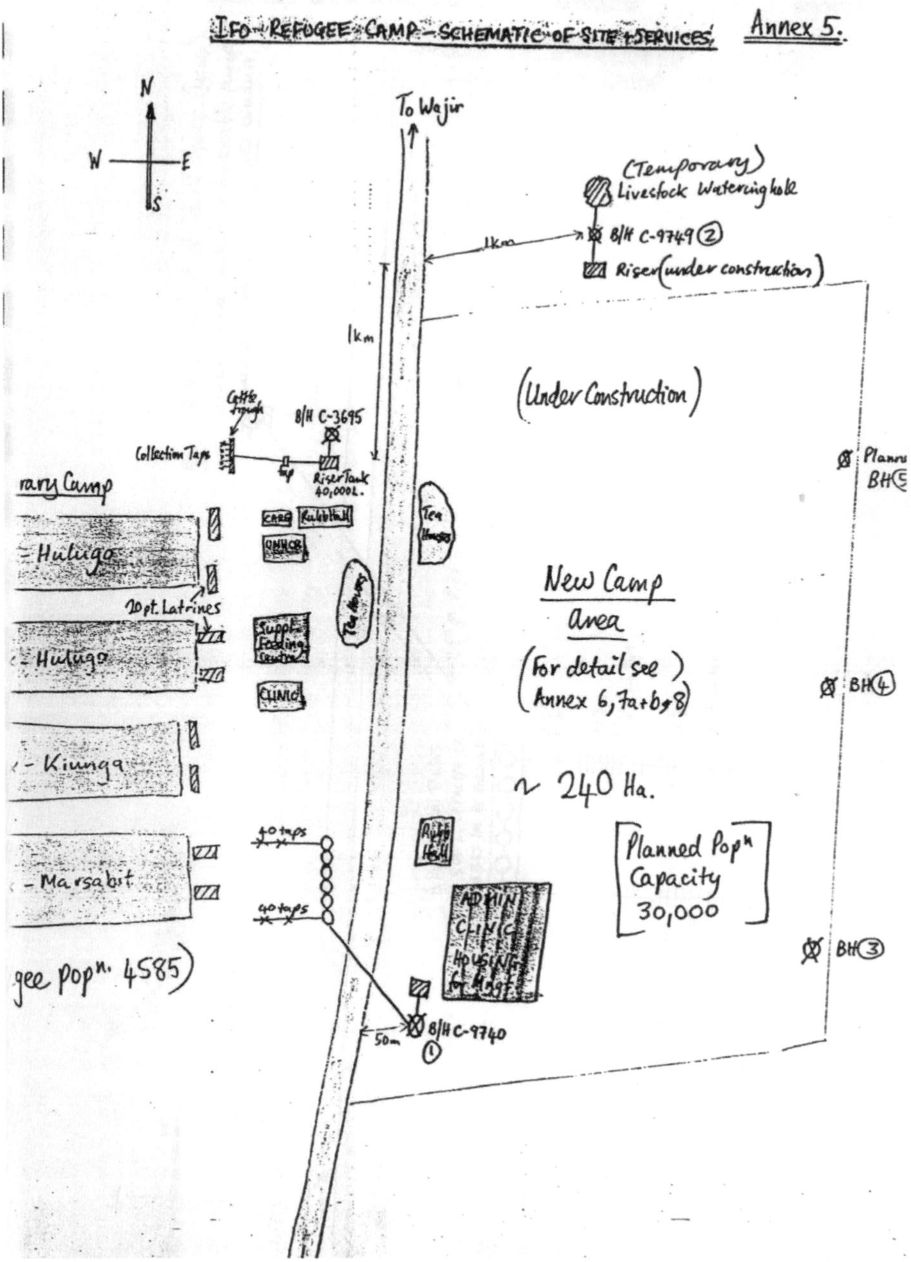

4.5. (*above*) Martin L. Taylor, plan of Ifo camp, 1991, from Lutheran World Federation Department of World Service report (November 1991), provided by Per Iwansson.
4.6. (*opposite*) Per Iwansson, hand-drawn sketch plan of Ifo camp, 1992, provided by Per Iwansson.

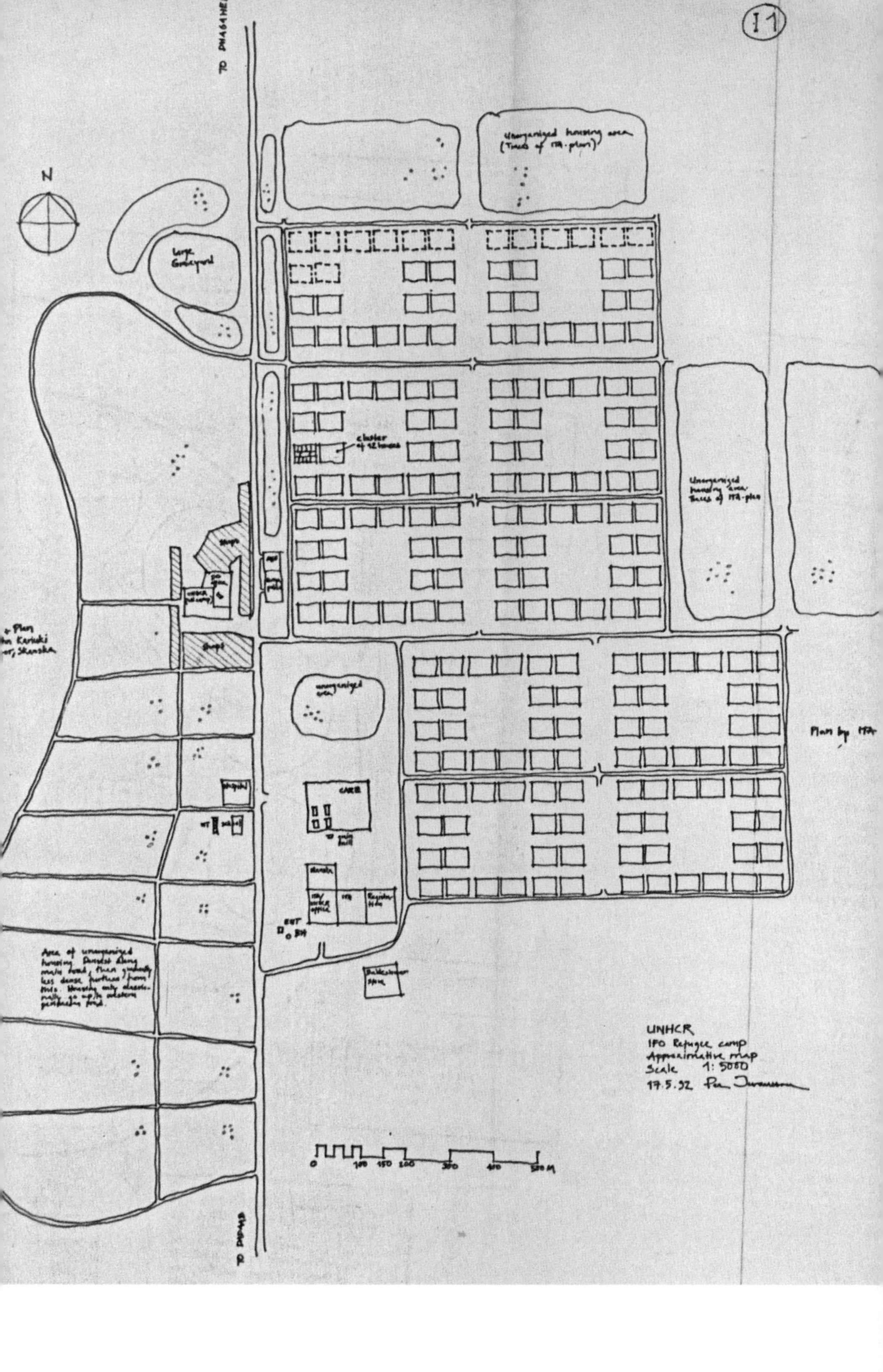

I1
TO DHAGAHELEY
N
Large Graveyard
Unorganized housing area (Traces of IFA-plan)
cluster of 12 houses
Unorganized housing area. Traces of IFA-plan
Shops
Shops
Plan by IFA
unorganized area
CARE
Area of unorganized housing. Densest along main road, then gradually less dense further from this. Housing only occasionally go up to western perimeter road.
TO DADAAB
UNHCR
IFO Refugee camp
Approximative map
Scale 1: 5000
17.5.92
0 100 150 200 300 400 500 M

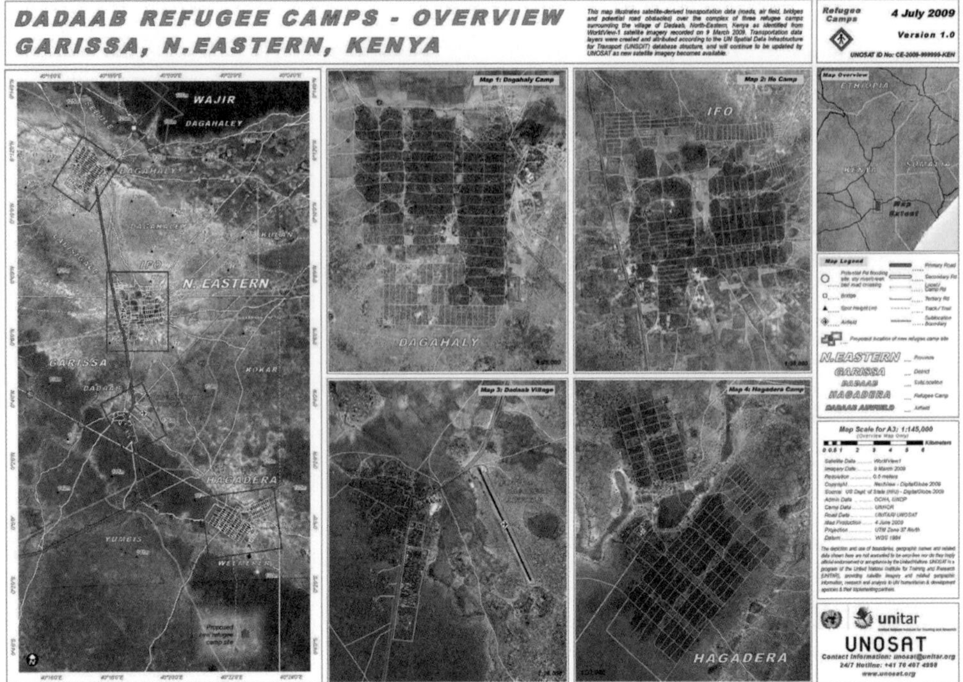

4.7. UNOSAT (a program of UNITAR, the UN Institute for Training and Research, "providing satellite imagery and related geographic information, research and analysis to UN humanitarian & development agencies & their implementing partners"), overview maps of Dadaab refugee camps, July 4, 2009.

Satellite mapping of Dadaab should be understood within the context that humanitarian geospatial mapping has become a prolific medium activated by a variety of organizations and agencies within their own research and to engage publics.[81] By the mid-2000s, among the imagery collected and published on Google Earth, high-resolution satellite views appeared of Ifo, Dagahaley, and Hagadera, each with a level of detail that added new visual and technical information to the public representations of these settlements. For example, the visual detail of Ifo camp demonstrated that the photos were taken prior to its flooding in late 2006.[82] At approximately the same time, the UNHCR created the Field Information and Coordination Support Section, a technical unit specializing in collating archival information, satellite imagery, and ground data into analytical maps intended to provide operational support to field units working at humanitarian sites.[83] The UN Institute for Training and Research (UNITAR) also launched the Operational Satellite

Applications Programme (UNOSAT), delivering elaborate analytical maps to the humanitarian and development sectors. As with the high-resolution aerial photography that preceded it, these new forms of imagery performed in an ethically problematic way, producing a database for complex problem-solving while heightening the capacity to surveil. The paradox is evident in a PhD dissertation written by James Kennedy, an architect who conducted research while working on emergency shelter in Dadaab in 2007, proposing design approaches for the new settlement of Ifo 2. His extensive, site-specific analysis of Ifo, observing in the IRD maps that habitable plots do not meet minimum UNHCR standards, names features in the aerial photos not previously detectable, such as a dense network of paths that had been used as routes for livestock, noting on later observation a series of new "vehicle routes, acting as back-roads (i.e. roads without regular police patrols) between the three camps, and also as direct roads to some of the older and at that time newly-establishing host-community villages in the area," as well as "non-residential structures whereby the non-central placement, and irregular shape of the space which they occupy, would imply that the locations for such infrastructures were chosen and built by the refugees (e.g. mosques)."[84] These descriptions demonstrate the quality of visual data previously unavailable for a refugee camp, which satellite imagery could provide to an interested viewer. Regardless of the intentions of individual makers or users, such universally accessible visual material must be understood as abstracting the lives and bodies of people; more information does not equate to more just forms of knowledge. Nevertheless, these photographs too form part of the critical archive.

A final body of material comprising depictions of Dadaab's built environment, most widely in circulation, includes the images produced for the promotion and marketing of humanitarian activity. Photos and films that capture the built environment generally abstract it, as in one public information video, titled "UNHCR Goodwill Ambassador Angelina Jolie visits Dadaab, Kenya," posted in 2009 by UNHCR on the video-sharing website YouTube.[85] The script does not name the distinct housing sectors, blocks, settlements, or host nation, and the filmed environment provides no visual features that locate the narrative within specific places. Instead, it presents an overview of the landscape, rare in this location and achievable only through the exertion of climbing water or cell towers or flying low to the ground. The overhead angle generates a perspective of scattered dwellings and highlights discordant colors and nonorthogonal lines in the roofscape, in contrast to the plan's hard edges depicted in the bird's-eye view. The material clutter gives the impression of disorder.[86] The additive fabric roof and wall elements and

4.8. Still from UNHCR promotional film, YouTube, 2009.

uneven wood-framed fences and mud-patched buildings emphasize ephemerality and fragility in the lightness of structures. Through a glimpse, the viewer is compelled to draw a metaphorical connection between the scenic and social structure, represented in the call for aid. Nevertheless, its many "walk-through" and "flyby" scenes contain a great deal of architectural information.

In assessing these selected components of the visual archive of the Dadaab refugee camps, I draw the important conclusion that its documentation results in a twinned depiction of a permanent built environment and an ephemeral one. Whether a lone sketch by an architect pacing the bush or a satellite depiction of textile roofs, the imagery traces a suspension of architecture between emergency and development, at once under construction and also fully conceived, planned, and executed. This tension between emergency and development has defined life in the camps and the shape of their built environment, reproduced in the humanitarian archive.

In the years between 1993 and 2006, as the government of Kenya reinforced an encampment strategy and the UNHCR aligned its mission with military peacekeeping and entrenched the policy of refugee repatriation, the stakes increased for refugee camps to produce a permanent ephemerality. To achieve this, they were called on to perform as instruments of signification. The visual legibility of refugee camps as temporary became tantamount, as architectural signs of refugee permanence threatened social stability in host countries, signaled a protracted state of uncertainty for the displaced, and politically complicated the interventions of humanitarians. The ephemerality of built structures and environments was needed to denote the temporariness of migration. However, for Dadaab, ephemeral architectures have belied a concrete infrastructure that monumentalizes the condition of emergency. Such problematics have not only impacted Dadaab, but also defined a global humanitarianism, whose built environments and forms of knowledge have been fraught with the politics of visibility and visuality.

2006–2011: An Archive of Humanitarian Settlement

My speculative periodization of the history of the Dadaab refugee camps, during the first twenty years in which its UNHCR files were classified, catalogs the construction of a conventional archive with which to "see" Dadaab. What can be seen is the transformation of a humanitarian intervention into an architecture, the entangling of emergency response and development practice. I have referred to a multiplicity of gazes. These not only order time and historicity, but also provide forms and methods for accessing the history of a provisional built environment. My critical archiving serves a heritage practice, in which I document Dadaab from my own ground view.

In 2006, the UNHCR and the government of Kenya began planning expansion of the Dadaab camps, eventually building Ifo 2 and Kambioos (the latter since decommissioned). That year, as the al-Shabaab movement took hold in southern Somalia, many more people fled to Kenya's northeast. Ifo camp flooded during the rainy season, occasioning the events discussed in chapter 3, irreversibly damaging the land and several structures and displacing the camp's residents, as the waters eliminated vehicular artery access for aid distribution to the settlement. These events catalyzed the planning and design of Ifo 2 (work initiated by Kennedy, the architect referred to earlier).

The planning of a new settlement, also discussed in chapter 3, culminated a long political process intended to alleviate the growth and density of Ifo's population and provide additional services to mollify a host community bristling at the many benefits they perceived refugees as receiving. In hand with the expansion of the settlements, the UNHCR diversified responsibility for them, replacing CARE's contract with several awarded to international and local NGOs, which brought a wide field of actors to Dadaab, to administer health, education, camp planning and management, shelter, youth programs, livelihoods, and a variety of other services. This significant shift in institutional structure in 2006 marks it as an inflection point in my speculative periodization of the history of the settlements, a moment during which the character of the camp complex changed. The following pictorial overview, including photos collected during my visit in March 2011, offers one more archive of the Dadaab refugee camps.

ROUTES INTO DADAAB

Travelers to the Dadaab refugee camps have primarily arrived on foot, by road in vehicles, or by air. Most refugees from Somalia journeyed overland by foot, crossing the western border of Somalia and the bush of Kenya's North Eastern Province. From the time when the al-Shabaab network took control of most of southern Somalia in 2006 to the profound regional drought of 2011 in the Horn of Africa, the Kenyan police presence along the state border increased the risks for asylum seekers, with rising reports of extortion, rape, and other forms of violence as greater numbers of people attempted to cross the border.[87] Many refugees spoke of assailants lining routes and endangering vulnerable bands of people, often lone women and children in flight. Many refugees crossed the porous political border between Somalia and Kenya via cattle paths or in the vehicles of human traffickers.

A highway connects Dadaab to the two capitals, Nairobi and Mogadishu, passing through county seat Garissa to the west and Liboi to the east, the site of the former UNHCR refugee reception and transit center described earlier. Short-term visitors to Dadaab travel by public bus or all-terrain vehicle for five hours on an asphalt-paved highway from Nairobi to Garissa and then for another two hours along a secondary road, as the verdant landscape of the highlands turns to a dusty, semiarid one. Police checkpoints stationed along this route monitor refugee movement in both directions. Secondary roads also lead to Dadaab from Mombasa and other southern coastal towns, as well as from Marsabit to the northwest and Mandera on the northeast border, all of which have been refugee-hosting areas in Kenya. Refugees from countries other than Somalia, primarily those resettled from other locations within and outside Kenya, have arrived by bus and occasionally by air, via one of the UNHCR transit centers at the borders or in Nairobi. From the establishment of the Dadaab settlements, aid supplies have primarily arrived by road, which has occasionally caused acute deprivation during the rainy season, when extreme flooding created impassable conditions, stranding vehicles in muddy waters.

Passage to Dadaab by official visitors and aid workers not based locally involves a one-hour flight chartered by interested agencies—for example, the twice-weekly UNHCR flight. Small passenger planes in the UN Humanitarian Air Service depart from Nairobi's Wilson Airport, a one-hall facility with a coffee stand and a small duty-free shop. They land on a stretch of tarmac at the airstrip near Dadaab town. Drivers meet visitors at the airport in all-terrain vehicles emblazoned with agency logos (UNHCR, IRC, MSF, and so on). A five-minute drive on the Garissa Road toward Nairobi leads to Dadaab town and, across from it, the main gate of the humanitarian compound that houses the UNHCR and NGOs. Through this metal gate, a sandy drive lies between the compound's razor-wire fence to the west, along the Garissa

4.9. Humanitarian Air Service, Wilson Airport, Nairobi, 2011.

Road, and subcompounds to the east surrounded by chain-link fence, each individually gated with guardhouses and armed patrols.

A view from outside the camps evidences little of the density within. The primary arteries that lead to Ifo, Dagahaley, and Hagadera, marked "Main road" on the UNHCR overview map, and the secondary roads around the perimeters of each settlement, marked "Feeder road," are wide, sandy trails with little foot traffic, few donkey carts, and periodic appearances of humanitarian vehicles—the three most common forms of transportation in the settlements. Herders can be seen taking goats, cows, and (occasionally) camels outside the perimeter or to the boreholes to graze and water in the mornings, returning in the late afternoons. Individuals on these roads are often traveling to collect firewood, using hand trucks or donkey carts. The surrounding reddish landscape is barren, with occasional trees or thorny acacia bushes growing in dark green, woody clumps. Marabou storks loom, always at some distance from human activity. Very few vertical elements mark the landscape, with the notable exception of man-made objects, such as the water towers providing gravity distribution of water through the settlements or the steel masts erected by Safaricom, Kenya's dominant mobile phone company.

From the roads at the periphery, plots within the settlement become visible through the bush. If the distribution of vegetation appears unplanned at first, a closer encounter reveals a planting scheme for area demarcation. This regional species of *Commiphora* is a thorn bush used as live fencing around residential plots. It grows in a thick brush, with spikes that can easily puncture the skin of humans and animals. Plots at the periphery of all the settlements are usually less densely planted than plots within. Interior plots are sometimes surrounded by high, neat fencing, architecturally modeled to incorporate gates, doors, and windows. The planting at the peripheral plots serves more as a trace of intention than a concrete delineation, creating a perforated border, if any, as this book's frontispiece shows.

The curfew to which people residing in the central humanitarian compound adhere imposes a graphic spectacle on the landscape three times each weekday, in the morning, just after lunchtime, and in the late afternoon, as the convoys of white Toyota Land Cruisers drive from the central compound to the camps and back, always surrounded by clouds of burnt orange dust,

4.10. (*opposite, top*) Road in Hagadera camp, with *Commiphora* fencing around family plots.

4.11. (*opposite, bottom*) Humanitarian convoy on the highway to Dagahaley camp, UNHCR vehicle with radio antenna in foreground.

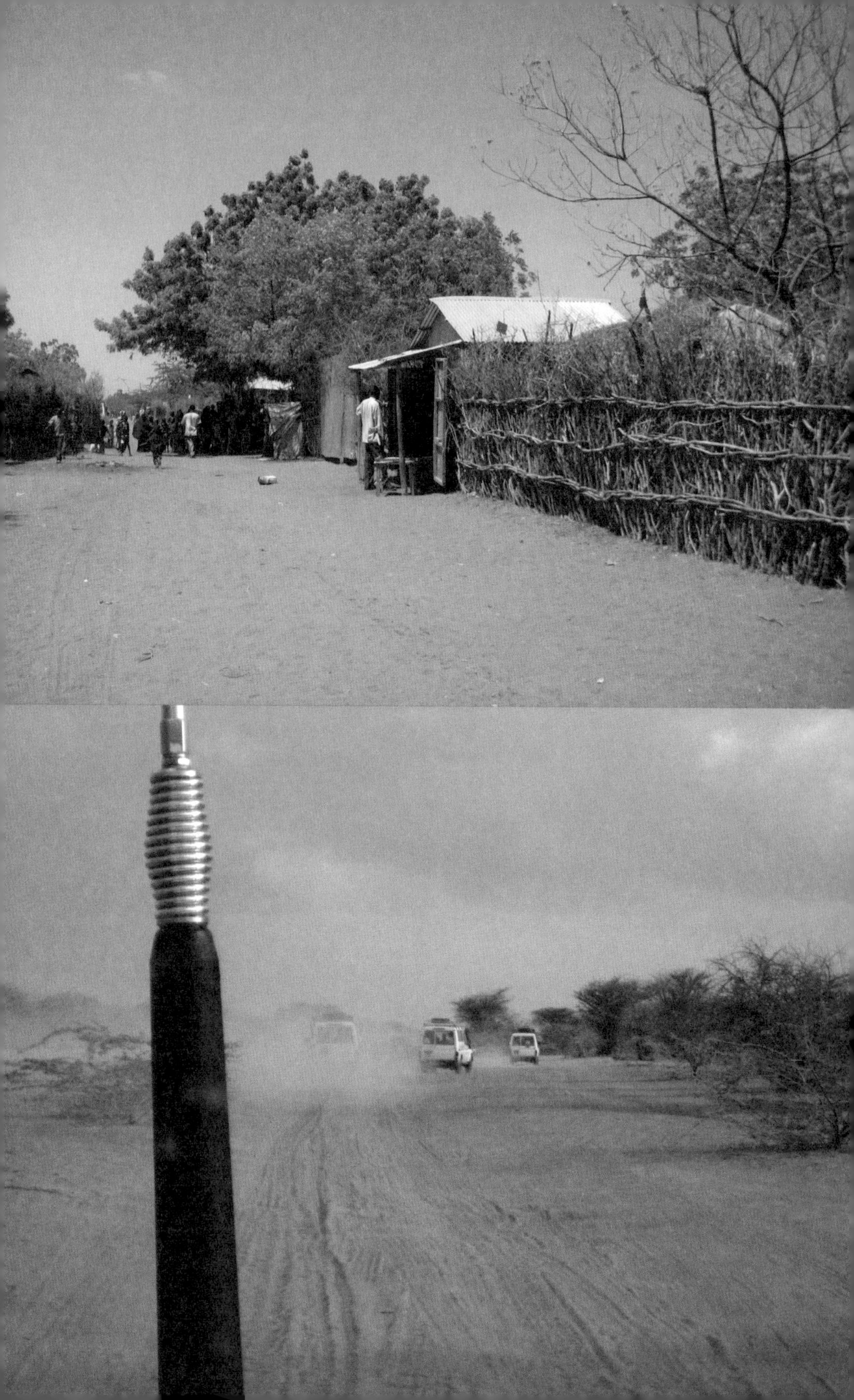

above which the tall black antennae of the vehicles poke out. The drivers stop at the Dadaab police station on the way to the camps to pick up the UNHCR-contracted escort, awaiting this escort's arrival at each settlement when returning to the central humanitarian compound. As aid workers have become targets for kidnappings and killings, agencies and organizations have secured police protection for international staff, with threats by al-Shabaab inspiring an acute security response around Dadaab after 2006. In addition to the vehicular escort, the UNHCR and most of the international organizations, excluding MSF, stopped allowing staff members into the settlements without a walking armed officer. Aid workers entering refugee neighborhoods in the company of a mostly male state police force with a reputation for hostility and extortion gives embodied form to one of the most problematic aspects of exchange between refugees and humanitarians. The presence of aid workers in refugee camps produces a daily time marker for residents, along with certain forms of security and order, as the humanitarian literature has noted.[88] Yet, some of the mothers I spoke to in Dadaab noted that if the departure of the humanitarian workforce prior to each sunset created immediate social tensions to negotiate, it also brought some measure of rest and relief.

ORGANIZATION OF THE SETTLEMENTS

The central humanitarian compound in Dadaab is divided into three subcompounds: the "UNHCR compound" (the first built), the "CARE compound" to its north, and another to its south, which have each housed multiple agency residences and offices. International staff from each organization reside in these compounds, some in tents and some in permanent structures. The UNHCR houses all of its staff in the central Dadaab compound. Most organizations house international staff in one of the subcompounds, while national staff, under less restrictive security requirements, live in a compound within the refugee settlement where they undertake their primary activity. All MSF staff from the various country branches that have worked in Dadaab have lived within a compound in the refugee settlements. These local geographies reflect worldwide policies and practices of agencies and organizations, with the UNHCR on one end of the spectrum, maintaining a standardized approach to staff security in all locations around the globe, and grassroots organizations and MSF on the other, putting staff members in

4.12. (*opposite, top*) UNHCR offices, UNHCR compound.
4.13. (*opposite, bottom*) Humanitarian residences, UNHCR compound.

4.14. Mess hall and recreational center, UNHCR compound.

proximity to the people they serve. Most organizations fall somewhere in the middle of this spectrum with regard to security.

The spatial organization of UNHCR settlements worldwide conforms to density standards based on water supply and sewage removal per person per area. "Blocks" (A, B, C, D, and so on) are further subdivided into "sectors" (1, 2, 3, 4, and so on). These divisions form the basic units for the census, food and nonfood item distribution, representative government, and most other aspects of social and political ordering and population management. Any sense of the settlements as bounded is suggested only in a view from above. The figure-ground relationship visible in high-resolution aerial photos suggests carefully demarcated boundaries around a dense massing of residential blocks, with several planes speckled white and gray adjacent to one another, reflecting the color and texture of corrugated tin, plastic sheeting, and other roofing materials. The most pronounced grid telegraphing through this mottle in the bird's-eye view is in the plan for Hagadera camp, whose wide green spaces and firebreaks separate the residential blocks. Such a grid is visible, if barely, in the plan of Dagahaley camp and on the east and north of Ifo camp.

The areas first settled by refugees at Dadaab were "A" and "D" blocks of Ifo camp. Ifo is the oldest of the settlements, largely self-settled on low ground just east of the adjacent highway when the first refugees arrived in 1991. In 2011, it was the only camp housing large groups of non-Somali refugees. The residential blocks on the west side of Ifo flood regularly; after the severe rainy season in 2006 mentioned earlier and discussed in chapter 3, a movement began to develop a new settlement, Ifo 2, to house people further displaced. Ifo is the settlement closest to Dadaab town and the central UNHCR compound. Its humanitarian compound at the south end and food distribution center at the north end, both adjacent to police stations, form two major nodes in its system of social services. Within Ifo's humanitarian compound, CARE's subcompound is the largest, and its community meeting areas are used regularly by aid workers and refugees alike. The UNHCR field office in Ifo camp includes an often-crowded refugee reception center.

The marketplace drives life in each camp. A large market sits centrally in each, except in Dagahaley camp, where it is located at the edge. As Kennedy writes, each settlement contains "large markets of 200–300 stalls, offering everything from fresh vegetables, to replica football shirts, to internet cafes to ice-making machines, and many services, including international currency exchange, which would otherwise not be normally available either at the local Kenyan village, or at the provincial capital Garissa, 110 kilometres back along the road towards Nairobi."[89] The metal roofs of the marketplace are spaced closely together, covering solid walls around the hundreds of stalls in each settlement, for the secure storage of goods.

Most camp planning guidelines call for even distribution across the blocks and sectors of amenities and social service facilities, from green space to water tap stands to schools to medical clinics. The proximity of a refugee's residential plot to such facilities may have profound effects, particularly in large settlements where the need for transportation of materials or access to services is a safety factor. Proximity to a medical facility can affect morbidity or mortality, just as distance from a school can preclude a family from providing a girl with an education. UNHCR overview maps show the concentration of social service facilities around each camp's humanitarian compound and the dispersal of schools, community centers, hospitals, graveyards, religious centers, police stations, and markets. The monochromatic orthogonality of prefabricated imported structures, easily distinguishable from those fashioned on-site, appear in aerial photos.

SHOP

4.15. People drinking chai in the shade of Amin shopping mall in Bosnia market, Ifo camp.

4.16. Kulmiye Lodge, Ifo market.

4.17. Mashallah Beauty Center, Ifo market.

4.18. Provisions seller in his shop, Dagahaley market.

4.19. Vegetable seller in her shop, Dagahaley market.

4.20. Building supplies warehouse, Hagadera market.

ESSENTIAL AID

Food and water distribution are central to life in a refugee camp. The water grid and access points drive the camps' spatial layout. Boreholes in Ifo's humanitarian compound and "D" block ("Borehole 0" and "Borehole 1" on UNHCR overview maps) were among the first to access the aquifer that supplies the settlements through pumped and gravity distribution of water. Tap stands were established at one of every two residential blocks, corresponding to the grids in Ifo's east and north blocks, and throughout the blocks of Dagahaley and Hagadera. The water tap stand is a node of conflict and negotiation in a context of scarcity, among the most charged points in space.

Proximity of a family plot to the food distribution center is possibly the most significant determinant of a person's chances to survive in Dadaab and make a life, or even a livelihood, as most refugees sell their rations within a

4.21. Mother holding her friend's place in the queue at a water tap stand in Ifo camp.

day of receiving them. A plot far from the food distribution center or attached market can be economically taxing, requiring hire of a donkey cart for transport, or even life-threatening, increasing the risk of physical attack to someone carrying rations across the settlement. For this reason, the UNHCR provides plots to the most vulnerable people—for example, children, single mothers, the elderly, and those with physical mobility challenges—in the vicinity of the distribution point. The refugee camp can be understood as a materialization of the food distribution cycle. The following photographs of the environments of food distribution draw from interviews conducted by the author and Bethany Young for the WRC.

✦

4.22. (*above*) Women moving through the food distribution center, Ifo camp.
4.23. (*below*) CARE food distribution sheds, Ifo camp, photo by Tom Corsellis, May 1995.

4.24. WFP warehouse, Ifo camp.

4.25. Food ration chart, food distribution center, Ifo camp.

USAID

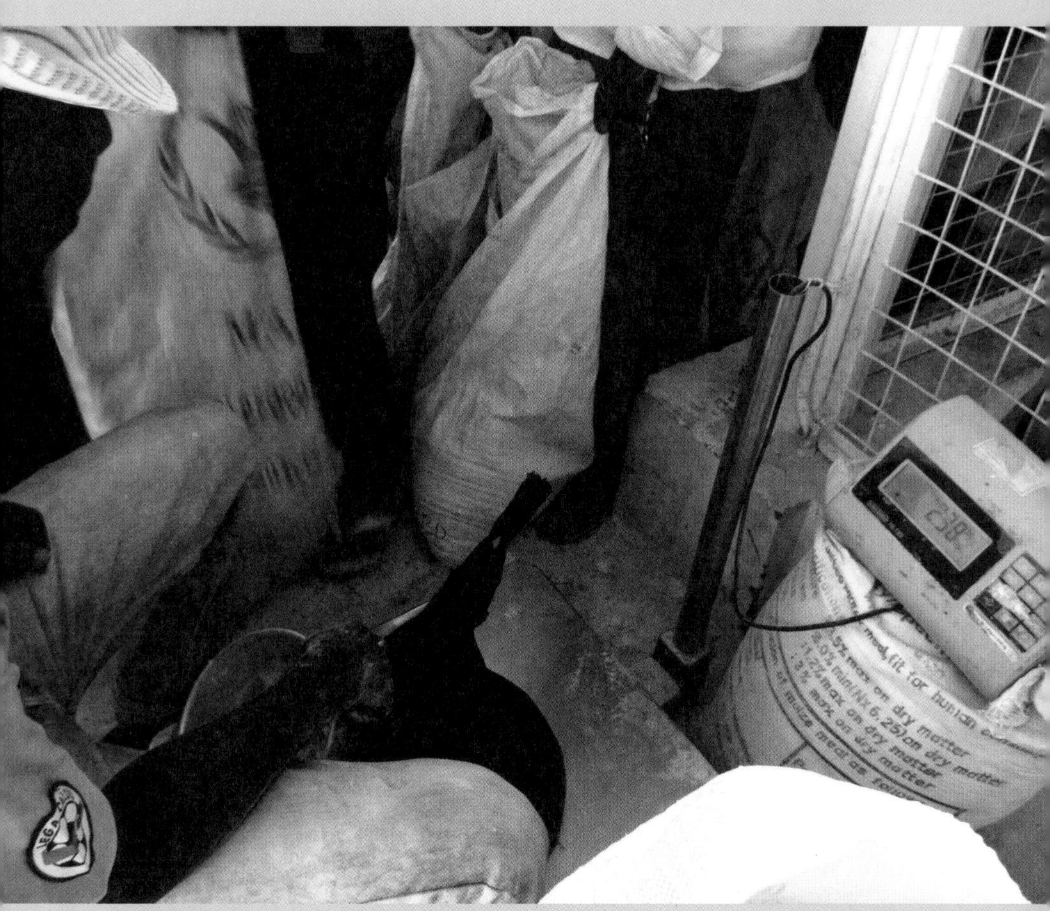

4.26 and 4.27. (*opposite and above*) Workers at the food distribution center, Ifo camp.

4.28. Boy reapportioning his family's rations in the food distribution center, Ifo camp.

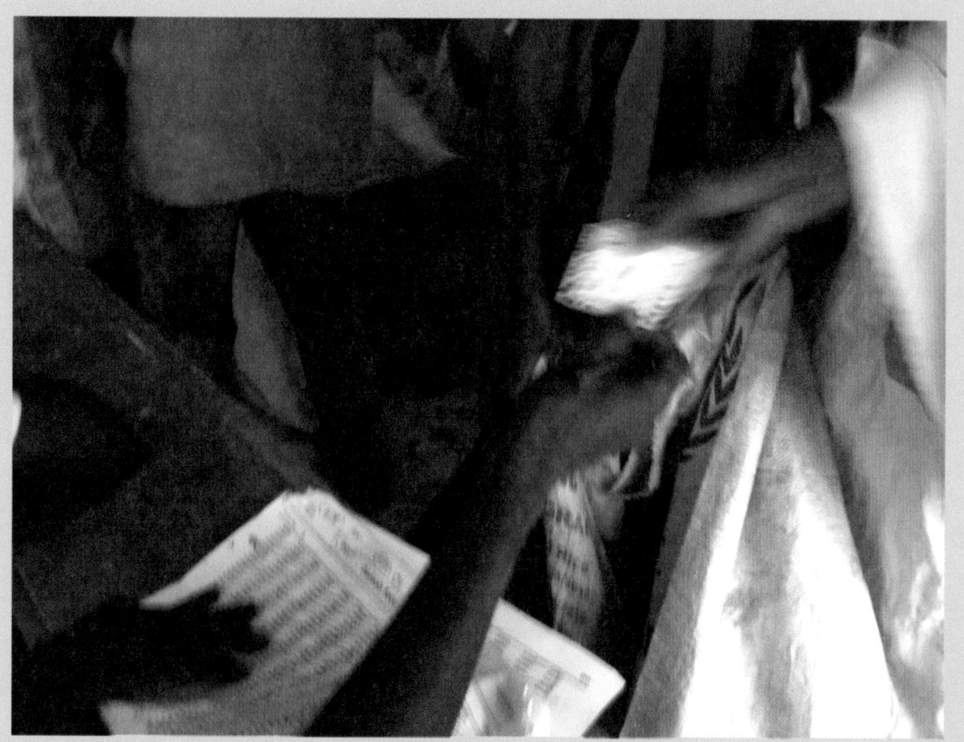

4.29. Ration card passing hands, food distribution center, Ifo camp.

4.30. Donkey carts outside the food distribution center, Ifo camp.

4.31. People leaving an aid distribution point in Ifo camp.

Figure 4.22. The physical footprint of UNHCR camps is determined by distribution of aid commodities and medical and social services. The former refer to food, water, and "nonfood items" (in humanitarian parlance), such as plastic sheeting, water jugs, soap, and shelters. The movement of raw commodities—flour, meal, beans, oil, salt—shapes the planning and constructed form of camps. Ifo camp was planned in 1991 for a population of 30,000. The UNHCR recommends allocating one aid distribution site per 20,000 people, well below the official numbers of people living in Ifo camp, and not accounting for thousands of unregistered migrants who participate in the trade of aid commodities.[90] In April 2017, the official population of this camp began to exceed 60,000 people.[91] In this photo, refugees move along a passage that traverses the ten "sheds" where food is distributed at Ifo camp. On this day, rations were being distributed to newly arriving people at shed 10, and, at the other sheds, to families categorized on their ration cards as "Size 1" and "Size 8."

Registered refugees arrive at the distribution area, where aid workers and refugee "incentive" workers immediately direct "clients" to a processing point according to their family size. According to UNHCR guidelines: "The family, as a natural unit, is the target of distribution."[92] The UNHCR attempts to house individuals and communities requiring extra protection—for example, unattended minors, single women, or people requiring assistance with mobility—close to food distribution areas. The agency recommends organizing individuals into "household groups" to facilitate commodity distribution and shelter provision.[93] The food distribution center is one of the only areas of the camp where all people gather: women with children, the elderly, boys, men, families, individuals, community representatives, and political and religious leaders. At the food distribution point, refugees acquire sacks to collect rations. They are made of a durable woven plastic, in order to be filled with dried goods. The sacks are typically repurposed as scrap material for cladding shelters or other purposes and enter the refugee economy as a unit of trade.

Figure 4.23. Tom Corsellis, photo of CARE food distribution sheds, May 1995, University of Oxford Bodleian Social Science Library, Refugee Studies Centre (RSC) Collection.[94] Food was originally delivered by road to Dadaab, and its distribution managed by CARE. According to a report by Corsellis in 1995, the method of food distribution had "not progressed significantly in approach beyond the initial relief phase" in 1991.[95] The food distribution system described in this report was essentially unchanged in 2011, although facilities had been constructed using more durable materials and designed to control people's movement.

Figure 4.24. Before dried foodstuffs and other commodities stock the sheds, they are warehoused in giant tents, themselves mass-produced, warehoused, and shipped around the world. The WFP canvas tent warehouses appear in aerial photos as rows of white rectangles, but the pronounced ridgelines of their roofs rise above the cleared expanses of land near the food distribution sites (see figure 3.7). The imposing iconography of the storage warehouses at once recalls immediate scarcity and foreign largesse: steel-framed, fabric-clad mobile architectures producing an unexpected aesthetic regime across the global landscape of UNHCR camps. Experienced singularly or grouped as they are in Ifo camp, their scale and placement represents the humanitarian lifesaving mission.

Figure 4.25. "FOOD RATION SCALE FOR 2ND CYCLE MARCH 2011 (printed elsewhere in Somali: "RAASHINKA LAQAADANHAYO DOORKAN LABAAD MARSO 2011 WAA SIDAN"), a chart with the distribution allotted for "Family Size" ("F/S") 1 through 15. Rations offer a basis for meals rich in proteins, carbohydrates, and overall calories, including dry uncooked foods such as: wheat flour, corn meal, pulses, oil, oatmeal, salt, and peanuts. Rations are distributed at different "shops" located in each "shed." In Ifo, as in other UNHCR-administered camps around the world, rations are distributed twice per month, around the first and around the fifteenth. At these moments, the camp swells in size as markets spring up around the food distribution center, and extended families and community members pay visits to each home. Ration cards are issued for a seventeen-month period, including thirty-four cycles, after which new cards must be obtained.

Figures 4.26 and 4.27. The WFP selects refugees for participation in the distribution of food aid, engaging in a contentious process that produces and reinforces asymmetries throughout the camp. In response to concerns that women were targeted during the distribution of food and nonfood items, sometimes with male staff members forcing the exchange of rations for sex, the agencies recommended placing women refugees as ration distributors. However, as people negotiate emergency within the humanitarian system, complexities arise from the condition of a patriarchy within a patriarchy; at the time of my visit, a WFP officer reported that a group of refugees had requested the removal of a woman in charge of rationing at one of the camps, accusing her of corrupt practices.

Women frequently registered complaints about the selection of a "head of household" as the person officially designated to collect rations for a family unit, rather than a community-recognized "head of family," because the appointment of the wrong person could engender inequalities and sometimes violent transactions. According to the UNHCR, each of these figures might be male or female, but had to be recognized and accepted by the family and society in these roles.[96] The overwrought definition of each role in the UNHCR field guide for commodity distribution testifies to the tensions of the positions.

Rations are weighed on distribution, and weighing stations for refugee use and for random checks by agency staff are located outside the sheds. The power of a single transaction as well as its coherence as a complex set of exchanges is inscribed within the scale. However simple this humanitarian technology, it has superseded scoops as a measure of food, given the perceived variability of scooping as a technique for ration distribution.

Figure 4.28. In addition to the inhospitable architecture of a route lined with chain-link fencing and barbed wire to keep people filing along individually or in easily watched groups, the accommodation of families of disparate sizes on the same day facilitates control of the distribution process. People can be monitored as they move through the shops at different sheds, so that they may not surreptitiously pass ration cards to others for double use, and to ensure the sacks they carry are filled with contents of comparable bulk after they pass through each shop. The food distribution point is a spectacularly public area in the camp, as well as within the visual spectrum of the commodities' circulation in the camps. The collection and transportation of food materials is a highly securitized process, on the one hand, and produces extreme vulnerability, on the other, especially among women. According to the UNHCR Commodity Distribution field guide, "a typical one month food ration for a family of 5 can weigh 75kg [165 pounds]."[97] Thus, transportation of commodities from the distribution center can create crisis and possible trauma. Here, a boy reapportions his family's rations after receiving them.

Figure 4.29. The ration card is the telos of the humanitarian aid environment, its fundamental form of currency, an embodiment of power, and a material artifact that gains significance with each pair of hands that grip it. After people pass through the sheds, with several weighings of rations at points along the way, their cards are stamped by staff members at the exit. The cards are numbered according to refugee family size (1 to 16) and the cycle of distribution (1 to 34).

Figure 4.30. A fleet of donkey carts waits outside the food distribution center, for hire by refugees who must carry rations some distance or to facilitate exchange with unregistered persons who may not enter the food distribution center. The ownership and rental of donkey carts forms a subsidiary economy in the region.

Usually what they do . . . they sell some portion of their rations, and hire a donkey cart to take the balance to the household. . . . Selling a part of the ration [is] not only about transportation. There are many other compelling factors. . . . In a given month, that's the only cash they get. If they need [a] tarpaulin . . . they have to sell their food. If they need [something] for their child, they have to sell. If they don't want this food and they want [something else,] they have to sell. If they want to buy milk, they have to sell. If they want to buy clothes—anything, ANYTHING, anything for the household. It's only the food that's available. Do you understand?
—WFP officer, Dadaab

Figure 4.31. Refugees arriving to Ifo in the days immediately prior to a food distribution cycle may be able to register, but they may find that food aid is unavailable. Even if the cash reserves from their journey to Dadaab remain intact, the supply of resold rations moving through the markets may be limited. If a person's registration or ration cards are not processed in time, multiple days prior to the next distribution may pass during which food simply cannot be accessed, even by children. Depending on need and stock, aid workers will often issue nonfood items to people, whether registered as refugees or not.

On our way here, we were attacked by bandits. They took everything we had when we were coming, even our clothes. . . . We are women with children. We were given registration . . . two days [after] our arrival. Today we have been given nonfood items . . . also some tents.
—Women outside the new arrivals area in Ifo camp

Humanitarian operations are predicated on refugee registration and the ensuing agreement on a population figure, which determines the provision of all forms of aid. As part of the process, in order to manage and count a fleeing population, the UNHCR prioritizes dissemination of sheltering materials "for the structuring of refugee sites" and to control "the fluidity of the population."[98] The women and men in this photo carry only blankets and plastic sheeting on their backs, the remaining elements in the aid distribution chain. They are walking to the outskirts of Ifo, to use the tarp and blankets to construct dwellings. Even during their first day in Ifo camp, they became its builders.

✦

This archive of the Dadaab refugee camps contests the invisibility of humanitarian settlement in the historical record. In Dadaab, from 1991 to 1993, as three transitional settlements were established to shelter refugees from Somalia, an architecture culture and planning project emerged as part of the activities of humanitarian spatiality, which established emergency territory. From 1993 to 2006, the population grew and fluctuated, as emergency relief and development coincided and led to a concentration of refugees in an architecture of permanent ephemerality. From 2006 to 2011, floods in Ifo camp and regime change in Somalia catalyzed the planned expansion of the settlements. In the years following this speculative periodization, as the settlements expanded and contracted, the humanitarian archive accessible to a wide public has been radically augmented through the contributions of many more people living in and visiting Dadaab.

The critical archive produced in these pages speaks to the many territorial strategies employed at Dadaab, whether by states exerting authority or individuals attempting to shift power relations and their own physical security, legal status, or proximity to resources.[99] These practices of humanitarian spatiality at Dadaab created forms of urbanity and monumentality.[100] Through them, people and institutions effected a process of humanitarian settlement. This interpretation of the refugee settlements at Dadaab speaks to the role that a critical study of architecture and heritage might play, in what has primarily been an operative discourse, rather than a humanistic one. I carry this approach through the next chapter, which examines the architectures of Dadaab at a scale that relates closely to the body, through acts of design that produce an infrastructure around the planet, building forms of knowledge and a common heritage.

(*previous page*) Somali and Sudanese women establishing a “hotel” (restaurant), Ifo camp, photos by Bethany Young.

Design as Infrastructure

5

Calling the global infrastructure of refugee camps an "architecture of migration" is a reclamation of terms. It is a way to relocate authority in forms born of dispossession, by reversing what we name as architecture and whom we name as architects. This nomenclature centers people whose crossing into the legal enclosures of refugee camps recalls those whose migratory ways of life and relationships to the land and ecology go far deeper than possession and extraction. It is ironic that in Dadaab and elsewhere in the refugee world where people are immobilized, the architectures and materials with which they most immediately interact are alienated from the land. These architectures are imported, designed to be mobile, and made to cross borders. This chapter examines these architectures and their authors. It examines designs and designers that make up an infrastructure of migration.

Thinking with design as infrastructure, this chapter zooms into Dadaab, and then perhaps further in, to examine design and construction practices in the camps and specific histories of Dadaab's component architectures. Through the design and adaptation histories of these infrastructural elements of contemporary refugee camps—tarps, tanks, and tents—I uncover understudied microhistories of humanitarian institutions. These institutions assiduously—if offhandedly or even inadvertently—assumed the role of designer, adopting positions of authorship and undertaking signature practices. Furthermore, this fine historical grain of the practice of design in emergency illuminates figures and spatial practices that themselves formed infrastructures.

Design—a noun and a verb, referring to people, things, and activities—is a critical problem-solving infrastructure in emergency contexts. Yet, it is also an expression of authorial intent. The most urgent, lifesaving infrastructures have been composed of practices and objects that, surprisingly, leave the trace of a distinct signature in emergency. They expose "the false notion that design is not a crucial, or even necessary, activity, and that art is not a substantial human need in times of life-threatening urgency," as architectural historians Elisa Dainese and Aleksandar Staničić argue.[1] They illuminate the principle, articulated by African studies scholars Chérie Rivers Ndaliko and Samuel Anderson, that "emergency is itself an art that we can begin to apprehend by studying the subjectivities of its various expert authors and the aesthetic distributions—whether purposeful or inadvertent—of its sensory experience."[2] This chapter follows many such expert authors and aesthetic distributions of experience, putting design and construction in Dadaab into conversation with global institutional histories.

The chapter traces the tension between systems and signatures in design initiatives undertaken by international humanitarian organizations and highlights how architectural accomplishment and utilitarian standardization together have produced conditions for the commodification of aid. This paradox writes these architectures of migration into and out of history and exposes the contradictions underlying a liberal discourse around the alleviation of suffering.

While the narrative presented here begins and ends tangibly in the Dadaab refugee camps, it makes a significant detour into a global history of design, which is yet tethered to the work of refugees and aid workers in Dadaab. Dadaab is a site of "field" operations that has anchored an institutionalization of *humanitarian spatiality*, a production and occupation of space by workers in agencies and organizations *and* refugees. Specifically, as chapters 3 and 4 demonstrate, Dadaab served in important ways as a training ground for the development of the humanitarian subfield of spatial practice known in aid parlance as "humanitarian shelter and settlements." The development of this subfield, likewise, has been predicated on a plethora of small-scale design initiatives to develop mobile architectures such as those to be examined in this chapter, which evince the creativity of designated humanitarian agencies and organizations to innovate as well as the drive to professionalize the spatial practices of emergency relief. The formation of "shelter and settlements" units in humanitarian NGOs from the 1990s to the present, and the related shelter and camp planning specializations of organizations such as the NRC, are developments predicated on the integration of professional planners, architects, and designers—and also, as we have seen, refugees—into the field of emergency relief. It is little understood that an unnamed touchpoint for these innovations was the substantive humanitarian operation at Dadaab; over the years, the camps not only served as the material test bed for design experiments, but also, more metaphorically, provided the raison d'être. Dadaab was not the UNHCR's only large refugee settlement operating during this period but offered a pronounced stability within the global infrastructure of humanitarian spatial practice. As a site integral to frameworks of thought and discourse, Dadaab made possible signature form-making in contexts of forced migration worldwide (notably, the much-referenced architecture and design of al-Za'atari camp established in Jordan in 2012). The significance of the Dadaab refugee camps is rarely defined in these terms. Yet, people living in these camps exercised their own drive and creativity in design and construction.

The Dadaab refugee camps have historical predecessors in past abolitionist settlements and detention camps of East Africa, yet the Dadaab camps have been composed of a contemporary constellation of artifacts, systems, practices, and people, which together constitute *humanitarian space,* a term that has come to denote the conceptual location of recognized humanitarian activity.[3] Humanitarian space is often theorized only in terms of the production of space by aid organizations. Yet, the opening photographs of this chapter narrate a very different version of how space is produced in a refugee camp. They show the proprietors of a "hotel" (a restaurant) who formed a collective in Ifo camp.[4] Initially composed of Sudanese women contributing to a collective purse, the group later sought the participation of their Somali neighbors. The decision to open a restaurant required appealing to the majority population, and because members of the Muslim community might not eat food that was not halal, the Christian Sudanese women invited their Somali neighbors to join their venture to help with the cooking, manage community perception, and attract customers. The hotel was located on the border between Sudanese and Somali blocks in Ifo camp. As a vital element of humanitarian space, the built form illustrates design as infrastructure, as does the collaboration behind it.

The collaboration produced an intangible infrastructure, intertwining forms of labor, care, and mutual aid. Unexpected commonalities grew out of the women's partnership, as this group of single mothers forged a cooperative to fund the business, design a restaurant, and build and manage it. They did so under the guidance and funding of CARE, through a microcredit program that encouraged collective labor scaffolded by humanitarian technical support and a monitoring process. The refugee partners described a landscape of bureaucratic struggle to establish the restaurant. They noted that CARE provided support to build the building, but not to procure materials, nor to launch the activities within. By the time the building was built, the women had worked for two full years to develop the project and formulate a focus for the business. After all this, the buying of foodstuffs, the organization of labor, and so on seemed to be afterthoughts. In our meetings, all of the women articulated a sense that they were required to bring an unsustainable level of entrepreneurship to the endeavor. CARE's approach was one of "self-help," rooted in development models. The organization expected refugees to become purveyors of what, in aid parlance, is termed an income-generating activity, a concrete aim of self-sustenance that formed a core professional focus for CARE. However, this approach little acknowledged constraints in Ifo camp. The women in the collective faced a sheer lack of cash and uncertain community support, among other things. Analyses of such structural challenges in other contexts have been a focus of studies of humanitarian aid in neoliberal economies.[5] Yet, what surfaced in our conversations was structural in a very different register. Even as these friends met to discuss their process and concerns, they laughed as they complained, telling stories of their trials and teasing one another. These sounds and this warmth projected the contours of a forged community. Without romanticizing that laughter, I would like to focus a brief analysis on that gendered process of forging a form of kinship, across religious and cultural lines, under the duress of living and working in a refugee camp, while designing and building a space for social activity. This construction of social relationships speaks to a phenomenon that holds meaning not only in the localized context of Ifo camp in Dadaab, or even internationally within the enclosure of humanitarian environments per se, but across the worlds of migration.

This processual, gendered forging of relation is a core example of design as infrastructure. For this insight, I draw on urban theorist AbdouMaliq Simone's formulation of "people as infrastructure," in which he pushed against (and with) the definitions of physical infrastructure in order to reflect on "complex combinations of objects, spaces, persons, and practices" as "conjunctions [that] become an infrastructure—a platform for providing for and reproducing life."[6] Turning from this theorization to the problem of gendered space, I would further posit that the affective aspect of this human infrastructure intensifies in the embodied practices of women's labor and mutual aid in a refugee camp. The work of this women's collective resolves, much as Simone articulated but with the added complexity of this gendered aspect, in the "conjunction of heterogeneous activities, modes of production, and institutional forms . . . highly mobile and provisional possibilities for how people live and make things, how they use the urban environment and collaborate with one another."[7] Putting aside the debate over whether or not the Ifo camp environment was urban, the process of making the hotel brimmed with this life-giving complexity, heterogeneity, provisionality, and mobility. It commingled, as the photographs show, women from the Somali and Sudanese communities (registered as refugees in Ifo camp); their children playing together (visible through the building window); a Kenyan aid worker for CARE (in the orange shirt); researchers from US-based universities and organizations (one seated at the table); lumber and plywood (sourced through local—that is, nonhumanitarian—supply chains from Garissa or Nairobi); corrugated sheet metal, one of the finest construction materials in the camp (whose source I could not ascertain, but possibly imported from outside of Kenya, whether or not through humanitarian networks); and various other people and things. The infrastructural quality of this combination of people and things, I argue, stemmed from the collaborative processes of envisioning, projection, abstraction, and articulation inherent in architectural design.

To further understand an infrastructure of design in the intersection of these people and things, I theorize these social crucibles of collaboration and incipient making in which these women participated as forming an archive on which to draw. That is, these collaborative spaces and moments formed a primary source for understanding an architecture of migration. They were sociospatial and temporal formations within which knowledge and consciousness were constructed and shared. I was privileged to be invited into one of these moments, in which women met within the four walls of an enclosure they dreamed and designed, to negotiate next steps. My research partner Bethany Young and I met the women in this collective while they were in a process of constructing an establishment, which had already taken architectural form before it could be properly programmed.[8] We asked them many questions. *Does it help to have a building? Why was the building built before there were any saucepans? Was there anyone in this group who was involved in making the decision?* Our questions and their answers are of less significance here than the way the conversation, as one among many they had been having with one another, shaped a space-time archive of design as infrastructure. This archive was constituted of many acts of care and labor—refugees befriending one another, building a structure, establishing a business and cultural center, relaxing the border between two neighborhoods, growing a mixed community, minding children, providing livelihoods for people living and laboring under a distinct sign of social difference as single women, and sharing, as the matter of their concern, a planned and built artifact: the hotel. This artifact, the processes and laughter behind it, and the collective of people who were its authors, should be understood as constitutive infrastructures of humanitarian settlement, connected to processes of design.

Design processes have anchored an infrastructure of historically specific materialities and signature activity, a dissonant concept, yet evident in the authorship documented in this book, by Isnina Ali Rage or Alishine Osman in chapter 1, Abdullah Susi or Johann Ludwig Krapf in chapter 2, Shamso Abdullahi Farah or Frederick Cuny in chapter 3, or Sabine Wähning or Per Iwansson in chapter 4. The chapters have charted structures such as the shelters in chapter 3 or the food distribution system in chapter 4, which resulted from practices in which refugees acted as architects, or collaborated with official planners and architects, building knowledge and designs together. In the following pages, I catalog emergency artifacts and practices within humanitarian institutions that demonstrate the trace of a particular hand, disaggregating named designers and unnamed authors contributing to technical and aesthetic experimentation and innovation. In this task, I am sympathetic to the research undertaken by artist and art historian Azra Akšamija and her team, which documents (in English and Arabic, in text and image) designs by refugees, humanitarians, and others in Azraq camp in Jordan that bring art and cultural precision into everyday life in emergency.[9] While acknowledging such localized worldmaking in refugee camps, my project diverges as I aim to comprehend the objects in this chapter within a global infrastructure, to recover the hands of makers outside the refugee camp alongside those within, and theorize them together as producing a signature. The design of lifesaving technologies has paradoxically and perhaps improbably involved aesthetic practices and forms operating in sensible, affective registers well outside the logistical and social constructs of emergency relief practice.[10] This history of design processes and the interactions of designers within an architecture of migration thus takes on an infrastructural capacity.

Humanitarian Iconography and Commodification

While this book's narrative privileges the architectures and spatial practices urgent to people who have made Dadaab home, the universal tarps, tanks, and tents—found across all UNHCR-administered refugee camps—are also critical to Dadaab's built environment. Such "meta pragmatic objects," as anthropologist Brian Larkin analyzes, belie "a world in movement and open to change where the free circulation of goods, ideas, and people created the possibility of progress."[11] For example, the WFP warehouses in the food distribution centers of the Dadaab camps that serve refugees or the Pumzika café in the UNHCR compound that caters to aid workers are part of the concrete footprint of an international humanitarian infrastructure across the liberal, progressive world of modernity Larkin describes.

Although they are mobile architectures, these objects behave differently when in stasis. Lisa Smirl's acute analysis of the material infrastructure of the humanitarian regime identifies the production of social space by the distinct hardware of humanitarian communications, transportation, accommodation, and leisure.[12] This chapter confronts the same phenomenon, but in contrast to her largely sociomaterial inquiry, mine seeks aesthetic, cultural, and political design histories of humanitarian objects that are at once mobile, circulatory, and legible across many landscapes, while also static anchors for the enclosures and built environments of emergency relief in specific places such as Dadaab. Whereas chapter 4 focused largely on the latter problem, this chapter tackles the former and attempts to resolve the two.

The politics of the *signature emergency artifact* lies in its reproduction and circulation as a form of humanitarian iconography that can be commodified. Such objects form infrastructures operating in material, spatial, visual, and aesthetic registers: beyond immediate function and toward symbolic representation. Their very circulation within the humanitarian regime reproduces them as semiotic markers. Infrastructures double as political and poetic, as Larkin proposes, working as "signs of themselves deployed in particular circulatory regimes to establish sets of effects."[13] Signature emergency artifacts, while material remnants of the infrastructure of humanitarian settlement, operate as aesthetic signifiers, as humanitarian iconography.[14] Their circulation shifts their use value to an exchange value, turning humanitarian iconography into commodity.[15] Thus, a lifesaving technology, such as a water tank, becomes an icon of lifesaving activity, functioning as the signifier to attract donors to this referent, or as the sign of the donor itself. These objects and images produce *desire*. This desire, at once related to the alleviation of suffering and to a concurrent commodification of objects, alienates people from participating in a mutual aid process. Instead, signature emergency artifacts manufacture a dialectical relationship between donors and recipients of aid, exacerbating various forms of political and social asymmetry, as the following episode illustrates.

The UNHCR and the IKEA Foundation inaugurated a financial partnership through diffuse initiatives in 2009, which advanced in 2011 to "knowledge sharing" concerning logistics, including product and warehousing network design, quality control, packaging, procurement, distribution, and information technology, accompanied by a $62 million donation for shelter in the Ifo 2 camp commissioned at Dadaab. The announcement of this donation followed in the week after reports of the publication of a new book exposing the corporation founder's ties to the Swedish Nazi party.[16] According to a UNHCR spokesperson, this was "the largest private donation that the UN refugee agency has received in its 60-year history, and the first time that a private body has chosen to directly support a major refugee complex."[17] The gift, a powerful representation of a humanitarianism positioned to cleanse a tarnished image of Nazi affiliation, enabled a massive sum of capital, itself an abstraction, to transform into a material iteration: a concrete, signature expression of patronage that operated both philanthropically and within the sphere of morality. That is, it alleviated suffering and produced desire around that action, transforming moral value into aesthetic value. As this patronage translated capital into a contained work of design and construction at a high-profile site, it revealed the complex practical and social life of architecture in humanitarian environments. Here, design, as a form of infrastructure, traversed ground between the financial and sociopolitical toward questions of authorship and aesthetics. Through the enactment of exchange and the aggrandizement of an object's value through the aesthetics of its moral value, design transformed a lifesaving humanitarian shelter into a fetishized commodity.

Several problems stem from such conditions, and I will target two. The first is the entanglement of urgent material concerns with aesthetic ones, linking technological innovation in emergency relief with the commodity's production of desire or fetish. The second is a reinscription of borders that stems from and fortifies this entanglement, as the design, fabrication, and installation of humanitarian architectures are predicated on *border-crossing artifacts*. Humanitarian mobile architectures descend from the promise of prefabrication and its application to emergency relief. The innovation of prefabrication—the production of mobile building components for rapid on-site assembly—forms a master narrative in the history of modern architecture, seen in the emergency response to the Lisbon earthquake discussed in chapter 1 and in iconic works by architects such as the Dom-Ino concrete slab structure that Le Corbusier proposed for housing to rehabilitate cities destroyed after World War I or, in an ideologically different vein, R. Buckminster

Fuller's Dymaxion House experiments for minimal dwellings deployable from the air. However, prefabrication's history is ultimately a military history. Based as such in the rise of the modern nation-state, prefabrication has rarely been thought through the problem of borders. Following the problem articulated in chapter 1, I argue that humanitarian tarps, tanks, and tents materialize the afterlife of a partition, as border-crossing artifacts and elements of humanitarian iconography with the capacity to cross between nation-states, as people often cannot. They reinscribe refugees' spatial relationships to borders.[18] They also reinscribe the cosmopolitanisms of humanitarian agencies, organizations, and workers; for example, in images of Red Cross trucks at border checkpoints that form a visual trope in "sans frontières" photographic representation.[19] Aspirations for transborder mobility intersect with humanitarian iconography, increasing the exchange value of humanitarian objects and precipitating the commodification of *design as infrastructure*.

The histories of design to follow enable close looking at processes of commodification and microhistories of institutions, and with them, I identify a pantheon of lifesaving architectures, part of a humanitarian iconography, which illuminates a tension between systematization and signature practice. The iconic architectures in this chapter are products of systems, both agents and terrain of this tension. If this thinking draws on the foundational theory that components of a technology can be "actors" and behave as protagonists in a story, it does not privilege a nonhuman approach and imagines affective objects and landscapes that relate to the humans dreaming, making, and using them.[20] A discussion of systems and signature practices follows, to pave the way for an exploration of specific objects.

Systems and Signature Practices

A history of tension between humanitarian systems and signature practice can be traced to the early 1990s, when the international practice of coordinated emergency relief expanded into a billion-dollar economy. The UNHCR operating budget peaked, coincident with the agency's express alignment with militarized peacekeeping.[21] The UN introduced an initiative to centralize international emergency relief funding, establishing direct streams for state and private support that facilitated explicitly "humanitarian" responses to designated crises.[22] As anthropologists Didier Fassin and Mariella Pandolfi discuss, a cyclical scheme of emergency and response emerged with ever more frequency.[23] Displacements of people at unprecedented scales and frequencies occurred due to global patterns of ecologically unsustainable habitation and interruptions of global supply chains causing sudden localized food and water scarcity. These pressures forced individuals, families, and communities into an international system, which categorically qualified them as displaced and assumed legal responsibility for them as such. In this system, events that had begun to be designated as "humanitarian" crises effected responses at the scale of building programs, even as the evidence presented by authorities underscored the negative aspects of refugee camps—not least, that they would likely endure for generations, regardless of quality or maintenance. Although the UNHCR and NGOs in this heterogeneous system of state and private actors established fewer camps overall, they systematized design and construction processes in highly professionalized and coordinated emergency interventions. State agencies and NGOs implemented physical planning on a large scale at individual locations, often not installing shelters, but instead employing a "sites-and-services" approach by designating space and offering basic civil infrastructure to displaced people, with the expectation that they would produce their own shelter using ready-made materials provided at the moment when they became registered as refugees—a mass housing development strategy taken up by many states. In this context, the humanitarian shelter sector and the commercial architecture and design disciplines converged.[24] As kits containing everything from household supplies to flat-packed dwellings and other prefabricated materials were deployed to sites of emergency via air or ground, enabling rapid assembly of large settlements, the work of the system became entangled with the signature of designers or of donors. The Norwegian roofline of Shamso Abdullahi Farah's shop in chapter 3 is one example of a donor signature, and many more appeared in the varieties of portable objects and mobile architectures created for use in displacement contexts.

The aesthetic burden on these architectures was to communicate ephemerality, to act as signifiers of impermanence. Architectural signs of permanence threatened societies and governments, complicating the activity of relief donors and aid organizations, irritating host communities, and reifying the displacement of people from home. During this period, when commercial design forces became entangled with humanitarian relief, the design of the camp and its material components assumed a semiotic function. This doubling of shelter and signifier did not find its way into the otherwise trenchant criticism of the UNHCR, for example, missing from comments in the *New Left Review*: "If it was originally a guarantor of refugee rights, UNHCR has since mutated into a patron of these prisons of the stateless: a network of huge camps that can never meet any plausible 'humanitarian' standard, and yet somehow justify international funding for the agency."[25] However percipient, such political criticisms overlooked a spatial politics in the twinned labor of the architectures of camp, tent, and tarp to materially protect and also convey meaning. Design was called on by refugees, humanitarians, and bystanders alike to effect a variety of solutions. This awkward demand resulted in a commingling of desire with the commodification of humanitarian aid, giving rise to *signature practices* in emergency contexts.

Signature practices may be considered along a spectrum. Some inhabit the spheres of art and design proper, constituting the epistemic tradition and the discourse that surrounds the work. In some, the author is nearly invisible, yet a trace of handiwork produces the commodifiable object. In both, signature activity forms the topography of exchange.[26] For example, professionally trained architects and refugee laborers, however recognized (or not) in institutional design contexts, together imagined and constructed built environments in many locations, undertaking roles as space planners, designers, construction contractors, and materials procurers—creating paradigmatic aesthetic identities for the camps at Dadaab and elsewhere. Aesthetic identity, in this formulation, works in conjunction with and also independent of systems. For historian of technology Gabrielle Hecht, whether strategic or not, design "shaped the ways in which those systems acted upon the world."[27] A spectrum of signature practices is critical to the infrastructure produced by design.

Renowned and lesser-known figures whose practices together inhabit this spectrum constitute an infrastructure of people whose creation of desire—not for human suffering, of course, but around the capacity to alleviate it—concretizes profound asymmetries through the production, even if inadvertent, of fetishization.[28] Humanitarian authorship creates philosophical and aesthetic problems around the consumption, exchange, and circulation of objects and imagery; however, as discussed in chapter 4, these authored objects and material culture produce epistemic and historical problems as well, as they constitute an archive of sorts. Such an archive, operating in the realm of the moral, forms a diverse infrastructure representing signature practices.

A Spectrum of Signature Practices

The office of architect Shigeru Ban offers a celebrated example of a signature humanitarian practice. Responding to the 1995 earthquake in Kobe, Japan, Ban worked for the UNHCR, an agency functioning independently from the UN General Assembly; he was contracted as an "architect consultant" under the unit of Wolfgang Neumann, the UNHCR's senior physical planner and first staff architect.[29] Shigeru Ban Architects had previously developed a design of paper structural tubes in a variety of cultural and commercial contexts. The structure of compressed cardboard adapted mass-produced formwork used in reinforced concrete construction, made to hold the plastic shape of uncured concrete poured into cylindrical columns. Ban's studio first tested the compressed cardboard construction technique in an indoor exhibition of the Finnish modernist architect Alvar Aalto's work in 1986, and later in an outdoor pavilion, Paper Arbor, for the World Design Expo in Nagoya, Japan, in 1989.[30] In 1995, after the UNHCR had begun working with architects but before it embarked on tent design initiatives in the 2000s or established a Shelter and Settlement Section in 2011, Ban's office designed a structural frame for a tent using this paper tube technology, with a cost estimated at over three dollars per unit, prototyped pro bono by the VITRA furniture company in Basel and implemented in Rwanda. Senior Physical Planner Wolfgang Neumann praised the "quite sophisticated" structure (pending waterproofing and strengthening the tubes), its precise welded aluminum joinery, and the feasibility of its fabrication and assembly in the field.[31] Ban's office built similar structures at Kobe and later in India and Turkey, affordably and sustainably using recyclable materials, aligning joined paper tubes to form bearing walls and roofs for shelters.[32] The tension between the signature practice described here and a broader systematicity registered in the machined, modular, replicable shelters, whose paper tube walls, plywood foundations, and plastic tarpaulin roofs referred to systems of production that were foreign to the locations of the devastated sites, requiring transregional communications networks and markets for the purchase and distribution of materials and supplies, as well as standardized international expertise. Children and bicycles in the architect's photographs imply the social life and effect of shelters transformed into humanitarian iconography through the global circulation and consumption of those images, via the career of a Pritzker Architecture Prize winner whose jury citation liberally referred to his emergency relief work. The UNHCR brought Ban into partnership in the years following the First International Workshop on Improved Shelter Response and Environment for Refugees, organized in 1993 by the architect responsible for site selection for the Dadaab camps. Although Ban's office did not design any shelters in Dadaab, the prominence of the site as an iteration of humanitarian spatiality at the time of the UNHCR's burgeoning attentiveness to architectural practice likely attuned the agency to Ban's signature practices of emergency relief.

Ban's work illustrates the practice of architecture as a fine art; in the examples that follow, artistic intentions may be unrecognized or unintended. The architect of Benaco camp, for example, was its emergency coordinator, Maureen Connelly. Its establishment in Tanzania in 1994 possesses a genealogical connection to Dadaab, as she developed the role of UNHCR emergency coordinator at Ifo camp in 1991.[33] The emergency coordination system she designed in Dadaab was a progenitor for Benaco's.

Benaco camp housed a quarter of a million refugees who crossed the border over the Rusumo Bridge from Rwanda into Tanzania's Ngara District in a single day, in April 1994. Many aspects of this event were extraordinary. For so many people to seek asylum and to be received by the UNHCR in such a short time was unprecedented, as was the semblance of order they presented, having kept entire villages intact while on foot. While a humanitarian settlement materialized nearly instantly to host the refugees, planned and constructed by aid agencies rather than with national or international military logistical support, this traumatized group of Hutu families, children, and communities were almost immediately exposed as having fled to avoid violent reprisal, having killed up to fifty thousand Tutsi people on the preceding day. The

5.1. Shigeru Ban Architects, Paper Emergency Shelters for UNHCR, Byumba Refugee Camp, Rwanda, 1999, © Shigeru Ban Architects.

complex and horrific circumstances sent shock waves throughout the world. In humanitarian spheres, the realization of complicity in the immediate context of violence ignited a burst of self-reflection and self-critique, in public discourse and scholarly literature.[34] These events precipitated reactionary responses, technocratic impulses, and ultimately a reckoning of humanitarian practice, resulting in the collective development and publication of standards for the delivery of humanitarian aid.

For aid workers, Benaco camp realized the impossible, the planning of a camp for a quarter of a million people over a matter of days, through the coordination of numerous international and local actors. In the face of this heterogeneity and the complex circumstances attending the refugees, this efficient planning became a storied feat, a referent for many aid workers I interviewed, and a refrain repeated in varying contexts (in humanitarian headquarters, at field sites, in conferences, and elsewhere). The aftermath of those days in Ngara may have contributed to this mythologizing, but so did a signature practice. The rapid and site-sensitive construction of a settlement in response to a daunting scale and suddenness of crisis is widely credited to the UNHCR emergency coordinator, Maureen Connelly, frequently named as the source of Benaco's exemplary management and lauded for leading collaborations across institutions and professional fields with a "strong" and "no-nonsense" approach.[35] In speaking to me, she was direct about the controversial episode at Benaco camp and full of humor about her "fame" (wondering aloud which "expletives" colleagues had used to describe her).[36] Her professional reputation expanded during her final position before retirement, at the UNHCR headquarters in Geneva, as younger colleagues within and outside the agency shared stories and grew the legend. If an emergency environment can have an architect, she was Benaco's.

Another architect of Benaco camp was the first-response organization MSF. The political crisis in the aftermath of genocide in Rwanda was formative and controversial in MSF's history, with MSF-France eventually removing its staff from field operations.[37] Yet, the organization was central to Benaco camp's physical planning. Maureen Connelly described an MSF-Spain engineer who snaked a pipe up the hill, so that refugees and humanitarian staff would not have to travel to the base on foot for water.[38] This inclination toward bricolage lies at the heart of MSF's signature practice, embodied in the pioneering prefabrication and logistics center, MSF Logistique.

The construction of a settlement at the scale and speed at which Benaco was realized owed a debt to this logistical capacity and developed into one of

MSF's core specializations through the Logistique satellite office. Anthropologist Peter Redfield's broader research on MSF's specialization in bricolage and development of a mutable and mobile kit identifies a culture of field logisticians "tinkering with the means at hand" to achieve results.[39] The head bricoleur, Jacques Pinel, a professional pharmacist and adviser to the division MSF Logistique, discussed with me his career transfer from the private sector into the world of MSF's medical relief operations in the Thai-Cambodian border region in the 1980s. He realized in later missions in Africa that a logistics system would be required to address the dearth of "things"—from pharmaceuticals to vehicles to telephones.[40] Pinel's work in organizing MSF Logistique, aside from developing humanitarian logistics as a field-wide operational paradigm, initiated a proprietary system of materials supply based on a singularly humanitarian scope and mission.[41] The fabrication of medical kits to supply camps later extended to the production of a variety of commodities. Today, a shipment from MSF Logistique's facilities near the Bordeaux-Mérignac Airport in France to a field site could contain an inflatable medical hospital and a package of ten thousand prefabricated shelters, or a Toyota Land Cruiser reconfigured for satellite communications and packed with medicines specific to the nutrition or disease profile of a particular region. Such innovations placed MSF at the forefront of a muscular field it had forged.

Professional logistics and the prefabricated kit drew from military systems with broad social service and commercial applications. However, within designated humanitarian contexts, they were ensconced in the service of a moral imperative. In other words, these methods and materials were the outcome of a philosophical orientation. This aesthetic impetus lies at the basis of a signature practice.[42] Like Connelly's practice at Benaco camp, Pinel's employed systematization across a large configuration. Nevertheless, it harkened back to signature practices by individuals or organizations, whose expertise undergirded the techniques used in humanitarian logistics. The design of emergency environments and the implementation of aid within them traces back to acts of spatial planning and experiences of spatial planners. These designs and designers configured the infrastructure of emergency environments and ordered the work within them.

These examples link signature practice to distinct individuals responsible for forms of creativity within emergency contexts. While Shigeru Ban's work produced a direct exchange value in two spheres—one concerned with the creation of desire and the other with emergency relief—the work at Benaco camp by UNHCR Emergency Coordinator Maureen Connelly or in Mérignac

5.2. Essential nonfood supplies laid out for distribution to ten thousand individuals, © ICRC / FICHARD, Philippe, August 8, 2009, District of Buner, Daggar, Sawari camp for displaced persons. Relief distribution organized by the ICRC jointly with the Pakistan Red Crescent Society. V-P-PK-E-00883.

by Jacques Pinel of MSF Logistique illustrates how leadership or technical proficiency in crisis produced a signature practice. In most emergency relief settings, in which such protagonists are elusive, the social lives of designed objects nevertheless instigate a process of commodification, independent of categorical networks of authorship or reception.

A photo posted in the 2009 gallery on the website of the ICRC illuminates this process. It is one of eleven photographs depicting the work of the ICRC and Red Crescent, and one of two depicting commodities, including nonperishable foods and essential supplies, laid out in a grid at a camp.[43] Each bundle included machined red plastic buckets, bedsheets prepackaged in plastic wrap, factory-manufactured tents, yellow cans of "Shama" brand ghee (clarified butter for cooking), and other essentials. Each object in the image was symptomatic of a hybrid interaction between emergency relief organizations and state, military, and commercial networks, within Pakistan and internationally. The ordering of the grid of objects makes visible the trace of the human hand, the aid workers who arranged these donated or procured items, the material remnants of a humanitarian manual labor force and its administrative and executive bodies. The ephemeral architecture of the shelters marked the camp's rapid construction, serving as the temporary footprint at the end of permanent supply chains supporting the mass manufacture and distribution of such items. Unlike other images by professional photographers who specialize in capturing such contexts, this one is not composed or rendered with artistic or photojournalistic intent. Credited to ICRC communications staff member Philippe Fichard (not a commissioned photographer or photojournalist), the photo depicts a common scene in an ordinary way, behaving as a stock image. Even absent an explicit signature, this humanitarian matter at the nexus of significant material and visual systems in circulation intersects with multiple economic, political, and social practices. The signature at the heart of these practices brings the relief site and its photographic artifacts into play with the monumentalization of a humanitarian ideology and the creation of desire around it.

Attention to such grammars of representation, design histories, and iconography behind humanitarian spatiality forms the core discussion to follow on the tarp, a tank, a tent, a hospital, and a logistics system. These objects offer lessons on signature practices behind the creation of desire in emergency. They are among the architectures and infrastructures that constitute the Dadaab refugee camps and essential components of humanitarian-built environments worldwide. They are organized, described, and theorized according to a conventional language of the patron-artist-artwork relationship. This approach is intended to produce reversals of thought. It estranges these objects, liberating them from being limited and abstracted by the mortal utilitarianism of functioning as essential, lifesaving objects, and allowing them to be analyzed as works of design. By putting them into dialogue with people who depend on them as well as people who make them, I aim to defamiliarize institutions, complicating monolithic readings of humanitarian agencies and organizations by naming and listening to individuals within them. In this way, I aim to deconstruct humanitarian commodification. Treating each of these designed objects as a small monument understood in terms of patronage enables us to take seriously what it means for emergency relief and design to work in cooperation. The following meditations consider designed objects as well as the infrastructures of their making as constitutive of an architecture of migration.

The UNHCR and the Tarp

Cawo Aden Yeru arrived at Ifo camp on March 12, 2011, under circumstances of extreme distress. That afternoon, in the hours before the curfew would be imposed, sending foreigners back to the UNHCR compound, she paused to explain to us her experiences of the day. She arrived at the camp along with dozens of others who had traveled a long distance on foot to escape danger. In Ifo, she was registered as a refugee immediately, according to prima facie law, which allows governments and the UNHCR to administer mass registrations in the face of ample evidence that the presenting groups face imminent persecution. If she had arrived on the fifteenth of the month, the humanitarian aid providers would have allotted her a food ration. Because she arrived within a day of the next food distribution, the aid providers who registered her could provide her only with "nonfood items," in aid parlance—that is, the blankets and other supplies she holds in this photograph. These items did not include a prefabricated shelter, as the camps had already been facing a shortage of shelters before the large numbers of people began arriving that month. I spoke with her only briefly, during which time her generosity and wherewithal were palpable. Then, she gathered her things to walk to the periphery of the camp to build a makeshift dwelling before dark. Among her new possessions was a tarp.

The tarpaulin that she was given was a machine-fabricated plastic-based textile. The fabric is light but not fragile and can be draped over structural supports to provide shade, be gathered at the ends to collect rainwater, approximate a medical stretcher when suspended over two pieces of bamboo or other wood, and wrap corpses for burial. These civil and cultural needs expand its material purpose well beyond emergency sheltering. The UNHCR did not invent lightweight plastic sheeting; however, since 1985, distributing it in emergency has been the agency's first response strategy, as part of its mandate to respond to a disaster within seventy-two hours. The UNHCR airlifts approximately 500,000 to one million reinforced polyethylene tarps per year to different parts of the world. These tarps are stockpiled in warehouses in Copenhagen, Durban, and Dubai. Dubai is the shipping hub for Dadaab, where distribution of tarps remains common, as Cawo Aden Yeru and other asylum seekers have experienced. The agency procures the finished materials from companies such as Qingdao Gyoha Plastics in China. The low bulk price of this textile creates a ubiquitous field of blue at emergency sites. Visually, the color has become synonymous with emergency and its relief. Materially, the textile, as a fabric that covers and encloses but houses no integrated structure, reproduces the condition of ephemerality.

5.3. Cawo Aden Yeru, Ifo camp.

The exhibition of this material in art museums speaks to its labor in the realm of aesthetics. For example, more than once the Museum of Modern Art (MoMA) in New York City, an institution that has historically played a significant role in arbitrating on iconicity and value in modern design, has named emergency materials as exemplary: in the 2016 exhibition "Insecurities: Tracing Displacement and Shelter" and in the 2005 exhibition "SAFE: Design Takes on Risk."[44] The latter exhibited the blue tarp with the curatorial conceit that "sometimes the best design is the simplest."[45] This appeal to a universal understanding of "best design" assigned aesthetic value to objects associated with displacement, categorizing them as fundamentally "modern." This act of cataloging placed this generation of lightweight plastic sheeting, the tarp favored by the UNHCR, among the broader set of artifacts of concern to a museum adjudicating on the stylistically modern.

This museum's attentiveness to the design of the tarp demonstrates this material's inhabitation of a social field of signature practices. The curators described it as a densely woven fabric, "stabilized against ultraviolet rays and excess heat for long outdoor exposure," and augmented with features such as aluminum eyelets to promote flexible use.[46] Such design refinements increased this textile's utility, transforming it socially and enabling it to engage aesthetic languages and negotiations. The "SAFE" curator, Paola Antonelli, discussed with me the museological narrative and taxonomy of objects, among the guiding principles of an exhibition displaying objects of human risk and security, articulating a curatorial objective to convey the preciousness of the tarp object.[47] Putting aside critiques of this or other design exhibitions and art institutions that use aesthetic practices to narrate emergency objects, I am concerned with the placement of systematically manufactured emergency objects within a regime of signature practices. This small and precise step is significant evidence of the construction of humanitarian iconography and the commodification of the most essential materials designed for emergency relief.

Oxfam and the Water Tank

The Oxfam water tank provides a study of a conspicuous object. It represents *adaptation*: a principle that is recognized and valued in a refugee camp, where social and material adjustment is urgent and lifesaving, and conditions the experience of migration. In many conversations with mothers and children in Dadaab and elsewhere, I heard descriptions of time spent adapting, as they spoke of arriving in the camp and building dwellings, renovating those dwellings, acclimating to new neighbors, or preparing for emigration to another place. Aid workers spoke of adapting with pride and respect—the very act of alteration amounting to a signature achievement in precarious environments, in which the material aim of innovation was not production of the new but modification of the existing. In this milieu, the visual conspicuousness of the Oxfam water tank was an echo of the organization's achievement in designing infrastructure—ironically, an inconspicuous act of integration of conspicuous objects.

The Oxfam water tank was designed for ready adaptation by nonspecialists on its installation in a camp. This principle enabled its quick installation by Hijra, an organization working with Oxfam in Badbaado camp established outside Mogadishu after the 2011 drought created extreme food and water scarcity, driving thousands of people out of the city. As indicated in a candid photograph contributed by Oxfam East Africa to an open-source database earlier that year, the installation process is embodied and interactive, with engineers in direct engagement with displaced people and their families. One might imagine the children involving themselves in all aspects of the process, invited or not. Within the global as well as local infrastructures in which the Oxfam water tank is integrated, it remains a recognizable object. If aesthetically unremarkable, it is nevertheless iconic—historically, socially, and even visually.

Among the sectors into which humanitarian physical planning operations are divided, that devoted to water and sanitation in emergency environments was among the first to develop iconic infrastructural objects and systems. Within the water and sanitation sector, the UK-originated organization Oxfam developed an unparalleled field expertise.[48] Its signature water tank became a commonly recognizable visual element at emergency sites around the world in the 1980s and 1990s.[49] However, this iteration of a water tank stemmed from an unexpected origin point, which related to the land and to development in different ways than a refugee camp does—or perhaps in ways that suggest subtle connections. As described to me by Sean Barton, the head of Oxfam Great Britain's humanitarian supply operations, the design of the Oxfam water tank drew from agricultural sources: "The leader of our technical team, back in the 70s and 80s, was someone called Jim Howard, who noticed that in British farms, farmers were storing their grain in circular prefabricated tanks. He thought to himself, well, couldn't this be used in emergency interventions for the storage of water if a bladder was put inside it? And that's essentially what happened. That agricultural use was transferred to humanitarian sector use. And now the suppliers we source our

5.4. Oxfam water tanks built by the NGO Hijra, Badbaado camp, Somalia, photo by Geno Teofino, September 28, 2011, © Geno Teofino/Oxfam.

5.5. Installation of an Oxfam water tank, Ifo camp, photo on Wikimedia Commons, July 18, 2011, credited to Oxfam East Africa, Jo Harrison/Oxfam.

tanks from and the internal bladders . . . are still in the agricultural sector."[50] Through this quiet transfer of agricultural knowledge, an infrastructural component of economic development in the United Kingdom and a visual motif in the English countryside during the Cold War found another life as an infrastructural component and visual motif in quite different settings of emergency and humanitarianism, geographically and conceptually far from England.

An earlier iteration of the object, pictured through the eyes of Per Iwansson, a Swedish architect working in Dadaab in 1992 (discussed in chapter 4), staked British claims among Somali refugees in a Kenyan settlement through an international technology.[51] On a purely spatial level, the water tank dominated the cross-section of the refugee settlements. It towered high over any other built or living object in Dadaab and its surroundings. The storage tank ordered the plan, setting nodal points that determined the spacing for the water distribution grid. Supply lines were established every forty feet.[52] This geometry materialized itself in structures composed of imported machined elements, such as the corrugated galvanized steel shell, rubber lining, and polyvinyl chloride roof. The grid, in turn, set the lot spacing for residential plots. It determined quotidian and yet vital matters—for example, the amount of space available on a residential plot for additional family shelters or for keeping livestock. A conspicuous, foreign, materially hybrid, essential object together marked the everyday and the exceptional. This meme from Britain's agro-industrial development produced a foreign imaginary in Dadaab, while the psychic primacy of an element in the pantheon of lifesaving equipment enacted a tension in each of its immediate environments.

The Oxfam water tank can be found in each settlement in Dadaab and refugee camps across the region and world. That recurrence contributes to a visual rhetoric. The recurring object is at once indispensable to the unique lives of individuals and common to many. From the perspective of a mobile viewer, whether refugee, aid worker, official, donor, or researcher—any of whom may have seen the object at multiple sites—the artifact concretized and reinforced collective perceptions of Oxfam's technical proficiency in the humanitarian water and sanitation sector through the ingenuity of the adaptation of an ordinary object. The object, meanwhile, occupied a synechdochal role, at any one site implying the transportation and communications networks, diplomatic relations, and geography of the international supply chain and marking the concrete presence of the state and international governmental order. It silently asserted Kenyan authority and relations with other states, even making national claims for Britain, while ultimately representing the

international humanitarian regime in Dadaab. Taken as a fragment as such, the object metonymically stands in for these material worlds, denoting a foreign system of aid, an industrialized system of food and water economies, and a hybrid system of governmental and nongovernmental caretaking and authority. This is not to claim that such signification was intentional, but that precisely through the *design* of the object and its surrounding environments, such signification and immanent power relations were enacted.

While the Oxfam water tank's representations do not supersede its actual use, its value as a usable object has been enmeshed with its value as a circulating object representing the multiple interests just discussed. As it has passed through various social environments and been "exchanged," the water tank's real and virtual circulation produces both a tangible and a mimetic layering, as the material object moves through global networks and its photos move through websites, humanitarian gray literature, reports, and so on. This layering produces a "concrete abstraction," a concept architectural historian Reinhold Martin uses to analyze architecture within the net of global finance capital, which he identifies as carrying certain "spatial and psychic equivalents."[53] The tangible abstraction of a piece of lifesaving equipment and the psychic ramifications of that object could hardly be more pressing than in the context of a refugee camp. Refugee camps are enclosures of trauma, which people associate with forcible removal from home. As mental health workers in Dadaab explained, a person's trauma is often translated into meaning-making through psychic investment in, or disinvestment from, objects.[54] Many people I spoke with—aid workers as well as refugees—attested to abstracting or disinvesting from meaningful objects and also imbuing ordinary ones with latent significance. They also commented on the circulation of architectures within and beyond the boundaries of a camp or a state, regularly referring to national imaginaries via objects and their associations, and articulating the representational layering that could be produced by a water tank as an image in circulation. Such nuances may have resulted from investing places and things with what anthropologist Liisa Malkki calls a "mythico-history," in the context of the bounded setting of Mishamo camp in Tanzania "enabling and nurturing an elaborate and self-conscious historicity among

5.6–5.8. (*opposite*) Oxfam water tank in Ifo camp, the construction crew clearing brush and marking the path for the line using their bodies as surveying tools, and the laying of the water pipeline, 1991, photos from slideshow provided by Per Iwansson.

its refugee inhabitants," as Hutu people developed new social "regimes of truth" culled from common narratives.[55] In settings of forced displacement, architectures and geographies retain chronicles of refuge. Through photographs of railway barracks, parks, and markets in Delhi, historian Ravinder Kaur shows where refugees from the Punjab arrived and made new lives after the territorial partition in 1947, and, in subsequent generations, continued to gather, reside, and perpetuate a shared narrative of flight.[56] In Ifo, Dagahaley, and Hagadera camps, refugees often returned to neighborhoods, spaces, and buildings in their conversations, impregnating the water tap stand, the corner shop, or the mosque with charged meaning through their continued narrations and inhabitations—real or imaginary—of these spaces. These investments are the many layers of a water tank.

The lives, displacement, and mobility of refugees and laborers in the humanitarian aid system are altogether incommensurate, yet certain commonly understood signs have emerged at Dadaab, unique to the setting and comprehended in the same ways by many due to their shared experiences of migration and their collective geographical and conceptual distance from home.[57] Their common worldmaking—a problematic idea but perhaps a possibility at Dadaab—was equally robust in the early 1990s, when refugees and humanitarians lived in barely separated spaces, and in the years that followed, when the Dadaab refugee camps became segregated. I argue that the common understanding of a water tank stems not only from the enclosure Dadaab has produced, in concert with other enclosed sites across a vast network, but also from receptions of architecture that have been shared across time and across asymmetries.

The UNHCR and the Family Tent

A certain tent, referred to by its designers as the "family tent," once populated the edges of each of the Dadaab refugee camps. A photograph from Dagahaley camp in 2011 of a tent occupying an open plot presents an image of the margin in a refugee settlement whose core and robust market had otherwise grown and densified over the course of decades. A group of tuquls and this family tent occupied land at the camp's outer edge, demarcated in places by young *Commiphora* growth planted in a line to form nascent fences. The people who had been issued the structure as part of their nonfood item aid package suggested that its interior temperature was uncomfortable in the hot, dusty summer.[58] My colleagues and I also noted that the family tent could not be disassembled and sold in parts, a strategy often used by people

5.9. UNHCR family tent, Dagahaley camp periphery.

in Dadaab to trade humanitarian materials in order to enter the economy of the camps. Reflecting on the residents' claims of discomfort, we wondered whether, in addition to seeking climate-related comfort, they preferred to sleep in tuquls because this type of home offered some sense of familiarity and intimacy that the adjacent foreign object could not.

The UNHCR family tent was nevertheless designed with concerns for its end user in mind. This end user has remained the universal, idealized target of a design process, even as its designers have acknowledged that "shelter is contextual and there exists no 'one-size-fits-all' solution which can be applied worldwide."[59] This tension between a universal end for design and a desire for adaptation (as explored, for example, by refugee studies scholar Tom Scott-Smith, in a study of the award-winning IKEA shelter), along with the problem identified by Redfield of a heterogeneous body of designed objects "participating in a wider humanitarian impulse to assist needy strangers rather than a utopian vision of social welfare," which furthermore "anticipate state failure and seek to provide a small-scale, self-contained alternative," offer starting points for interpreting the UNHCR family tent.[60] My concern is not with the technical success of solutions; crises in designing for the universal; questions of dignity, human rights, and the social—to which many nongovernmental actors as well as shelter designers are necessarily committed—or even the important critiques of actual designs by humanitarians, architects, and others. To different ends, I take in hand what would be considered a "failed" experiment by the UNHCR, examining its aspirations, its tests and evaluations, its forms, its internationalization of local problems, and its adherence to the patterns of empire in applying identical practices in vastly different settings. My concern with the UNHCR's attempts to make a family tent lies in the production of moral economies and materialities inherent to a humanitarian signature practice of design as infrastructure.

The first family tent authored by the UNHCR was the outcome of a series of design initiatives between 2002 and 2008, eventually involving the IFRC and other partners. The UNHCR aimed to update the expedient portable shelter unit, of whose military precedents the Quonset hut most obviously lent the tent's external shell its ribbed barrel-vaulted form.[61] However, this structure differed radically from its predecessors in design details that quoted other architectures. Specifically, it was modeled from commercial recreational tents. Moreover, many of its design elements aspired to functions well beyond basic sheltering. They engaged concerns about universal human rights and proposed expressions of dignity. They attempted to mitigate the threat of domestic violence. They offered protections against the elements and disease. With such grand aims, this tent was not only an aim of design, but the vehicle for its realization.

In his 2002 job interview for the position of UNHCR senior physical planner (after the retirement of architect Wolfgang Neumann, the first person to hold this position), Ghassem Fardanesh was asked to develop a "lightweight tent," a need the UNHCR had identified since 1993.[62] Fardanesh updated the previous model, revising the military surplus canvas ridge tent in collaboration with a supplier in Pakistan to produce a structure with greater durability, shelf life, storage capacity, cost efficiency, longevity up to twenty years, and—above all—lighter weight. A plane carrying emergency shelters could accommodate four hundred canvas ridge tents, each weighing one hundred kilograms.[63] In 2006, the UNHCR design initiative produced a lightweight emergency tent (LWET), to be delivered in chartered planes with capacity for only a third as many canvas tents. Fardanesh directed the prototype, batch rollout, and delivery phases of design development. An Iranian-born mechanical engineer who worked for the UNHCR from 1989 to 2006 in Iran, Pakistan, and Sri Lanka before moving to the headquarters in Geneva, he spoke at length about the agency's information-gathering process, his collaborative design with a supplier, and his own technical training, and he highlighted the expertise he gained in years of observing living patterns and health, social, and human rights conditions among displaced people in diverse settings and regions.[64] He spoke sensitively of the need to be familiar with the exact situation people may be facing in order to design for them; the differences between cultures in the humanitarian contexts in which he had worked; and the pragmatic challenges of domesticity in emergency, specifically for women. He referred to his aspiration to gather knowledge and its ultimate dispersal, that "shelter does not lend itself to having a body of organized information."[65] He intimated that the lightweight tent he envisioned would be conversant, in form and humaneness, with local dwellings in communities in various parts of the world where he worked.

For the UNHCR senior physical planner, the successor to an architect, to mount a design initiative may have been expected, but to mobilize a voice and signature, drawing from diverse experiences of social difference, evidenced an exertion of moral interests. My concern here, given a senior staff member's purview to direct policy, is not necessarily with its outcome—the success or failure of the initiative—but with the exercise of authority in the humanitarian interest. Notwithstanding the questionable objectives of making a recreational-model tent for refugees in severe circumstances, a cost-saving measure displacing other demonstrations of solidarity, the exercise evidences how the UNHCR brought into being a moral economy and, with it, an infrastructure *through design*.

The design specifications as listed in the LWET manual followed those for commercial recreational tents.[66] The final design, a waterproof polyester exterior shell with a breathable cotton interior liner, and the same sixteen-square-meter usable floor space as its canvas predecessor, was intended to sleep "a family of four to five persons," though it could accommodate many more.[67] It reduced the weight by half, equal to a bag of cement, and was packaged with tote handles for individual distribution, for example, on the back of a bicycle, following airdrops.[68] Its technical details enhanced physical comfort and protection from disease, pollution, and the elements, promoting a sense of privacy and integrating several architectural elements. Woven high-density polyethylene fibers were laminated on both sides to make a "bathtub" floor, with a similar low-density material for dampproofing. Integrated textile doors and windows were "glazed" with fine-mesh insecticide-treated mosquito netting (to prevent malaria), encircled by a perimeter of double pull slider zipper openings. Fiberglass integral fabric chimneys released smoke, enabled safe cooking inside the tent, and produced a hearth inside the temporary home. For durability, all fabric elements were double-lock stitched, taped at the seams, and stabilized against decomposition. An interior partition was added to create privacy for women, an acknowledgment of the gendered experience of camps. The hung fabric partition separated private from public spaces for families clustering their tents to care jointly for children, mitigating some of the stress of close quarters that could lead to domestic violence.[69] These architectural details brought commercial recreational tents into dialogue with human rights.

During the following years, the UNHCR engaged in an iterative design process. The first ten thousand units of the LWET were deployed to Banda Aceh after the 2006 tsunami by the Pakistani manufacturer, which was invited to participate in the initiative though originally prequalified to fabricate and supply canvas tents. Fardanesh later canceled the contract, based on substandard performance of the structures, and awarded contracts to four fabricators in Shanghai, Ningbo, and Shenzhen, China, experienced in commercial recreational tent production.[70] His team visited each factory, issuing a report on capacity, technology, and human rights conditions—for instance, noting that "the mission did not see any child labor."[71] The next order was shipped to East Timor, in order to stockpile fifty thousand units for emergencies.[72] Units were later sent to several locations in Africa, but after reports showed poor test performance against lateral wind forces, the design initiative was temporarily discontinued.[73] With Fardanesh retiring, the UNHCR postponed any immediate upgrade.[74] The succeeding senior physical planner, Manoucher Lolachi, a civil engineer by training with a focus in structural design and water and sanitation, discussed the development of a new prototype for the lightweight emergency tent in 2008. Its tightly closing polyester-cotton blend outer shell doubled its weight from the previous model but allowed for greater breathability in extremely hot climates; it had an entry vestibule. The UNHCR continued to test and assess design features, finding excessive problems with stability, lack of durability, the outer shell not being fire-retardant, and low ultraviolet resistance in the material, as well as various concerns about the tunnel shape. These problems led to the UNHCR's discontinuation of the lightweight emergency tent model and the start of new strands of design research with the IFRC.[75] In the UNHCR's 2016 *Shelter Design Catalogue*, a new model for the family tent was introduced, of a different shape and size altogether.

The methodology of prototyping, testing, monitoring and evaluation, revision, and even discontinuation—that is, the overall design process—became infrastructural. It evolved through many phases, providing organization, materials, and facilities—a spine for operations and policy—eventually supporting partnerships across agencies and contributing to the structuring of the Shelter and Settlement Section within the UNHCR. This design infrastructure was composed of singular signature practices, including those of prominent authors such as Fardanesh and those with diffuse interests such as the companies in Qingdao that manufactured outdoor recreation tents for corporations such as REI alongside lifesaving humanitarian equipment for the UNHCR.

This design infrastructure performed within a domain of the moral, producing economies of scale, substance, and relations. Disaggregating the moral infrastructure shows that the design process exposes *autonomy* at work within humanitarian bureaucracies. A practitioner's concerns for refugees' lived experience translated itself into institutional policy. Human rights standards not articulated in common UNHCR documents such as the Invitation to Bid or Prequalification of Suppliers appeared in a mission report. No clear, transparent process emerged for awarding contracts; rather, an affective, iterative, collaborative practice prevailed. These instantiations of humanitarian autonomy complicate any reading of a monolithic, technocratic practice within the UNHCR or any other agency or organization commissioning design.

These slippages point to a quality that philosopher Adi Ophir has described as a "moral residue."[76] The real, active, human moral interests at work within "untamed events, undercodified interactions, hybrid situations, and positions that evade the classifying power of the sovereign, or of any other authority" return to the tensions around design of the universal object and the work of those designs in the interstitial and peripheral spaces of state failure referred to earlier.[77] Emergency response depends on a field of uniform standardization. Humanitarian design extracts from this field labor practices operating with intellectual independence, in the realm of the moral. I argue that this autonomy, characterized by individual discretion, is the limit concept for a moral economic infrastructure based in design labor.

The design process for the LWET disambiguates this infrastructure, its affect rendered in a photo from the periphery of Dagahaley camp. In this end destination in the tent's social and physical trajectory, the desires of a technical professional with humanist aspirations for intimate, anchoring architectures came into full expression. Despite questions on the effectiveness of the design and on whether humanistic aims were met, the LWET produced a landscape of humanitarian desire in Dadaab, replete with moral residue, entangling utility and symbolism in an architectural object. Refugee desire and domesticity in emergency surfaced less directly, yet not merely as latent aspects of a design process. The home in this photograph is the gravity to the moral economic infrastructure. Its social, philosophical, and material dissonances reverberate throughout a global chain, alighting here in the interstices and peripheries of Dadaab.

MSF and the Architecture of Logistics

In a conversation with WRC researchers, Jean-Pierre Mapela, the logistics team leader in Dadaab for MSF, described to us the organization's material commitment: that all staff members live in Dagahaley camp.[78] Most of the approximately eighty staff members working for MSF-Switzerland in Dadaab, including twelve to fifteen expatriate aid workers, resided in the MSF compound in Dagahaley. "Our action is based on the principle that you should be accepted by the beneficiaries," he explained, "to be accepted by people . . . to whom you are providing services. . . . This we cannot compromise. That's the reason for what we are, the only NGO with expatriates living in the camp, because we should be near, close to our beneficiaries."[79] If this language repeated the binaries of donor/beneficiary, aider/aided, rescuer/rescued, it nevertheless distinguished MSF's humanitarian orientation in Dadaab, very different from the UNHCR policy for staff members to reside in a segregated and fortified compound, divided from both refugees and the Kenyan host community. MSF staff members not staying in the Dagahaley compound were from Dadaab or Garissa, or sometimes Nairobi or elsewhere, living in the town of Dadaab or nearby within the host community. Workers from the refugee community, who lived in blocks in the camp, constituted another a workforce that MSF (like many international organizations) retained, in a form of mutual aid, paying "incentive" wages rather than salaries. This was the local landscape of asymmetries within which MSF worked and injected its moral and medical commitments.

In Dadaab, local asymmetries often mapped directly onto geopolitical conflict, with ramifications on regional and international levels. MSF's characteristically spirited, uncontented engagement with politics, a "culture of internal argument and critical reflection" elucidated in Redfield's intellectual biography of the organization, came to crisis in its own negotiations with al-Shabaab, in the decisions it made in order to continue work in Somalia,

5.10. Women waiting for their friend outside MSF hospital, Dagahaley camp.

as its research and reflection unit CRASH analyzed and reported.[80] Yet, MSF made no agreements with the police. As far as we could make out, MSF staff members did not carry weapons. They were advised to limit travel between the camps within the curfew, from 8:00 a.m. to 5:00 p.m., because of the presence of criminal elements in the vicinity. Mapela could not have known the extent of the threat at the time of our conversation in March 2011, but the stakes became clear by October, when al-Shabaab soldiers kidnapped two foreign MSF aid workers. The event caused the state authorities to enforce extreme restrictions on all foreign aid workers and camp personnel and to further limit all movement between the camps. The drought and extreme food insecurity earlier in the year, declared a famine by the UN, and the continuing violent attacks and abduction and conscription of youths into al-Shabaab's army had forced so many people to flee their homes and seek asylum in Dadaab that the density of settlement in Ifo, Dagahaley, and Hagadera reached a saturation point, leaving unprecedented numbers of people seeking shelter at the peripheries of the camps.

In the months before this event cast its shadow, Mapela's work involved supplying MSF's newly built hospital, serving the 100,000 people living in Dagahaley camp. It was time for a permanent building, he noted, as the temporary infrastructure in Dagahaley had been built twenty years ago. His work as acting field coordinator and logistics team leader required relationships with five sources. In the Dagahaley market, the team acquired basic items for construction. They went to Dadaab, or beyond to Garissa, for what they could not find in the camp. For furniture, stationery, and some pharmaceuticals, they would have to travel to Nairobi. For most pharmaceuticals, and for tents, generators, and communications items, they would await shipments of kits from France. They regularly received plastic sheeting in bulk from the UNHCR to distribute to the least resourced: asylum seekers who had settled near the MSF compound in Dagahaley camp.

In order to meet the continued need for a variety of supplies, the Dagahaley team coordinated with the central MSF supply unit in Mérignac, a small French town near the airport in Bordeaux. The story of the work in Mérignac is a central design history for Dadaab. This design history also extends well beyond Dadaab, contouring an infrastructure of humanitarian intervention around the world.

Fewer than six kilometers from a subdivision of workers' housing in Pessac designed by Le Corbusier, from just atop a hill on the motorway as I approached the facilities that Mapela depended on, a scarlet MSF logo appeared, screen-printed on the side of an aluminum-clad warehouse ensconced in a big-box retail and office park landscape surrounding the town of Bordeaux. The cluster of offices, workshops, and storage facilities at the source of the organization's global supply chain in the village of Mérignac housed nearly half of the approximately one hundred employees of MSF Logistique, responsible for the reception and processing of pharmaceutical and other supplies from manufacturers; the quality control inspection; the custom assembly of medical, architectural, vehicular, and other mobile kits; and the shipment of those kits to sites of MSF's operations.[81] In February 2012, I toured the site with technical specialists and administrators involved in local and global operations, attended the all-staff weekly meeting, and visited MSF Logistique's airport site, where architectural kits—shelters, water tanks, hospitals—were packaged and shipped to the field.

A prototype of MSF's hôpital gonflable (inflatable hospital) sat on a bed of rubber palettes in a tree-lined corner of the grounds of the Mérignac headquarters facility. Among its mobile equipment and structures, the inflatable hospital has been MSF's most architecturally ambitious. The MSF Logistique staff credits its design to an in-house architect, Hocine Bouhabib, a member of a team developing mobile structures, which includes others with similar professional training.[82] The one-hundred-square-meter tent is constructed of PVC fabric; sewn together with integral floors, openings, and partitions for nearly hermetic sealing; and supported by pneumatic rolls that inflate to a structural ridge four meters off the ground. A single hospital may include a freestanding nursing station; beds; sinks and their water supply and waste disposal; high-beam surgical lamps and other lighting fixtures; devices for air conditioning and heat control; the electric generator to power a pump to inflate the structure; and, not least, the kits of biomedical equipment, tools, and pharmaceuticals housed by this architecture. The specialized personnel, aside from physicians, surgeons, and nurses, include the technicians—such as electricians, plumbers, and a variety of other logisticians—who assemble the building and its components in the field.

The assembly of the prototype at MSF Logistique in 2005, prior to its first field test after the earthquake that year in Pakistan, illustrates a construction process under ideal conditions. The logisticians began by laying a foundation of palettes within an eight-by-twelve-meter floor plan. The interconnectable tiles could also form more complex configurations, for hospitals with smaller, multipurpose forty-five-square-meter tents. After the logisticians unrolled the tent atop the foundation, they used generators to inflate it, a three-hour process producing standing arched PVC rolls, which formed the primary roof support ridges, possessing the material strength and stability of life rafts. After tying and hanging a ceiling from the roof structure and erecting examination bays, surgeries, and recovery areas, logisticians installed wiring and water infrastructure connecting to the major medical equipment. In the field, the hospital becomes operational following a commissioning process in which all networking and equipment is tested.

The structures were deployed for a large operation following the 2010 earthquake in Haiti, where logisticians assembled nine joined units into a hundred-bed hospital amid international scrutiny in new social media forms. MSF Logistique attracted attention with its innovative hospital—earthquake-responsive, portable, reusable, and rapidly assembled. Its installation and commissioning process took half the time it had taken five years earlier in Pakistan, according to Bouhabib.[83] Videos of the inflation process were posted by MSF on YouTube.[84] As I argue in relation to the Oxfam water tank discussed earlier, the inflatable hospital demonstrated

5.11. Inflatable hospital prototype, before inflation process, Mérignac, photo provided by MSF Logistique.

5.12. Inflatable hospital prototype, Mérignac, photo provided by MSF Logistique.

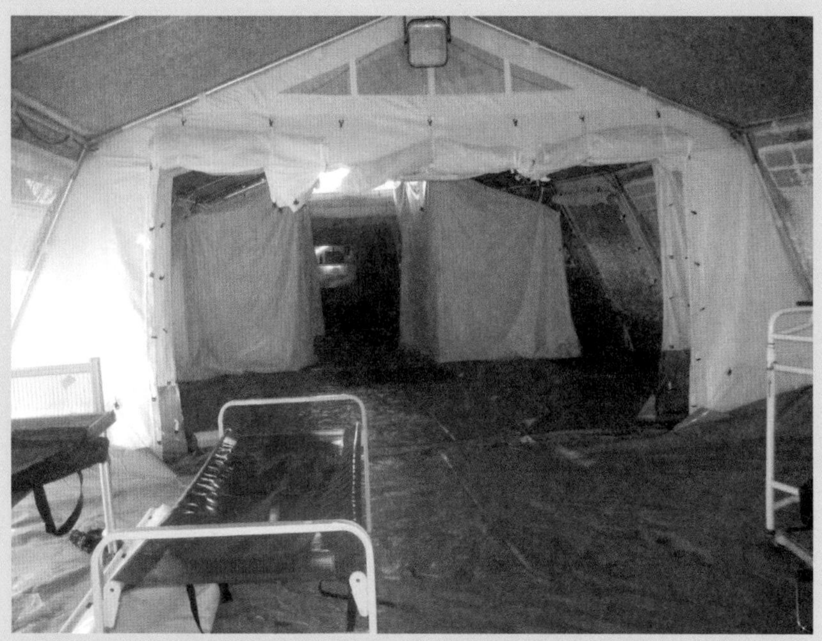

5.13. Inflatable hospital prototype, interior, Mérignac, 2012.

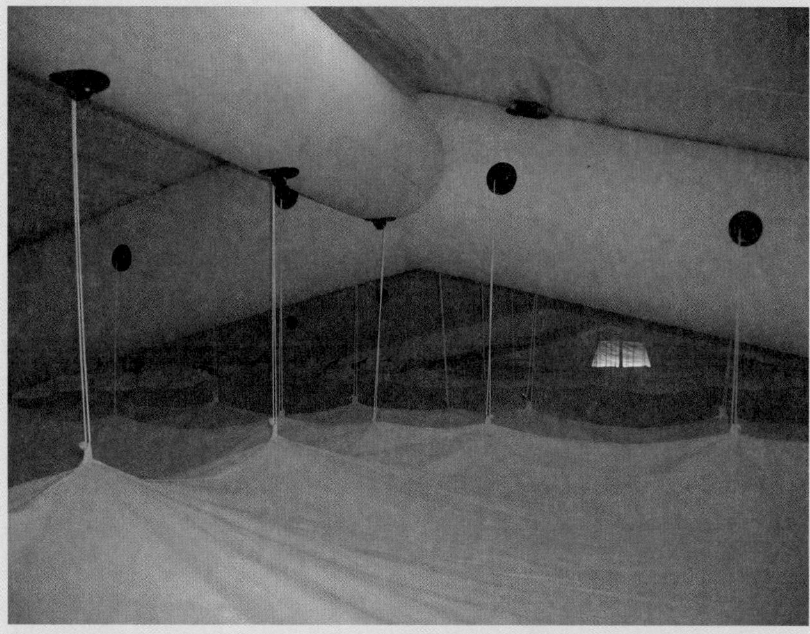

5.14. Inflatable hospital prototype, roof beam detail, Mérignac, photo provided by MSF Logistique.

5.15. Inflatable hospital kits, MSF Logistique warehouse near Bordeaux-Mérignac International Airport.

how the imbrication of architecture with its image transformed its use value as a critical lifesaving object into a high exchange value as media in circulation.

Emergency response to the Haiti earthquake shifted paradigms for humanitarian fundraising and self-narration.[85] Sophisticated publicity, celebrity intervention, and the proximity of Haiti to the United States—the Office of Foreign Disaster Assistance maintaining robust aid streams—encouraged spectacle around design culture. The photogenic inflatable hospital provided a quantifiable form of relief in a context of complex private sector funding, in which donations from philanthropic and corporate foundations as well as individuals contributing small amounts (via internet or phone messaging technologies) encouraged intensive programs of communications, reporting, and publicity by humanitarian organizations. Among the spectacles, philanthropies including the Clinton Foundation, led by the former US president, worked outside their areas of expertise to build shelters and schools, with undesirable outcomes attracting explosive media attention; meanwhile, US-based professional architectural organizations such as Architecture for Humanity competed to contribute to the relief effort.[86] As powerful optics balanced against the high unit costs of architectures of emergency relief, MSF's skill and visual rhetorical facility enabled it to foreground design alongside urgent medical work. In urban stagings such as the "Refugee Camp in the Heart of the City," MSF developed a spatial method for narrating its work and mission, merging a spectatorial consumption of architecture and media with the promotion of lifesaving activity.[87] This is not to suggest that MSF's infrastructural labor in design as ascribed here is the organization's intent, nor that its proponents agree with my diagnosis. I situate this aesthetic labor as a microcosm of that which an architecture of migration engenders. The work creates a different spatial politics, as a merging of design infrastructures and emergency relief within the act of humanitarian self-narration is one of the microscopic processes in humanitarian settlement.

The architectural and structural details of the inflatable hospital enabled rapid deployment of a hygienic vessel offering flexible configurations for outpatient and inpatient examination, critical care, and the more specific needs of surgery, while providing shock resistance against tremors, for envi-

5.16. MSF "Refugee Camp in the Heart of the City," Tokyo, 2004, photo provided by MSF.

THE HOSPITAL THAT

Complete field surgical hospital lands on a field in Thailand during a recent SEATO exercise. As many as 20 parachutes must be used in a "dandelion seed" cluster to support the heaviest pieces of equipment

Photos by French Air Ministry, James Pickerell

Members of the French 10th Airborne Division Surgical Team go into action, inflating their "hospital" as soon as they hit the ground. Compact, generator-powered blower pumps inflate the tents in three minutes

COMBAT EXPERIENCE in North Africa taught the French Army the difficulty of providing medical support to troops during the early hours of an airborne assault. Shown on these pages is their answer—a complete field surgical hospital that can be parachuted from a single transport aircraft and set up in minutes near the drop zone, ready to handle battle casualties in the all-important first few minutes after injury.

Two officers and seven enlisted men make up the special Airborne Surgical Team that is now a regular part of each French airborne division. The key to their fast operation is three inflatable hospital tents of the British "Numa" type—one large unit of 1750 cubic feet volume and two smaller tents of 430 cubic feet each. For ground transportation they are supplied with a quarter-ton Jeep ambulance, a motor scooter and a collapsible trailer.

A single French Air Force Nord Atlas, their version of the U. S. C-119 transport, delivers the entire hospital unit—nine men, 400 pounds of tents and equipment, three vehicles and 3000 pounds of medical equipment and supplies—by parachute.

Medics assemble the lightweight folding operating table as the other team members inflate the tents

DROPS FROM THE SKY

Inflatable rubber ribs form the framework of the fabric tents. Once on the ground, the team spreads the tent walls and floors in position, starts a portable 0.5 kilowatt power unit, and uses blower pumps to inflate the framework. The job only takes about three minutes, and in the meantime other team members assemble the folding hospital gear, including a full-scale operating table, which is ready to wheel into the "hospital" by the time it's inflated.

The entire operation, from the time the chutes touch down until the hospital is ready to receive casualties, takes only 20 minutes. ★ ★ ★

Above, airman starts 0.5 kilowatt generator. Below, hospital and ward tent ready to handle casualties

NOVEMBER 1959 163

5.17 and 5.18. (*opposite and above*) "The Hospital That Drops from the Sky," *Popular Mechanics* (November 1959), 162–63.

Revue de sociologie de l'urbain

Catalogue de l'exposition

structures gonflables

mars 1968

Précédé d'un

Essai sur technique et société

de

Considérations inactuelles sur le gonflable

et de

Particularité des structures gonflables

animation recherche confrontation
Musée d'Art Moderne
de la ville de Paris

5.19 and 5.20. *Structures Gonflables* ("Inflatable Structures") exhibition catalog cover (*opposite*) and interior image (*above*), provided by Jean-Louis Cohen.

ronments in which earthquakes or shelling could threaten lateral stability. The specialized medical goals expanded this object's field—in plan rather than in section, much in the spirit of modern architecture—situating it not as an autonomous, enclosed building but as a fully networked infrastructure covering local and global territory. The building connected to local infrastructures for electrification, plumbing, and climate control and to global systems of mobile people and things—both the professional facilitators and experts, such as the logisticians or surgeons, and the sinks, operating tables, and other artifacts that made the inflatable architecture hygienic and operational as a hospital and a surgery.

MSF Logistique's inflatable hospital joins a history of mobile architectures, border-crossing artifacts. The nomadic surgical hospital, for instance, existed in a consistent form in the MASH (mobile army surgical hospital) unit deployed by the US military from World War II through Operation Iraqi Freedom at the beginning of the 2000s. The pages of *Popular Mechanics* celebrate an inflatable hospital in a French military operation in a drop zone in Thailand in 1959. Pneumatics entered the culture in Paris at the time that Bernard Kouchner, one of MSF's prominent founders, studied at the Sorbonne, when architects in the group Utopie, from the École Nationale Supérieure des Beaux-Arts, mounted the 1968 exhibition "Structures

Gonflables" at the Musée d'Art Moderne. They displayed forms such as the hangar, the individual domicile, and the climate-controlled room, expressing the quotidian and discursive potential of pneumatic architecture.[88] If Utopie and MSF shared little else in common, each may be said to have pioneered iconic forms of spatial resistance.[89] The former proffered architectural materialities and forms to counter homogenizing modernist urbanization. The latter challenged national borders through a mobile infrastructure of people and things. Spatial resistance for each appeared in the border-transgressing technology of pneumatics.

Inflatable architectures constitute only one prong of research and development behind MSF Logistique's catalog of flexible kits. This portfolio was initiated with Pinel's designs for pharmaceutical supply prior to the founding of the MSF satellite unit in 1986.[90] He built on lessons from the commercial sector to develop the prototype logistics system for pharmaceutical distribution, which eventually facilitated a cold-temperature chain.[91] The medical kit had military predecessors; as outlined by Redfield, the humanitarian model was the *Materia Medica Minimalis*, a 1944 Red Cross document issued in Latin to field stations around Europe, which estimated pharmaceutical quantities in units of 100,000 persons per six months.[92] In Redfield's terms, this "mobile template for crisis response around a principle of flexible standardization" produced a concept that sociologist Nicolas Dodier analyzes as "'adjustable' (based on the user's view of the situation in the field) and 'evolutive' (with some adaptations resulting in changes to the kit)."[93] Mapela's work in Dagahaley camp would have involved either form of knowledge construction: whether adapting a model into the object used on-site or transforming the model itself, as informed by site-based conditions. Because Mapela was charged to serve high numbers of people, representing a large-scale or protracted intervention, it might be assumed that a direction from Dadaab would impact a centralized policy or design process emanating from Mérignac. MSF Logistique has designed kits according to the medical and population profile of specific territories, calibrated to the scale of the humanitarian interventions. Logisticians have preassembled kits in Mérignac from materials in the warehouse, including instruction booklets whose technical and operational focus targeted nonspecialized readers in unpredictable circumstances. The system was intended to "function as a form of materialized memory whereby previous experience extends directly into every new setting without having to be actively recalled."[94] It also encouraged improvisation in particular situations and extra cataloging of design modifications, so that knowledge could be retained and future kits revised as necessary. In both of

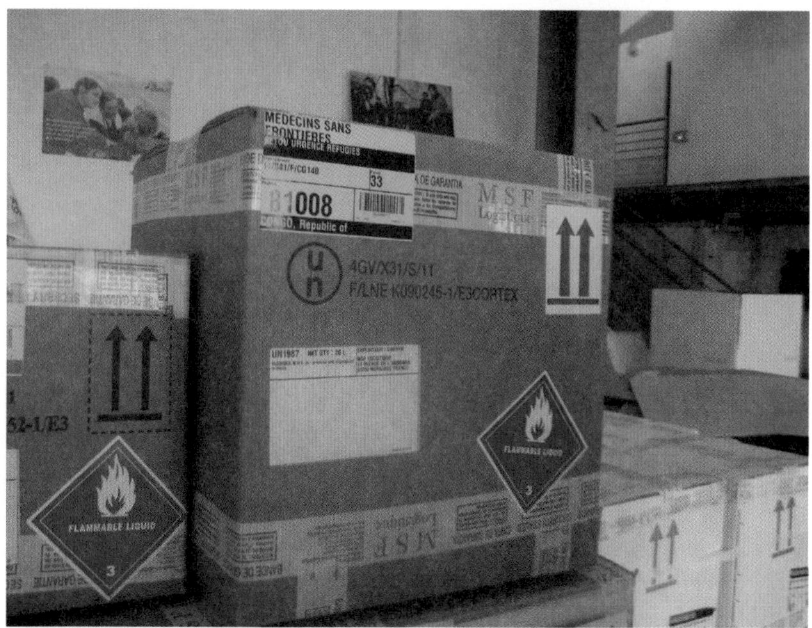

5.21. Pharmaceutical kit, "Alcohols (propanol and isopropanol mixture)," to be shipped to the Republic of Congo, MSF Logistique, Mérignac, France.

5.22. Toyota Land Cruiser being outfitted with antenna for satellite communications, front and rear bumper, silk-screened bug screen to protect front vent, and other devices for emergency operations, MSF Logistique garage, Mérignac, France.

these orientations, the research and development—the design—resulted in a recombinant process.

MSF Logistique's design innovation, or authorship, lies in two aspects. One is the recombinant process behind the kits. The other is the packaging of artifacts to move through the global supply chain. MSF Logistique's approach to fleet management provides a rich illustration. The Toyota Land Cruiser, a four-wheel-drive vehicle fundamental to humanitarian fleets, has made emergency response possible in areas with little preexisting transportation or communications infrastructure. Gilles Perroud, from MSF Logistique's Quality Service division, and Rockson, who worked on a vehicle in MSF Logistique's garage during my visit, explained the logisticians' precise adaptation of vehicles directly acquired from manufacturers and warehoused at the facility in Mérignac. Technicians add front and rear bumpers, internal seats serving an ambulance function, and satellite antennae that enable communication between headquarters and field locations. Through mosquito nets, stickers, and screening, the scarlet MSF logo occupies strategic, visible locations, which convert the vehicle into mobile, marked "humanitarian space." MSF has supported fleet sharing as a strategy at new operation sites; the Mérignac office has facilitated acquisition of vehicles by field logisticians from regional suppliers and Toyota's headquarters in Japan. MSF Logistique offers a catalog of additional materials that may be ordered from Mérignac for direct alteration of vehicles (such as "Basic Equipment for Ambulance Conversion" or "Ballistic Blanket Kit").[95] A vehicle ordered by a logistician such as Mapela might arrive as both vehicle and shipping container. The order might ship via chartered plane from the Bordeaux-Mérignac airport or as a single package by boat, equipped with a high-frequency radio, generator, and several kits of pharmaceuticals, traveling through a transition station, such as the MSF warehouse in Dubai, or directly to Dagahaley camp. These shipments, capable of holding one thousand kilograms, contain pharmaceuticals more often than shelters. While not all the kits operate as matryoshka dolls, their mutability and the fluidity enabled by the closed MSF-only supply chain have created nimble pathways for the transfer of MSF's mobile architectures of tents, reservoirs, and hospitals, and formed a basis for the global spatialization of MSF's operations. Thus, *design* for MSF Logistique lay at two levels: that of invention, in the creative expansiveness of the recombinant kits, and efficiency, in the modularity and logistics of the kits and their shipping containers. Both orientations demonstrate complex and iterative design thinking, fully integrated with technical and professional responses to emergency, amounting to a signature infrastructure.

How to understand a humanitarian signature practice of design? When asked whether the volume of supplies MSF drove through the supply chain warranted requesting modified product designs from a supplier such as Toyota, Perroud demurred. Companies exist that can install these accessories, he answered, "but there are specific MSF things, and . . . we prefer to keep it here."[96] This proprietary approach to the design of the system and its components may not have been claimed as a form of authorship per se, but raises just that question. What does a signature practice mean for the designers at MSF Logistique and those in the logistics units at Dadaab, or for the people in Dagahaley camp who are the specific—and precisely *not* universal—subjects for whom design is intended?

Turning again to the notion that "there are specific MSF things," the question of authorship must be confronted as signature practices of design are embedded in infrastructures of placemaking and architectural realizations of refugee camps such as those at Dadaab. MSF's signature forms and practices circulated widely. The use of MSF Logistique's kit proliferated, with the World Health Organization adopting it in 1988 and the ICRC purchasing many of the guideline booklets.[97] MSF's own material and spatial footprint expanded globally through the proprietary supply chain and attendant architectures, representing only a fraction of a vast scope of multiagency humanitarian logistics in the world. The medical supply kit and the guidelines for field operations materialized an increased capacity for public health evaluation and emergency response, part of broader professional humanitarian standardizations. The form they took in MSF Logistique ultimately concretized a split in the organization's priorities—on the one hand, a political passion associated with figures such as Kouchner and, on the other, desires by those such as Pinel "to overcome amateurism" producing the turn to pragmatics and the capacity to spatialize operations on a grand scale.[98] With that capacity, I argue, MSF Logistique coproduced emergency territory, effecting humanitarian settlement. It did so by forging a set of artifacts, systems, and practices, which, as noted by former MSF-France President Rony Brauman, accidentally turned humanitarians into "city planners."[99] The conclusivity of the built environment he alludes to, stemming from the "accident" of city planning—Dadaab providing a vivid articulation—paradoxically resolves the tensions I identify in MSF's work between infrastructure and authorship, systems and signature practice. Ironically, MSF's architectures in concrete environments such as that at Dadaab were themselves ephemeral.

This ephemerality is iterated not only in provisional inflatable hospitals, but also in the expedient architecture of MSF Logistique's warehouses. They

5.23. MSF Logistique warehouse near Bordeaux-Mérignac International Airport.

recall a provocation in international relations scholar Fiona Terry's passionate book, *Condemned to Repeat? The Paradox of Humanitarian Action*, on humanitarian actors contracting private security forces to deliver aid. She writes, "if humanitarian action has been reduced to a logistical exercise, better to contract a supermarket chain to deliver aid . . . and at least avoid the humanitarian pretense."[100] A chain such as Walmart indeed offers an aesthetic analog to an MSF warehouse. International relations scholar Stephen Hopgood poses a related question, measuring the neoliberal pragmatism of the corporation's approach to logistics: "Can Wal-Mart be a humanitarian organization?"[101] To this, I add another. In the systems and signature practices of humanitarian space—in its design—how will we know the difference between the ephemeral architectures of MSF and Walmart?

I argue that, if Walmart's architecture is bereft, MSF's is monumental. It has imbricated design with humanitarian relief in the realization of a signature infrastructure. These thrusts can be perceived as dissonant. I prefer to understand the signature they create as a strategic and urgent alloy: concrete architectures making ephemeral environments, and ephemeral architectures making concrete environments. These paradoxes leave behind fuller questions of what we can learn when we look closely at a refugee camp. To take these questions to a conclusion, let us return to Dagahaley camp, to follow a final signature practice, which demonstrates how the ephemeral infrastructures of design resolve in humanitarian settlement.

Coda: Concrete Architectures and Ephemeral Infrastructures

The architectures in this chapter, even those with a seemingly light footprint, have driven humanitarian settlement. These concrete architectures have entangled humanitarian spatiality with the land beneath refugee camps, as material anchors for settlement. These architectures have inscribed as infrastructures design processes and designers themselves. Yet, this infrastructural network of people and things has been largely ephemeral. This chapter ends on this ephemeral infrastructure, as an archive for an architecture of migration.

Dadaab's built environment has been constituted of many infrastructures of design and designers—in Dagahaley, the cooperatives established by refugees obtaining contracts for construction work within and outside the camps. Bethany Young and I interviewed the leaders of two construction cooperatives led by women. Women are the architects of the Dadaab refugee camps; their work has been fundamental to the construction of this built environment. Habiba Abdurahman Mursan chaired Dagahaley Girls United Center and described its formation in an interview with us in the Dagahaley office of the NRC, which offered sponsorship and training relevant to the work of construction cooperatives.[102] Her words form a discursive archive, recording events, relationships, and economies behind the design and shaping of the built environment of the camps.

ANOORADHA IYER SIDDIQI: How long have you run your cooperative?

HABIBA ABDURAHMAN MURSAN: Two years.

ANOORADHA IYER SIDDIQI: All the cooperatives started at the same time?

HABIBA ABDURAHMAN MURSAN: Yes.

ANOORADHA IYER SIDDIQI: How many were you?

HABIBA ABDURAHMAN MURSAN: Twenty-two.

ANOORADHA IYER SIDDIQI: Is it for women who are working?

HABIBA ABDURAHMAN MURSAN: No, women who are not working, those who work, and those who are in school.

ANOORADHA IYER SIDDIQI: It's a support group?

HABIBA ABDURAHMAN MURSAN: Yes.

ANOORADHA IYER SIDDIQI: Did this group help you earn income to start the cooperative?

HABIBA ABDURAHMAN MURSAN: Yes, it really helped. In the first place when we started to have a business, it was a very long stage.

ANOORADHA IYER SIDDIQI: Did [the NRC] give you a loan or did they grant the money to you?

HABIBA ABDURAHMAN MURSAN: No, among ourselves, we all collected the money to start a business. We applied for the cooperative, then we were given [the funds by NRC], and we are doing the work.

ANOORADHA IYER SIDDIQI: You are actually doing the physical labor? Were all the women trained in construction?

HABIBA ABDURAHMAN MURSAN: We had camp management training.

ANOORADHA IYER SIDDIQI: What about in actual construction, brick making, foundations . . . ?

HABIBA ABDURAHMAN MURSAN: We normally supervise the work.

ANOORADHA IYER SIDDIQI: How many people do each of you manage?

HABIBA ABDURAHMAN MURSAN: It's two of us. Me and another lady normally supervise. Three men are working for us.

ANOORADHA IYER SIDDIQI: I thought you said that in the Dagahaley United Girls Center, all twenty-two women raised the money for the cooperative. Is that correct?

HABIBA ABDURAHMAN MURSAN: No, I said, in the first place, we came together as [a group of] girls. We collected some money to start a business. When we started a business, we requested to be given a contract from NRC.

ANOORADHA IYER SIDDIQI: What business did you start?

HABIBA ABDURAHMAN MURSAN: We have a small shop at the market. After that we applied for this.

ANOORADHA IYER SIDDIQI: With the idea that two of you would be supervisors. Two of you did the training?

HABIBA ABDURAHMAN MURSAN: Yes, two of us did the training. . . . For the training in camp management, all the girls did this training.

ANOORADHA IYER SIDDIQI: All twenty-two of you?

HABIBA ABDURAHMAN MURSAN: All twenty-two, yes, by [the] camp management team within NRC. But specifically as a cooperative, two of our girls were trained on how to select construction items from the center to give to our subcontractors, the men who normally work with us. It's two of us who normally supervise.

ANOORADHA IYER SIDDIQI: Two of you got technical training about what happens in the field. The two of you are acting as foremen on the job? Do you go to the site to supervise? Are there any challenges being a woman and doing that kind of work?

HABIBA ABDURAHMAN MURSAN: Sometimes, but not always.

ANOORADHA IYER SIDDIQI: Can you talk about that?

HABIBA ABDURAHMAN MURSAN: You know, where we are coming from is very far. Sometimes the work will be quick, to distribute the items. The subcontractors normally help us to collect items from the center.

ANOORADHA IYER SIDDIQI: You have to pay them extra for that?

HABIBA ABDURAHMAN MURSAN: No.

ANOORADHA IYER SIDDIQI: Are there any challenges working directly with men?

HABIBA ABDURAHMAN MURSAN: I never faced any challenge.

ANOORADHA IYER SIDDIQI: Do you have children?

HABIBA ABDURAHMAN MURSAN: Yes.

ANOORADHA IYER SIDDIQI: Where are your children when you are working?

HABIBA ABDURAHMAN MURSAN: Some of them are in school, others are at home. My family members normally take care of them.

ANOORADHA IYER SIDDIQI: What are the hours of your work?

HABIBA ABDURAHMAN MURSAN: It depends on getting the items. Sometimes it's slow. When there is activity, you have to go at 8:00 in the morning and get the items and give them to the subcontractors. Then you go home. Then you come back in the afternoon for supervision. After they finish the work, you have to report to the office.

ANOORADHA IYER SIDDIQI: What time do they finish the work?

HABIBA ABDURAHMAN MURSAN: In the afternoon, 4:30. Then you come back to the center and report.

ANOORADHA IYER SIDDIQI: What time do you usually go home?

HABIBA ABDURAHMAN MURSAN: After 5:00.

ANOORADHA IYER SIDDIQI: Is it safe to go home at that hour?

HABIBA ABDURAHMAN MURSAN: In Dagahaley, it's safe.

ANOORADHA IYER SIDDIQI: Is it safe in the morning? We've been reading about risks to women walking by themselves.

HABIBA ABDURAHMAN MURSAN: Sometimes there's risk. The community where we are now, they don't want women to work with the men. Sometimes they challenge, but they never come out and talk to you.

ANOORADHA IYER SIDDIQI: Is there anything else you can tell us about your experience?

HABIBA ABDURAHMAN MURSAN: The pay is low. Whatever you get, you have to divide in two, for the subcontractors and you. . . . To build a latrine is [only] six hundred shillings.

ANOORADHA IYER SIDDIQI: When you bring [your share of] the money home, do you and your husband make decisions together about how to spend the money?

HABIBA ABDURAHMAN MURSAN: This money belongs to the group.

ANOORADHA IYER SIDDIQI: The group gives each of its members a little bit of money?

HABIBA ABDURAHMAN MURSAN: If it's needed. Otherwise, there's a treasurer who normally keeps the money for us. She has to record everything. Whenever we agree, we divide it among the group.

ANOORADHA IYER SIDDIQI: How do you earn income for your family?

HABIBA ABDURAHMAN MURSAN: We depend on the camp distribution.

ANOORADHA IYER SIDDIQI: There is no extra income?

HABIBA ABDURAHMAN MURSAN: No.

ANOORADHA IYER SIDDIQI: You are not just doing hard work, but you are doing something unique. Thank you for taking the time to talk.

HABIBA ABDURAHMAN MURSAN: Thank you.

If infrastructure can be theorized through design and designers and their artifacts and practices, it is worth noting that the construction cooperatives led by refugee women occasioned parallel initiatives outside the camps, with cooperative-based construction labor and women-led businesses entering the building sector to form a meaningful spatial practice outside Dadaab. Meanwhile, the NRC broadened its experiments not only in shelter but also in other industries in which refugees might engage in an environment where they may not have earned wages for labor but did significant work for compensation. Beyond producing microeconomies in architectural design and construction, the Dagahaley Girls United Center and its sister cooperatives symbolized something monumental, even if ephemeral, forging social relationships establishing other materialities and historical trajectories. These cooperatives lay behind "signature" activity in a refugee camp. Their work operated in sensible, affective registers, within but also well outside the social constructs of emergency.[103] In the end, it is this ephemerality, on such a scale and with such intention, that marks the architecture of Dadaab and, indeed, all humanitarian settlement. It is precisely an ephemerality in the design labor and signature practices of Habiba Abdurahman Mursan, Maureen Connelly, Jacques Pinel, and Jean-Pierre Mapela that impregnates the built environment, investing it with intense meaning. Their material and aesthetic constructions show us where the history of an architecture of migration stops and a common heritage begins.

cultures like liquid gold
stories that were never
told this is our
liquid gold will fade

(*previous page*) Deqa Abshir, *Fragmented II*, mixed media on canvas, 90cm × 120cm, 2015. Courtesy of the artist.

Afterword

"POETRY IS A WEAPON THAT WE USE IN BOTH WAR AND PEACE"

I came across a powerful remark by the noted Somali poet and elder Hadraawi when I began the research for this book in 2010. "Poetry is a weapon that we use in both war and peace," he told his interviewer.[1] My attempt to understand the meaning of this seemingly straightforward statement has accompanied years of examining an architecture of migration, during which I found myself substituting the word *architecture* for the word *poetry*, as the weapon that we use in both war and peace. As a coda to the arguments in the preceding chapters, I will endeavor to explain this substitution.

In the research for this book, I attempted to learn, together, from people I spoke with and people whose work I read, understanding the theory offered by each as intertwined. I initiated discussions with many migrants, in Africa and elsewhere. I had the privilege of meeting people who had lived or were living in Dadaab or in refugee camps in other parts of East Africa and the rest of the world. Many were forced to negotiate political status and living conditions over the course of years. In this book, I have attempted to work with their words and the narratives they shared with me. Each of the chapters hinges on excerpts from one or more conversations with people from Dadaab; some of these excerpts represent our only meeting, and some are an amalgamation of multiple discussions. Their presentation may raise questions inadequately answered. My coalescing interviews, archives, literature, and reflections may create slippage rather than balance. I take responsibility for these moments. Yet, I turn to these seams, as the trace of a historiographical practice of inclusion and restitution. This is the undercurrent for this book. This ethos underwriting the text is crucial to understanding architecture as symbolizing not only the power of states or empires with the capacity to usurp people's lives but also the power of other orders: that of people whose domesticity is worldmaking, whose architecture can be the basis of our common histories.

To imagine and construct common histories, migration offers an important method for analyzing epistemological foundations and countering the typical privileging of histories premised on archives that represent landed, settled institutions. While this book has used empirical lessons from Dadaab to construct arguments on the restriction of migration at borders and the encampment and immobilization of people, its narratives of an architecture of migration have lain not in the carceral detention spaces of the nation-state, but in the constructed forms and landscapes of people's open migration. I question the epistemological faith in fixity, asking how the archive can be based on conditions of openness. In the architecture of migration I theorize, constructed environments and landscapes *generated by* and *imposed on* people overlap with one another. Building on this complexity, I put the humanitarian macroenvironment and refugee camp in dialogue with the single individual's work or domain. Vice versa, I intimate the work of an architect by extrapolating and narrating wider architectures, histories, and epistemes that it organizes and gives rise to. My epistemic practice offers an alternative to depending exclusively on official archives by seeking multiplicity, constructing a multivocal and pluralistic approach. The many architectures of migration that this book has excavated demand interpretive commitment from the reader. When looking closely at an architecture of migration, one can at once see and also not see. An architecture of migration offers the opportunity to examine and understand that architecture is not fixed.

To acknowledge this problem and culminate my research, I engaged in a critical practice of knowledge production by working with artists and architects to *draw Dadaab* in its myriad forms. They directed their own creative practices, conceiving works that turned to Dadaab as a referent (in dialogue with me and informed by my feedback). My methodological aim was to study how knowledges promised in a concept history of the Dadaab refugee camps and humanitarian settlement might be built through independently cultivated practices. This experiment in artistic and architectural knowledge production demonstrates ways that Dadaab, as an object lesson and basis for intellectual history, offers a springboard for theory.

I was inspired to undertake this iterative process on learning of the work of artist Deqa Abshir, who applied her graduate study in expressive arts therapy to a practice of trauma relief for former residents of Dadaab living in the

Eastleigh neighborhood of Nairobi—"the Nairobi home of Somalis even before it had been named Eastleigh," as anthropologist Neil Carrier writes of "Little Mogadishu."[2] Her double-canvas painting opening this chapter, *Fragmented II*, recalls a heritage of migration through the tuqul, an object that has transformed from a symbol of tradition to one of refugee life.[3] She splits the painting into two "fragments," which purposely misalign the image, offsetting the geometric lines and planes just as the canvas edges are arranged in alignment. The aligned canvases produce a series of shifted, broken lines and planes, disrupting the compositional narrative across the break between canvases, just enough to sow visual discord. This fragmented rendering of the domed tuqul dwelling translates Abshir's perspective of homemaking in the bush, built over years of growing up in Nairobi in a refugee family in diaspora, positioned as a visitor when returning to Somalia. In the lower painting, she excerpts and reinterprets text from the poem "Gold" by her sister Idil Abshir, writing by hand on the canvas:

> cultures like liquid gold
> stories that were never
> told, this is our africa
> our children will be born
> with golden glitter on
> their faces never knowing why

Deqa Abshir's work reckons with visits to her relatives in the Somali countryside and the alienation from her grandmothers' building traditions as they were imposed upon her. "Will we conserve, restore and rebuild traditions honouring forgotten principles," she asks, "or will we keep creating a new city and culture, pressing our foundations ever further into the earth?"[4] I have similarly argued that architecture performs critical heritage work, keeping custody of history through war and peace, and building foundations for knowledge and for constructing new futures.

I take the Dadaab refugee camps as a basis for a concept history of settlement, in this book's chapters examining partition, sedentarization, domesticity, archives, and design, starting in the introduction with a seemingly simple question of what we learn when we look closely at a refugee camp. Although generic understandings of the camp cast it as a space of abjection, of racialized lack, and of political, social, and aesthetic marginality, the camp instead opens profound questions of architecture and history. Theorizations of the refugee camp, based on foundational work by social theorist Hannah Arendt and political theorist Giorgio Agamben, often limit the narrative to one of politics without aesthetics and without the sensible. Space is understood without land, time, or materiality. The refugee figure is abstracted. Before becoming the subject of development and humanitarian aid, this figure is the subject of an impossibility of minority belonging within the nation-state, as Arendt analyzed, and of political exception—of bare life—as Agamben theorized.[5] I have tried to move beyond these important diagnoses and indeed beyond crisis, expressed at the periphery of the nation-state and in the center of humanitarian government, to take a step toward asking who a refugee might be if embodied—and if not exclusively embodying lack. For this, I turn to the people named in this book who have lived their lives in camps and for whom a camp is unequivocally a site of architecture and history, as well as to humanitarian laborers, the aid workers with whom refugees imagined and built settlements. I further refer to scholars who situate refugee worlds not exclusively as spaces of displacement or shelter from it, but, indeed, as architectures with which to think.[6] Through all of these perspectives, I argue, the Dadaab refugee camps allow us to theorize, to mark time and space, to see, and to learn.

The Dadaab refugee camps are not a teleological end in themselves and instead represent the architectural afterlife of partitions. Partitions of land have contributed to the systematic control and rationing of resources, forming the empirical conditions and the metanarrative of what historian Walter Rodney calls "underdevelopment," a concept rooted in the alienation of people from the land and places with which they identify.[7] In a conversation in chapter 1, Alishine Osman and I bring the Dadaab refugee camps into full color through a discussion of the partitions the camps enact by confining people on lands that have been unbordered in the past. We examine photographs together that we each took in the camps, Osman as a resident for much of his life and I as a brief visitor, and I draw from this collaboration to analyze partitions of land and of the self that have divided Dadaab and the people living there. I argue that the siting of the refugee camps in the divided Jubaland reinscribes a historical partition, and also demonstrates a model for reproducing partition. Conceptually, such a model marks the agendas of states, rather than people's politics.[8] The refugee in Dadaab, and no doubt elsewhere, is further subjected to a partitioning of the self as she undergoes a negotiation described by political philosopher Frantz Fanon as the colonizer's distorted recognition of the colonized, forcing her to perform a doubling akin to that analyzed by social historian W. E. B. Du Bois as an effect of racial consciousness.[9] The camp frames these processes through an architecture that comes from partitions. The partitions set the terms for the camp. Chapter 1 invites the reader to move beyond partition thinking.

Beyond enacting confinement, the Dadaab refugee camps mark the recurrence of imposed sedentarization. Refugee camps form enclosures that enact their own temporal and spatial markers, which can be used for subjugation and control through architectures of immobilization. Chapter 2 opens with a photo of clustered tuquls in Dadaab, which bring into view the paradoxes of humanitarian settlement through the sedentarization of architectures intended for migration, disallowing pastoralist economies and social lives. Through abolitionist missions and detention camps for Mau Mau and shifta alike, I underscore a recurring sedentarization of dispossessed people and the erasure and criminalization of nomadic and pastoralist ways of relating to the land. The interruption of the pastoralist economy and social life has colonial ramifications, to borrow architectural historian Samia Henni's argument on the myriad ways that colonial violence reproduces itself, invoking literary scholar Bhakti Shringarpure's demand, "isn't it time to stop feeling ambivalent about empire?"[10] That it fundamentally disrupts the *political* capacity of borderless or transborder structures and ways of life stands among the ways that the shifta war continues into the present day in East Africa.

Architect AbdulFatah Adam builds out this argument in a body of works that quietly describe ways of seeing Dadaab from outside the humanitarian perspective, from the ground of Somalia. Through four works he produced for this book as a countermapping exercise, he draws Dadaab from his situated and embodied perspective—as a person raised in the Kibera neighborhood of Nairobi, trained in architecture at the University of Nairobi, practicing professionally in Kenya and Somalia, and self-identifying within multiple communities. The works, titled *Origins*, *Partitions*, *Borders*, and *Migrations*, tell a serial story. Each appropriates drawing and mapping techniques. *Origins* is a watercolor rendering of the contemporary African and Middle Eastern states that represent a wider region of relationships for many people in the Dadaab refugee camps. The subtle watery gradation in color saturation, which distinguishes one place concretely from another, is overwritten by his overlay of abstract Cartesian coordinates locating Dadaab. *Partitions* gestures to Soomaliweyn, the area of Greater Somalia discussed in chapter 1. The earthy multitonal leather collage peers out from behind a plexiglass shield, cut to disobey colonial territorial borders and articulate the space of Soomaliweyn, which is further inscribed by stitching along the shadow line of the plexiglass cut. *Borders* speaks of the distance and roughness of fleeing from one border town, Dhobey in Somalia, to another, Liboi in Kenya. This traversal is made across terrain modeled in crumpled paper and conceptualized as a steep climb in the work's vertical orientation, representing the path of a person's flight from Somalia to Kenya. Adam drafted *Migrations*, punctuating the series, using the Morpholio Trace computer program over a Google Earth map of Ifo camp, overwriting an image of surveillance with his own. The drawing suggests the primacy of the livestock grazing trails made by the hands and feet of people and animals over the foreign vehicular routes. Together, these paths suggest the multiple infrastructures scaffolding the camp, some "hard," some "soft." Adam's accompanying texts weave a story of partition and sedentarization behind the refugee camps at Dadaab:

> *Origins*. Some historians claim Somalis are descendants of the pharaohs. Geologists have also claimed the oil deposits in Somalia are greater than those in any other country in the region, even on the Arabian Peninsula. The existence of Dadaab could be attributed to this gift, or curse.
>
> *Partitions*. Colonialist and neocolonialist policies have divided the Somali nation over the years, troubling integration and identity. The business acumen of Somalis, with their emergence as an economic force, is, however, putting these divisions to the test.
>
> *Borders*. Border towns are typically developed and integrated urban areas, with local people's mobility unaffected by administrations on either side. Kenya's borders with Somalia demonstrate intentional separations of communities otherwise connected across the administrative lines.
>
> *Migrations*. The networks for migration and circulation highlight the contrast between natural and man-made processes. Footpaths leading into the center of Dadaab are organic like the homesteads and tuquls, weaving around trees and landscapes. The planning of Dadaab is artificial like the roads designed for vehicle access, making false boundaries and territories. Somalis' migration patterns are as contingent as their circulation paths, leading them to settle all over the world and in the most unexpected places.

Building on theorizations of partition and sedentarization, I examine domesticity in emergency in chapter 3, expanding the architectural terms of shelter. Shelter in emergency masks underlying radical practices of domesticity. Drawing from collaborative scholarship, I develop the concept of insurgent domesticities to theorize practices of homemaking in Dadaab, from the design and construction of the dwelling to its inhabitation.[11] For this effort, Abshir's broader body of work is instructive. Her painting *Fragmented II* draws from a series titled *Foundations*, which speaks to the interiority of

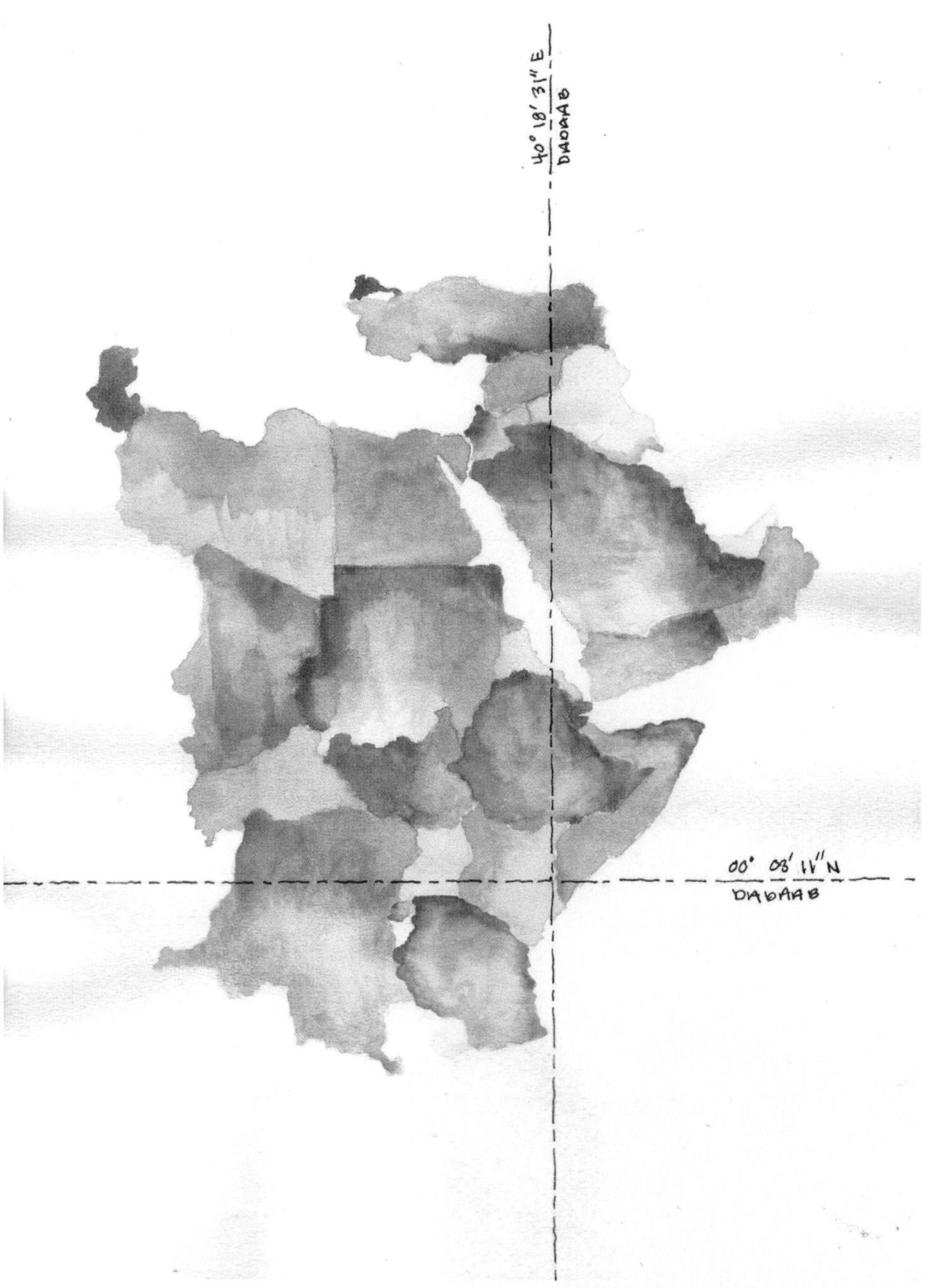

A.1. AbdulFatah Adam, *Origins*, watercolor and ink on paper, 420mm × 197mm, 2022.

A.2. AbdulFatah Adam, *Partitions*, leather, acrylic, and string on mahogany wood, 420mm × 197mm, 2022.

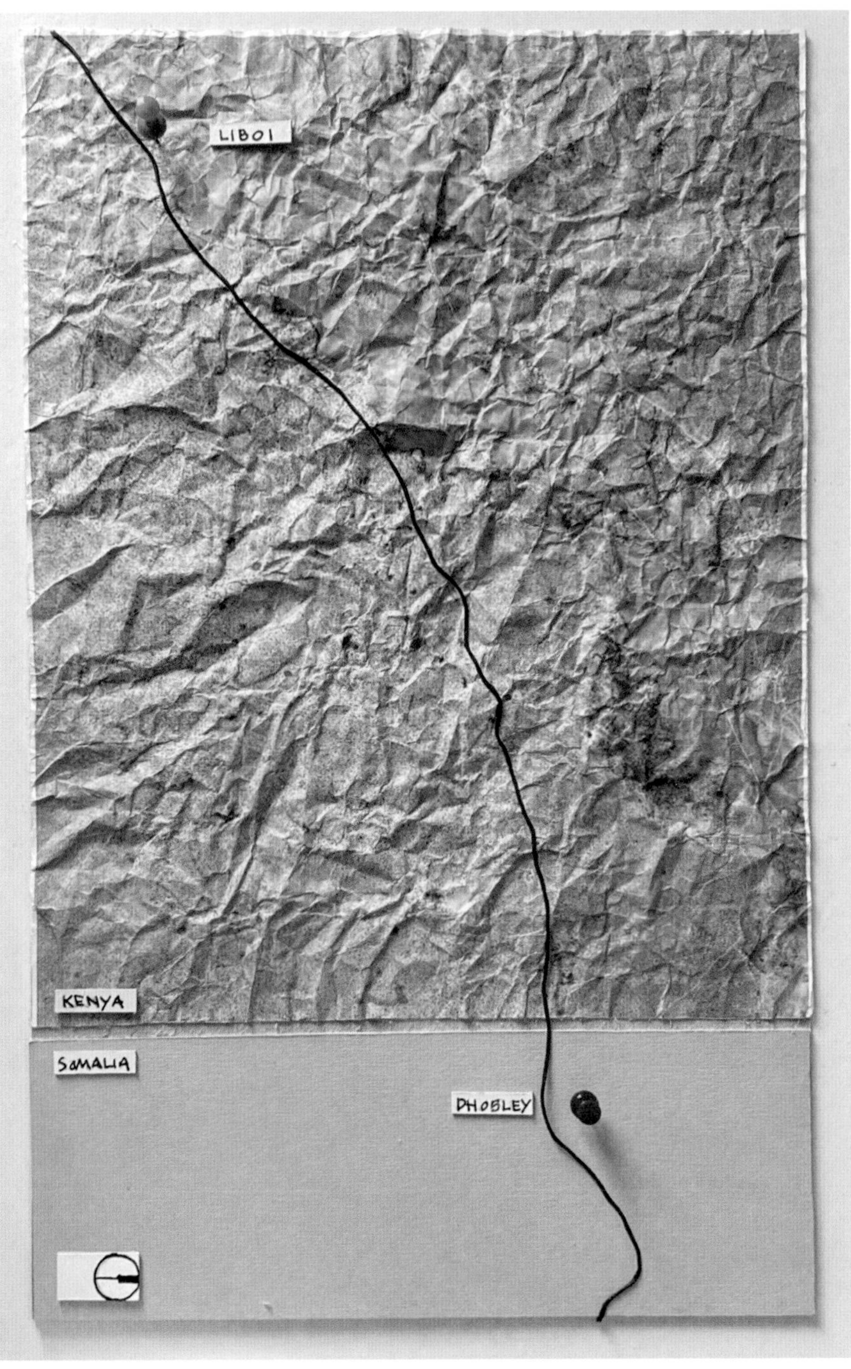

A.3. AbdulFatah Adam, *Borders,* ink on paper and museum board, plastic thumbtacks, and string, 420mm × 197mm, 2022.

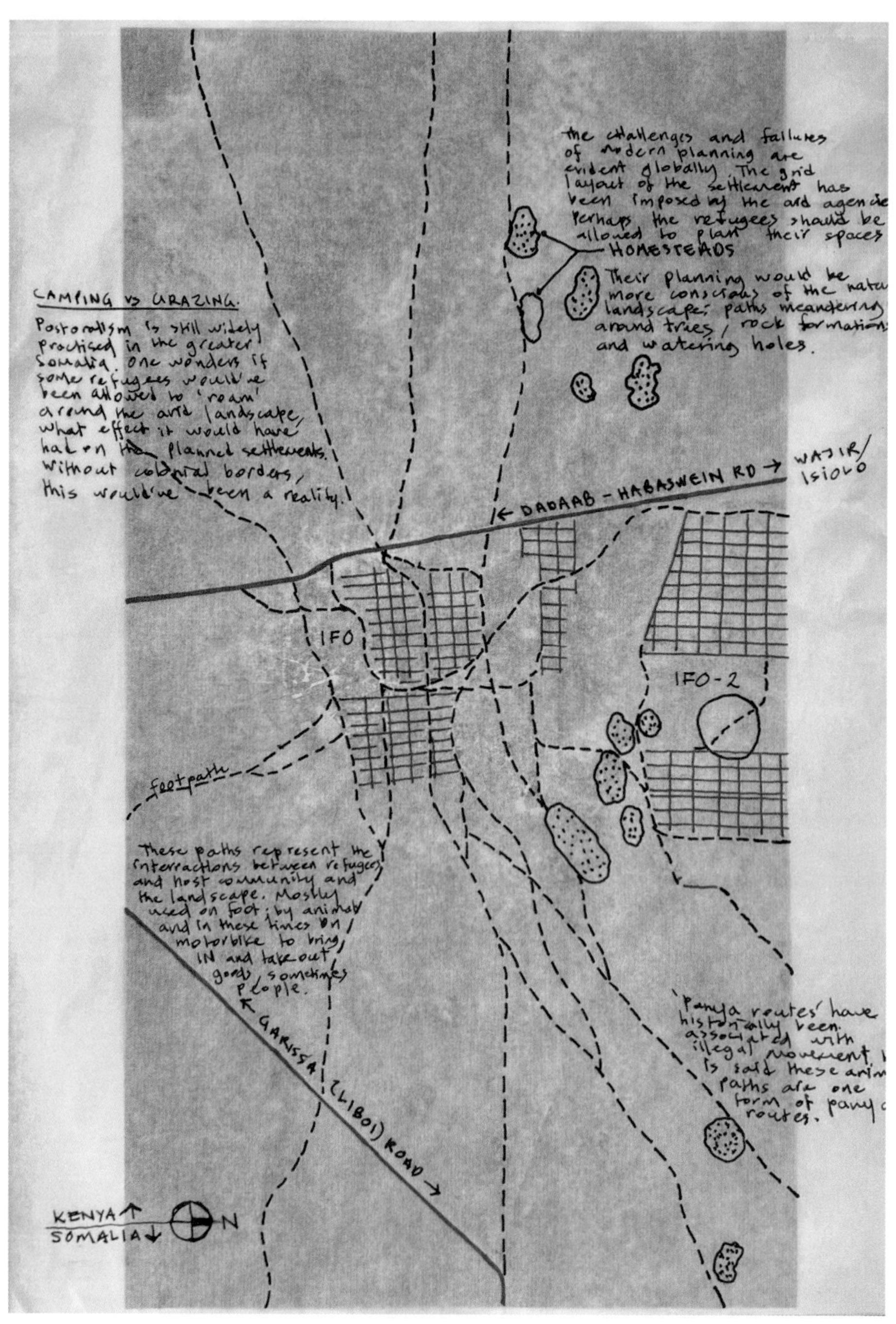

A.4. AbdulFatah Adam, *Migrations*, ink on tracing paper, overlaying a printed Google Earth map, 420mm × 197mm, 2022.

the dwelling as well as the camp.[12] The domesticities inherent in one home in Dadaab provide insight into the camp as a whole domestic space—as an architecture working at the level of people's homes and of nation-states. I argue that domesticity is itself the camp's *theory*, its immanent form of knowledge.

Partition, sedentarization, and domesticity serve as foundational concepts to critically engage a history and ethnography of the architecture and planning of the Dadaab refugee camps in chapter 4. I explore the history of the establishment of the refugee camps and a process of humanitarian settlement by periodizing the growth and structuring of this built form. This counter-appropriation of a historiographic practice allows the renarration of a site most often framed within the humanitarian temporalities of urgency. Such framings disallow *historicity*, or even the mere discursive register of longer periods of time, which might, in turn, disassociate the camps from their ready depiction exclusively as an emergency spatial response to perpetual war. My counternarration instead foregrounds an environment with its own normativities—a humanitarian settlement, which I examine through the construction of an archive. This archive counters the ephemerality of this settlement and its architectures. I recuperate documentary materials that produce fixities, making possible a historiography of Dadaab's planning and design, and also archive the camps themselves through photographic depictions of their architecture and infrastructure. This strategy exposes the archival biases in our writing of histories of architecture and urbanism, by constructing an archive of Dadaab as an urgent historiographical practice.

The book's chapters move from territory to region to nation-state to settlement to architecture, landing in chapter 5 on an infrastructure of humanitarian designs and designers analyzed through connected episodes. My narrative includes the refugee designers and designs in the Dadaab camps, as well as those belonging to various institutions, such as MSF Logistique, the satellite of MSF that produces medical and architectural kits for deployment around the world. In this chapter, I think with humanitarian agencies and organizations in the model of the patron, but not as monoliths; I am interested in individuals and their signature practices, which form the signature practices of the institutions for which they work. I follow an infrastructure of designers, those trained in academies and those living and working in refugee environments, all of whom I name throughout this book as architects. I also follow an infrastructure of designs, understanding them through the construction of signature emergency artifacts, as forms of humanitarian iconography reproduced and commodified. My focus on the signature, the *design*, in contexts of emergency underscores the premise that a refugee camp is a site of architecture and history. The construction of desire for a better humanitarian architecture is an incipient form of commodification that supports the will to rescue, which underlies liberal humanitarian intervention. That design itself forms an infrastructure of humanitarian thought and practice gives us the material and aesthetic means by which to examine the social and political effects of each. Among these effects is an ongoing aesthetic response to perpetual war.

This returns to the question of architecture as the weapon that we use in both war and peace. The concept of an architecture of migration provides an analytic with which to understand war and peace. Architecture—whether understood conceptually or materially, as a building or an environment, as practices or sites—offers empirical terms with which to recalibrate our understanding of normative sociopolitical conditions, war, and emergency, but also remains the concrete site of spatial violence, in need of restoration. This is not an Afropessimistic stance, but rather a tempered comprehension of futurities conditioned by compromise, and a recognition of complex African sociopolitical temporalities, as articulated by anthropologists Brian Goldstone and Juan Obarrio, in that "long term political imaginations of the future seem to be engulfed by a continuous present, composing a mélange of precolonial, colonial, and postcolonial fragments."[13] To resolve this problem, I think with architectural historian Itohan Osayimwese on the possible roles of historical scholarship, design, and cultural heritage practices as critical forms of restitution and repair, and with architect Emanuel Admassu, who asks in the same vein if architecture can be rescued by contemporary art.[14] In a parallel spirit, the exercises in drawing Dadaab that I invited artists to conduct attest to a potential strategy to cast beyond war and partitions, toward wider ecologies.

I close on two works by artists exploring planetary ecologies, each setting the Dadaab refugee camps within wider ecosystems. Architectural designer Elsa MH Mäki (Anishinaabe and Finnish) directly confronts the act of gazing on refugee camps from afar. Her spare line and color patterns examine a satellite's survey and process of image production. Her text comments on artistry and authorship. She developed these images by tracing and layering UNHCR maps of Hagadera using the Rhino (Rhinoceros 3D) drawing program, and reformatting them in the Adobe Illustrator program using information from UNHCR maps and Google Earth's satellite imagery of Hagadera from approximately 2003 to 2021. While she maps Dadaab's relation to the sky, Cave Bureau, the studio founded by principal architects Kabage Karanja and Stella Mutegi, maps Dadaab's relation to the earth.[15] Cave Bureau studies the in-

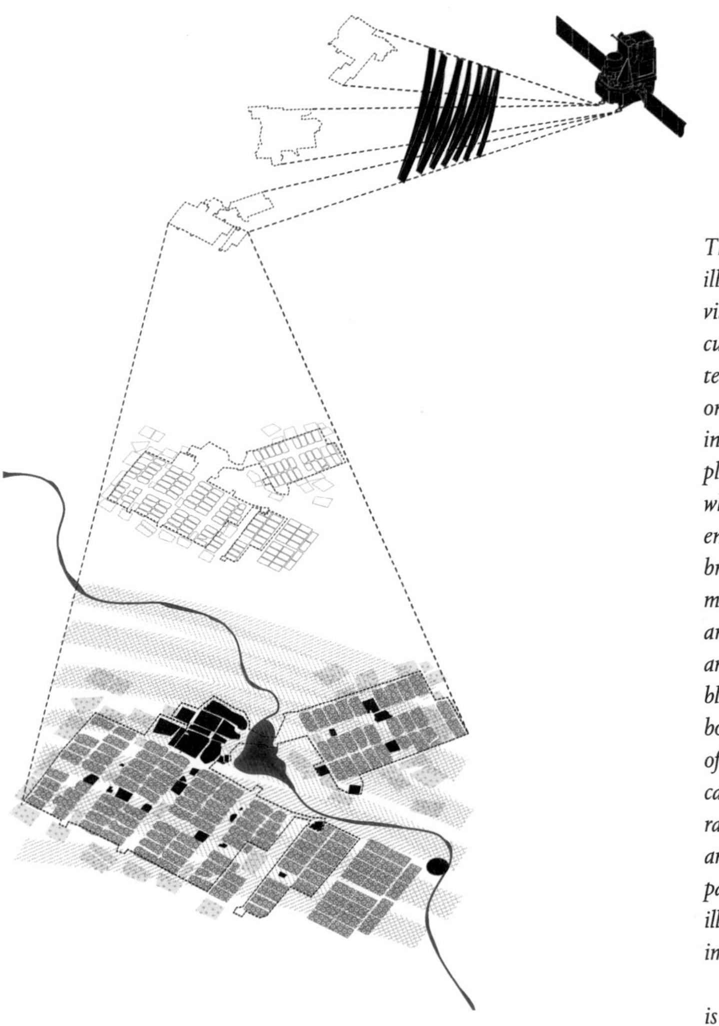

This map of Hagadera illustrates satellite vision. To begin, the cutaway shows a pattern inversion of things on the ground. Dots in green (agricultural planting) contrast with white rings (homes encircled by myrrh brush fencing). Blue marks the seasonal lake and river. Markets and amenities appear in black. The dashes and bold hatching at the top of the drawing depict camp outlines desaturated of information and the erratic flight path of a satellite above, illustrating a process of image construction.

While the ground is saturated with color, texture, and patterns, the satellite captures only pixels to reconstruct a data picture. A satellite operator "cleans" and rearranges this data into a picture resembling the earth, adding bounding benchmarks (including consistent scale at ground level, latitude/longitude, and so on). Individual and corporate entities purchase the data and use additional software to add demographic and other information to produce the maps they value. For example, maps of the Dadaab refugee camps depict the administrated space of the camps, demography, and other data. Everyday ecologies and materialities—wells, homes, and seasonal surface water—are less transmissible through this process.

Things on the ground are imaged by the jagged cloud of a satellite's glitchy motion and extracted to form the dashed lines of the administrative boundaries. The satellite producing public imagery from 1999, the US Geological Survey (USGS) and National Aeronautics and Space Administration's (NASA) Landsat 7, has a sensor failure producing an uneven picture with both gaps and overlaps. This condition demonstrates some of the compositional logic behind the technology, betraying its nature as neither photographic nor veristic, but instead, like all maps and representations of mass data, an authored picture.

A.5. Elsa MH Mäki, satellite study, 2022.

DAGAHALY
IFO
IFO II
DADAAB
HAGADERA
A
B
C
D
E
Pump head
Spout
Handle
Top flange
Pump stand
Cement platform
Ground
Casing pipe
Rising main
Pump rod
Plunger
Cylinder
Footvalve
Suction pipe
Suction pipe

frastructure of the Dadaab settlements in relation to the Merti aquifer. Through diagrams of settlements, hardware, stone, and water, the architects narrate the connection of the camps to the prehistoric interlocking underground cave system. Their text explains the impact of borewell drilling on the aquifer and, conversely, the occasion of its eruption above ground: the water tap stand in the camps. These images were generated through the collaging of textures in the Adobe Photoshop image design program, overlaid after a loose modeling process in the drafting program SketchUp, and built on hand drawings converted into accurate linework in MicroStation.[16] The drawings by Elsa MH Mäki and Cave Bureau offer ways that architecture, like Hadraawi's poetry, can act as a restitutive "weapon." These artworks critically restore the Dadaab refugee camps from emergency subjecthood to a different ecological belonging. It is in those larger forms of belonging that Dadaab has something to teach.

What do we learn when we see a refugee camp? The Dadaab refugee camps have shaped history, heritage, and temporalities. They contain multiple architectures of migration, which demand foregrounding pluralities of perspective, interpretation, and vocality as urgent for historiography and theorization. Was the poet Hadraawi speaking of the comfort that poetry

A.6. (*opposite*) Cave Bureau, architectural analytical cross-section of the Merti Aquifer, the camp settlement, and extractive infrastructure; construction of a Jurassic-era structure of the earth sustaining life on the surface, 2022. Ink on paper freehand sketch, digital linework in MicroStation, modeling in SketchUp, collage of textures in Photoshop.

KEY

A. Main lithology: Semiconsolidated sandstones and limestones.

B. Salinity distribution in the Merti aquifer (see the introduction, note 27). Little data is available on water chemistry of the southwestern flank of the Merti aquifer. This is likely the result of poor yields and water quality in this area, leading to few completed boreholes.

C. The aquifer is situated in the Anza Rift, which was formed in the Jurassic period of the Mesozoic era.

D. The average depth to the top of the aquifer is 114 meters, and the average vertical thickness of the aquifer system varies between 78 and 130 meters (Oord, Collenteur, and Tolk, "Hydrogeological Assessment," in introduction, note 27).

E. There is some anthropogenic pollution occurring, but the data is not available to determine the percentage of the aquifer area that has been affected, although this is over a significant part of the aquifer within Somalia (Oord, Collenteur, and Tolk, "Hydrogeological Assessment," in introduction, note 27).

gives in any context? Or the power and security of a weapon? The precise answer may be less important than the knowledge that architecture has a similar diffractive potential to generate many meanings. I therefore insist on a discussion that enables multiplicities to surface, whether by the many interlocutors or past figures who appear in these pages, the artists whose work has formed the backbone of this afterword, or future thinkers. A lesson I take from Dadaab is to trust the many connections that persist in spite of partitions. Because of that, this work is dedicated to the elders and communities who have lived in Dadaab and in refugee camps around the world, who demonstrate the fine grain of how we may live together, owing each other debts, and together building common heritages, knowledges, and futures.

Acknowledgments

My book speaks of migration, displacement, dispossession, and colonialism, and can do so because of people who came before me, cited in these pages, as well as people who lifted me up, whose second gift is this occasion to reflect on the intellectual solidarities and accountabilities behind this work. My coming of age (as a student, and later as an architect, in diaspora in the United States and in India before economic liberalization) occurred in the worldwide wake of the South African struggle against apartheid. The luminosity of this African accomplishment changed me. It gave me historical consciousness and a sense of belonging. While ten years as an architect and five in humanitarian organizations led me very practically to this book's research, the imagination for it was seeded in a childhood attunement to worlds dreamed in this struggle, with its expectations of abolition and border-crossing solidarities against oppression. I am proud to have been raised by worldmakers who, despite extensive sacrifices and burdens, demanded that we maintain such expectations and visions of how to live together with one another. This book is the materialization of the love, trust, care, and power of my mother, Shanta Raman, and my father, Dr. K. Venkata Raman. It is a horizon of their migrations.

Researching and writing this book has not been without implication in landed institutions enmeshed in colonial practices or the imperial interests of the country where I work and live as an immigrant settler. My present institutional position at Barnard College, Columbia University, is indebted to the elders, relatives, and children of Lenapehoking on whose unceded land I work and who have been stewards of this land. I am mindful that I have conducted research in Kenya on lands that are home to generations of people who have endured removals, detentions, flight, and many other terrors, and have continued to struggle for peaceful relations to those lands, for their homes. My work is infused with the wisdom of elders and communities in Dadaab and elsewhere, whose migrations, worldbuilding, homemaking, and aesthetic labors hold meaning for us all. In my scholarship, I have tried to be conscious of colonial practices that we have allowed to persist, holding people and ecologies at risk. I write more about this here: https://barnard.edu/profiles/anooradha-iyer-siddiqi.

My words here offer a threadbare account of the labor and attentiveness of others, which brought this book into being. There is not room to acknowledge twelve years of unpayable debts. My path to and through the academy has been circuitous and precarious, and people supported this research when I could offer little equal in return. I have cherished every invitation to discuss my scholarship in a classroom or public lecture, every conversation with a colleague or student that provided insight or sustenance to continue this difficult research and writing, every collaboration, every cup of tea, every care shown for my children. I remember and reflect on these relations every day. They constructed a choral environment around my work (a powerful clarifying concept I heard emphasized in Saidiya Hartman's seminar "black poesis/radical composition").

The ideas in these pages were developed alongside inspiring processes of cowriting and collaboration with Hollyamber Kennedy, Vazira Zamindar, Rachel Lee, Somayeh Chitchian, Andrew Herscher, and members of the Insurgent Domesticities working group (listed in chapter 3, note 5). My awe is forever reserved for these scholars. My argumentation was further sharpened by editorial feedback on chapters, the full book manuscript, or related articles (under my name in the references) by the following excellent scholars: Carli Coetzee, Miriam Ticktin, Esra Akcan, Anupama Rao, Zirwat Chowdhury, Itohan Osayimwese, Ikem Okoye, Delia Wendel, Juliana Maxim, Can Bilsel, Radha d'Souza, Prathama Bannerjee, Ravi Sundaram, Patricia Morton, Michael Waters, Steven Pierce, Shahd Seethaler-Wari, Maja Momić, Ashika Singh, Alessandra Gola, Luce Beeckmans, Hilde Heynen, Ijlal Muzaffar, Daniel Abramson, Zeynep Çelik Alexander, Michael Osman, Meredith Tenhoor, Pamela Karimi, Alexandra Pereira-Edwards, Albert Ferré, Tania Sengupta, Johan Lagae, Ricardo Agarez, Dana Cuff, Will Davis, Alessandro Petti, Eduardo Rega, Daniel Barber, Nick Axel, Mahdi Sabbagh, Meghan McCallister, Lucia Allais, Daniel Monk, Steven Pierce, Casey Primel, Angela Naimou, Iftikhar Dadi, James Graham, Léopold Lambert, two reviewers of this book, and reviewers of my articles.

The following academic collaborations and their culminating publications (see the notes and the references) provide a significant foundation for this work: "Concept Histories of Settlement" (Hollyamber Kennedy, Nitin Bathla, Debjani Bhattacharyya, S. E. Eisterer, Rafico Ruiz, Manuel Shvartzberg-Carrió); "Insurgent Domesticities" (see chapter 3, note 5); "Feminist Architectural Histories of Migration" (Rachel Lee; for others, see the references); "The Art and Architecture of Partition" (Zirwat Chowdhury, Farhan Karim, Maristella Casciato; for others, see the references); "Architecture and the Housing Question" (Juliana Maxim, Can Bilsel; for others, see the references); "Caregiving as Method" (Can Bilsel, Garnette Cadogan, Jay Cephas, Lilian Chee, Elis Mendoza, Ana Miljački, Ikem Okoye, Itohan Osayimwese, Kush Patel, Peg Rawes, Delia Wendel); and "Cohabitations" (Namita Dharia, Peg Rawes, Ikem Okoye, Daniel Barber). These multi-institutional, multiyear collaborations have educated me. Together and individually, their participants have anchored scholarly frameworks for my book.

The privilege of academic employment and its networks enabled my writing and refinement of arguments. My book took its present form in the Mellon Migration Seminar at the Harvard University Mahindra Humanities Center, which I joined upon experiencing a devastating injury, after which I thought I might not walk again. While in the following months I learned much about "ability" and "disability," people nurtured my work while nursing me. I will forever hold dear these empathic and passionate scholars: Nick Estes, Lowell Brower, S. E. Eisterer, and my postdoctoral cohort (Sumayya Kassamalli, Valeria Castelli, Jon Connolly, Onur Günay, Matthew Kruer, with graduate fellows Neelam Khoja and Argyro Nicolaou). I thank Homi K. Bhabha, Steve Biel, Diane Davis, Lisa Lowe, Jacqueline Bhabha, and Mary Halpenny-Killip for supporting the fellowship, and readers in my book manuscript workshop for labor that was transformative for me: Ana María Léon, Durba Mitra, Sai Balkrishnan, Lauren Jacobi, Ed Eigen, and George Meiu. I received feedback crucial for my book in presentations in the Mahindra Humanities Center, African Studies Workshop, Radcliffe Institute for Advanced Study, and Graduate School of Design.

At Barnard College and Columbia University, many inspired colleagues have helped me think through this book's questions by engaging my work and inviting me into their own remarkable conversations. My thinking and research owe a debt to discussions in the Columbia University Seminar "Studies in Contemporary Africa" (especially acknowledging my co-chairs Abosede George, Robyn d'Avignon, and Laura Fair; rapporteurs Anusha Sundar, Jessie Cohen, and Luz Colpa; and an initial invitation from Rhiannon Stephens and Abosede George); the "Unsettlement" workshop (Yvette Christianse, Rosalind Morris) organized by the University of the Witwatersrand; the Barnard College Willen Seminars "Bombay!" (co-organized with Anupama Rao, Shayoni Mitra, Debashree Mukherjee, Kavita Sivaramakrishnan), "Urban Studies" (Nick Smith, Aaron Passell), and "Traditional Ecological Knowledge" (Elizabeth Hutchinson); the "Decoloniality and the Politics of

History" symposium (Alex Alberro, Pujan Karambeigi); the Buell dissertation colloquium (Reinhold Martin); Critical, Curatorial, and Conceptual Practices program reviews (Felicity Scott, Mark Wasiuta); the Refugee Cities working group (Amy Chazkel, Bahia Munem); the Common Circle workshop (Andrés Jacque, Laura Kurgan); the "Feminist Architectural Histories of Migration" launch by the Barnard Center for Research on Women and the Graduate School of Architecture, Planning, and Preservation Dean's Lecture Series (Rebecca Siqueiros, Anais Halftermeyer, Sophia Strabo, Bryony Roberts, Ateya Khorakiwala, Premilla Nadesan, Janet Jakobsen, Andrés Jacque); the Historic Preservation lecture series (Jorge Otero-Pailos); and courses taught by Celia Naylor, Debra Minkoff, Kavita Sivaramakrishnan, Michael Waters, Emanuel Admassu, Bryony Roberts, Mario Gooden, Diana Cristobal Olave, Kadambari Baxi, Ralph Ghoche, Ignacio Galán, and Karen Fairbanks. Each and every one of these opportunities has been meaningful and forms part of the diverse intellectual and scholarly support that has grown my work. In addition to those named thus far, I am terribly thankful for Mabel Wilson, Brian Larkin, Monica Miller, Neferti Tadiar, Manijeh Moradian, Beck Jordan-Young, Rosalyn Deutsche, Jonathan Reynolds, Irena Haiduk, Meg McLagan, Irina Verona, Jennifer Wenzel, Elleni Centime Zeleke, Zoë Strother, Avinoam Shalem, Joseph Slaughter, Manan Ahmed, Mana Kia, Maria José de Abreu, Paige West, and Lila Abu-Lughod. Gregory Bryda made sure I would write a book. I have worked through this book's complexities in dialogue with incisive, generous scholars gracing my classrooms to assist in teaching: Sourav Chatterjee, Ana G. Ozaki, Rochelle Malcolm, Zainab Najeeb, Samaya Mansour, Ingrid Lao, Javairia Shahid, Megan Eardley, Jonah Rowen, and Navid Zarrinnal. Along the way, gifted students and advisees have read and thought with me and helped me process the ideas in these pages.

My gratitude is bottomless for mentors, colleagues, and students in my prior academic positions, without whose early development of my work this book would not exist. At New York University, Vasuki Nesiah, Eve Meltzer, Robyn d'Avignon, Jini Kim Watson, Crystal Parikh, Emily Bauman, Rosalind Fredericks, Sophia Azeb, and Andrea Gadberry read and enriched my work; Meleko Mokgosi, Ritty Lukose, Millery Polyné, Kwami Coleman, and C. Cybele Raver advised me; and Alishine Osman, Samar al-Bulushi, AbdouMaliq Simone, Ben Rawlence, and Rachel Stern expanded my scholarly imagination in the public discussion "Dadaab Is a Place on Earth." At Bryn Mawr College, my work benefited from the attention of Ellen Stroud, Alicia Walker, Joel Schlosser, Gary McDonough, Andrew Friedman, Barbara Miller Lane, and Carola Hein. Jilly Traganou, Joseph Heathcott, and other colleagues at The

New School invited me to present my work and join their discussions, and Carol Krinsky at New York University brought me into my first architectural history classroom.

Ideas for this study emerged in the New York University Institute of Fine Arts, where my PhD dissertation was carefully and spiritedly supervised by three fine scholars: Jean-Louis Cohen, Sally Engle Merry, and Thomas Keenan. (To Sally's memory I dedicate chapter 3, "Shelter and Domesticity." To the memory of Jean-Louis, I dedicate this book's archive of Dadaab.) My approaches were contoured in rigorous coursework, especially with Felicity Scott, Linda Gordon and Mary Nolan, Finbarr Barry Flood, and Glenn Wharton; in New York University interdisciplinary exchanges in the Institute of Fine Arts, the Humanities Initiative, and the Institute for Public Knowledge (with Crystal Parikh, Patrick Deer, Sally Merry, Nicholas Guilhot, Ravinder Kaur, and David Ludden); and in multiyear studies with the Duke University Franklin Humanities Institute FOCUS cluster on Humanitarian Challenges/Borderwork(s) Lab (Claudia Koonz, Erika Weinthal) and École des Hautes Études en Sciences Sociales project "Un Paysage Global de Camps" (Michel Agier, Clara Lecadet). This work matured alongside that of a particular cohort of radical art historians—Ileana Selejan, Clare Davies, AnnMarie Perl, Rashmi Vishwanathan—who continue to bring camaraderie and cheer.

The manuscript for this book was completed in a residency at Denniston Hill, a gift beyond my wildest dreams. I am exceptionally moved to have been nominated by Lawrence Chua and to have spent incomparable days with Lacey Romano and Julie Mehretu. I hope to do for others what the artists and thinkers behind this warm environment have done for me.

My writing has been impacted by arresting critical remarks and championship by scholars and intellectuals whom I admire. I have referenced many already and further mention: Nicole King, Brett St. Louis, Dubravka Sekulić, Sarover Zaidi, Garnette Oluoch-Olunya, Lydia Muthuma, Zoé Samudzi, Romola Sanyal, Madiha Tahir, Saloni Mathur, Garnette Cadogan, Jill Casid, Christina Sharpe, Sandi Hilal, Olga Touloumi, Omar Berrada, Nora Akawi, Bhakti Shringarpure, Samia Henni, Mpho Matsipa, Nida Rehman, Daniel Cardoso-Llach, Liza Oliver, Claire Zimmerman, Barbara Penner, Juan Du, Kajri Jain, Prita Meier, Kishwar Rizvi, Naomi Stead, Ross Exo Adams, Armaghan Ziaee, Catalina Mejia Moreno, Huda Tayob, Warebi Brisibe, Mahmoud Keshavarz, Irit Katz, Juliet Koss, Markus Stock, Srinivas Krishna, Emily Bauman, Simon Addison, Loren Landau, Marnie Thomson, Matt Swagler, Marta Caldeira, María González Pendás, Alicia Imperiale, Gina Greene, Ginger

Nolan, Kate Brideau, Dina Siddiqi, Vyjayanthi Rao, Deen Sharp, Ipek Türeli, Sonali Dhanpal, Rochelle Malcolm, Shivani Shedde, Curt Gambetta, Julien Lafontaine Carboni, Charlotte Grace, Divya Kumar-Dumas, Ishani Dasgupta, Tapati Guha-Thakurta, Rohit Mujumdar, Rupali Gupte, Prasad Shetty, Samprati Pani, Raqs Media Collective, Mustansir Dalvi, Ishita Shah, Spyros Papapetros, Keller Easterling, Nasser Rabbat, Huma Gupta, David Joselit, Ashley Dawson, and Emma Shaw Crane.

One day I received a life-changing invitation from Elizabeth Ault. I have been astonished time and again by her attentive editorial custodianship and honored by the commitment of Benjamin Kossak, James Moore, Lisa Lawley, Aimee Harrison, David Rainey, Lalitree Darnielle, Christopher Robinson, Lee Willoughby-Harris, Chad Royal, Laura Sell, Malai Escamilla, and others on the marketing and editorial, design, and production teams; John Donohue and the teams at Westchester Publishing Services and Antares Publishing Services; Jayashree Anand and Prathima Rajan at Sanam Solutions; and the Duke University Press Editorial Advisory Board and "Theory in Forms" series editors, Nancy Rose Hunt, Achille Mbembe, and Todd Meyers. The dedication and acumen of all of these individuals brought this politically, ethically, emotionally, and aesthetically complex book into its finest form on the page, honoring its subjects. I am humbled by Lisa Lowe for recommending my work to this publisher.

I am indebted to people whose lives and work have put them in the humanitarian system as refugees or laborers. They are cited in the primary sources unless they requested to be omitted. This research depended upon the insights and camaraderie of Bethany Young and Elettra Legovini, without whom my travels would have been lonely indeed. Alishine Osman, our trust has been my cornerstone.

This book culminated in shared practices with creative intellectuals who showed me that we can *draw differently*, that we are not consigned to inscribe colonial practices and instead can lay different footprints in the earth. I am inspired by the citizens of the GoDown Arts Centre—Henry Omondi, Catherine Mujomba, Nyambura Muiruri, Deborah Wanjugu, M. K. Mbugua, Rehema Kabare, Lima Mbai, Salome Ndung'u, Roseline Mugo, Dennis Simiyu, John Waswa, Garnette Oluoch-Olunya, and Joy Mboya—and in companionship, Lydia Muthuma, Abdullahi Abdulkadir Sheikh Nur, Peterson Kamwathi, Flora Mutere-Okuku, and Yvonne Adhiambo Owuor. I have learned from wonderful teachers about Nairobi and East Africa: from the Jua Kali Association on material landscapes and soundscapes of labor; Siyama Ismail Medi on Kibera; Clive Wanguthi on Eastleigh; Member of Parliament

Yusuf Hassan Abdi on Kamukunji; Professor Erastus Abonyo on histories of academic institutions; and, not least, from participants in my lectures and seminars at the Technical University of Kenya, Kenyatta University, Rift Valley Institute, British Institute in Eastern Africa, and the course "Architecture as a Form of Knowledge." For bringing meaning to our mazingira, my everlasting respect belongs to Diana Lee-Smith and Davinder Lamba, as well as my partners in drawing Dadaab in these pages: Deqa Abshir, Abdulfatah Adam, Kabage Karanja, Stella Mutegi, and Elsa MH Mäki.

Scholarly books stand on the shoulders of archivists, librarians, curators, and many academic workers. My work before and after we shared an institutional umbrella has been impacted by efforts in the libraries of Columbia University and Barnard College by Zak Rouse, Kitty Chibnik, Yuusuf Caruso, Shannon O'Neill, Martha Tenney, Vani Natarajan, Madiha Choksi, and Meredith Wisner. In Kenya, I benefited from the advocacy of Richard Ambani and Alfred Anangwe in the Kenya National Archives and Immelda Kithuke and Julius Mambo in the National Museums of Kenya, as well as the vision of Eastleigh's Awjama Omar Cultural Research and Reading Center and Nairobi bookstores Cheche (Ubax Abdi) and BookStop (Chan Bahal). Montserrat Canela Garayoa and Jeff Crisp at the UNHCR and Tom Corsellis at the Shelter Centre supported research (in Geneva), as did Sarah Rhodes at the University of Oxford Bodleian Social Science Library and Gwendolyn Blin at Médecins Sans Frontières (in Paris). Serubiri Moses and Naeem Mohaiemen provided important curatorial advice for exhibiting the work in this book. Professor Kimani Njogu helped me consider Somali and Kiswahili translations of this book. My special thanks to Mwalimu Abdul Nanji, Mwalimu Anne Munuku, Sanghita Sanyal, Sanjutha Thiraviyanayagam, Aude Eretta, and Olivier Garrel for instruction in Kiswahili, Bangla, Tamil, and French. The staff of the Columbia University Center for the Study of Social Difference and Barnard Center for Research on Women have provided crucial project assistance, and Rachel Garcia-Grossman and Elisabeth Sher have offered invaluable daily administrative support.

While I remain mindful that selective grants and fellowships structurally favor those working within powerful states and institutions by augmenting their capacity to research and positioning their work to circulate in sophisticated scholarly communities, a book with the complex methodology and scope of this one would not have been written without a variety of supports. Publication of the color image archive and open-access distribution was supported by a Graham Foundation for Advanced Studies in the Fine Arts Grant to Individuals, the Columbia University Seminar Schoff Fund, and Barnard

College (Linda Bell, Reshmi Mukherjee). Grants and fellowships at Barnard College, Columbia University, Harvard University, New York University, the University of Basel (Kenny Cupers), and The New School, as well as a Social Science Research Council International Dissertation Research Fellowship and a Graham Foundation for Advanced Studies in the Fine Arts Carter Manny Award Citation of Special Recognition supported research and writing. My travels depended on the hospitality and critical companionship of Nicole King, Brett St. Louis, Mutheu Mbondo, Simon Addison, Danielle Bishop, Annemarie van Roessel, Nick Eckert, Miren Atela, Anula Shetty and Michael Kuetemeyer, Nelun Harassgama and Luxshmanan Nadaraja, and Léopold Lambert and Mariam Shivangi Raj.

In the background, elders have cared for us and continue to do so. I am so grateful for the warmth of my parents-in-law; Amma and Baba, I miss you very much. I love our unfolding family reunions in India, Bangladesh, Sri Lanka, Kenya, England, and the United States, with periammas, periappas, chithis, chithappas, akkas, annas, khalas, mamas, apas, bhaiyas, aunties, uncles, and cousins in our big family. For cheering this book on (and often housing and feeding me/us), thanks to Renuma, Kalyani Chithi, Gnana Periamma, Mali Chithappa, Thiagu Periappa, Sanckar Periappa, Shanta Periamma, Radha Akka, Jaya Akka, Pattu Periamma, Ajeet, Murali, Menaka, Situ Khala and Ranu Mama, Tariq Bhai, Shampa Apa, Sheesh Bhai, Luva Apa, Rochona, David, Mohona, Sarat, Suzi, Sonia, and Ashwin. Our domestic infrastructure in New York is fortified by Audra Robb, Lisa Putignano, Diane Bradshaw, Kate Hillis, Ercu Dedelioglu, Kristin Johansen, Isaiah Stannard, Sanjive Vaidya, Elena Monzón, Maria Fuentes, Isaac St. Louis, Nkili Birmingham, Grace Sandoval, Shveta Dogra, Rachel Leary, Rachel Shoemake, Candi Rodriguez, Tatiana Hoover, and the teachers of P.S. 333. Our home is filled with the love and floppy ears of our nyota ya asubuhi, Mister Darcy.

My greatest treasures are the joy, the sigh, and the soul that begin and end my days. Sahil Iyer Siddiqi and Ruhi Iyer Siddiqi, the horizons of my migrations, if this book took me away from you, I return to you the intellectual and political commons it honors and imagines. Dr. Asif Azam Siddiqi, because a single question about the special theory of relativity led to a conversation for the ages, you are on every page.

Notes

INTRODUCTION

1 The largest numbers of refugees in the world are hosted in Africa, in spite of the international mandate for responsibility sharing by UNHCR signatories.
2 Michelle Shephard, "World's Largest Refugee Camp in Kenya Could Be 'the Future,'" *Toronto Star*, September 21, 2015, https://www.thestar.com/news/world/2015/09/21/worlds-large-refugee-camp-in-kenya-could-be-the-future.html. Mohamed Olow Odowa "calls Dadaab his 'open-air prison.' He has lived here since 1992. Odowa, 28, is a chairman of the camp's volunteer security force. 'We're cops without guns,' he says."
3 See Espiritu et al., *Departures*.
4 Tamale, *Decolonization and Afro-Feminism*; D'Souza, "Decolonizing Knowledge"; Mahmood, *Politics of Piety*.
5 Akcan, *Open Architecture*, 38.
6 Iheka, *African Ecomedia*, 10.
7 Lopez, *Remittance Landscape*, 21.
8 Trouillot, *Silencing the Past*, 23, 24.
9 Isnina Ali Rage, interview by author; Siddiqi, "Ephemerality."
10 McKittrick, *Demonic Grounds*, 121–22.
11 I am grateful to Prathama Banerjee on discussions of constructions and constitutions of "history," Delhi, 2018. See Banerjee, *Politics of Time*.
12 I am grateful to Abdullahi Abdulkadir Sheikh Nur for research and translation assistance. "Hagar" may refer to Abraham's wife, significant in Muslim traditions, the mother of Ishmael who was banished and for whom Allah brought forth a well.
13 Corsellis, "Selection of Sites," 150; Horst, *Transnational Nomads*.
14 Pérouse de Montclos and Kagwanja, "Refugee Camps or Cities?," 207.
15 "Dadaab—World's Biggest Refugee Camp 20 Years Old," *UNHCR News*, February 21, 2012, https://www.unhcr.org/en-us/news/makingdifference/2012/2/4f439dbb9/dadaab-worlds-biggest-refugee-camp-20-years-old.html.
16 Government of Kenya, Royal Danish Embassy, and Norwegian Embassy, *In Search of Protection and Livelihoods: Socio-economic and Environmental Impacts of Dadaab Refugee Camps on Host Communities*, September 2010, 7, 9, https://www.alnap.org/system/files/content/resource/files/main/1396.pdf.

17 See Walia, *Border and Rule*; Bradley and De Noronha, *Against Borders*; Pallister-Wilkins, *Humanitarian Borders*.

18 Binaifer Nowrojee, "Seeking Refuge, Finding Terror: The Widespread Rape of Somali Women Refugees in North Eastern Kenya," in "Africa Watch," *Human Rights Watch* 5, no. 13 (October 4, 1993); Gerald Simpson, Meghan Rhoad, Agnes Odhiambo, and Human Rights Watch, *"Welcome to Kenya": Police Abuse of Somali Refugees* (New York: Human Rights Watch, 2010).

19 The concept of the clan is imprecise, is contingent on social context, and fails to account for many forms of belonging and identification in Somali worlds. Samatar, "Somalia"; Abdi, *Elusive Jannah*, 33; Harper, *Getting Somalia Wrong?*, 14–43.

20 Martin L. Taylor, "Refugees in Kenya: Current Status" (n.p.: Lutheran World Federation Department of World Service, November 1991, provided by Per Iwansson), 11.

21 Government of Kenya, Royal Danish Embassy, and Norwegian Embassy, *In Search of Protection*, 7–10.

22 Interviews with aid workers worldwide reflected this bias.

23 Figures are given in US dollars. Government of Kenya, Royal Danish Embassy, and Norwegian Embassy, *In Search of Protection*, 9.

24 Pérouse de Montclos and Kagwanja, "Refugee Camps or Cities?," 212.

25 For a sociomaterial study of humanitarian infrastructure, see Smirl, *Spaces of Aid*.

26 *The Option*, Safaricom newsletter, December 2009–February 2010, 39, https://docplayer.net/49938857-December-february-2010-think-safaricom-business-win-internet-on-the-move-a-year-s-subscription-to-your-favourite-magazine.html.

27 W. V. Swarzenski and M. J. Mundorff, prepared in cooperation with the Water Department, Kenya Ministry of Agriculture, under the auspices of the U.S. Agency for International Development, "Geohydrology of North Eastern Province, Kenya," *Contributions to the Hydrology of Africa and the Mediterranean Region*, Geological Survey Water-Supply Paper 1757-N (Washington, DC: US Government Printing Office, 1977); Fred K. Mwango, B. C. Muhangú, C. O. Juma, and I. T. Githae, "Groundwater Resources in Kenya," in *Managing Shared Aquifer Resources in Africa*, ed. Bo Applegreen (Tripoli: General Water Authority of the Libyan Arab Jamahiriya, 2004), 93–100; Arjen Oord, Raoul Collenteur, and Lieselotte Tolk, "Hydrogeological Assessment of the Merti Aquifer, Kenya," technical report no. 1 of ARIGA, *Assessing Risks of Investment in Groundwater Development in Sub-Saharan Africa*, August 5, 2014, https://www.worldagroforestry.org/sites/default/files/TR1%20ARIGA-%20Hydrological%20Assessment%20of%20the%20Merti%20Aquifer%20Kenya.pdf; David Ndegwa Kuria and Henry Njau Kamunge, "Merti Aquifer Recharge Zones Determination Using Geospatial Technologies," *Journal of Applied Sciences, Engineering and Technology for Development* 1, no. 1 (July 15, 2013): 24–31.

28 Purpura, "Framing the Ephemeral," 11–15.

29 On the recalcitrance of material things—a vital capacity to obstruct—see Bennett, *Vibrant Matter*, 1–19.

30 Siddiqi, "Ephemerality."

31 I build on a literature on refugee urbanisms and materialities, stemming from foundational studies of constructed environments and landscapes of subaltern, Southern, and/or Muslim worlds. Ananya Roy, "Slumdog Cities"; Pasquetti and Sanyal, *Displacement*; Sanyal, "An Architecture of Displacement"; Seethaler-Wari, Chitchian, and Momić, *Inhabiting Displacement*; Beeckmans et al., *Making Home(s) in Displacement*; Desai and Sanyal, *Urbanizing Citizenship*; Katz, Martín, and Minca, *Camps Revisited*; Katz, *Common Camp*; Sanyal, "Squatting in Camps"; Agha, "Emotional Capital"; Abourahme, "Assembling and Spilling-Over"; Abourahme, "Beneath the Concrete"; Katz, "Spreading and Concentrating"; Bilsel and Maxim, *Architecture and the Housing Question*; Gharipour and Kılınç, *Social Housing*; Abu-Hamdi and Allweil, "Beyond the Camp." Scholarly analysis of Dadaab as "urban" is limited and terming it as such is debated. Siddiqi, "Ephemerality"; Siddiqi, "Dadaab (Kenya)"; Siddiqi, "Emergency or Development?"; Agier, "Camp-Towns: Somalia in Kenya," in *Managing the Undesirables*, 132–46; Pérouse de Montclos and Kagwanja, "Refugee Camps or Cities?"; Jansen, *Kakuma Refugee Camp*. Narrating the camps broadly as a "city" is common in journalistic and humanitarian gray literature: "If counted as a city, Dadaab would be Kenya's third largest—the economic possibilities are tremendous." Melanie Teff, "Kenya Can Turn the Dadaab Refugee Camps into an Asset," *The Guardian*, April 18, 2012, https://www.theguardian.com/global-development/poverty-matters/2012/apr/18/kenya-turn-dadaab-into-asset. See also Rawlence, *City of Thorns*; Alain Beaudou, Luc Cambrézy, and Marc Souris, *Environment, Cartography, Demography and Geographical Information System in the Refugee Camps: Dadaab, Kakuma-Kenya: Final Report: Major Findings* (n.p.: UNHCR/IRD (ORSTOM), October 1999); Jim Lewis, "The Exigent City," *New York Times Magazine*, June 8, 2008, https://www.nytimes.com/2008/06/08/magazine/08wwln-urbanism-t.html.

32 Agier, *Managing the Undesirables*, 145.

33 Mire, "Role of Cultural Heritage," 152.

34 Al-Bulushi, "Kenya's Refugee 'Problem.'"

35 The Refugees Act, 2006, *Kenya Gazette Supplement* No. 97 (Acts No. 13), January 2, 2007.

36 On this poetic condition of Swahili coast architecture, see Meier, *Swahili Port Cities*. On syncretic Indian Ocean identities and pluralistic East African imaginaries of South Asia, see Desai, *Commerce with the Universe*; Aiyar, *Indians in Kenya*; Shankar, *An Uneasy Embrace*.

37 Warah, *War Crimes*.

38 I am grateful for discussions with Nick Estes on land and territorialization during a Harvard University Mahindra Humanities Center fellowship, 2017–2018; with Miriam Ticktin on the anticapitalist history of the "feminist commons" in the Columbia University Center for the Study of Social

Difference working group, Insurgent Domesticities, 2020–2022; and with Zoé Samudzi on genocide and African Indigenous struggle during her Columbia University seminar "Studies in Contemporary Africa" presentation, "Camps, Archives, and Ancestors," January 26, 2021. Estes, *Our History Is the Future*; Ticktin, "Building a Feminist Commons"; Samudzi, "Capturing German South West Africa."

39 For a concise explanation of post-independence politics and civil breakdown in Somalia, see Abdi, *Elusive Jannah*, 32–40; see also Kapteijns, *Clan Cleansing in Somalia*.

40 For a history of contested belonging in Kenya, see Weitzberg, *We Do Not Have Borders*. For a history of the partitioned Jubaland (present-day Kenya, Somalia, and Ethiopia), see Cassanelli, *Shaping of Somali Society*; Bestemann, *Unraveling Somalia*; Casanelli and Bestemann, *Struggle for Land*; Kapteijns, *Clan Cleansing in Somalia*; Ogot and Ochieng, *Decolonization and Independence*; Donham and James, *Southern Marches*; James et al., *Remapping Ethiopia*.

41 Geeldoon, *We Kissed the Ground*, 8.

42 Aidid, "Pan-Somali Dreams"; Laitin and Samatar, *Somalia*; Ahmed, *Invention of Somalia*.

43 Weitzberg, "Unaccountable Census," 409–28; on eliding the governmental view, see also Scott, *Art of Not Being Governed*.

44 Mburu, "The Imperial Partition," in *Bandits on the Border*, 23–42.

45 Weitzberg, *We Do Not Have Borders*.

46 D'Avignon, *Ritual Geology*, 13–20.

47 Okoye, "Enigmatic Mobilities / Historical Mobilities." See also Matsipa, *African Mobilities*.

48 East Africa Protectorate Ordinance No. 21 and No. 25 of 1902, "Crown Lands" and "Outlying Districts" (with Ordinance No. 22 of 1926, "An Ordinance to Amend the Crown Lands Ordinance"), Kenya National Archives.

49 I am grateful to Frederick Cooper for discussions on these differences, New York, April 19, 2019.

50 Whittaker, *Insurgency and Counterinsurgency*.

51 Prussin, *African Nomadic Architecture*.

52 El-Bushra and Gardner, *Somalia*; S. Roy, "Ethical Ambivalence"; De Alwis, "Moral Mothers"; Samuel, Slatter, and Gunasekara, *Political Economy*; Lorentzen and Turpin, *Women and War Reader*.

53 Dharia, *Industrial Ephemeral*, 22.

54 Wilson, "Provisional Demos." See also the essay by the same author in Blanco, et. al. *After Belonging*, 179–85.

55 Rodney, *How Europe Underdeveloped Africa*.

56 Wynter, "On How We Mistook the Map."

57 Khagram, Riker, and Sikkink, *Restructuring World Politics*. See also Keck and Sikkink, *Activists beyond Borders*.

58 For a critical contextualization, see Incite!, *Revolution Will Not Be Funded*; Sclar, *You Don't Always Get*; McNeish and Lie, *Security and Development*.

59 Terry, *Condemned to Repeat?*; Rieff, *Bed for the Night*.

60 On a performance theory of "architectural spatiality," see Carboni, "Undrawn Spatialities." See also Musmar, "Witnessing." The term *l'espace humanitaire* came into usage in the 1990s, widely credited to former president of MSF-France, Rony Brauman. It can refer to a camp, the inside of a vehicle, or a supply chain; see Smirl, *Spaces of Aid*; Fredriksen, "Emergency Shelter Topologies," 2–3.

61 Samuel Moyn argues that the international human rights movement filled an ideological space vacated by leftist politics. Radhika Coomaraswamy argues against a universal theory of human rights, attending to its diverse iterations in the postcolonial world. ("Not every war is about Americans fighting terrorists," she critiques of a northern, masculinist subjectivity in human rights discourses.) Mainstream architectural discourses have depended on the space Moyn describes; discourses on vernacular, self-help, and user-driven design have depended on that which Coomaraswamy identifies. Moyn, *Last Utopia*; see also A. Clapham, *Human Rights*, 133–37, 182–89. Coomaraswamy, "Reclaiming Parts."

62 Siddiqi, "Architecture Culture, Humanitarian Expertise"; Jamison, "Humanitarian Intervention," 365.

63 Abdi, *Elusive Jannah*; Kapteijns, *Clan Cleansing in Somalia*; De Waal, *Famine Crimes*.

64 Siddiqi, "Architecture Culture, Humanitarian Expertise."

65 Based on Organisation for Economic Co-operation and Development (OECD) data, emergency relief aid rose sharply in the 1990s, jumping eight billion dollars and rising with overall development aid in the next decade, so that humanitarian aid "moved from a tight oligopoly to a highly competitive market," separate from peacekeeping operations. Fearon, "Rise of Emergency Relief Aid," 69.

66 Jain, "Whose Emergency?," 17.

67 Mire, *Divine Fertility*; Deegan, *Mogadishu*; Wendel, *Rwanda's Genocide Heritage*.

68 I held an internship with the Women's Refugee Commission in 2010–2011, in order to study in the locations where the organization worked. For further explanation, see notes 70 and 75.

69 See, for example, critical ethnographic work in refugee camps by Malkki, *Purity and Exile*; Thomson, "Black Boxes of Bureaucracy," "'Giving Cases Weight,'" "Mud, Dust, and Marougé," and "What Documents Do Not Do." See also ethnographic perspectives on Somali life in Dadaab and the diaspora. Ikanda, "Animating 'Refugeeness' through Vulnerabilities," "Deteriorating Conditions," "Somali Refugees in Kenya," and "Good and Bad Muslims"; Abuye, "Askar."

70 Women's Refugee Commission, *Preventing Gender-Based Violence, Building Livelihoods: Guidance and Tools for Improved Programming* (New York: Women's Refugee Commission, December 2011). This report was partly funded by the US Department of State Bureau of Population, Refugees, and Migration, the US governmental unit providing humanitarian protection.

71 Because my work required that I move between refugee communities in which different languages were spoken, I rarely used the Kiswahili I was trained in. I learned enough Somali to play with children in the camps, while meeting with their parents.

72 On "hierarchies of humanity," see Fassin, *Humanitarian Reason*, 223–43. See also a distillation on the asymmetry of lives in Keenan, "Do Something."

73 Borderless Higher Education for Refugees, https://www.bher.org. In 2013, the organization Film Aid launched "Dadaab Stories," an evolving online documentary and collaborative community media project combining video, photography, poetry, music and journalism in an artistic oral history, at www.dadaabstories.org. The web initiative has since been discontinued.

74 I am grateful to staff members at all of these institutions and organizations for supporting my study and facilitating my visits.

75 I have attended to a wide range of sources, requiring a great deal of time and mobility. My initial research on this project, up to and during the internship with the Women's Refugee Commission, was self-funded through student loans. My later research benefited from grant and fellowship awards, adjunct teaching contracts at multiple academic institutions, and brief paid consultancies with the Women's Refugee Commission, the United Nations Foundation, and the Coalition for Adolescent Girls. Research for this book later received stable institutional support associated with my position on the faculty of Barnard College, Columbia University.

76 This thinking owes a debt to hooks, *Yearning*; Puig de la Bellacasa, *Matters of Care*; Haraway, "Situated Knowledges"; Haraway, *Staying with the Trouble*.

77 On the archival fragment, see Siddiqi, "Crafting the Archive."

78 Berger and Mohr, *Seventh Man*; Said, *After the Last Sky*. I am grateful to Elleni Centime Zeleke for conversations on Berger, and to Dubravka Sekulić for introducing me to his first collaboration with Mohr. See Berger and Mohr, *A Fortunate Man*; Zeleke, *Ethiopia in Theory*; Sekulić, "Constructing Non-Alignment."

79 See Herscher, introduction to *Violence Taking Place*.

80 Anonymous, interview by author, November 30, 2011.

81 I am grateful to Ana María Léon and S. E. Eisterer for the opportunity to present a paper in their session "No Small Acts: Spatial Histories of Imprisonment and Resistance," in the Society of Architectural Historians 2021 annual meeting, and the accompanying 2021 Princeton-Mellon Research Forum on the Urban Environment workshop. See also Oliver, *Carceral Humanitarianism*; Pieris and Horiuchi, *Architecture of Confinement*; Perera, *Australia and the Insular Imagination*; Fleetwood, *Marking Time*; Lopez, "States of Incarceration"; Kirkham-Lewitt, *Paths to Prison*; Jaskot, *The Architecture of Oppression*.

82 A coedited version of our discussion appears in chapter 1 and in Siddiqi and Osman, "Traversals."

83 Siddiqi, "Dadaab Is a Place."

84 Siddiqi, "Dadaab (Kenya)"; see Gramsci, *Selections from the Prison Notebooks*, 5–14.

85 I draw on diverse analyses of epistemic, environmental, and spatial violence as colonial practices. Spivak, "Can the Subaltern Speak?"; Nixon, *Slow Violence*; Herscher and Siddiqi, "Spatial Violence"; Wendel and Aidoo, *Spatializing Politics*; Brun and Jazeel, *Spatialising Politics*; Anderson and Ferng, "The Detention-Industrial Complex."

86 Jeff Crisp, interviews by author. The volume of visitors to Dadaab—an international security site of interest proximate to the state capital and regional commercial and humanitarian hub of Nairobi, in an anglophone African country—has occasioned UNHCR suboffice staffing for hospitality and press outreach.

87 Smith, *Decolonizing Methodologies*. Smith draws from Ngũgĩ wa Thiong'o, whose detention was executed by some of the same authorities that later incarcerated people at Dadaab. Thiong'o, *Decolonizing the Mind*.

88 Smith, *Decolonizing Methodologies*.

89 H. Kennedy, "Spatial Writing"; Osayimwese, *Colonialism and Modern Architecture*; Henni, *Architecture of Counterrevolution*.

90 See Siddiqi, "Heritage as Restitution"; Siddiqi, "In Favor of Seeing Specific Histories."

91 Siddiqi, "Writing With."

92 Lorde, "Master's Tools."

93 Lorde, "Uses of Anger."

94 Herscher and Siddiqi, "Spatial Violence."

95 Trouillot, *Silencing the Past*, 2.

96 Pollock, preface to *Differencing the Canon*.

CHAPTER ONE. FROM PARTITIONS

Epigraph: Owuor, *Dust*, 26.

1 The analysis of territory as a concept is not the aim here, and my orientation to key terms (*land, terrain, space, territoriality*) differs, but on territory as a "political technology," see Elden, "Land, Terrain, Territory"; Elden, *The Birth of Territory*.

2 Fanon, *Black Skin, White Masks*, 185–97; Rodney, *How Europe Underdeveloped Africa*.

3 I am grateful to Carli Coetzee for discussions on a global imaginary of Blackness, 2021, and to Lydia Muthuma, Rohit Mujumdar, and participants from Nairobi, Mumbai, Colombo, and Karachi in our 2022 seminar, "Architecture as a Form of Knowledge," for concerns with Afro-Asian and Indian Ocean consciousnesses.

4 Siddiqi and Osman, "Traversals."

5 Horst, *Transnational Nomads*.

6 Furthermore, on inequalities between expatriates and nationals in the aid labor system (in salaries, contractual terms, and value placed on lives), see Fassin, *Humanitarian Reason*, 239.

7 The market is called "Bosnia," a place in the headlines when Ifo was established.

8 Atellah, "Toa Kitambulisho!" The kipande system, comprising an infrastructure and material culture, controlled the movement of people in British colonies, reproducing forms of division in South Africa under apartheid and in Kenya after independence.

9 A matatu is a shared minibus taxi in East Africa. Mutongi, *Matatu*.

10 Damien McSweeney, "Conflict and Deteriorating Security in Dadaab," *Humanitarian Exchange* 53 (February 2012): 26–27.

11 Women's Refugee Commission, *Preventing Gender-Based Violence, Building Livelihoods: Guidance and Tools for Improved Programming* (New York: Women's Refugee Commission, December 2011).

12 Siddiqi, "Architecture Culture, Humanitarian Expertise." See chapter 3 for more on this history and Osman's NRC work.

13 Kenya acceded to the 1951 UN Convention Relating to the Status of Refugees in 1966.

14 "Kenya to Close All Refugee Camps and Displace 600,000 People," *The Independent*, May 9, 2016, http://www.independent.co.uk/news/world/africa/kenya-refugee-camp-closure-dadaab-worlds-largest-a7019461.html; "UNHCR Appeals to Kenya over Decision to End Refugee Hosting," *UNHCR News*, May 9, 2016, http://www.unhcr.org/news/latest/2016/5/5730b5f36/unhcr-appeals-kenya-decision-end-refugee-hosting.html; Nanjala Nyabola, "Closing Dadaab," Rift Valley Institute Nairobi Forum Meeting Report, September 2015, https://riftvalley.net/sites/default/files/publication-documents/Closing%20Dadaab%20%23U2013%20RVI%20Nairobi%20Forum%20Meeting%20Report%20%282015%29.pdf. This part of the discussion took place before the High Court intervened to stay the closure of the camps.

15 Khat (or miraa) is a heavily traded narcotic in East Africa.

16 To win elections, refugees must receive not only broad support but backing from particular Somali communities. Humanitarian workers describe Somali social structure in terms of "clan" affiliation, the category by which the UNHCR settles refugees in blocks in the camps (for their protection and security). This terminology stems from scholarship on segmentary lineage systems in Somali society, particularly Lewis, *Understanding Somalia and Somaliland*. For a critical perspective, see Besteman, "Primordialist Blinders."

17 "Kenya Says Go Home," *The Economist* 412, no. 8985 (May 14, 2016).

18 Noting the wide geographical and theoretical range of border studies and histories examining the partitioning of Ireland, India, and Palestine, I draw from critical art, architectural, and urban studies. The Getty Research Institute, "Art and Architecture"; Dadi and Nasar, *Lines of Control*; Decolonizing Art Architecture Art Residency (DAAR) et al., *Architecture after Revolution*; Pieris, *Architecture on the Borderline*; Zamindar, *Long Partition*; Weizman, *Hollow Land*. Similarly, I note humanistic studies of xenophobia that speak of borders from the perspective of storytellers crossing them, including architects, historians,

and urbanists; see, for example, Akcan, *Abolish Human Bans*; Landau and Pampalone, *I Want to Go Home Forever.*

19 Besteman and Cassanelli, *Struggle for Land*, 7–10.

20 Besteman, *Unraveling Somalia*, 10.

21 "More than any other part of the country, the peoples of the inter-riverine paid the heaviest human and material costs . . . farming communities of this region died by the tens of thousands." Samatar, "Somalia," 223.

22 Zamindar, *Long Partition*, 4.

23 Zamindar, *Long Partition*, 3–6. For another argument on urban transformations categorically produced by refugees, see Alimia, *Refugee Cities*.

24 Sen, *Citizen Refugee*, 4–5. Similarly, the muhajir is conceptually essential to postpartition citizenship in Pakistan. Muzaffar, "Boundary Games"; Karim, "Between Self and Citizenship."

25 Arendt, *Origins of Totalitarianism*; Arendt, "We Refugees"; Agamben, *Homo Sacer*.

26 Through critical ethnographic practices, Zamindar and Sen construct theory by talking to people, electing a politically committed, fulsome research method of centering refugee personhood. Zamindar, *Long Partition*; Sen, *Citizen Refugee*. Simply speaking to people does not constitute an ethnographic practice, nor reflect rigorous tracing of a social group or encounter, but has become a recognized method of gathering architectural knowledge relating to matters of use, social impact, and emotional understanding of design. Gosseye, Stead, and van der Plaat, *Speaking of Buildings*; Singh et al., *Displacement and Domesticity*; Cupers, *Use Matters*; Karim, *Routledge Companion to Architecture*; Agha, "Emotional Capital."

27 Siddiqi and Zamindar, "Partitions."

28 A copious literature on borders informs my research, especially on their materiality and aesthetics. Brown, *Walled States, Waning Sovereignty*; Perera, *Australia and the Insular Imagination*; Perera, "Oceanic Corpo-graphies"; Perera, "Sexual Violence"; Rael, *Borderwall as Architecture*; Forman and Cruz, *Top Down / Bottom Up*; Nugent and Asiwaju, *African Boundaries*; Mezzadra and Nielson, *Border as Method*; Mostov, *Soft Borders*.

29 Mezzadra and Nielson, *Border as Method*, 1–26.

30 Siddiqi, "Ephemerality"; Siddiqi, "On Humanitarian Architecture."

31 Weizman, *Hollow Land*.

32 Katz, *Common Camp*; Katz, "Spreading and Concentrating."

33 Balibar, "What Is a Border?," 79.

34 "Transgressive Circulations 1: The Land as Medium," in H. Kennedy, "Infrastructures of 'Legitimate Violence.'"

35 Azoulay, *Potential History*, 21.

36 See arguments in Rizvi, "Contingency and Architectural Speculation"; Lopez, *Remittance Landscape*.

37 Rehman, "Primary Materials."

38 Rawlence, *City of Thorns*.

39 Ho, *Graves of Tarim*, 8.

40 Hartman, "Venus in Two Acts," 12, 11; Hartman, *Wayward Lives, Beautiful Experiments*.

41 Hartman, *Lose Your Mother*, 17.

42 United Nations High Commissioner for Refugees (UNHCR), "Implementing Registration within an Identity Management Framework: 5.3 Documentation," https://www.unhcr.org/registration-guidance/chapter5/documentation/, accessed March 16, 2023.

43 I am grateful to Hollyamber Kennedy for discussions on a "politics of arithmetic."

44 Atellah, "Toa Kitambulisho!"

45 Keshavarz, *Design Politics*, 5, 23. On the material emergence and execution of the national border through documentation and its restriction of mobility, see also Alimia, "Performing the Afghanistan-Pakistan Border."

46 Jansen, *Kakuma Refugee Camp*, 44–45.

47 Sandvik, "Physicality of Legal Consciousness"; Ticktin, *Casualties of Care*; Ticktin, "From Redundancy to Recognition."

48 I am grateful to Najib Khalif for descriptions of the process of prima facie recognition of refugees, based on his work for UNHCR Ethiopia (camps in Jigjiga and Dollo Ado). Najib Khalif, interviews by author; Najib Khalif, emails to author, 2012.

49 Mamdani, *Citizen and Subject*.

50 Sandvik, "Physicality of Legal Consciousness"; Ticktin, *Casualties of Care*; Ticktin, "From Redundancy to Recognition"; Wilson and Brown, *Humanitarianism and Suffering*; Fassin, *Humanitarian Reason*.

51 Rao and Pierce, "Discipline and the Other Body," 12.

52 I draw this conclusion based on extensive conversations with refugees in Kenya and Ethiopia, who had come from Somalia, Somaliland, Eritrea, Sudan (since reconstituted as South Sudan), Uganda, Rwanda, and Burundi. Najib Khalif, interviews by author; Najib Khalif, emails to author, 2012.

53 Anonymous, interview by author, Dagahaley camp, 2011.

54 Anonymous, interview by author, Nairobi, 2016; emphasis added.

55 Anonymous, interviews by author, 2011.

56 Wilson, "Notes on the Virginia Capitol"; Cheng, Davis, and Wilson, *Race and Modern Architecture*. On race, architecture, and culture, see also Lokko, *White Papers, Black Marks*; Tayob, Hall, and Loewenson, "Race, Space, and Architecture"; Wilson, *Negro Building*; Cadogan, "Walking While Black"; Admassu and Bateman, *Where Is Africa*; Matsipa, "African Mobilities"; Gooden, *Dark Space*; Barton, *Sites of Memory*.

57 Mbembe, *Critique of Black Reason*, 32.

58 Du Bois, "Strivings of the Negro People."

59 People living in Dadaab sometimes enjoy social privilege, erudition, lineage, or other positions and resources more substantial than that of African and non-African aid workers they encounter, complicating the construction of race and its intersection with power.

60 Butler, *Frames of War*, 6–7.

61 This conceptualization draws on discussions and collaboration on "cohabitations" since 2019, with Ikem Okoye, Namita Dharia, Peg Rawes, and Daniel Barber.
62 Anonymous, interviews by author, UNHCR compound, Dadaab, 2011.
63 Anonymous, interviews by author, UNHCR compound, Dadaab, 2011; anonymous, interview by author, UNHCR offices, Nairobi, 2011.
64 Atanasoski, *Humanitarian Violence*, 1–31.
65 Puar, *Terrorist Assemblages*.
66 Simms and Trim, *Humanitarian Intervention*. Their interpretation moves past a well-known constellation of points in human rights or humanitarian history: the Treaty of Westphalia in the seventeenth century, the Declaration of the Rights of Man and of the Citizen in the eighteenth, Henri Dunant's experience at Solferino and the founding of the Red Cross in the nineteenth, and the construction of the League of Nations and UN in the twentieth.
67 Trim, "'If a Prince Use Tyrannie,'" 29.
68 Ticktin, "Humanitarianism's History of the Singular"; Siddiqi, "Humanitarian Homemaker, Emergency Subject."
69 International Commission on Intervention and State Sovereignty, *The Responsibility to Protect: Report of the International Commission on Intervention and State Sovereignty* (Ottawa: International Development Research Centre, 2001).
70 Oliver, *Carceral Humanitarianism*, 47–49; see also Calhoun, "Imperative to Reduce Suffering," 73–97.
71 Hunt, *Inventing Human Rights*, 82.
72 Du Bois, "Strivings of the Negro People"; Fanon, *Black Skin, White Masks*; Mbembe, *Critique of Black Reason*.
73 Anonymous, interview with author, Ifo camp, 2011.
74 Mbembe, *Critique of Black Reason*, 14; Hibou, *La bureaucratization du monde*.
75 Sliwinski, "Aesthetics of Human Rights," 27; Sliwinski, *Human Rights in Camera*, ch. 2.
76 Kostof, *City Assembled*, 247–49.
77 Dos Santos, *A Baixa Pombalina*; Tavares, *O pequeno livro*. I am grateful to Marta Caldeira for her insights and discussion on this subject.

CHAPTER TWO. LAND, EMERGENCY, AND SEDENTARIZATION IN EAST AFRICA

1 "Transgressive Circulations 1: The Land as Medium," in H. Kennedy, "Infrastructures of 'Legitimate Violence,'" 59–63; H. Kennedy, "Wastelands of Empire."
2 I am grateful to Juliana Maxim for discussions on Siddiqi, "Humanitarian Homemaker, Emergency Subject." Maxim, email to author, June 1, 2019. The mixed media works by artist and architect Saba Innab on the Nahr el Bared camp in Lebanon confront similar paradoxes; see Innab, "How to Build without a Land," Art Institute Chicago, Architecture and Design holdings, https://www.artic.edu/artists/116831/saba-innab, accessed April 3, 2023.

3 Maganai Saddiq Hassan, interview by author.
4 Casid, *Sowing Empire*, 32.
5 Zeller, "African Borderlands," 1.
6 Aidid, "Pan-Somali Dreams," 3. See also Williams, *Long Revolution*; Williams, "Structures of Feeling."
7 Aidid, "Pan-Somali Dreams," 6.
8 C. Clapham, "Boundary and Territory," 240; see also Brownlie and Burns, *African Boundaries*; Drysdale, *Somali Dispute*.
9 Cassanelli, *Shaping of Somali Society*, 3.
10 Weitzberg, *We Do Not Have Borders*.
11 Abdi, *Elusive Jannah*.
12 Horst, "Buufis amongst Somalis." Somalis on all sides of political borders fuel "economies of corporeal displacement and transnational capital," per Hyndman, "Border Crossings," 159. Systems of care lie behind "Somali malls" in Africa and worldwide; see Tayob, "Transnational Practices of Care."
13 Khadiagala, "Boundaries in Eastern Africa," 267.
14 Khadiagala, "Boundaries in Eastern Africa," 268; Khadiagala cites McEwen, *International Boundaries of East Africa*, 40.
15 The shifta war impacted Somali, Samburu, Boran, and other pastoralists in the region. Whittaker, *Insurgency and Counterinsurgency*; Whittaker, "Legacies of Empire"; Whittaker, "Socioeconomic Dynamics." I draw on literature on the Mau Mau detention schemes that examines cartographies and demographies of confinement and landscapes of collective memory and ongoing struggle. Kĩnyattĩ, *Kenya's Freedom Struggle*; Kĩnyattĩ, *Mwakenya*; Odhiambo and Lonsdale, *Mau Mau and Nationhood*; Ogot, "Decisive Years 1956–63"; Elkins, "Detention, Rehabilitation"; Elkins, *Imperial Reckoning*; D. Anderson, *Histories of the Hanged*; Miyonga, "Colonial Afterlives"; Kĩnyattĩ, *Pen and the Gun*; Osborne, *Ethnicity and Empire in Kenya*; MacArthur, *Cartography and the Political Imagination*. See also the recent reception in James, "Epilogue."
16 East Africa Protectorate Ordinance No. 25 of 1902, "Outlying Districts," by F. J. Jackson, Acting Commissioner, Mombasa, October 24, 1902.
17 British Library, Maps MOD GSGS 4050. Map note: "All Roads in the N.F.D. [Northern Frontier District] must be regarded as likely to become impassable after rains." Map redrawn and revised 1938 by (Sd.) M. Unwin Heathcote Capt. R.A.(T.A.) and (Sd.) J. A. Powell Lieut. R.E. with the assistance of the Kenya Survey Department. Geographical Section, General Staff, No. 4050, published at the War Office, 1938.
18 East Africa Protectorate Proclamation, by D. Stewart, His Majesty's Commissioner, Nairobi, February 4, 1905. Under East Africa Protectorate Ordinance No. 25 of 1902, "Outlying Districts."
19 East Africa Protectorate Proclamation, by D. Stewart, His Majesty's Commissioner, Nairobi, April 26, 1905. Under East Africa Protectorate Ordinance No. 25 of 1902, "Outlying Districts."
20 The archives of the National Museums of Kenya, Nairobi, contain photographic albums capturing the manyatta in the eighteenth and nineteenth

centuries. The National Museum of Tanzania Makumbusho / Village Museum collections include full-scale built replicas. A Samburu manyatta appears in Meiu, *Ethno-erotic Economies*.

21 East Africa Protectorate Ordinance No. 21 of 1902, "Crown Lands," September 27, 1902, and East Africa Protectorate Ordinance No. 25 of 1902, "Outlying Districts," established crown lands and outlying districts, beginning the process of delineating lands for native reserves. Land reservations for "native tribes" were called out in East Africa Protectorate Ordinance No. 12 of 1915, "An Ordinance to make further and better provision for Regulating the Leasing and other disposal of Crown Lands, and for other purposes," Part VI, May 18, 1915, indicating boundaries in an amendment to the Crown Lands ordinance, East Africa Protectorate Ordinance No. 22 of 1926, September 28, 1926.

22 The government-missionary abolitionist settlement was previously modeled in Sierra Leone, Gabon, and Liberia. Everill, "Freetown, Frere Town," 24.

23 Cooper, "What Is the Concept," 204.

24 Julius Mambo, interview with author. Krapf's wife, Rosine Dietrich Krapf, died soon after arriving in Africa; her grave and tombstone remain in the Krapf Memorial Heritage Park in Freretown.

25 They were an "elaboration of an extensive Kamba commercial system . . . a pattern of trade that closely linked for the first time the economies of the interior with those of the Swahili coast and the world beyond East Africa." Strayer, *Making of Mission Communities*, 4.

26 This refers to historian Clifford Pereira's research for the 2007 Royal Geographical Society exhibition, "Bombay Africans: 1850–1910," whose boards are displayed in the National Museums of Kenya, Rabai.

27 Royal Geographical Society exhibition, "Bombay Africans: 1850–1910," section titled "Liberation." The Royal Navy attempted to pressure India's princely states to restrict trade based on enslavement.

28 In western India, enslaved people were most often put to work as domestic laborers, and thus, this community is understood to have included children more than the communities displaced as part of the Atlantic slave trade did.

29 Everill, "Freetown, Frere Town," 26.

30 Everill, "Freetown, Frere Town," 29. She cites the East African Slave Trade Committee, First Report of the Proceedings of the East African Slave Trade Committee (London, July 1874), 17.

31 Ochieng and Maxon, *Economic History of Kenya*, 130–31.

32 Strayer, *Making of Mission Communities*, 15.

33 Cooper, *Plantation Slavery*, 108–11. Meier, "Difference Set in Stone: Place and Race in Mombasa," in *Swahili Port Cities*.

34 Ozaki, "Afro-Brazilian Lenses," 101, 104.

35 Lowe, *Intimacies of Four Continents*, 35.

36 Cooper, *Plantation Slavery*, 100, 148. This was "part of a long-term and coastwide process of economic development" through 1890 (long after the ratification of abolition laws for sea and land). Cooper cites Krapf's comments

in 1844 on the inland hamlets settled by Mombasa slaveowners, and British Consulate of Zanzibar notations of agricultural production in the coastal and inland shambas around Mombasa that enslaved people from Kilwa (in present-day Tanzania) up to 1874. Published research on the coastal communities affected by plantations largely centers colonial archives and interpretations of social life. The National Museums of Kenya, Rabai, serves as an important repository of local perspectives and sources. See Willis, *Mombasa*; Spear, "Traditional Myths"; Dingley, "Kinship, Capital, and the Occult."

37 Everill, "Freetown, Frere Town," 35–37; West, "New Cultural Politics."

38 For related work on development, see Eade and Vaux, *Development and Humanitarianism*; Dutta et al., *Architecture in Development*; Dutta, *Second Modernism*; Nolan, *Neocolonialism*. I draw on work that links pastoralism, building craft, and land politics with extraction or forced migration—mediated through architecture, and connecting development-related craft practices with war. See Scott, *Outlaw Territories*; W. Davis, "Palm Politics."

39 Mburu, *Bandits on the Border*; Whittaker, *Insurgency and Counterinsurgency*; Weitzberg, *We Do Not Have Borders*; Sheik, *Blood on the Runway*; Kibinge et al., *Scarred*.

40 Several interviews with the author in the Dadaab refugee camps reflected this circumstance.

41 This was in part due to the broad spectrum of political repression in Kenya; see, for example, Kĩnyattĩ, *Pen and the Gun*.

42 See definitions in Whittaker, *Insurgency and Counterinsurgency*, 50. The term *shaffata* "has been used to describe common criminal bandits as well as 'noble' rebels." Whittaker, *Insurgency and Counterinsurgency*, 51.

43 For a sensitive discussion of the 1962 *Report of the Northern Frontier District Commission* (chapter 2, note 69), see Weitzberg, *We Do Not Have Borders*, 112–25. The commission attended to some aspects of the heterogeneity of the population in the NFD and elided others.

44 As in India and Pakistan, subordination of competing nationalisms enabled the British to elide responsibility for decolonization, and the OAU adopted the former colonial borders during its inaugural meeting in Addis Ababa in 1963 and its second meeting in Cairo in 1964.

45 Besteman, *Unraveling Somalia*. Weitzberg, *We Do Not Have Borders*, 112–22. See also Schlee and Shongolo, "Pax Borana."

46 Chatterjee, *Nation and Its Fragments*; Rao, *Caste Question*.

47 Weitzberg, *We Do Not Have Borders*, 122; Mburu, *Bandits on the Border*, 75–106.

48 Handing-over report, Isiolo District, Kenya National Archives PC/NFD/1/4/2.

49 "Re-vote on NFD Emergency: Crisis Is Averted," *Daily Nation*, January 1, 1964; "Shifta Supporters Held in Security Swoop on Garissa," *Daily Nation*, January 8, 1964.

50 Kenya, National Assembly, *Official Record (Hansard)*, June 4, 1965, 226–27; Geoffrey Gitahi Kariuki, member of parliament for Laikipia-Nanyuki. See Whittaker, *Insurgency and Counterinsurgency*, 108–9.

51 Whittaker, *Insurgency and Counterinsurgency*, 89–106; De Waal, *Famine Crimes*, 40–41; Weitzberg, *We Do Not Have Borders*, 129.

52 Franklin, *Pied Cloak*.

53 Odhiambo and Lonsdale, *Mau Mau and Nationhood*; see Elkins, "Detention, Rehabilitation."

54 R. J. M. Swynnerton, *The Swynnerton Report: A Plan to Intensify the Development of African Agriculture in Kenya* (Nairobi: Government Printer, 1955); Thurston, *Smallholder Agriculture*; Atieno-Odhiambo, "Formative Years 1945–55"; Ogot, "Decisive Years 1956–63"; Kanogo, *Squatters*; Berman and Lonsdale, *Unhappy Valley*; Nolan, "Cash-Crop Design." On the "land hunger" sharpened by the displacement of agrarian Gĩkũyũ people, see Oluoch-Olunya, "Contextualizing," 256.

55 Nyerere, "The Arusha Declaration"; Hydén, *Beyond Ujamaa in Tanzania*; Jennings, *Surrogates of the State*. On the relation of architecture and socialist ideology to development in Africa (in practices from prefabrication in design and construction to city planning), see Stanek, *Architecture in Global Socialism*.

56 Kenya, National Assembly, *Official Record (Hansard)*, November 4, 1966, 1720; G. F. O. Oduya, Member of Parliament for Elgon West. See Whittaker, *Insurgency and Counterinsurgency*, 113.

57 From 1946 to 1966, Garissa had the only primary school in the region. Whittaker, *Insurgency and Counterinsurgency*, 115–17, 119.

58 No images of the shifta detention villages had surfaced, as of 2015, per Whittaker, discussion with author, January 15, 2016. For firsthand accounts from witnesses of the Wagalla Massacre, in which hundreds of Somali residents of Wajir were tortured, murdered, and raped by Kenyan security personnel between February 10 and 14, 1984, see Kibinge et al., *Scarred*.

59 Henni, *Architecture of Counterrevolution*.

60 Thiong'o, "English Master."

61 They also did so through aid, for which development practices became vehicles, as critiqued in Moyo, *Dead Aid*.

62 Whittaker, *Insurgency and Counterinsurgency*, 113–14.

63 Manji, *Struggle for Land and Justice*. See also Operation Firingi documents and pamphlets, on people's actions against land grabbing, Mazingira Institute archives; Lee-Smith, "'My House Is My Husband.'"

64 Whittaker, *Insurgency and Counterinsurgency*, 108.

65 Whittaker, *Insurgency and Counterinsurgency*, 119–20.

66 Whittaker, *Insurgency and Counterinsurgency*, 116; D. Anderson, *Histories of the Hanged*.

67 Kenya National Archives, District Monthly Reports for Wajir, Isiolo, Marsabit, Garissa, March, April, and May 1967.

68 Whittaker, *Insurgency and Counterinsurgency*, 115–16.

69 *Report of the Northern Frontier District Commission: Presented to Parliament by the Secretary of State for the Colonies by Command of Her Majesty* (London: Her Majesty's Stationery Office, 1962); Whittaker, *Insurgency and Counterinsurgency*, 115.

70 De Waal, *Famine Crimes*, 42. As another example, President Moi, who was part of the Tugen Kalenjin pastoralist community from the Rift Valley (later understood to have presented him as a viable non-Gĩkũyũ minority opponent and successor to Gĩkũyũ majority party leader Jomo Kenyatta, Kenya's first president), may have wished to demonstrate a show of power against other pastoralist communities. Lynch, *I Say to You*.

71 Whittaker regularly uses this framing; Whittaker, *Insurgency and Counterinsurgency*, 108. De Waal, *Famine Crimes*, 35–43. See also Baxter and Hogg, *Property, Poverty and People*; Carrier and Quaintance, "Frontier Photographs"; Carrier, O'Leary, and Palsson, "Paul T. W. Baxter."

72 De Waal, *Famine Crimes*, 40.

73 For more, see Weitzberg, *We Do Not Have Borders*, 6.

74 Anonymous, interviews by author, Ifo and Dagahaley camps, 2011.

75 See Umbach and Hüppauf, *Vernacular Modernism*; Crinson, "Dossier."

76 Turton, "Somali Resistance," 129.

77 Elleh, *African Architecture*, 148–49; K. B. Anderson, *Traditional African Architecture*, 82; Makumbusho / Village Museum, Dar es Salaam, Sambaa exhibit, 2016.

78 Wendel, "Materiality of Interpellation."

79 Kenya, National Assembly, Assembly Debates, *Official Record (Hansard)*, November 13, 1991, 580–81; Geoffrey Gitahi Kariuki, member of parliament for Laikipia-Nanyuki.

80 Prussin, *African Nomadic Architecture*.

81 Ibrahim, "Women's Role."

82 Ibrahim, "Women's Role," 28–33.

83 Najib Khalif, interviews by author.

84 Multiple interviews, Aw Bare and Kebribeyah camps, Ethiopia. See also Ibrahim, "Women's Role," 28–33.

85 Najib Khalif, interviews by author.

86 Maureen Connelly, interview by author.

87 Cephas, "Critical Closeness."

CHAPTER THREE. SHELTER AND DOMESTICITY

1 I owe a debt and have contributed substantial research to several collaborations dedicated to this analysis, cited in this chapter; they build on foundational literature on the connections between architecture, migration, and displacement, including Akcan, *Open Architecture*; Pieris, *Architecture on the Borderline*; Lozanovska, *Migrant Housing*; Lozanovska, *Ethno-architecture*; Lopez, *Remittance Landscape*; Siddiqi and Lee, "On Margins"; Siddiqi and Lee, "On Diffractions"; Siddiqi and Lee, "On Collaborations"; Herscher, *Displacements*.

2 Beeckmans et al., *Making Home(s) in Displacement*, 5.

3 Chitchian, Momić, and Seethaler-Wari, "Architectures of an 'Otherwise,'" 253; see also "Inside Out—Outside In: Shifting Architectures of Refugee Inhabitation," Max Planck Institute for the Study of Religious and Ethnic

Diversity, Göttingen, January 24–25, 2019, a conference including papers by refugees recently displaced from home.

4 Bilsel and Maxim, "Introduction," 7.

5 Collaboration is a grounding methodology and theory for my scholarship, and I am privileged to participate in a multiyear collaboration on domesticities: "Situating Domesticities" (2017 symposium organized by Lilian Chee, National University of Singapore, https://situatingdomesticities.com), Global Domesticities (2019 working group organized by Naomi Stead, Monash University), and Insurgent Domesticities (2020 working group organized by the author, Columbia University Center for the Study of Social Difference, https://www.socialdifference.columbia.edu/projects-/insurgent-domesticities). Chapter 3 draws on Siddiqi, "Insurgent Domesticities," Cooper Union Student Lecture Series, November 5, 2020, https://cooper.edu/events-and-exhibitions/events/student-lecture-series-anooradha-iyer-siddiqi-insurgent-domesticities. Collaborations among the Insurgent Domesticities working group have been invaluable to the development of this chapter, and I am indebted to discussions with Lilian Chee, M Constantine, Aastha Deshpande, S. E. Eisterer, Annapurna Garimella, Abosede George, Gil Hochberg, Hollyamber Kennedy, Nadrah Mohammed, Mignon Moore, Debashree Mukherjee, Corinna Mullin, Lydia Waithira Muthuma, Garnette Oluoch-Olunya, Ana Gisele Ozaki, Barbara Penner, Natalie Swan Reinhart, Akira Drake Rodriguez, Felicity D. Scott, Javairia Shahid, Kavita Sivaramakrishnan, Iulia Statica, Naomi Stead, Rhiannon Stephens, Neferti Tadiar, Madiha Tahir, Rishav Kumar Thakur, Miriam Ticktin, Ife Salema Vanable, Delia Duong Ba Wendel, Melanie Yazzie, and Sarover Zaidi.

6 Insurgent Domesticities.

7 Siddiqi and Chitchian, "To Shelter in Place."

8 Naimou, "Preface," 511, 516.

9 Tsing, *Mushroom.*

10 Tsing, *Mushroom.*

11 Naimou, "Preface," 516.

12 Povinelli articulates a theory of "an otherwise" in a number of writings. Povinelli, *Geontologies*; Povinelli, "Will to Be Otherwise"; Povinelli, "Routes/Worlds."

13 Foucault articulated the concept of biopower in a series of lectures in the 1970s as the political rationale for the administration and regulation of life and populations as a governmental practice of ordering society. Foucault, "Society Must Be Defended"; Foucault et al., *Security, Territory, Population*; Foucault, "Birth of Biopolitics." I draw broadly on a study catalyzed by Foucault's theory of biopower, on poetic and ecofeminist practices in the arts and architecture; Rawes, Loo, and Mathews, *Poetic Biopolitics.*

14 Foucault discusses "a thoroughly heterogeneous ensemble consisting of discourses, institutions, architectural forms, regulatory decisions, laws, administrative measures, scientific statements, philosophical, moral and

philanthropic propositions" and "the system of relations that can be established between these elements." Foucault, "Confession of the Flesh," 194. See also Cock, *Le dispositif humanitaire*.

15 Ophir, "Sovereign."

16 Povinelli, "Will to Be Otherwise," 456.

17 hooks, *Yearning*, 8.

18 Chitchian, Momić, and Seethaler-Wari, "Architectures of an 'Otherwise.'"

19 hooks, *Yearning*, 8.

20 hooks, *Yearning*, 8.

21 Siddiqi and Lee, "On Collaborations."

22 Siddiqi and Lee, "On Collaborations"; hooks, "Choosing the Margin."

23 Seethaler-Wari, Chitchian, and Momić, "Introduction," 13.

24 Postmodernist theory was extended through architecture schools in the twentieth century due to the North American reception of Martin Heidegger's writings, especially on "dwelling." Otero-Pailos, *Architecture's Historical Turn*.

25 Arundhati Roy, "Pandemic Is a Portal."

26 See note 6. On dissidences and disobediences in homemaking and housing, see also Zaidi, "Homing and Unhoming"; Chee, "Keeping Cats, Hoarding Things." I am grateful to Anoma Pieris for discussions on Holston, *Insurgent Citizenship*, Singapore, December 7–8, 2017.

27 On the ambivalences of violence, I am grateful for the substantial research, scholarly caregiving, and knowing kindness of Sally Engle Merry. Merry, *Gender Violence*; Merry, "Introduction." On the gravity of joy and collective social possibility that attends disaster, see Solnit, *Paradise Built in Hell*.

28 Siddiqi and Lee, "On Margins"; Siddiqi and Lee, "On Collaborations."

29 On Farah's work in relation to housing, see Siddiqi, "Humanitarian Homemaker, Emergency Subject"; in relation to decolonizing epistemologies, see Siddiqi, "Reversals"; as a basis for collaborative narration, see Siddiqi, "Writing With"; for a biography, see Siddiqi, "Shamso Abdullahi Farah."

30 Shamso Abdullahi Farah, interview by author.

31 Anonymous, interview by author, on behalf of the Women's Refugee Commission, 2011.

32 "Shelter and settlements" expertise is a stated and recognized core competence of the NRC, confirmed in multiple interviews; Norwegian Refugee Council, "Shelter and Settlements," https://www.nrc.no/what-we-do/activities-in-the-field/shelter/, accessed June 8, 2020.

33 For example, architect Øyvind Nordlie was seconded to the UNHCR Shelter and Settlement Section. Email from Nordlie to author (confirming a one-year appointment beginning in March 2012), January 24, 2012.

34 Norwegian Refugee Council, *The Camp Management Toolkit*, 2008, https://cms.emergency.unhcr.org/documents/11982/47942/Norwegian+Refugee+Council,+The+Camp+Management+Toolkit/a718d47b-5906-4adb-9735-dc8009e9b2a0. The guide was intended to establish an industry standard,

culling information from recognized experts such as architects Tom Corsellis of the Shelter Centre and Øyvind Nordlie of the NRC, in a digital platform. Drawing on humanitarian practices not yet standardized across sites, it offered brief, instructive chapters on several aspects of managing a camp, including physical planning and construction ("Camp Set-Up and Closure" and "Shelter"), social services ("Food Distribution and Non-food Items," "Livelihoods," and "Education"), implementation of legal frameworks ("Registration and Profiling" and "Protection in a Camp Setting"), and social and cultural techniques for camp managers to help displaced people adjust ("Participation and Community Involvement" and "Prevention of and Response to Gender-Based Violence").

35 Many NRC shelter project managers in Dadaab had trained in architecture or construction—for example, Joanna Cameira (Portugal), Mitchell Sipus (United States), Jake Zarins (England), and Unni Lange (Norway). Hashim Keinan, interview by author, Ifo camp; Unni Lange, interview by author; Jake Zarins, interview by author; Mitchell Sipus, interview by author.

36 Jake Zarins, interview by author.

37 Alishine Osman, multiple interviews by author; email from Osman to author, February 6, 2014. Osman discussed the structure of life in the Dadaab camps in chapter 1.

38 Jake Zarins, interview by author; he discussed events in 2009 and 2010.

39 Unni Lange, interview by author; she discussed events in 2011.

40 Siddiqi, "Humanitarian Homemaker, Emergency Subject," 47.

41 Fraiman, *Extreme Domesticity*, 164.

42 Siddiqi, "Architecture Culture, Humanitarian Expertise"; Muzaffar, "God's Gamble"; Karim, *Routledge Companion to Architecture*; Gyger, *Improvised Cities*.

43 The UN section on Housing, Town, and Country Planning was proposed in 1946 by planner Catherine Bauer and CIAM secretary Jacqueline Tyrwhitt, with CIAM member architect Ernest Weissman acting as its first head. It provided "experts" for UN missions in the global South, who helped to determine modern development agendas and contour a relationship between the "developed" and underdeveloped worlds. Muzaffar, "Periphery Within"; Gyger, *Improvised Cities*.

44 UNHCR, *The UNHCR Tool for Participatory Assessment in Operations*, http://www.unhcr.org/pages/4a2698b86.html, accessed February 8, 2014.

45 Muzaffar, "Periphery Within," 25–26.

46 The contracting of the multinational security firm G4S is but one form of "disaster capitalism" in Dadaab. Klein, *Shock Doctrine*; Kimathi, "Securitization of Humanitarian Aid."

47 Siddiqi, "Humanitarian Homemaker, Emergency Subject."

48 Muzaffar, "Periphery Within," 27, 261–67. Quotation, 27.

49 Roger Zetter, "Interview with Dr. Barbara Harrell-Bond," *Forced Migration Online*, August 2007, http://www.forcedmigration.org/podcasts-videos-photos/podcasts/harrell-bond; "Memorandum of Understanding to Establish

Collaboration between Centre for Refugee Studies, Moi University and Refugee Studies Programme, University of Oxford, represented by Professor S. O. Keya, Vice-Chancellor, Moi University, and Dr. Barbara Harrell-Bond, Director, Refugee Studies Programme, University of Oxford," University of Oxford Bodleian Social Science Library Refugee Studies Centre Collection.

50 The following section draws from the research behind Siddiqi, "Architecture Culture, Humanitarian Expertise."

51 Lee, "Negotiating Modernities"; Damm, Fenk, and Lee, *OK —Otto Koenigsberger*; Baweja, "Messy Modernisms"; Baweja, "Pre-history of Green Architecture"; Otto Koenigsberger, "The Story of a Town, Jamshedpur," *Marg* 1, no. 1 (October 1946): 18–29.

52 I. Davis, *Shelter after Disaster*.

53 Cuny, Abrams, and Oxfam America, *Disasters and Development*; Mendoza, "From Refuge to Shelter."

54 United Nations Disaster Relief Office (UNDRO), *Shelter after Disaster: Guidelines for Assistance* (New York: United Nations, 1982); United Nations High Commissioner for Refugees (UNHCR), *Handbook for Emergencies*, 2nd ed. (New York: United Nations, 2002).

55 Siddiqi, "Architecture Culture, Humanitarian Expertise."

56 The forum was created to share knowledge on building for cold climates, after escalating conflicts in the former Yugoslavia had driven refugees into environments where the technologies of plastic sheeting and temporary settlements offered little protection against frigid winters.

57 Zetter, *Shelter Provision*, 29–106.

58 Zetter, *Shelter Provision*, 36–43; "Workshop Folder: First International Workshop on Improved Shelter Response and Environment for Refugees," participant's copy, courtesy of Roger Zetter.

59 Zetter, *Shelter Provision*, 2–3.

60 The inaugural meeting of the CIAM in 1928 focused on contemporary housing to serve "the greater number," and the La Sarraz Declaration discussed modern architectural practice in relation to economics, the state, and the public. Somer, *Functional City*.

61 In 1981, the UNHCR Workshop on Rural Refugees in Africa included a talk on implementing rural settlements. Physical planning modules were included in two training workshops for emergency managers, one led by UNICEF in Nairobi in 1985 and one held in 1987 at the Disaster Management Center at the University of Wisconsin–Madison, where D. K. Hardin from UNHCR presented and distributed a paper. Roger Zetter, "Refugees—An Overview of Shelter Provision and Settlement Policy," paper presented at the First International Workshop on Improved Shelter Response and Environment for Refugees, Geneva, June 29–July 1, 1993; D. K. Hardin, "Physical Planning," paper presented at the UNHCR/Disaster Management Center Emergency Managers Workshop, 1987; Corsellis, "Selection of Sites," 95–96. Corsellis refers to Hardin's paper as "Refugee Camp Planning."

62 Rony Brauman and Fabrice Weissmann, interviews by author; Sean Barton, interview by author.

63 Today, the comprehensive libraries of Intertect and Shelter Centre archive this knowledge.

64 Lola Gostelow, "The Sphere Project: The Implications of Making Humanitarian Principles and Codes Work," *Disasters* 23, no. 4 (December 1999): 318. The participants in the Sphere Project drafted a charter and standards that reaffirmed core human rights principles through a strategy that integrated planning and building with other humanitarian relief categories, "set out in the five core sectors: water supply and sanitation; nutrition; food aid; shelter and site planning; and health services." Gerald Martone, interview by author.

65 Tom Corsellis, interview by author.

66 Tom Corsellis and Antonella Vitale, *Transitional Settlement: Displaced Populations* (Oxford: Shelter Centre, Oxfam GB, 2005), http://www.humanitarianlibrary.org/resource/transitional-settlement-displaced-populations. Many interviews confirmed a wide acknowledgment of Corsellis and the Shelter Centre's leadership.

67 On the Shelter Meeting, see the Shelter Centre website, http://sheltercentre.org, accessed August 15, 2015. To include participants who could not travel to Geneva, the Shelter Meeting began using an interactive online format after 2011, long before such formats became common. People from thirty-four countries participated in the first hybrid in-person and online meeting, May 24–25, 2012; "Shelter Meeting 12a," http://sheltercentre.org/meeting/shelter-meeting-12a, accessed February 14, 2014.

68 Lee, "Negotiating Modernities"; Mendoza, "From Refuge to Shelter."

69 Mendoza, "Tracing Humanitarian Work."

70 Bauman, "Naive Republic of Aid."

71 Bauman, "Naive Republic of Aid."

72 Alishine Osman, multiple interviews by author; email from Osman to author, February 6, 2014.

73 This section draws from Siddiqi, "Humanitarian Homemaker, Emergency Subject."

74 Chowdhury, "Imperial Mughal Tent."

CHAPTER FOUR. AN ARCHIVE OF HUMANITARIAN SETTLEMENT

Epigraph: Hartman, *Lose Your Mother*, 16.

Section epigraphs and other text epigraphs: Fax cable issued by UNHCR Nairobi branch office, May 8, 1991, UNHCR Central Registry Project Files, UNHCR archive, Geneva; Stephen Redding, Paul Sitnam, Graham Wood, and Care International in Kenya, *The Refugee Assistance Project of* CARE*-Kenya, 1991–1993* (n.p.: CARE-Kenya, 1994), 10; CARE internal memo, N. Kenya (Graham W. to Camp Managers Jill, Kaylo, Isabelle, Phil, and Paul), October 29, 1993, 2, University of Oxford Bodleian Social Science Library Refugee Studies Centre Collection;

WFP officer, anonymous interview with author, Dadaab; community members, anonymous interview with author, Ifo camp.

1 I may be the last researcher able to make out the words on these pages, raising enormous problems of primary source access supporting collective scholarship among peers able to study the same materials. Siddiqi, "Dadaab Is a Place on Earth."

2 Siddiqi, "Architecture as a Form."

3 Individuals named in documents are no longer expected to be in immediate danger after twenty years.

4 Siddiqi, "Dadaab Is a Place on Earth."

5 hooks, "Liberation Scenes: Speak this Yearning," 1–13, and "The Politics of Radical Black Subjectivity," 15–22, in *Yearning*; Puig de la Bellacasa, *Matters of Care*; Haraway, "Situated Knowledges."

6 Doucet, "Understanding Social Engagement," 14.

7 Blier, *The Anatomy of Architecture.*

8 Curation of archival fragments is taken up in various art and architectural historical studies. See, for example, Lavin, *Architecture Itself*. See also cultural scientist and art historian Aby Warburg's *Mnemosyne's Atlas*, an image map intended to document the recurrence of powerful images from antiquity. Johnson, *Memory, Metaphor*; Cornell University Library, Warburg Institute, Cornell University Press, and Signale, *Mnemosyne: Meanderings through Aby Warburg's Atlas*, https://live-warburglibrarycornelledu.pantheonsite.io, accessed March 20, 2023.

9 OAU Convention Governing the Specific Aspects of Refugee Problems in Africa, Article I, numbers 1 and 2, adopted September 10, 1969, with forty-one signatory states, including Kenya and each of its bordering nations. Kenya acceded to the 1951 Convention relating to the Status of Refugees in 1966.

10 Dale Buscher, interview by author.

11 Rony Brauman and Fabrice Weissmann, interviews by author.

12 Fassin and Pandolfi, *Contemporary States of Emergency*; Calhoun, "Idea of Emergency."

13 Bonaventure Rutinwa, "The End of Asylum? The Changing Nature of Refugee Policies in Africa," *New Issues in Refugee Research*, Working Paper no. 5, UNHCR (May 1999), 1.

14 Ahmed and Green, "Heritage of War," 113–27, 121.

15 Horst, *Transnational Nomads*, 19.

16 Verdirame, "Human Rights and Refugees," 56–57.

17 Fax cable issued by UNHCR Nairobi, May 8, 1991.

18 Per Iwansson, interview by author. I learned about Wähning's training and practice during my research in Addis Ababa, where she happened to be stationed in 2011; she declined to provide an interview for this research.

19 M. Dualeh, D. Mora-Castro, and S. Wähning, "Kenya: Technical Mission for Site Selection and Planning of Ifo and Walde Camps for Ethiopian and

Somali Refugees, 10–28 June 1991," Programme and Technical Support Section (PTSS), Mission Report 91/14, UNHCR archive, Geneva, 1–2.

20 Dualeh, Mora-Castro, and Wähning, "Kenya," 8; OAU Convention Governing the Specific Aspects of Refugee Problems in Africa, Article II, number 6.

21 Dualeh, Mora-Castro, and Wähning, "Kenya," 1; Martin L. Taylor, "Refugees in Kenya: Current Status" (n.p.: Lutheran World Federation Department of World Service, November 1991, provided by Per Iwansson), 11.

22 Corsellis, "Selection of Sites," 150; Horst, *Transnational Nomads*, 78.

23 Maureen Connelly, interview by author.

24 I am grateful for insights from numerous refugees; Richard Aclund, interview by author; Unni Lange, interview by author; Focus group discussion, Dadaab community members; Debriefing, multiple agencies.

25 Siddiqi, "Architecture Culture, Humanitarian Expertise."

26 Dualeh, Mora-Castro, and Wähning, "Kenya," 10.

27 Dualeh, Mora-Castro, and Wähning, "Kenya," 7.

28 Fax cable issued by UNHCR Nairobi, May 8, 1991.

29 See also Jaji, "Social Technology."

30 Dualeh, Mora-Castro, and Wähning, "Kenya," 8.

31 Taylor, "Refugees in Kenya," 11, 13, Annex 5.

32 Taylor, "Refugees in Kenya," 11, 13, Annex 5.

33 Taylor, "Refugees in Kenya," 11–14. Presumably this police force consisted of refugees, but the report does not specify.

34 Per Iwansson, interview by author.

35 Per Iwansson, "Kenya: Site Planning Consultancy, 12 April–15 June 1992," *Programme and Technical Support Section (PTSS) Mission Report 92/44*, UNHCR archive, Geneva, 3–4, Annex D, E; architectural documents, Dagahaley and Hagadera settlements, 1992, courtesy of Per Iwansson.

36 I am grateful to Claire Zimmerman for discussions in preparation for the session "The Stagecraft of Architecture," Society of Architectural Historians annual meeting, 2018.

37 The organizations included the Department of Refugee Affairs (DRA) (camp coordination and management); WFP (food distribution and food-related income generation); UNICEF (food, operation of child-friendly spaces in camps and Dadaab town); Handicap International (people living with disabilities in Dadaab, medical referrals to Garissa); NRC (shelter and latrine construction, youth education, gender development and counseling); CARE-Kenya (food distribution, water supply, sanitation, education, community and gender development and counseling); GTZ (health in Ifo camp, environment, firewood distribution); FilmAid International (mass information); International Organization for Migration (IOM) (voluntary repatriation by air or road, resettlement); Lutheran World Federation (LWF) (camp management and coordination, community policing, camp planning, transit centers, safe havens, Fafi host community agro-forestry); National Council of Churches of Kenya (NCCK) (peace education, prevention/combating/destigmatization

of HIV/AIDS, reproductive health); Windle Trust Kenya (secondary education); Save the Children UK (child protection); IRC (health care, hospital in Hagadera camp); MSF Switzerland (health care, hospital in Dagahaley camp); Kenya Red Cross Society (child tracing and family reunification); Cooperazione e Sviluppo (CESVI) (sanitation facility rehabilitation); Cooperazione Internazionale (COOPI) (refugee and host community water projects); Associazione Volontari per il Servizio Internazionale (AVSI) (school classroom rehabilitation, teacher training); Danish Refugee Council (DRC) (shelter, construction).

38 UNHCR memo, "Dadaab—Brief Overview," from visitor orientation packet, March 23, 2010.

39 Memorandum from S. Awuye, Representative, UNHCR Branch Office in Kenya, to P. Meijer, Head, Desk II, UNHCR Headquarters, Geneva, December 9, 1991; original agreements signed by Government of Kenya, 23 July 1991, CARE-Kenya, July, 19, 1991, and UNHCR, July 17, 1991.

40 Redding et al., *Refugee Assistance Project*, 3. See also Memo from Ben Hoskins, World Vision Relief and Development (WVRD)/DC, to Tsega Mariam, Aba Mpesha, Dick Venegoni, Carolyn Rose-Avila, Jerry Levin, Scott Solberg (CARE), Joe Siegle, Ian Wishart (WVRD/Australia), Jim Carrie (WVRD/Canada), Jeff Thindwa (WVRD/Great Britain), October 16, 1992, 1.

41 World Food Programme, *Project Kenya 4961(Exp. 3): Food Assistance for Somali and Sudanese Refugees* (Rome: World Food Programme, 1997), 3.

42 Redding et al., *Refugee Assistance Project*, 3.

43 United Nations 1993 Consolidated Inter-Agency Appeal: Kenya, Special Emergency Programme for the Horn of Africa (SEPHA), January 1993, 1.

44 Jacobsen, *Economic Life of Refugees*.

45 Maureen Connelly, interview by author; Christian Gad, interview by author.

46 Memo from Ben Hoskins, October 16, 1992.

47 CARE internal memo, October 29, 1993, 6.

48 CARE internal memo, October 29, 1993, 3.

49 CARE internal memo, October 29, 1993, 4–8. Quotation, 8.

50 CARE internal memo, October 29, 1993, 6–7. Quotation, 6.

51 Ruiz, *Slow Disturbance*.

52 Jansen, *Kakuma Refugee Camp*, 9.

53 CARE internal memo, October 29, 1993, 6–7. Quotation, 5.

54 Derek Nurse, Bajuni Database General Document, Department of Linguistics, Memorial University of Newfoundland, Canada, 4–5, http://www.ucs.mun.ca/~dnurse/bajuni_database/general_document.pdf, accessed March 16, 2023.

55 UNHCR press release, July 28, 1992.

56 Fax from S. Kimbimbi, Division of International Protection, UNHCR Geneva, to Mr. Awuye, UNHCR Kenya, August 15, 1991, 260–62. Extracts of *Africa Watch* enclosed. Quotations, 262.

57 Verdirame, "Human Rights and Refugees," 68.

58 Verdirame, "Human Rights and Refugees," 69.

59 UNHCR press release, December 22, 1998; see also Verdirame, "Human Rights and Refugees," 70.

60 The following studies provide spatial knowledge of the Dadaab refugee camps at multiple points in the past: mid-1990s (Hyndman and Corsellis), 1999–2000 (Horst), 2000 (Agier), 2006 (Kennedy), mid-2000s to 2011 (Rawlence), and 2010s (Ikanda). Hyndman, *Managing Displacement*; Corsellis, "Selection of Sites"; Horst, *Transnational Nomads*; Agier, *Managing the Undesirables*; J. Kennedy, "Structures for the Displaced"; Rawlence, *City of Thorns*; Ikanda, "Deteriorating Conditions"; Ikanda, "Good and Bad Muslims."

61 Malkki, "An Ethnography of Displacement in the National Order of Things," in *Purity and Exile*.

62 Thomson, "Mud, Dust, and Marougé"; Thomson, "Stories of Darkness."

63 Ikanda, "Deteriorating Conditions," 46.

64 Horst, *Transnational Nomads*, 130–31. Quotation, 9.

65 Horst, *Transnational Nomads*, 132.

66 Horst, *Transnational Nomads*, 134–35; Siddiqi, "Radio Free Refugee Camp."

67 Horst, *Transnational Nomads*, 132.

68 Agier, *Managing the Undesirables*, 141–42.

69 Agier, *Managing the Undesirables*, 136.

70 Agier, *Managing the Undesirables*, 136.

71 For a 2008 overview of on the planning and design of the Dadaab settlements, see J. Kennedy, "Structures for the Displaced," 142.

72 Dualeh, Mora-Castro, and Wähning, "Kenya."

73 Taylor, "Refugees in Kenya."

74 Maureen Connelly, interview by author.

75 Per Iwansson, interview by author.

76 Iwansson, "Kenya," 5.

77 The humanitarian use of overhead photography draws on military precedents. See Cohen, *Architecture in Uniform*; Ramirez, "Airs of Modernity."

78 I did not obtain these documents. On the Ethiopian context in the decades prior to the establishment of refugee camps in the Somali Region, see Aidid, "Pan-Somali Dreams."

79 Alain Beaudou, Luc Cambrézy, and Marc Souris, *Environment, Cartography, Demography and Geographical Information System in the Refugee Camps: Dadaab, Kakuma-Kenya: Final Report: Major Findings* (n.p.: UNHCR/IRD (ORSTOM), October 1999), 2.

80 Beaudou, Cambrézy, and Souris, *Environment, Cartography, Demography*, 2.

81 Kurgan, *Close Up*; Herscher, "Surveillant Witnessing"; Antonopoulou, "Situated Knowledges."

82 J. Kennedy, "Structures for the Displaced," 163.

83 UNHCR Demographic Projection Tool, https://demographicprojection.unhcr.org/#_ga=2.208330386.103758707.1649345159-1426980980.1649345159, accessed March 9, 2023.

84 J. Kennedy, "Structures for the Displaced," 157.

85 UNHCR, "Angelina Jolie Visits UNHCR Operation in Dadaab, Kenya," YouTube, September 14, 2009, www.youtube.com/watch?v=2L6VJKYnefc.

86 This effect is reinforced by filmic clichés (e.g., voice-overs, subject positions of celebrities versus refugees), not related to depiction of the built environment.

87 Gerald Simpson, Meghan Rhoad, Agnes Odhiambo, and Human Rights Watch, *"Welcome to Kenya": Police Abuse of Somali Refugees* (New York: Human Rights Watch, 2010).

88 Pia Vogler, "In the Absence of the Humanitarian Gaze: Refugee Camps after Dark," *New Issues in Refugee Research*, Working Paper no. 137, UNHCR (December 2006).

89 J. Kennedy, "Structures for the Displaced," 10.

90 UNHCR, "Commodity Distribution: A Practical Guide for Field Staff," June 1997, 8, http://www.unhcr.org/en-us/publications/operations/3c4d44554/commodity-distribution-practical-guide-field-staff.html.

91 UNHCR, "Refugees in the Horn of Africa: Somali Displacement Crisis. Information Sharing Portal," http://data.unhcr.org/horn-of-africa/region.php?id=3, accessed May 28, 2017.

92 UNHCR, "Commodity Distribution," 8.

93 UNHCR, "Commodity Distribution," 10.

94 Tom Corsellis, "Description of Food Aid Distribution: Dadaab Refugee Complex, Kenya," University of Oxford Bodleian Social Science Library Refugee Studies Centre Collection, Kenya papers, file number LK 51 COR.

95 Corsellis, "Description of Food Aid Distribution."

96 "Head of family" and "head of household" are defined, representative, and recognized roles. See UNHCR, "Commodity Distribution," 6.

97 UNHCR, "Commodity Distribution," 18.

98 UNHCR, "Commodity Distribution," 8.

99 Addison, "Spaces of Protection."

100 Siddiqi, "Humanitarianism and Monumentality."

CHAPTER FIVE. DESIGN AS INFRASTRUCTURE

1 Dainese and Staničić, "Introduction," 5.

2 Ndaliko and Anderson, introduction to *Art of Emergency*, 22.

3 The term *l'espace humanitaire* came into usage in the 1990s. It can refer to a camp, the inside of a vehicle, or a supply chain; see Fredriksen, "Emergency Shelter Topologies," 2–3.

4 The refugees in this chapter's opening photos participated in a focus group discussion led by Bethany Young and the author, on behalf of the Women's Refugee Commission. The Sudanese partners in the venture were Abuk Mora, Grace Alor Francis, Rose Narod, Elizabeth Adyutuch, Salome, Margaret, and Mary; the Somali partners were Halima, Fardoza, Sara, and Halima. The income-generating activity was sponsored by the organization CARE. We visited the hotel accompanied by Lucy Mwihaki Njenga, CARE-Ifo assistant livelihoods officer (Information, Communication, and Technology). Transla-

tion and interpretation were provided in real time by Roda Awak (Kiswahili) and Faiza Suleiman (Somali).

5 Monk and Herscher, *Global Shelter Imaginary*.

6 Simone, "People as Infrastructure," 407, 410.

7 Simone, "People as Infrastructure," 407, 410.

8 Bethany Young was a student from Jamaica in the Columbia University School of International and Public Affairs, working with the Women's Refugee Commission on a capstone project toward her degree. Her photographs appear in this book.

9 Akšamija, *Design to Live*.

10 McLagan and McKee, *Sensible Politics*.

11 Larkin, "Politics and Poetics."

12 Smirl, *Spaces of Aid*.

13 Larkin, "Politics and Poetics."

14 I am grateful to Emily Bauman for discussions on humanitarian iconography, Nairobi, March 2016.

15 Marx, "Fetishism of the Commodity." See also Scott-Smith, "Fetishism of Humanitarian Objects."

16 Adrian Edwards, "IKEA Foundation Gives UNHCR US $62 Million for Somali Refugees in Kenya," *UNHCR News*, August 30, 2011, http://www.unhcr.org/4e5cbaa99.html. The IKEA Foundation's description of "knowledge donation" can be found here: https://ikeafoundation.org/story/ikea-flat-pack-solutions-are-making-a-big-difference-to-refugees/, accessed March 12, 2023. See also Associated Press, "Ikea Founder Ingvar Kamprad Involved in New Nazi Claims," *Guardian*, August 25, 2011, http://www.guardian.co.uk/world/2011/aug/25/ikea-ingvar-kamprad-new-nazi-claims. The book is *And in Wienerwald the Trees Remain*, by journalist Elisabeth Asbrink.

17 Edwards, "IKEA Foundation."

18 UNHCR, *1951 Convention Relating to the Status of Refugees*, Chapter 1: General Provisions, Article I: Definition of the Term "Refugee," Paragraph A. This instrument delimited the legal and political categories of displacement, locating the refugee outside a national territorial boundary. On the insurgency and counterinsurgency of architecture at frontiers as a reinscribing force (and for more on R. Buckminster Fuller's border-crossing experiments in prefabrication), see Scott, *Outlaw Territories*; Scott, *Architecture or Techno-Utopia*.

19 Ironically, the ICRC once gave rise to MSF and the broader oppositional "sans frontières" solidarity movement, each symbolized by transnational mobility in the second half of the twentieth century.

20 Latour, *Pasteurization of France*; Gell, introduction to *Art and Agency*.

21 Loescher, "The Post–Cold War Era and the UNHCR under Sadako Ogata," in *UNHCR and World Politics*, 272–347.

22 Frederiksen, "Making Humanitarian Spaces Global," 11–12.

23 Fassin and Pandolfi, *Contemporary States of Emergency*.

24 Scott-Smith, "Beyond the Boxes"; Redfield, "Bioexpectations."

25 Stevens, "Prisons of the Stateless," 54–55.

26 I am grateful to many refugees and aid workers for conversations that tested this reasoning. Habiba Suleiman Abdi and Habiba Abdurahman Mursan, interview by author and Bethany Young; Halima Hassin Dair, interview by author; Hashim Keinan, interview by author; Unni Lange, interview by author; Jake Zarins, interview by author.

27 Technopolitics, "a concept that captures the hybrid forms of power embedded in technological artifacts, systems, and practices," positions technological systems or assemblages as enacting intentional political goals or redistributing authority and agency unintentionally. Hecht, introduction to *Entangled Geographies*; Mitchell, *Rule of Experts*.

28 Marx, "Fetishism of the Commodity." According to Marx, during the process of exchange, an object attains a value beyond the mere sum of its materials, labor, and usefulness, due to the social relations and perceptions around it.

29 Wolfgang Neumann, "Paper Tube / Emergency Shelter Project Technical Meetings/Prototype Assembly 20 and 21 April 1995," 4. Note for the File, Ref: 596, PTSS Mission Report 95/09/N, UNHCR archive, Geneva.

30 McQuaid, *Shigeru Ban*, 14.

31 Neumann, "Paper Tube / Emergency Shelter Project," 2–4. The architect's website (http://www.shigerubanarchitects.com/works/1999_paper-emergency-shelter/index.html) describes the Paper Emergency Shelters for UNHCR in Byumba Refugee Camp, Rwanda: "More than 2 million people became homeless when civil war broke out in Rwanda in 1994. The office of the United Nations High Commissioner for Refugees (UNHCR) normally supplied plastic sheets and aluminum poles to be rigged as temporary shelters. Rwandan refugees would sell the aluminum poles and then proceed to cut down trees to use branches for structural support. Contributing to already critical deforestation, it was obvious that alternative materials had to be found. A low-cost alternative, paper tubes, was introduced. The proposal was adopted, and development of prototype shelters began. Three prototype shelters were designed and tested for durability, assessed for cost and termite-resistance. Since paper tubes can be manufactured cheaply and by small and simple machinery, the potential to produce the materials on-site to reduce transportation costs [*sic*]. In 1998, fifty emergency shelters were constructed in Rwanda and monitored to evaluate the system in practical use."

32 Jodidio, *Shigeru Ban*, 166–171. The architect's website describes the Paper Log House in Kobe as follows: "The foundation consists of donated beer crates loaded with sandbags. The walls are made from 106mm-diameter, 4mm-thick paper tubes, with tenting material for the roof. The 1.8m space between houses was used as a common area. For insulation, a waterproof sponge tape backed with adhesive is sandwiched between the paper tubes of the walls. The cost of materials for one 52 square meter unit is below $2000. The unit are easy to dismantle [*sic*], and the materials easily disposed or recycled."

33 Sommers, "Dynamics of Coordination," 16–17; Maureen Connelly, interview by author, September 16, 2010.

34 This event prompted massive reforms in humanitarian practice and the development of standards in aid implementation.

35 Myriam Houtart, telephone interview by author; Jacques Franquin, telephone interview by author; Christian Gad, interview by author.

36 Maureen Connelly, interview by author, May 3, 2012.

37 Terry, *Condemned to Repeat?* MSF's rationale for pulling out was an opposition to being instrumentalized by *génocidaires* for health care, food, shelter, and other essentials; others criticized the abrupt exit for the increase in danger it caused to all on the ground.

38 Maureen Connelly, interview by author, September 16, 2010. Quotation taken from Ngara camp coordinator Jacques Franquin; see Philippe Lamair, "Cooperation Crucial in Rwanda Crisis," *Refugees Magazine* 97 (September 1, 1994), http://www.unhcr.org/3b5402fa1.html. It is important to understand that national sections of MSF operated independently from one another, beginning with the creation of MSF-Belgium in 1980, coordinating with each other as necessary in the field. The nationalization of the organization persisted in the creation of each new section (at variance with the "sans frontières" concept), operating in association through a general assembly of MSF International in Geneva.

39 Redfield, *Life in Crisis*; Redfield, "Cleaning Up the Cold War," 280.

40 Jacques Pinel, interview by author. The ICRC also began to develop logistics in the 1970s; Redfield, "Cleaning Up the Cold War," 290n44.

41 Phelan, "From an Idea to Action," 8–9.

42 Redfield, *Life in Crisis*; Redfield, "Cleaning Up the Cold War," 282.

43 "Pakistan: ICRC and Red Crescent Help People Displaced by Violence in North-West Frontier Province," International Committee of the Red Cross, October 20, 2009, http://www.icrc.org/eng/resources/documents/photo-gallery/photos-pakistan-201009.htm.

44 The 2005 exhibition was curated by Paola Antonelli and the 2016 exhibition by Sean Anderson for MoMA. Siddiqi, "Tracing Insecurities."

45 *UNHCR Plastic Sheeting c. 1985*, photograph from online exhibition "SAFE: Design Takes on Risk," MoMA multimedia audiofile featuring interview with Bernard Kerblatt (chief of the Emergency Preparedness and Response Section, UNHCR) from online audio, http://www.moma.org/explore/multimedia/audios/20/501, and exhibit, http://www.moma.org/interactives/exhibitions/2005/safe/safe.html.

46 *UNHCR Plastic Sheeting c. 1985*.

47 Paola Antonelli, interview by author.

48 Slim, "Establishment Radicals." Jim Howard and Paul Sherlock were water and sanitation engineers responsible for Oxfam's specialization and reputation in refugee camp water and sanitation systems design, participants in the UNHCR workshop discussed in chapter 3 and identified in photos by Roger Zetter, emails to author, September 4, 2013; Mandinda Zimba, "Summary of Proceedings: First International Workshop on Improved Shelter Response

and Environment for Refugees," UNHCR Publications Files, UNHCR archive, Geneva.

49 Photographs and documents on the design development and field use of the water tank may be held in the Oxfam Great Britain archives (closed during the period of my visits, and thus not consulted).

50 Sean Barton, interview by author.

51 Per Iwansson, interview by author.

52 "Please do not ask me why the number forty." Per Iwansson, interview by author.

53 Martin, "Financial Imaginaries," 73–74.

54 My research partner Bethany Young and I conducted interviews with mental health workers whom I render anonymous for the purpose of publication. See also Scarry, *Body in Pain*.

55 Malkki, *Purity and Exile*, 52–53, 104.

56 Kaur, "Claiming Community through Narratives," 54–67.

57 Multiple interviews reflected these impressions.

58 My research partner Bethany Young and I, along with aid workers, conducted a series of interviews in Dagahaley camp with many people who had arrived in Dadaab very recently and declined to provide their names for publication.

59 United Nations High Commissioner for Refugees (UNHCR) Shelter and Settlement Section, Division of Programme Management, *Shelter Design Catalogue* (Geneva: UNHCR, January 2016), 3.

60 Scott-Smith, "A Slightly Better Shelter?"; Redfield, "Bioexpectations," 178.

61 Cohen, *Architecture in Uniform*.

62 Ghassem Fardanesh, telephone interview by author; Zimba, "Summary of Proceedings."

63 The UNHCR chartered planes at the time at the cost of $200,000. Ghassem Fardanesh, telephone interview by author.

64 Ghassem Fardanesh, telephone interview by author.

65 Ghassem Fardanesh, telephone interview by author.

66 UNHCR, *Light-Weight Emergency Tent (LWET) Specifications, Version 4.0* (June 2006) and *Specifications and Requirements, Version 4.2* (May 2007).

67 Ghassem Fardanesh, telephone interview by author (including quotation); Olivier Siegenthaler, interview by author.

68 Ghassem Fardanesh, telephone interview by author.

69 UNHCR, *Light-Weight Emergency Tent*. "Family tents comparison table—May 2008," unpublished document attributed to IFRC Tent Development project, Patrick Oger, May 27, 2008, DRAFT V.1, courtesy of IFRC.

70 Ghassem Fardanesh, telephone interview by author.

71 Ghassem Fardanesh, "Mission to China: Visiting of the LWET Manufacturers and Intertek Inspection Agency, 26 November–08 December 2005" (n.p.: UNHCR Technical Support Section / DOS Mission Report, December 19, 2005), courtesy of Fardanesh.

72 Ghassem Fardanesh, email to author, April 24, 2009.

73 Manoucher Lolachi, telephone interview by author.

74 Manoucher Lolachi, telephone interview by author.

75 Corinne Treherne, telephone interview by author. "Comparative table of new Family Tents," unpublished document attributed to Tent Development Project, Comparative AWT and LWET, Patrick Oger, May 5, 2008, courtesy of IFRC. "Family tents comparison table—May 2008."

76 Ophir, "Sovereign," 169.

77 Ophir, "Sovereign," 169.

78 Jean-Pierre Mapela, interview by author.

79 Jean-Pierre Mapela, interview by author.

80 Redfield, *Life in Crisis* (MSF's bildungsroman, in his words); Magone, Neuman, and Weissman, *Humanitarian Negotiations Revealed*; Peter Beaumont, "Médecins sans Frontières Book Reveals Aid Agencies' Ugly Compromises," *Guardian*, November 20, 2011, https://www.theguardian.com/global-development/2011/nov/20/medecins-sans-frontieres-book.

81 Philippe Cachet, interview by author; Gilles Perroud, interview by author.

82 For example, an architect and construction specialist, Chloé Decazes, gave me a tour of the prototype.

83 The inflatable hospital was frequently discussed in sensational terms in humanitarian settings; World Humanitarian Studies Conference, 2011, Coalition for Adolescent Girls meetings, 2011, 2012 (participants included Haiti Adolescent Girls Network); International Council of Voluntary Agencies annual conference, 2012. See also Stephanie Schomer, "Doctors Without Borders . . . with Inflatable Hospitals," *Fast Company* 147 (July/August 2010), http://www.fastcompany.com/1659051/doctors-without-borders-inflatable-hospitals; Hicks, "Inflatable Hospitals Bring Medical Care to Where It's Needed," *Triple Pundit*, August 23, 2010, http://www.triplepundit.com/2010/08/inflatable-hospitals-bring-medical-care/; "Tentes gonflables: Une capacité de réponse en chirurgie plus rapide et plus économique," MSF articles, January 29, 2009, http://www.msf.fr/actualite/articles/tentes-gonflables-capacite-reponse-en-chirurgie-plus-rapide-et-plus-economique.

84 Doctors Without Borders / MSF-USA, "MSF Haiti Inflatable Hospital Tent Setup," January 21, 2010, https://www.youtube.com/watch?v=kkhGTQhVMKo.

85 UN-OCHA (United Nations Office for the Coordination of Humanitarian Affairs) reports the total funding response to this humanitarian emergency, including to a flash appeal, at $3.52 billion, nearly a billion dollars more than the second most funded crisis of that year, the flooding in Pakistan, and significantly higher than the commitment to any emergency in the years preceding or following; UN-OCHA Financial Tracking Service Report, "HAITI—Earthquakes—January 2010. Table A: List of all commitments/contributions and pledges as of 09 January 2014," http://fts.unocha.org (Table ref: R10), accessed January 8, 2014. Many actors noted that the largesse directed toward the emergency did not match programmatic capacity on the ground.

86 Isabel McDonald and Isabeau Doucet, "The Shelters That Clinton Built," *The Nation*, July 11, 2011, https://www.thenation.com/article/archive/shelters-clinton-built/; Steve Rose, "Haiti and the Demands of Disaster-Zone Architecture," *The Guardian*, February 14, 2010, section G2, 17. The robust response stemmed from a social justice and environmental sustainability culture and professional networks. See the annual Structures for Inclusion conference and SEED initiative ("Social Economic Environmental Design"—after the LEED initiative, "Leadership in Energy and Environmental Design"), initiated by Design Corps' founder, architect Bryan Bell (trained by architect Samuel Mockbee, whose pedagogical and service initiative, the "Rural Studio," positioned architecture students to design and build with structurally marginalized Alabama communities). After Hurricane Katrina, this network built wide professional and financial support. Bell and Wakeford, *Expanding Architecture*; Dean et al., *Rural Studio*.

87 The first exhibition was in Paris, followed by others worldwide—notably, in Central Park in New York City. Stephanie Davies, telephone interview by author; Alain Fredaigue, interview by author; McKee, "'Eyes and Ears.'"

88 Utopie, *Catalogue de l'Exposition: Structures Gonflables*, Musée d'Art Moderne de la ville de Paris, March 1968, 71–84.

89 Jacques Pinel did not indicate that MSF had any knowledge of the Utopie group or the exhibition, and Antoine Stinco of Utopie did not indicate any connection with MSF or any humanitarian work, although their circles may have crossed through Bernard Kouchner and members of Utopie in Paris. (Kouchner and Pinel represent quite different orientations of the organization, on the spectrum between politics and pragmatics.) Jacques Pinel, interview by author; Antoine Stinco, interview by author.

90 Vidal and Pinel, "MSF 'Satellites,'" 22.

91 Jacques Pinel, interview by author.

92 Redfield, *Life in Crisis*; Redfield, "Cleaning Up the Cold War," 270–71.

93 Redfield, "Cleaning Up the Cold War," 271; Dodier, "Contributions by Médecins Sans Frontières," 208.

94 Redfield, "Cleaning Up the Cold War," 276–77; Dodier, "Contributions by Médecins Sans Frontières," 208.

95 Gilles Perroud, interview by author; Garage Rockson, interview by author. The kits are listed in the password-protected online catalog for MSF Logistique, www.msflogistique.org, accessed March 1, 2014.

96 Gilles Perroud, interview by author.

97 Redfield, "Cleaning Up the Cold War," 280–81.

98 Dodier, "Contributions by Médecins Sans Frontières"; Phelan, "From an Idea," 7–8.

99 Brauman, "Planning Emergency."

100 Terry, *Condemned to Repeat?*, 234–35.

101 Hopgood, "Saying 'No' to Wal-Mart?"

102 Habiba Suleiman Abdi was also present, as another female chair of a construction cooperative, this one composed of male laborers. The author and Bethany Young interviewed her prior to Mursan, with translation and interpretation provided by NRC staff members as well as Mursan.

103 See also McLagan and McKee, *Sensible Politics*.

AFTERWORD

1 McConnell, "Inside Somalia."

2 Carrier, *Little Mogadishu*, 27. Please note recent studies by scholars (sometimes themselves refugees) using architectural methods in displacement contexts in order to recast drawing or mapping as a collaborative technique for knowledge building and healing. Dalal, *From Shelters to Dwellings*; Carboni, "(From) the Repertoire."

3 This painting is also known as *Fragments II*, from the exhibition "Foundations" at the One Off Contemporary Art Gallery, Nairobi, 2015.

4 Abshir, "Foundation."

5 Arendt, *Origins of Totalitarianism*; Arendt, "We Refugees"; Agamben, *Homo Sacer*; Agamben, *Means without End*.

6 See the discussion in Siddiqi, Katz, and Keshavarz, "Emplacing Displacement"; on the refugee within a global history of displacement, see Gattrell, *Making of the Modern Refugee*.

7 Rodney, *How Europe Underdeveloped Africa*.

8 Siddiqi and Zamindar, "Partitions."

9 Du Bois, "Strivings of the Negro People"; Fanon, "The Black Man and Recognition," in *Black Skin, White Masks*.

10 Henni, "Colonial Ramifications"; Shringarpure, "Empire and Ambivalence."

11 Insurgent Domesticities.

12 Abshir, "Foundation."

13 Goldstone and Obarrio, "Introduction: Untimely Africa?," in Goldstone and Obarrio, *African Futures*, 13. See also the perpetual reconciliation of historical tensions and melancholies invoked in Etoke, *Melancholia Africana*.

14 Osayimwese, "On Architecture"; Admassu, "Afterimages."

15 At the time of this writing, the other architects, designers, and researchers of Cave Bureau include Mtamu Kililo, Priscillah Msafari, and Kevin Mwangi. Balmoi Abe was another cofounder and worked with Cave Bureau from 2014 to 2018.

16 Kabage Karanja describes Sketchup as a grossly underrated design modeling software, treated as if it were a rudimentary obsidian tool in the present age. Karanja, email to author, June 2023.

Primary Sources

ARCHIVES, LIBRARIES, AND COLLECTIONS

The research for this book was informed by study in the following archives, libraries, and collections, as well as in agencies and organizations that appear in the abbreviations list.

Art, Resources, and Teaching Trust, Bengaluru
Barnard Archives and Special Collections, New York
Bibliothèque Nationale de France, Paris
British Institute in Eastern Africa, Nairobi
The British Library, London
Cambridge University Library Royal Commonwealth Society Collections, Cambridge
Canadian Centre for Architecture, Montréal
Centre de Réflexion sur l'Action et les Savoirs Humanitaires (CRASH), Paris
Centre for the Study of Developing Societies (CSDS), Delhi
Centre for the Study of Social Sciences, Calcutta (CSSSC), Kolkata
Columbia University Libraries, Avery Archives and Special Collections, Butler Library African Studies Reading Room, New York
Department of National Archives of Sri Lanka, Colombo
Duke University Libraries Human Rights Archive, Durham, NC
GoDown Arts Centre, Nairobi
Harvard University, Widener Library Sub-Saharan African Collection, Cambridge, MA
International Committee of the Red Cross, Geneva
International Rescue Committee (IRC), New York, Nairobi, Dadaab, Addis Ababa, Jigjiga, and Shimelba
Kenya National Archives, Nairobi
Mazingira Institute archives, Nairobi
Médecins Sans Frontières (MSF), Paris and New York
Museum of Modern Art (MoMA), New York
National Archives of India, Delhi
National Archives UK, London
National Museum of Tanzania, Dar-es-Salaam
National Museums of Kenya, Nairobi and Rabai
Nehru Memorial Museum and Library, Delhi

Oxfam, Oxford
Private Collection of Anonymous 1
Private Collection of Anonymous 2
Private Collection of Anonymous 3
Private Collection of Maureen Connelly
Private Collection of Per Iwansson
Rift Valley Institute (RVI), Nairobi
Shelter Centre, Geneva
United Nations (UN), Geneva
United Nations High Commissioner for Refugees (UNHCR), Dadaab, Nairobi, Geneva, Addis Ababa, Cox's Bazaar, New York
United Nations High Commissioner for Refugees (UNHCR) Archives and Records section, Geneva
United States Holocaust Memorial Museum, Washington, DC
University of Oxford, Bodleian Social Science Library Refugee Studies Centre (RSC) Collection, Oxford
Women's Education and Research Centre (WERC), Colombo
Women's Refugee Commission (WRC), New York
Yivo Institute, New York

INTERVIEWS

The research for this book was informed by people occupying diverse positions across the asymmetries of the humanitarian system as well as institutional spheres of knowledge production. The publication of their names is a complex and burdened task. Such a list risks misuse by those intending harm. Yet, naming contributors follows an urgently generous practice of citation. This list writes into the record names of protagonists and cowriters of a history of humanitarian settlement and of the Dadaab refugee camps, inscribing a historiographical method of *listening and writing with*. Providing a list of primary interlocutors quantitatively signifies an epistemic foundation to other researchers, just as naming individuals may qualitatively interest those directly connected to the sites of research. Naming a person honors her signature and acknowledges her authorship. The insights in this book are drawn from many discussions at once. Interviews articulated in these pages engaged figures who were well known in their contexts, understood the potential publication of our discussions, offered to pose for photographs (sometimes involving those in their care), and provided their full names for citation. I understand my responsibility in knowledge production as, on the one hand, accepting their expression of agency in granting permissions, and, on the other, recognizing the structural violence inherent in the environments where I worked and from which my presence was not disconnected. I have relied on the passage of time to diminish risks associated with any interview in its immediacy.

The list that follows illuminates the spatial methodology and geography of this research, acknowledges signature and historically significant practices across asymmetries and with citational parity, and limits identification of participants when needed. I utilize neither anonymization nor conventional citation fully. For the reader to comprehend the scope of the undertaking, the list is organized according to interview site, and each individual or group is cited separately. An asterisk next to a name denotes multiple communications at that location with the cited individual or group. Interviewees are named under multiple sites when interviewed in more than one location, as many were. Interviews occurred between 2010 and 2021, with the majority between 2011 and 2014. I note this date range rather than providing a date for each interview in order not to identify individual interviewees beyond their stated agreement. Many people opted to grant interviews and many opted not to. Although every person below permitted being cited, I remain mindful that public exposure can pose unknown risks to anyone adjacent to armed conflict, especially, though not limited to, those in flight. With the aim of constructing an inclusive citational structure, rather than omitting those I ascertained as requiring additional privacy, I take extra steps to list them by first name only, by initials, or as "Anonymous." I follow this practice as conservatively as possible, aware that in enclosed spaces people are known to each other, and the interview location may inevitably disclose even anonymized details. I list interviewees by name in an attempt to cite refugees, aid workers, and others together equitably, acknowledging all as authors in the architectures, spatial practices, and infrastructures within this book, and protagonists in its historical narratives. Interviews in conjunction with the WRC, whether conducted by me or Columbia University School of International and Public Affairs research team members (Bethany Young, Elettra Legovini, Maame Ofosuhene, Modupe Onemola, Nicole Schilit, Sarah Wilson, and Nicholas Winslow), are listed in *italics* and used in this book courtesy of the WRC. The Duke University Libraries Human Rights Archive holds these recordings. Interviews I conducted independently are held in the GoDown Arts Centre archive.

Dadaab

Individuals: *Anonymous WFP (World Food Programme) Officer, "Abdullahi" [Hashim] Keinan (Norwegian Refugee Council, NRC), Bettina Schulte (UNHCR), George Auma (Lutheran World Federation, LWF), Jane Maina (UNHCR), Julianna Bloodgood (Great Globe Foundation)*, Michael Littig (Great Globe Foundation)*, Richard Aclund (UNHCR)*, Rose Kanana (Danish Refugee Council, DRC), Sinead Murray (IRC)*, Unni Lange (NRC)*.*

Groups: *Agency representatives (sectors: gender-based violence, livelihoods, food security, water and sanitation, shelter, camp management)*, Dadaab town community members, UNHCR [Robert Ikoha, Daniel Kamau, Nyawira].*

Dagahaley Camp

Individuals: *Anonymous Garden, Anonymous Shopowner 1, Anonymous Shopowner 2, Bashir Ahmed Birri, Habiba Abdurahman Mursan, Habiba Suleiman Abdi, Jean-Pierre Mapela (MSF), Dr. Josiah Oyieke (MSF), Maganai Saddiq Hassan, Mohammed Osman Mohammed, Mohammed Absura (CARE).*

Groups: *Anonymous Community Members*, Anonymous Greenhouse Workers, Anonymous Shopowners, Dagahaley United Girls Center*.*
Translation/Interpretation: *Fardosa Abdullahi Mohammad, Mohammed Osman Mohammed.*

Hagadera Camp

Individuals: *Anonymous F4, Anonymous Together Women Group, Abdullahi, Fatuma Aden, Jactone, Jeremy, Joseph Kiai (LWF), Nimo Osman Mohammed, Sara, Soudo Ali Hassan, Wadajirke Ururka Hawenka (Together Women Group), Walter Oduogi (IRC), Zeleke Bacha (IRC).*
Groups: *Anonymous N10 residents, F4 residents, K4 residents, Together Women Group.*
Translation/Interpretation: *Abdullahi, Sadia Diriye.*

Ifo Camp

Individuals: *Anonymous Donkey Cart, Anonymous Market 1, Anonymous Market 2, Anonymous Market 3, Cawo Ahmed Mohammed, Halima Hassin Dahir, Hashim "Abdullahi" Keinan (NRC)*, Isnina Ali Rage*, Lucy Mwihaki Njenga (CARE)*, Lucy Waweru (CARE), Mohmina Hassan Ali, Shamso Abdullahi Farah.*
Groups: *Anonymous Community Members 1, Anonymous Community Members 2, Anonymous Incentive Workers, Anonymous N Block, Anonymous Security, Country Plan contributors, Greenhouse workers, Hotel workers [Abuk Mora, Elizabeth Adyutuch, Fardoza, Faiza Suleiman (CARE), Grace Alor Francis, Halima, Halima, Margaret, Mary, Rose Narod, Salome, Sara], Incentive workers, Lucy Mwihaki Njenga and Faiza Suleiman, WFP food distribution center workers and community members.*
Translation/Interpretation: *Anonymous Interpreter, "Abdullahi" [Hashim] Keinan (NRC), Ahmed Abdir Shuriye, Faiza Suleiman, Roda Awak.*

Ifo 2 Camp

Individuals: *Henoch (UNHCR), Antony Ondicho (DRC).*
Groups: *Anonymous Community Members.*
Translation/Interpretation: *Anonymous Interpreter.*

Addis Ababa

Individuals: *Anonymous Interpreter*, Ahmed Adan (MCDO, Mothers and Children Development Organization), *Amaha Altaye*, Amare Gebre-Egziabher, PhD, Anthony Mulenga (UNHCR), Berhanu Minassie (Africa Humanitarian Action, AHA), Catherine Evans (UNHCR), David Johnson (formerly IRC and MSF), David Murphy (IRC)*, Dereje Wubishet (UNHCR), Girma Yadeta (UNHCR), Heather Blackwell (DRC), Jappi Yilma (AHA), Jody Myrum (IRC), Magda Medina (UNHCR), Mustafa, Tigist Ayalew (Danish embassy), Zena Estifanos (AHA).*

Groups: *UNHCR [Almaz Degefu, Amaha Altaye, Amare Gebre-Egziabher, PhD], UNHCR Physical Planning and Community Services [Amaha Altaye, Magda Medina, Sardhanand Panchoe].*
Translation/Interpretation: *Anonymous Interpreter.*

Bangkok / Mae Sot / Mae La Camp

Individuals: *Dave Brown (Thailand Burma Border Consortium, TBBC), Madeline Sahagun (American Refugee Committee, ARC).*
Groups: *IRC [Art Carlson, Christine Petrie, Joel Harding], Jesuit Refugee Service [Anne Samson, Jennifer Titmuss], TBBC [Justin Foster, Khun Chirat, Sally Thompson, Thitrat Borerakwana], ZOA (Zuid Oost Asië) [Josef Czikl, Toe Toe Parkdeekhunthum].*

Dhaka / Cox's Bazaar

Individuals: Anonymous 1, Anonymous 2, *Arjun Jain (UNHCR Bangladesh),* Rear Admiral Harunur Rashid (Research, Training, and Management International), *Jane Williamson (UNHCR Cox's Bazaar),* Meghna Guhathakurta (Research Initiatives, Bangladesh), Dr. Zahid Jamal (Muslim Aid).
Groups: *Boyet and Siddique (UNHCR).*

Geneva

Individuals: Anonymous 1*, Anonymous 2*, Elisa Martinez, Graham Saunders (International Federation of Red Cross and Red Crescent Societies, IFRC)*, Jeff Crisp (UNHCR)*, Kim Roberson (UNHCR), Manoucher Lolachi (UNHCR)*, Mirjam Sorli (IASC, Inter-Agency Standing Committee), Rosa da Costa (UNHCHR), Sandra d'Urzo (IFRC)*, Tom Corsellis (Shelter Centre).
Groups: UNHCR Shelter and Settlement section [Gonzalo Vargas, Kim Roberson, Manoucher Lolachi, Naveed Hussain, Sivanka Dhanapala, Tim Irwin].

Lund / Copenhagen

Individuals: Christian Gad (DRC), Per Iwansson.

Mombasa / Rabai

Individuals: Anonymous 1*, Anonymous 2*, Julius Mambo (National Museums of Kenya).

Nairobi

Individuals: *Anonymous 1, Anonymous 2, Anonymous UNHCR,* AbdulFatah Adam, Abdullahi Abdulkadir Sheikh Nur, *Angela Kasili (DRC),* Danielle Bishop, Davinder Lamba (Mazingira Institute), Deqa Abshir, Diana Lee-Smith

(Mazingira Institute), Federica D'Andreagiovanni (United Nations Office for the Coordination of Humanitarian Affairs, UN-OCHA/RVI), Immelda Kithuke (National Museums of Kenya), *James Karanja (UNHCR), Jeanne Ward, Kellie Leeson and Prafulla Mishra (IRC), Laura Muema (PCEA Eastleigh Community Center), Leith Baker (NRC), Matthys Uys (IRC),* Minister of Parliament Moheshimiwa Yusuf, *Olivier Siegenthaler (UNHCR),* Patrick Gathara, *Peter Klansøe (DRC),* Peterson Kamwathi, Simon Addison, Suzy Price (UN Press).

Groups: British Institute of East Africa, Cave Bureau [Kabage Karanja, Stella Mutegi], GoDown Arts Centre, RVI.

New York / Philadelphia / Washington, DC

Individuals: Anonymous 1, Anonymous 2, Aaron Levy (Slought Foundation), *Abie Gacusana (WRC),* Alishine Osman*, Anne Cubilié (formerly UNHCR), Chuck Setchell (United States Agency for International Development, USAID), *Dale Buscher (WRC)*,* Deborah Gans (Gans Jelacic Architects), *Diana Quick (WRC), Erin Patrick (WRC)*,* Erol Kekic (Church World Service)*, *Gerald Martone (IRC)*,* Gonzalo Vargas Llosa (UNHCR), *Jeanne Annan (IRC), Jennifer Schlect (WRC)*, Jennifer Schulte (WRC)*, Jina Krause-Vilmar (WRC)*, Josh Chaffin (WRC),* Kevin Phelan (MSF USA)*, *Leora Ward (IRC),* Mark Ferdig (Mercy Corps)*, Nicole Nummelin (MSF USA)*, Paola Antonelli (MoMA), *Sandra Maignant (IRC),* Sivanka Dhanapala (UNHCR), Tim Irwin (UNHCR).

Groups: *WRC [Ada Williams, Jina Krause-Vilmar, Sarah Costa], WRC Reproductive Health team.*

Oxford / London

Individuals: Jake Zarins (NRC), Kinsi Abdulleh (Numbi Arts), Roger Zetter (RSC)*, Sean Barton (Oxfam).

Paris / Mérignac

Individuals: Alain Fredaigue (MSF France), Antoine Stinco (formerly Utopie), Chloé Decazes (MSF Logistique), Fabrice Weissmann (CRASH)*, Gilles Perroud (MSF Logistique), Jacqueline Wilbert (MSF Logistique), Jacques Pinel (MSF Logistique), Patrick Coulombel (Architectes de l'Urgence), Phillippe Cachet (MSF Logistique), Rockson (MSF Logistique), Rony Brauman (CRASH).

Tigray Region, Ethiopia

Shimbela Camp

Individuals: *Anonymous 1, Anonymous 2, Anonymous 3, Anonymous 4, Anonymous 5, Anonymous 6, Anonymous 7, Anonymous 8, Anonymous 9, Anonymous 10, Anonymous 11, Anonymous 12, Anonymous 13, Anonymous 14, Anonymous 15, Anonymous 16,*

Anonymous 17, Anonymous Administration for Refugee and Returnee Affairs, A., Behailu (IRC), Gebrehiwet Mezgebo (IRC), Mulugeta Abay (IRC), P., S. A., T.*, T. A., Tesfamichael Giday (IRC)*.*

Groups: *Anonymous Kunama Community Members*, Anonymous Laborers, Anonymous Tigrinya Community Members*, Tesfamichael Giday (IRC) and Kinfe (IRC)*, Tewolde and Tesfamichael Giday.*

Translation/Interpretation: *Gebrehiwet Mezgebo, Tesfamichael Giday.*

Somali Region, Ethiopia

Jigjiga

Individuals: *Antony Mulenga (UNHCR), Audrey Crawford (UNHCR), Dereje Wubishet (UNHCR).*

Groups: UNHCR *Physical Planning and Community Services team [Anchinesh, Antony Mulenga, Audrey Crawford, Dereje, Dereje, Mulugeta],* UNHCR *Protection and Gender-Based Violence team [Anchinesh, Mohan, Mulugeta].*

Aw Bare Camp

Individuals: *Ahmed Nur (IRC), Najib Khalif (formerly UNHCR)*.*

Groups: *Anonymous Aw Bare Community Members, Aw Bare Business Owners 1, Aw Bare Business Owners 2, Refugee Central Committee, Refugee community leaders, Refugee Women's Association.*

Kebribeyah Camp

Individuals: *Anonymous ZOA, Adan Abdul Mohammed, Ahmed Nur (IRC)*, Anthony Mulenga (UNHCR), Arish Fid'n Yusuf, Asha Abdi Muhummad, Audrey Crawford (UNHCR), Bashir (IRC), London Shop owner, Memphis, Muluken, Najib Khalif (formerly UNHCR)*, Sa'ada Omer Hassen*, Sheik Bashir*.*

Groups: *Anonymous Business Owners, Anonymous Community Members, Anonymous Laborers, Anonymous Shopowners, Electronics shop workers [Abdirazak Yasin Ibrahim, Ahmed Muse Olad, Ferhan Mohamed Muhamed, Mohammed Mahmoud Ibrahim], Najib Khalif (formerly* UNHCR*) and Bashir (IRC), Refugee Women's Association, Religious leaders [Abdirahman Sheikh Allahi, Ismail Osman Salah, Sheik Bashir], Teachers [Abdi Qasim, Hassan Abdi, Mohamed Abdi, Mohammed Beddel, Sahra Mohamed].*

Translation/Interpretation: *Ahmed Nur Mohamed, Najib Khalif, Sa'ada Omer Hassen, Shafi.*

Sheder Camp

Individuals: *Anonymous 1, Anonymous 2, Anonymous 3, Anonymous 4, Anonymous 5, Anonymous 6, Anonymous 7, Anonymous 8, Anonymous 9, Anonymous 10, Anonymous 11.*

Groups: *Anonymous Laborers, Refugee Women's Committee.*

Desk Interviews (Conducted Remotely by Phone or Video Call)

Individuals: Anonymous 1, Anonymous 2, Alishine Osman*, *Andrea Rodericks (CARE), Bartel (CARE), Charlotte Watts, Cody Donahue (UNICEF, United Nations Children's Fund),* Corinne Treherne (IFRC), Diana Lee-Smith (interviews conducted by author and Garnette Oluoch-Olunya)*, *Doris (CARE), Erin Gerber (IRC),* Ghassem Fardanesh (UNHCR)*, *Henrietta Miers (WISE, Women in Sustainable Economic Development),* Jacques Franquin (UNHCR), James Kennedy*, *Jeanne Annan (IRC), Jeanne Ward, Jennifer Schulte (IRCW, International Center for Research on Women)*, Judith Bruce (Population Council), Julia Kim (UNDP, United Nations Development Programme),* Laura Buffoni (UNHCR), *Laura Meissner (USAID-Office of U.S. Disaster Assistance), Leora Ward (IRC), Lisa Butenhoff (ARC), Maha Muna (United Nations Population Fund),* Mark Cutts (UN-OCHA), Matthew Jelacic (Gans Jelacic Architects), Maureen Connelly (formerly UNHCR)*, *Mendy Marsh (UNICEF),* Mitchell Sipus, Myriam Houtart (UNHCR), Øyvind Nordlie (NRC)*, *Radha Iyengar (London School of Economics)*, Stephanie Davies (MSF USA), Tom Corsellis (Shelter Centre)*.

Groups: *Janet Meyers and Leigh Stefanik (CARE), USAID-OFDA.*

References

Abdi, Cawo M. *Elusive Jannah: The Somali Diaspora and a Borderless Muslim Identity*. Minneapolis: University of Minnesota Press, 2015.

Abourahme, Nasser. "Assembling and Spilling-Over: Towards an 'Ethnography of Cement' in a Palestinian Refugee Camp." *International Journal of Urban and Regional Research* 39, no. 2 (2015): 200–217.

Abourahme, Nasser. "Beneath the Concrete: Camp, Colony, Palestine." PhD diss., Columbia University, 2019.

Abshir, Deqa. "Foundation." http://deqaart.com/?portfolio=foundation. Accessed February 8, 2022.

Abu-Hamdi, Eliana, and Yael Allweil. "Beyond the Camp: The Unbounded Architecture and Urbanism of Refugees (20th–21st Century)." Session in European Association for Urban History international conference, 2018.

Abuye, Mohamed. "Askar: Militarism, Policing and Somali Refugees." PhD diss., University of California, San Diego, 2017.

Addison, Simon. "Spaces of Protection." Concept note, unpublished manuscript, 2011.

Admassu, Emanuel. "Afterimages: On Restitution, Animism, and Diaspora." Syllabus, Columbia University Graduate School of Architecture, Planning, and Preservation, New York, Spring 2022.

Admassu, Emanuel, and Anita N. Bateman, eds. *Where Is Africa?* New York: Center for Art, Research and Alliances, 2022.

Agamben, Giorgio. *Homo Sacer: Sovereign Power and Bare Life*. Stanford, CA: Stanford University Press, 1998.

Agamben, Giorgio. *Means without End: Notes on Politics*. Minneapolis: University of Minnesota Press, 2000.

Agha, Menna. "Emotional Capital and Other Ontologies of the Architect." *Architectural Histories* 8, no. 1 (2020): 1–13.

Agier, Michel. *Managing the Undesirables: Refugee Camps and Humanitarian Government*. Translated by David Fernbach. Cambridge: Polity Press, 2011.

Ahmed, Ali Jimale. *The Invention of Somalia*. Lawrenceville, NJ: Red Sea, 1995.

Ahmed, Ismail I., and Reginald Herbold Green. "The Heritage of War and State Collapse in Somalia and Somaliland: Local-Level Effects, External Interventions and Reconstruction." *Third World Quarterly—Journal of Emerging Areas* 20, no. 1 (1999): 113–27.

Aidid, Safia. "Pan-Somali Dreams: Ethiopia, Greater Somalia, and the Somali Nationalist Imagination." PhD diss., Harvard University, 2020.

Aiyar, Sana. *Indians in Kenya: The Politics of Diaspora*. Cambridge, MA: Harvard University Press, 2015.

Akcan, Esra. *Abolish Human Bans: Intertwined Histories of Architecture.* Montreal: Canadian Centre for Architecture, 2022.

Akcan, Esra. *Open Architecture: Migration, Citizenship, and the Urban Renewal of Berlin-Kreuzberg by IBA-1984/87*. Basel: Birkhäuser, 2018.

Akšamija Azra, Raafat Majzoub, and Melina Phillippou, eds. *Design to Live: Everyday Inventions from a Refugee Camp.* Cambridge, MA: MIT Press, 2021.

Al-Bulushi, Samar. "Kenya's Refugee 'Problem.'" *Africa Is a Country*, May 25, 2016. http://africasacountry.com/2016/05/kenyas-refugee-problem/.

Alimia, Sanaa. "Performing the Afghanistan–Pakistan Border through Refugee ID Cards." *Geopolitics* 24, no. 2 (2019): 391–425.

Alimia, Sanaa. *Refugee Cities: How Afghans Changed Urban Pakistan*. Philadelphia: University of Pennsylvania Press, 2022.

Anderson, David. *Histories of the Hanged: Britain's Dirty War in Kenya and the End of Empire*. London: Weidenfeld and Nicolson, 2005.

Anderson, Kat Blegvad. *Traditional African Architecture*. London: Oxford University Press, 1977.

Anderson, Kay, and Susan Smith. "Editorial: Emotional Geographies." *Transactions of the Institute of British Geographers* 26, no. 1 (2001): 7–10.

Anderson, Sean, and Jennifer Ferng. "The Detention-Industrial Complex in Australia." *Journal of the Society of Architectural Historians* 73, no. 4 (December 2014): 469–74.

Antonopoulou, Aikaterini. "Situated Knowledges and Shifting Grounds: Questioning the Reality Effect of High-Resolution Imagery." *Field: A Free Journal for Architecture* 7, no. 1 (2017): 53–63.

Arendt, Hannah. *The Origins of Totalitarianism*. San Diego: Harcourt Brace, 1966.

Arendt, Hannah. "We Refugees." *Menorah Journal* 31, no. 1 (1943): 69–77.

Atanasoski, Neda. *Humanitarian Violence: The U.S. Deployment of Diversity*. Minneapolis: University of Minnesota Press, 2013.

Atellah, Juliet. "Toa Kitambulisho! Evolution of Registration of Persons in Kenya." *The Elephant*, June 14, 2019. https://www.theelephant.info/data-stories/2019/06/14/toa-kitambulisho-evolution-of-registration-of-persons-in-kenya/.

Atieno-Odhiambo, E. S. "The Formative Years 1945–55." In *Decolonization and Independence in Kenya, 1940–93*, edited by Bethwell A. Ogot and William Robert Ochieng', 25–47. London: James Currey, 1995.

Atieno-Odhiambo, E. S., and John Lonsdale, eds. *Mau Mau and Nationhood: Arms, Authority and Narration.* Oxford: James Currey, 2003.

Azoulay, Ariella Aïsha. *Potential History: Unlearning Imperialism*. London: Verso, 2019.

Balibar, Étienne. "What Is a Border?" In *Politics and the Other Scene*, translated by Christine Jones, James Swenson, and Chris Turner, 75–86. London: Verso, 2012.

Banerjee, Prathama. *Politics of Time: "Primitives" and History-Writing in a Colonial Society.* London: Oxford University Press, 2006.

Barton, Craig Evan. *Sites of Memory: Perspectives on Architecture and Race*. New York: Princeton Architectural Press, 2001.

Bauman, Emily. "The Naïve Republic of Aid: Grassroots Exceptionalism in Humanitarian Memoir." In *Global Humanitarianism and Media Culture,* edited by Michael Lawrence and Rachel Tavernor, 83–102. Manchester: Manchester University Press, 2019.

Baweja, Vandana. "Messy Modernisms: Otto Koenigsberger's Early Work in Princely Mysore, 1939–41." *South Asian Studies* 31, no. 1 (2015): 1–26.

Baweja, Vandana. "A Pre-history of Green Architecture: Otto Koenigsberger and Tropical Architecture, from Princely Mysore to Post-colonial London." PhD diss., University of Michigan, 2008.

Baxter, P. T. W., and Richard Hogg, eds. *Property, Poverty and People: Changing Rights in Property and Problems of Pastoral Development*. Manchester: Department of Social Anthropology and International Development Centre, University of Manchester, 1991.

Beeckmans, Luce, Alessandra Gola, Ashika Singh, and Hilde Heynen, eds. *Making Home(s) in Displacement: Critical Reflections on a Spatial Practice*. Leuven, Belgium: Leuven University Press, 2022.

Bell, Bryan, and Katie Wakeford, eds. *Expanding Architecture: Design as Activism.* New York: Metropolis Books, 2008.

Bennett, Jane. *Vibrant Matter: A Political Ecology of Things*. Durham, NC: Duke University Press, 2010.

Berger, John, and Jean Mohr. *A Fortunate Man: The Story of a Country Doctor*. London: Penguin, 1967.

Berger, John, and Jean Mohr. *A Seventh Man: Migrant Workers in Europe*. New York: Viking, 1975.

Berman, Bruce, and John Lonsdale. *Unhappy Valley: Conflict in Kenya and Africa*. London: James Currey, 1992.

Besteman, Catherine Lowe. "Primordialist Blinders: A Reply to I. M. Lewis." *Cultural Anthropology* 13, no. 1 (1998): 109–20.

Besteman, Catherine Lowe. *Unraveling Somalia: Race, Violence, and the Legacy of Slavery*. Philadelphia: University of Pennsylvania Press, 1999.

Besteman, Catherine Lowe, and Lee V. Cassanelli, eds. *The Struggle for Land in Southern Somalia: The War behind the War*. London: Haan, 2000.

Bilsel, Can, and Juliana Maxim, eds. *Architecture and the Housing Question*. London: Routledge, 2022.

Bilsel, Can, and Juliana Maxim. "Introduction: Architecture and the Housing Question: Specific Histories." In *Architecture and the Housing Question*, edited by Can Bilsel and Juliana Maxim, 1–18. London: Routledge, 2022.

Blanco, Lluís Alexandre Casanovas, Ignacio G. Galán, Carlos Mínguez Carrasco, Alejandra Navarrete Llopis, and Marina Otero Vezier, eds. *After Belonging: The Objects, Spaces, and Territories of the Ways We Stay in Transit.* Exhibition catalog, Oslo Architecture Triennale, 2016. Zurich: Lars Müller, 2016.

Blier, Suzanne Preston. *The Anatomy of Architecture: Ontology and Metaphor in Batammaliba Architectural Expression.* Chicago: University of Chicago Press, 1987.

Bradley, Gracie Mae, and Luke De Noronha. *Against Borders: The Case for Abolition*. London: Verso, 2022.

Brauman, Rony, interviewed by Eyal Weizman. "Planning Emergency: Urbanism for the Displaced?" Hosted by Laura Kurgan and Peter Marcuse, Graduate School of Architecture, Planning, and Preservation, Columbia University, February 4, 2008.

Brown, Wendy. *Walled States, Waning Sovereignty*. New York: Zone, 2010.

Brownlie, Ian, and Ian R. Burns. *African Boundaries: A Legal and Diplomatic Encyclopaedia*. London: Hurst, 1996.

Brun, Cathrine, and Tariq Jazeel, eds. *Spatialising Politics: Culture and Geography in Postcolonial Sri Lanka*. Los Angeles: Sage, 2009.

Butler, Judith. *Frames of War: When Is Life Grievable*? London: Verso, 2009.

Cadogan, Garnette. "Walking While Black." In *Freeman's: Arrival*. New York: Grove, 2015.

Calhoun, Craig. "The Idea of Emergency: Humanitarian Action and Global (Dis)Order." In *Contemporary States of Emergency: The Politics of Military and Humanitarian Interventions*, edited by Didier Fassin and Mariella Pandolfi, 29–58. New York: Zone, 2010.

Calhoun, Craig. "The Imperative to Reduce Suffering: Charity, Progress, and Emergencies in the Field of Humanitarian Action." In *Humanitarianism in Question: Politics, Power, Ethics*, edited by Michael Barnett and Thomas G. Weiss, 73–97. Ithaca, NY: Cornell University Press, 2008.

Carboni, Julien Lafontaine. "(From) the Repertoire: An Architectural Theory of Operations: Oral and Embodied Knowledge in Architectural and Spatial Practices." PhD diss., École Polytechnique Fédérale de Lausanne, 2022.

Carboni, Julien Lafontaine. "Undrawn Spatialities: The Architectural Archives in the Light of the History of the Sahrawi Refugee Camps." *Architecture and Culture* 9, no. 3 (2021): 505–22.

Carrier, Neil. *Little Mogadishu: Eastleigh, Nairobi's Global Somali Hub.* Oxford: Oxford University Press, 2016.

Carrier, Neil, Michael O'Leary, and Gisli Palsson. "Paul T. W. Baxter: Photographing the Other-than-Human." *Ethnos* 86, no. 1 (2021): 69–93.

Carrier, Neil, and Kimo Quaintance. "Frontier Photographs: Northern Kenya and the Paul Baxter Collection." In *Photography in Africa: Ethnographic Perspectives*, edited by Richard Vokes, 81–103. Woodbridge, UK: James Currey, 2012.

Casid, Jill. *Sowing Empire: Landscape and Colonization.* Minneapolis: University of Minnesota Press, 2005.

Cassanelli, Lee V. *The Shaping of Somali Society: Reconstructing the History of a Pastoral People, 1600–1900*. Philadelphia: University of Pennsylvania Press, 1982.

Cephas, Jay. "A Critical Closeness." In "Caregiving as Method" dossier, Anooradha Iyer Siddiqi, Can Bilsel, Ana Miljački, and Garnette Cadogan, with Javairia Shahid. In "Care," guest edited by Torsten Lange and Gabrielle Schaad. *gta Papers* 7 (2022): 108–12.

Chatterjee, Partha. *The Nation and Its Fragments: Colonial and Postcolonial Histories*. Princeton, NJ: Princeton University Press, 1993.

Chee, Lilian. "Keeping Cats, Hoarding Things: Domestic Situations in the Public Spaces of the Singaporean Housing Block." *Journal of Architecture* 22, no. 6 (2017): 1041–65.

Cheng, Irene, Charles L. Davis II, and Mabel O. Wilson, eds. *Race and Modern Architecture*. Pittsburgh, PA: University of Pittsburgh Press, 2020.

Chitchian, Somayeh, Maja Momić, and Shahd Seethaler-Wari. "Architectures of an 'Otherwise': Inhabiting Displacement." In "Contingency," guest edited by Dana Cuff and Will Davis. *Ardeth* 6 (July 2020): 249–55.

Chowdhury, Zirwat. "An Imperial Mughal Tent and Mobile Sovereignty in Eighteenth-Century Jodhpur." *Art History* 38, no. 4 (September 2015): 668–81.

Clapham, Andrew. *Human Rights: A Very Short Introduction*. Oxford: Oxford University Press, 2007.

Clapham, Christopher. "Boundary and Territory in the Horn of Africa." In *African Boundaries: Barriers, Conduits, and Opportunities*, edited by Paul Nugent and A. I. Asiwaju, 237–50. London: Pinter, 1996.

Cock, Emil, and Institut Universitaire d'Ètudes du Dèveloppement. *Le dispositif humanitaire*. Geneva: IUED, 2003.

Cohen, Jean-Louis. *Architecture in Uniform: Designing and Building for the Second World War*. Paris: Hazan Editeur, 2011.

Coomaraswamy, Radhika. "Reclaiming Parts of the Enlightenment: South Asia and Human Rights." Lecture, University of Edinburgh Centre for South Asian Studies, October 5, 2021.

Cooper, Frederick. *Plantation Slavery on the East Coast of Africa*. New Haven, CT: Yale University Press, 1977.

Cooper, Frederick. "What Is the Concept of Globalization Good For? An African Historian's Perspective." *African Affairs* 100 (April 2001): 189–213.

Corsellis, Tom. "The Selection of Sites for Temporary Settlements for Forced Migrants." PhD diss., King's College, University of Cambridge, 2001.

Crinson, Mark, ed. "Dossier: Dynamic Vernacular." *ABE Journal: Architecture beyond Europe* 9–10 (2016). https://doi.org/10.4000/abe.3002.

Cuny, Frederick C., Susan Abrams, and Oxfam America. *Disasters and Development*. New York: Oxford University Press, 1983.

Cupers, Kenny. *Use Matters: An Alternative History of Architecture*. London: Routledge, 2013.

Dadi, Iftikhar, and Hammad Nasar, eds. *Lines of Control: Partition as a Productive Space*. London: Green Cardamom, 2012.

Dainese, Elisa, and Aleksandar Staničić. "Introduction: Critical Themes of Design after Destruction." In *War Diaries: Design after the Destruction of Art and*

Architecture, edited by Elisa Dainese and Aleksandar Staničić, 1–15. Charlottesville: University of Virginia Press, 2022.

Dalal, Ayham. *From Shelters to Dwellings: The Zaatari Refugee Camp*. Bielefeld: Transcript Verlag, 2022.

Damm, Tile von, Anne-Katrin Fenk, and Rachel Lee, eds. *OK—Otto Koenigsberger: Architecture and Urban Visions in India*. Liverpool: TAG Press, 2015.

D'Avignon, Robyn. *A Ritual Geology: Gold and Subterranean Knowledge in Savanna West Africa*. Durham, NC: Duke University Press, 2022.

Davis, Ian. *Shelter after Disaster*. Oxford: Oxford Polytechnic Press, 1978.

Davis, William Michael. "Palm Politics: Warfare, Folklore, and Architecture." PhD diss., University of California, Los Angeles, 2021.

De Alwis, Malathi. "Moral Mothers and Stalwart Sons: Reading Binaries in a Time of War." In *The Women and War Reader*, edited by Lois Ann Lorentzen and Jennifer Turpin, 254–71. New York: New York University Press, 1998.

Dean, Andrea Oppenheimer, Timothy Hursley, Lawrence Chua, and Cervin Robinson. *Rural Studio: Samuel Mockbee and an Architecture of Decency*. New York: Princeton Architectural Press, 2002.

Decolonizing Architecture Art Residency (DAAR), Alessandro Petti, Sandi Hilal, and Eyal Weizman. *Architecture after Revolution*. Berlin: Sternberg, 2013.

Deegan, Omar. *Mogadishu: Through the Eyes of an Architect*. Self-published, 2020.

Desai, Gaurav Gajanan. *Commerce with the Universe: Africa, India, and the Afrasian Imagination*. New York: Columbia University Press, 2016.

Desai, Renu, and Romola Sanyal, eds. *Urbanizing Citizenship: Contested Spaces in Indian Cities*. Thousand Oaks, CA: Sage, 2012.

De Waal, Alex. *Famine Crimes: Politics and the Disaster Relief Industry in Africa*. London: African Rights and the International African Institute in association with James Currey, 1997.

Dharia, Namita Vijay. *The Industrial Ephemeral: Labor and Love in Indian Architecture and Construction*. Oakland: University of California Press, 2022.

Dingley, Zebulon. "Kinship, Capital, and the Occult on the South Coast of Kenya." PhD diss., University of Chicago, 2018.

Dodier, Nicolas. "Contributions by Médecins Sans Frontières to Changes in Transnational Medicine." In *Medical Innovations in Humanitarian Situations: The Work of Médecins Sans Frontières*, edited by Jean-Hervé Bradol and Claudine Vidal, 200–224. Paris: MSF, 2011.

Donham, Donald L., and Wendy James, eds. *The Southern Marches of Imperial Ethiopia: Essays in History and Social Anthropology*. Oxford: James Currey, 2001.

Dos Santos, Riberio. *A Baixa Pombalina: Passado e futuro*. Lisbon: Livros Horizonte, 2005.

Doucet, Isabelle. "Understanding Social Engagement in Architecture: Toward Situated-Embodied and Critical Accounts." In *The Routledge Companion to Architecture and Social Engagement*, edited by Farhan Karim, 14–26. London: Routledge, 2018.

Drysdale, John. *The Somali Dispute*. London: Pall Mall Press, 1964.
D'Souza, Radha. "Decolonizing Knowledge: Science, Scientists, and Science Education." In *Decolonising Knowledge: Looking Back, Moving Forward*, edited by Radha D'Souza and Sunera Thobani (forthcoming).
Du Bois, W. E. B. "Strivings of the Negro People." *Atlantic* 80 (August 1897): 194–98.
Dutta, Arindam. *A Second Modernism: MIT, Architecture, and the "Techno-Social" Moment.* Cambridge, MA: MIT Press, 2013.
Dutta, Arindam, Ateya Khorakiwala, Ayala Levin, Fabiola López Durán, and Ijlal Muzzaffar, eds., for Aggregate Architectural History Collaborative. *Architecture in Development: Systems and the Emergence of the Global South*. London: Routledge, 2022.
Eade, Deborah, and Tony Vaux, eds. *Development and Humanitarianism: Practical Issues*. Bloomfield, CT: Kumarian Press, 2007.
Elden, Stuart. *The Birth of Territory*. Chicago: University of Chicago Press, 2013.
Elden, Stuart. "Land, Terrain, Territory." *Progress in Human Geography* 34, no. 6 (December 2010): 799–817.
Elkins, Caroline. "Detention, Rehabilitation, and the Destruction of Kikuyu Society." In *Mau Mau and Nationhood: Arms, Authority and Narration*, edited by E. S. Atieno-Odhiambo and John Lonsdale, 191–226. Oxford: James Currey, 2003.
Elkins, Caroline. *Imperial Reckoning: The Untold Story of Britain's Gulag in Kenya*. New York: Henry Holt, 2005.
Elleh, Nnamdi. *African Architecture: Evolution and Transformation*. New York: McGraw-Hill, 1996.
Espiritu, Yen Le, Lan Duong, Ma Vang, Victor Bascara, Khatharya Um, Lila Sharif, and Nigel Hatton. *Departures: An Introduction to Critical Refugee Studies.* Oakland: University of California Press, 2022.
Estes, Nick. *Our History Is the Future: Standing Rock versus the Dakota Access Pipeline, and the Long Tradition of Indigenous Resistance*. London: Verso, 2019.
Etoke, Nathalie. *Melancholia Africana: The Indispensable Overcoming of the Black Condition*. Translated by Bill Hamlett. London: Rowman & Littlefield International, 2019.
Everill, Bronwen. "Freetown, Frere Town and the Kat River Settlement: Nineteenth-Century Humanitarian Intervention and Precursors to Modern Refugee Camps." In *The History and Practice of Humanitarian Intervention and Aid in Africa*, edited by Bronwen Everill and Josiah Kaplan, 23–42. Houndmills, UK: Palgrave Macmillan, 2013.
Fanon, Frantz. *Black Skins, White Masks*. Translated by Richard Phillcox. New York: Grove, 1952.
Fassin, Didier. *Humanitarian Reason: A Moral History of the Present*. Berkeley: University of California Press, 2012.
Fassin, Didier, and Mariella Pandolfi, eds. *Contemporary States of Emergency: The Politics of Military and Humanitarian Interventions.* New York: Zone, 2010.

Fearon, James. "The Rise of Emergency Relief Aid." In *Humanitarianism in Question: Power, Politics, Ethics*, edited by Michael Barnett and Thomas G. Weiss, 49–72. Ithaca, NY: Cornell University Press, 2008.

Feher, Michel, Gaëlle Krikorian, and Yates McKee, eds. *Nongovernmental Politics*. New York: Zone, 2007.

Fleetwood, Nicole R. *Marking Time: Art in the Age of Mass Incarceration*. Cambridge, MA: Harvard University Press, 2020.

Forman, Fonna, and Teddy Cruz. *Top Down / Bottom Up: The Political and Architectural Practice of Estudio Teddy Cruz + Forman*. Ostfildern, Germany: Hatje/Cantz, 2017.

Foucault, Michel. *The Birth of Biopolitics: Lectures at the Collège De France 1978–79*. Edited by Michel Senellart and translated by Graham Burchell. New York: Palgrave Macmillan, 2008.

Foucault, Michel. "The Confession of the Flesh." A conversation with Alain Grosrichard, Gerard Wajeman, Jaques-Alain Miller, Guy Le Gaufey, Dominique Celas, Gerard Miller, Catherine Millot, Jocelyne Livi, and Judith Miller. In *Power/Knowledge: Selected Interviews and Other Writings, 1972–1977*, edited by Colin Gordon, 194–228. New York: Pantheon, 1980.

Foucault, Michel. *The History of Sexuality*. Vol. 1: *The Will to Knowledge*. Translated by Robert Hurley. New York: Pantheon, 1978.

Foucault, Michel. *Society Must Be Defended: Lectures at the Collège de France, 1975–1976*. Edited by Mauro Bertani and Alessandro Fontana and translated by David Macey. New York: Picador, 2003.

Foucault, Michel, Michel Senellart, François Ewald, and Alessandro Fontana. *Security, Territory, Population: Lectures at the Collège de France, 1977–78*. New York: Picador, 2007.

Fraiman, Susan. *Extreme Domesticity: A View from the Margins*. New York: Columbia University Press, 2016.

Franklin, Derek Peter. *A Pied Cloak: Memoirs of a Colonial Police Officer (Special Branch), Kenya, 1953–66, Bahrain, 1967–71, Lesotho, 1971–75, Botswana, 1976–81*. London: Janus, 1996.

Fredriksen, Aurora. "Emergency Shelter Topologies: Locating Humanitarian Space in Mobile and Material Practice." *Environment and Planning D: Society and Space* 32, no. 1 (2014): 147–62.

Fredriksen, Aurora. "Making Humanitarian Spaces Global: Coordinating Crisis Response through the Cluster Approach." PhD diss., Columbia University, 2012.

Gardner, Judith, and Judy El Bushra, eds. *Somalia—the Untold Story: The War through the Eyes of Somali Women*. London: Pluto, 2004.

Gattrell, Peter. *The Making of the Modern Refugee*. Oxford: Oxford University Press, 2015.

Geeldoon, Maxamed Xuseen. *We Kissed the Ground: A Migrant's Journey from Somaliland to the Mediterranean* [*Carrada Ayaan Dhunkannay: Waa socdaalkii tahriibka ee Somaliland ilaa badda Medhitereeniyanka*]. London and Nairobi: Rift Valley Institute, 2016.

Gell, Alfred. *Art and Agency: An Anthropological Theory*. Oxford: Clarendon, 1998.

The Getty Research Institute. "The Art and Architecture of Partition and Confederation, Pakistan and Beyond, 1933–1971." Research project and workshop organized by Maristella Casciato, Zirwat Chowdhury, and Farhan Karim, October 15–16, 2018.

Gharipour, Mohammad, and Kıvanç Kılınç, eds. *Social Housing in the Middle East: Architecture, Urban Development, and Transnational Modernity*. Bloomington: Indiana University Press, 2019.

Goldewijk, Berma Klein, Georg Frerks, and Els van der Plas, eds. *Cultural Emergency in Conflict and Disaster*. Rotterdam: NAi, 2011.

Goldstone, Brian, and Juan Obarrio, eds. *African Futures: Essays on Crisis, Emergence, and Possibility.* Chicago: University of Chicago Press, 2017.

Gooden, Mario. *Dark Space: Architecture Representation Black Identity*. New York: Columbia Books on Architecture and the City, 2016.

Gosseye, Janina, Naomi Stead, and Deborah van der Plaat, eds. *Speaking of Buildings: Oral History in Architectural Research*. New York: Princeton Architectural Press, 2019.

Gramsci, Antonio, Quintin Hoare, and Geoffrey Nowell-Smith. *Selections from the Prison Notebooks of Antonio Gramsci*. New York: International Publishers, 1972.

Gyger, Helen. *Improvised Cities: Architecture, Urbanization, and Innovation in Peru.* Pittsburgh, PA: University of Pittsburgh Press, 2019.

Haraway, Donna. "Situated Knowledges: The Science Question in Feminism and the Privilege of Partial Perspective." In *Simians, Cyborgs and Women: The Reinvention of Nature*, 183–201. New York: Routledge, 1991.

Haraway, Donna. *Staying with the Trouble: Making Kin in the Chthulucene.* Durham, NC: Duke University Press, 2016.

Harper, Mary. *Getting Somalia Wrong? Faith, War, and Hope in a Shattered State*. London: Zed, 2012.

Hartman, Saidiya. *Lose Your Mother*. New York: Farrar, Straus, and Giroux, 2008.

Hartman, Saidiya. "Venus in Two Acts." *Small Axe*, no. 26 (June 2008): 1–14.

Hartman, Saidiya. *Wayward Lives, Beautiful Experiments: Intimate Histories of Riotous Black Girls, Troublesome Women, and Queer Radicals*. New York: W. W. Norton, 2019.

Hecht, Gabrielle. *Entangled Geographies: Empire and Technopolitics in the Global Cold War*. Cambridge, MA: MIT Press, 2011.

Henni, Samia. *Architecture of Counterrevolution: The French Army in Northern Algeria*. Zürich: GTA Verlag, 2017.

Henni, Samia. "Colonial Ramifications." *e-flux Architecture,* October 2018. https://www.e-flux.com/architecture/history-theory/225180/colonial-ramifications/.

Herscher, Andrew. *Displacements: Architecture and Refugee*. Berlin: Sternberg, 2017.

Herscher, Andrew. "Surveillant Witnessing: Satellite Imagery and the Visual Politics of Human Rights." *Public Culture* 26, no. 3 (September 1, 2014): 469–500.

Herscher, Andrew. *Violence Taking Place: The Architecture of the Kosovo Conflict*. Stanford, CA: Stanford University Press, 2010.

Herscher, Andrew, and Anooradha Iyer Siddiqi. "Spatial Violence." *Architectural Theory Review* 19, no. 3 (2014): 269–77.

Hibou, Béatrice. *La bureaucratization du monde à l'ère néolibérale*. Paris: La Découverte, 2012.
Ho, Engseng. *The Graves of Tarim: Genealogy and Mobility across the Indian Ocean.* Berkeley: University of California Press, 2006.
Holston, James. *Insurgent Citizenship: Disjunctions of Democracy and Modernity in Brazil*. Princeton, NJ: Princeton University Press, 2008.
hooks, bell. "Choosing the Margin as a Space of Radical Openness." *Framework: The Journal of Cinema and Media* 36 (1989): 15–23.
hooks, bell. *Yearning: Race, Gender, and Cultural Politics*. New York: Routledge, 2014.
Hopgood, Stephen. "Saying 'No' to Wal-Mart? Money and Morality in Professional Humanitarianism." In *Humanitarianism in Question: Politics, Power, Ethics*, edited by Michael Bennett and Thomas G. Weiss, 98–123. Ithaca, NY: Cornell University Press, 2008.
Horst, Cindy. "Buufis amongst Somalis in Dadaab: The Transnational and Historical Logics behind Resettlement Dreams." *Journal of Refugee Studies* 19, no. 2 (2006): 143–57.
Horst, Cindy. *Transnational Nomads: How Somalis Cope with Refugee Life in the Dadaab Camps of Kenya*. New York: Berghahn, 2006.
Hunt, Lynn. *Inventing Human Rights: A History*. New York: W. W. Norton, 2008.
Hydén, Göran. *Beyond Ujamaa in Tanzania: Underdevelopment and an Uncaptured Peasantry*. London: Heinemann, 1982.
Hyndman, Jennifer. "Border Crossings." *Antipode* 29, no. 2 (1997): 149–76.
Hyndman, Jennifer. *Managing Displacement: Refugees and the Politics of Humanitarianism*. Minneapolis: University of Minnesota Press, 2000.
Ibrahim, Rhoda M. "Women's Role in the Pastoral Economy." In *Somalia—the Untold Story: The War through the Eyes of Somali Women*, edited by Judith Gardner and Judy El Bushra, 24–50. London: Pluto, 2004.
Iheka, Cajetan. *African Ecomedia: Network Forms, Planetary Politics.* Durham, NC: Duke University Press, 2021.
Ikanda, Fred Nyongesa. "Animating 'Refugeeness' through Vulnerabilities: Worthiness of Long-Term Exile in Resettlement Claims among Somali Refugees in Kenya." *Africa* 88, no. 3 (August 2018): 579–96.
Ikanda, Fred Nyongesa. "Deteriorating Conditions of Hosting Refugees: A Case Study of the Dadaab Complex in Kenya." *African Study Monographs* 29, no. 1 (October 2008): 29–49.
Ikanda, Fred Nyongesa. "Good and Bad Muslims: Conflict, Justice, and Religion Among Somalis at Dagahaley Refugee Camp in Kenya." In *Pursuing Justice in Africa: Competing Imaginaries and Contested Practices*, edited by Jessica Johnson and George Hamandishe Karekwaivanane, 222–42. Athens: Ohio University Press, 2018.
Ikanda, Fred Nyongesa. "Somali Refugees in Kenya and Social Resilience: Resettlement Imaginings and the Longing for Minnesota." *African Affairs* 117, no. 469 (October 2018): 569–91.
Incite! Women of Color against Violence, ed. *The Revolution Will Not Be Funded: Beyond the Non-Profit Industrial Complex.* Cambridge: South End Press, 2007.

Insurgent Domesticities. Columbia University Center for the Study of Social Difference Working Group. https://www.socialdifference.columbia.edu/projects-/insurgent-domesticities. Accessed March 16, 2023.

Jacobsen, Karen. *The Economic Life of Refugees.* Bloomfield, CT: Kumarian, 2005.

Jain, Kajri. "Whose Emergency?" In *Art History and Emergency: Crises in the Visual Arts and Humanities*, edited by David Breslin, Darby English, and Sterling and Francine Clark Art Institute, 12–22. Williamstown, MA: Sterling and Francine Clark Art Institute, 2016.

Jaji, Rose. "Social Technology and Refugee Encampment in Kenya." *Journal of Refugee Studies* 25, no. 2 (2012): 221–38.

James, C. L. R. "Epilogue: The History of Pan-African Revolt: A Summary, 1939–1969." In *Living with Ghosts: A Reader*, edited by Kojo Abudu, 25-43. London: Pace Publishing, 2023.

James, Wendy, Donald L. Donham, Eisei Kurimoto, and Alessandro Triulzi, eds. *Remapping Ethiopia: Socialism and After*. Oxford: James Currey, 2002.

Jamison, Matthew. "Humanitarian Intervention since 1990 and 'Liberal Interventionism.'" In *Humanitarian Intervention: A History*, edited by Brendan Simms and D. J. B. Trim, 365–80. Cambridge: Cambridge University Press, 2011.

Jansen, Bram. *Kakuma Refugee Camp: Humanitarian Urbanism in Kenya's Accidental City*. London: Zed, 2018.

Jaskot, Paul B. *The Architecture of Oppression: The SS, Forced Labor, and the Nazi Monumental Building Economy*. London: Routledge, 2000.

Jennings, Michael. *Surrogates of the State: NGOs, Development, and Ujamaa in Tanzania*. Bloomfield, CT: Kumarian, 2008.

Jodidio, Philip. *Shigeru Ban: Complete Works 1985–2010*. Köln: Taschen, 2010.

Johnson, Christopher D. *Memory, Metaphor, and Aby Warburg's Atlas of Images*. Ithaca, NY: Cornell University Press, 2012.

Kanogo, Tabitha. *Squatters and the Roots of Mau Mau, 1905–63*. London: James Currey, 1987.

Kapteijns, Lidwien. *Clan Cleansing in Somalia: The Ruinous Legacy of 1991*. Philadelphia: University of Pennsylvania Press, 2013.

Karim, Farhan. "Between Self and Citizenship: Doxiadis Associates in Postcolonial Pakistan 1958–68." *International Journal of Islamic Architecture* 5, no. 1 (2016): 135–61.

Karim, Farhan. *The Routledge Companion to Architecture and Social Engagement*. London: Routledge, 2018.

Katz, Irit. *The Common Camp: Architecture of Power and Resistance in Israel-Palestine*. Minneapolis: University of Minnesota Press, 2022.

Katz, Irit. "Spreading and Concentrating: The Camp as the Space of the Frontier." *City* 19, no. 5 (2015): 727–40.

Katz, Irit, Diana Martín, and Claudio Minca, eds. *Camps Revisited: Multifaceted Spatialities of a Modern Political Technology*. London: Rowman and Littlefield International, 2018.

Kaur, Ravinder. "Claiming Community through Narratives: Punjabi Refugees in Delhi." In *The Idea of Delhi*, edited by Romi Khosla, 54–67. Mumbai: Marg, 2005.

Keck, Margaret E., and Kathryn Sikkink. *Activists beyond Borders*. Ithaca, NY: Cornell University Press, 1998.

Keenan, Thomas. "Do Something." In "Humanism without Borders: A Dossier on the Human, Humanitarianism, and Human Rights." *Alphabet City* 7, "Social Insecurity" (2000): 44–46.

Kennedy, Hollyamber. "Infrastructures of 'Legitimate Violence': The Prussian Settlement Commission, Internal Colonization, and the Migrant Remainder." *Grey Room* 76 (Summer 2019): 58–97.

Kennedy, Hollyamber. "A Spatial Writing of the Earth: The Design of Colonial Territory in South-West Africa." In *German Colonialism in Africa and Its Legacies*, edited by Itohan Osyayimwese, 89–119. London: Bloomsbury, 2023.

Kennedy, Hollyamber. "Wastelands of Empire, Sites of 'Salvation': Landscapes of 'Reform' in Late 19th Century Germany." In "Territories of Incarceration," guest edited by Sabrina Puddu and Francesco Zuddas. *Journal of Architecture* (forthcoming 2024).

Kennedy, James. "Structures for the Displaced: Service and Identity in Refugee Settlements." PhD diss., Technische Universiteit Delft, 2008.

Keshavarz, Mahmoud. *The Design Politics of the Passport: Materiality, Immobility, and Dissent*. London: Bloomsbury, 2019.

Khadiagala, Gilbert M. "Boundaries in Eastern Africa." *Journal of Eastern African Studies* 4, no. 2 (2010): 266–78.

Khagram, Sanjeev, James V. Riker, and Kathryn Sikkink, eds. *Restructuring World Politics: Transnational Social Movements, Networks and Norms*. Minneapolis: University of Minnesota Press, 2002.

Kibinge, Judy, Marius Van Graan, Jason Corder, and Kevin McCloud. *Scarred: The Anatomy of a Massacre*. Los Angeles: Seven Productions, 2015.

Kimathi, Leah. "The Securitization of Humanitarian Aid: A Case Study of the Dadaab Refugee Camp in Kenya." In *Refugees and Forced Migration in the Horn and Eastern Africa: Trends, Challenges, and Opportunities*, edited by Johannes Dragsbaek Schmidt, Leah Kimathi, and Michael Omondi Owiso, 65–80. Cham, Switzerland: Springer, 2019.

Kĩnyattĩ, Maina wa, ed. *Kenya's Freedom Struggle: The Dedan Kimathi Papers*. London: Zed, 1987.

Kĩnyattĩ, Maina wa. *Mwakenya: The Unfinished Revolution: Selected Documents of the Mwakenya-December Twelve Movement (1974–2002)*. Nairobi: Mau Mau Research Center, 2014.

Kĩnyattĩ, Maina wa. *The Pen and the Gun: Selected Essays, Letters, and Poems*. Nairobi: Mau Mau Research Center, 2006.

Kirkham-Lewitt, Isabelle, ed. *Paths to Prison: On the Architectures of Carcerality*. New York: Columbia University Press, 2020.

Klein, Naomi. *The Shock Doctrine: The Rise of Disaster Capitalism*. New York: Metropolitan / Henry Holt, 2007.

Kostof, Spiro. *The City Assembled: The Elements of Urban Form through History*. Boston: Little, Brown, 1992.

Kurgan, Laura. *Close Up at a Distance: Mapping, Technology, and Politics*. New York: Zone, 2013.

Laitin, David D., and Said S. Samatar. *Somalia: Nation in Search of a State*. Boulder, CO: Westview Press, 1987.

Landau, Loren, and Tanya Pampalone, eds. *I Want to Go Home Forever*. Johannesburg: Wits University Press, 2018.

Larkin, Brian. "The Politics and Poetics of Infrastructure." *Annual Review of Anthropology* 42 (2013): 327–43.

Latour, Bruno. *The Pasteurization of France*. Cambridge, MA: Harvard University Press, 1988.

Lavin, Sylvia. *Architecture Itself and Other Postmodernization Effects*. Montreal: Canadian Centre for Architecture, 2020.

Lawrence, Michael, and Rachel Tavernor, eds. *Global Humanitarianism and Media Culture*. Manchester: Manchester University Press, 2019.

Lee, Rachel. "Negotiating Modernities: Otto Koenigsberger's Works and Network in Exile (1933–1951)." PhD diss., TU Berlin, 2017.

Lee-Smith, Diana. "'My House Is My Husband': A Kenyan Study of Women's Access to Land and Housing." PhD diss., Lund University, 1997.

Lewis, I. M. *Understanding Somalia and Somaliland: Culture, History, Society*. New York: Columbia University Press, 1893.

Loescher, Gil. *The UNHCR and World Politics: A Perilous Path*. Oxford: Oxford University Press, 2001.

Lokko Lesley Naa Norle, ed. *White Papers Black Marks: Architecture, Race, Culture*. Minneapolis: University of Minnesota Press, 2000.

Lopez, Sarah Lynn. *The Remittance Landscape: Spaces of Migration in Rural Mexico and Urban USA*. Chicago: University of Chicago Press, 2014.

Lopez, Sarah Lynn. "States of Incarceration: An Architectural Perspective on Immigrant Detention in Texas." *Museums & Social Issues* 12, no. 1 (2017): 33–40.

Lorde, Audre. "The Master's Tools Will Never Dismantle the Master's House." In *This Bridge Called My Back: Writing by Radical Women of Color*, edited by Cherríe Moraga and Gloria Anzaldúa, 98–101. Watertown, MA: Persephone Press, 1981.

Lorde, Audre. "The Uses of Anger: Women Responding to Racism." *Blackpast*, August 12, 2012. https://www.blackpast.org/african-american-history/speeches-african-american-history/1981-audre-lorde-uses-anger-women-responding-racism/.

Lorentzen, Lois Ann, and Jennifer Turpin, eds. *The Women and War Reader*. New York: New York University Press, 1998.

Lowe, Lisa. *The Intimacies of Four Continents*. Durham, NC: Duke University Press, 2015.

Lozanovska, Mirjana. *Ethno-architecture and the Politics of Migration*. London: Routledge, 2016.

Lozanovska, Mirjana. *Migrant Housing: Architecture, Dwelling, Migration*. London: Routledge, 2019.

Lynch, Gabrielle. *I Say to You: Ethnic Politics and the Kalenjin in Kenya*. Chicago: University of Chicago Press, 2011.

MacArthur, Julie. *Cartography and the Political Imagination: Mapping Community in Colonial Kenya*. Athens: Ohio University Press, 2016.

Magone, Claire, Michael Neuman, and Fabrice Weissman, eds. *Humanitarian Negotiations Revealed: The MSF Experience*. New York: Columbia University Press, 2011.

Mahmood, Saba. *Politics of Piety: The Islamic Revival and the Feminist Subject*. Princeton, NJ: Princeton University Press, 2011.

Malkki, Liisa Helena. *Purity and Exile: Violence, Memory, and National Cosmology among Hutu Refugees in Tanzania*. Chicago: University of Chicago Press, 1995.

Mamdani, Mahmood. *Citizen and Subject: Contemporary Africa and the Legacy of Late Colonialism*. Princeton, NJ: Princeton University Press, 2018.

Manji, Ambreena. *The Struggle for Land and Justice in Kenya*. Woodbridge, UK: James Currey, 2020.

Martin, Reinhold. "Financial Imaginaries: Toward a Philosophy of the City." *Grey Room* 42 (Winter 2011): 60–79.

Marx, Karl. "The Fetishism of the Commodity and the Secret Thereof." In *Capital*, vol. 1. Alexandria, VA: Chadwydk-Healey, 1999.

Matsipa, Mpho, ed. *African Mobilities: This Is Not a Refugee Camp Exhibition*. Exhibition catalog, Arkitekturmuseum der TUM, April 26–August 19, 2018.

Mbembe, Achille. *Critique of Black Reason*. Durham, NC: Duke University Press, 2017.

Mburu, Nene. *Bandits on the Border: The Last Frontier in the Search for Somali Unity*. Lawrenceville, NJ: Red Sea, 2005.

McConnell, Tristan. "Inside Somalia: Where Poetry Is Revered." *The World*. GlobalPost from Agence France-Presse, February 12, 2010. https://theworld.org/stories/2010-02-12/inside-somalia-where-poetry-revered.

McEwen, A. C. *International Boundaries of East Africa*. Oxford: Clarendon, 1971.

McKee, Yates. "'Eyes and Ears': Aesthetics, Visual Culture, and the Claims of Nongovernmental Politics." In *Nongovernmental Politics*, edited by Michel Feher, with Gaëlle Krikorian and Yates McKee, 326–55. New York: Zone, 2007.

McKittrick, Katherine. *Demonic Grounds: Black Women and the Cartographies of Struggle*. Minneapolis: University of Minnesota Press, 2006.

McLagan, Meg, and Yates McKee, eds. *Sensible Politics: The Visual Culture of Nongovernmental Activism*. New York: Zone, 2012.

McNeish, John-Andrew, and Jon Harald Sande Lie, eds. *Security and Development*. New York: Berghahn, 2010.

McQuaid, Matilda. *Shigeru Ban*. London: Phaidon, 2003.

Meier, Prita. *Swahili Port Cities: The Architecture of Elsewhere*. Bloomington: Indiana University Press, 2016.

Meiu, George. *Ethno-erotic Economies: Sexuality, Money, and Belonging in Kenya*. Chicago: University of Chicago Press, 2017.

Mendoza, Elis. "From Refuge to Shelter: Frederick Cuny's Humanitarian Architecture as Deferred Utopia." PhD diss., Princeton University, 2022.

Mendoza, Elis. "Tracing Humanitarian Work: Caring about the Gaps in Documenting Knowledge Production." In "Caregiving as Method" dossier, Anooradha Iyer Siddiqi, Can Bilsel, Ana Miljački, and Garnette Cadogan, with Javairia Shahid. In "Care," guest edited by Torsten Lange and Gabrielle Schaad. *gta Papers* 7 (2022): 119–24.

Merry, Sally Engle. *Gender Violence: A Cultural Perspective.* Malden, MA: Wiley-Blackwell, 2009.

Merry, Sally Engle. "Introduction: States of Violence." In *The Practice of Human Rights: Tracking Law Between the Global and the Local*, edited by Mark Goodale and Sally Engle Merry, 41–48. Cambridge: Cambridge University Press, 2007.

Mezzadra, Sandro, and Brett Nielson. *Border as Method, or, the Multiplication of Labor*. Durham, NC: Duke University Press, 2013.

Mire, Sada. "Comment 2: The Role of Cultural Heritage in the Basic Needs of East African Pastoralists." Supplement, *African Study Monographs*, no. 53 (March 2017): 152.

Mire, Sada. *Divine Fertility: The Continuity in Transformation of an Ideology of Sacred Kinship in Northeast Africa*. London: Routledge, 2020.

Mitchell, Timothy. *Rule of Experts: Egypt, Techno-Politics, Modernity*. Berkeley: University of California Press, 2002.

Miyonga, Rose. "Colonial Afterlives: Land and the Emotional History of the Mau Mau War." *Funambulist*, February 22, 2022. https://thefunambulist.net/magazine/the-land/colonial-afterlives-land-and-the-emotional-history-of-the-mau-mau-war.

Monk, Daniel Bertrand, and Andrew Herscher. *The Global Shelter Imaginary: IKEA Humanitarianism and Rightless Relief.* Minneapolis: University of Minnesota Press, 2021.

Monk, Daniel Bertrand, and Jacob Mundy, eds. *The Post-Conflict Environment: Investigation and Critique*. Ann Arbor: University of Michigan Press, 2014.

Mostov, Julie. *Soft Borders: Rethinking Sovereignty and Democracy*. New York: Palgrave Macmillan, 2008.

Moyn, Samuel. *The Last Utopia: Human Rights in History*. Cambridge, MA: Belknap Press of Harvard University Press, 2010.

Moyo, Dambisa. *Dead Aid: Why Aid Is Not Working and How There Is a Better Way for Africa.* New York: Farrar, Straus, and Giroux, 2009.

Musmar, Aya. "Witnessing as a Feminist Spatial Practice: Encountering the Refugee Camp beyond Recognition." PhD diss., University of Sheffield, 2020.

Mutongi, Kenda. *Matatu: A History of Popular Transportation in Nairobi*. Chicago: University of Chicago Press, 2017.

Muzaffar, M. Ijlal. "Boundary Games: Ecochard, Doxiadis, and the Refugee Housing Projects under Military Rule in Pakistan, 1953–1959." In *Governing by Design: Architecture, Economy, and Politics in the Twentieth Century*, edited by Aggregate Architectural History Collaborative, 142–78. Pittsburgh, PA: University of Pittsburgh Press, 2012.

Muzaffar, M. Ijlal. "God's Gamble: Self-Help Architecture and the Housing of Risk." In *Architecture in Development: Systems and the Emergence of the Global South*, edited by Arindam Dutta, Ateya Khorakiwala, Ayala Levin, Fabiola López Durán, and Ijlal Muzaffar, for Aggregate Architectural History Collaborative, 47–62. London: Routledge, 2022.

Muzaffar, M. Ijlal. "The Periphery Within: Modern Architecture and the Making of the Third World." PhD diss., Massachusetts Institute of Technology, 2007.

Naimou, Angela. "Preface." *Humanity* 8, no. 3 (Winter 2017): 511–17, 580.

Ndaliko, Chérie Rivers, and Samuel Anderson. Introduction to *The Art of Emergency: Aesthetics and Aid in African Crises*, edited by Chérie Rivers Ndaliko and Samuel Anderson, 1–29. Oxford: Oxford University Press, 2020.

Nixon, Rob. *Slow Violence and the Environmentalism of the Poor*. Cambridge, MA: Harvard University Press, 2011.

Nolan, Ginger. "Cash-Crop Design: Architectures of Land, Knowledge, and Alienation in Twentieth-Century Kenya." *Architectural Theory Review* 3 (December 2017): 280–301.

Nolan, Ginger. *The Neocolonialism of the Global Village*. Minneapolis: University of Minnesota Press, 2018.

Nugent, Paul, and A. I. Asiwaju. *African Boundaries: Barriers, Conduits and Opportunities*. London: Pinter, 1996.

Nyerere, Julius Kambarage. "The Arusha Declaration: Socialism and Self-Reliance." In *Freedom and Socialism / Uhuru Na Ujamaa: A Selection from Writings and Speeches 1965–1967*. Dar Es Salaam: Oxford University Press, 1968.

Ochieng, William Robert, and Robert M. Maxon, eds. *An Economic History of Kenya*. Nairobi: East African Educational Publishers, 1992.

Ogot, Bethwell A. "The Decisive Years 1956–63." In *Decolonization and Independence in Kenya, 1940–93*, edited by Bethwell A. Ogot and William Robert Ochieng, 48–71. London: James Currey, 1995.

Ogot, Bethwell A., and William Robert Ochieng, eds. *Decolonization and Independence in Kenya, 1940–93*. London: James Currey, 1995.

Okoye, "Enigmatic Mobilities / Historical Mobilities." In *African Mobilities*, edited by Mpho Matsipa, 2018. https://archive.africanmobilities.org/discourse/2018/05/enigmatic-mobilities-historical-mobilities/.

Oliver, Kelly. *Carceral Humanitarianism: Logics of Refugee Detention*. Minneapolis: University of Minnesota Press, 2017.

Oluoch-Olunya, Garnette. "Contextualising Post-Independence Anglophone African Writing: Ayi Kwei Armah and Ngugi wa Thiong'o Compared." PhD diss., University of Glasgow, 2000.

Ophir, Adi. "The Sovereign, the Humanitarian, and the Terrorist." In *Nongovernmental Politics*, edited by Michel Feher, Gaëlle Krikorian, and Yates McKee, 161–66. New York: Zone, 2007.

Osayimwese, Itohan. *Colonialism and Modern Architecture in Germany*. Pittsburgh, PA: University of Pittsburgh Press, 2017.

Osayimwese, Itohan. "On Architecture and the Restitution of Cultural Heritage." Eduard F. Sekler talk delivered at the Society of Architectural Historians annual meeting, April 28, 2022. https://www.sah.org/2022/sekler-talk?_zs=7XjhX&_zl=xsIv2.

Osborne, Myles. *Ethnicity and Empire in Kenya: Loyalty and Martial Race among the Kamba, c. 1800 to the Present*. New York: Cambridge University Press, 2014.

Otero-Pailos, Jorge. *Architecture's Historical Turn: Phenomenology and the Rise of the Postmodern*. Minneapolis: University of Minnesota Press, 2010.

Owuor, Yvonne Adhiambo. *Dust*. London: Granta, 2014.

Ozaki, Ana G. "Afro-Brazilian Lenses: Quilombo Urbanism in Rio de Janeiro's Pequena África." In *Decolonizing the Spatial History of the Americas*, edited by Fernando Luiz Lara, 100–113. Austin: Center for American Architecture and Design at the University of Texas at Austin, 2021.

Pallister-Wilkins, Polly. *Humanitarian Borders: Unequal Mobility and Saving Lives*. London: Verso, 2022.

Pasquetti, Silvia, and Romola Sanyal, eds. *Displacement: Global Conversations on Refuge*. Manchester: Manchester University Press, 2020.

Perera, Suvendrini. *Australia and the Insular Imagination: Beaches, Borders, Boats, and Bodies*. New York: Palgrave Macmillan, 2009.

Perera, Suvendrini. "Oceanic Corpo-graphies, Refugee Bodies and the Making and Unmaking of Waters." In "Water," guest edited by Rutvica Andrijasevic and Laleh Khalili, *Feminist Review* 103 no. 1 (March 2013): 58–79.

Perera, Suvendrini. "Sexual Violence and the Border: Colonial Genealogies of US and Australian Immigration Detention Regimes." *Social & Legal Studies* 30, no. 1 (2021): 66–79.

Pérouse de Montclos, Marc-Antoine, and Peter Mwangi Kagwanja. "Refugee Camps or Cities? The Socio-Economic Dynamics of the Dadaab and Kakuma Camps in Northern Kenya." *Journal of Refugee Studies* 13, no. 2 (2000): 205–22.

Phelan, Kevin P. Q. "From an Idea to Action: The Evolution of Médicins Sans Frontières." In *The New Humanitarians: Inspiration, Innovations, and Blueprints for Visionaries*, edited by Chris E. Stout, vol. 1, *Changing Global Health Inequities*, 1–29. London: Praeger, 2009.

Pieris, Anoma, ed. *Architecture on the Borderline: Boundary Politics and Built Space*. Abingdon, UK: Routledge, 2019.

Pieris, Anoma, ed., and Lynne Horiuchi. *The Architecture of Confinement: Incarceration Camps of the Pacific War*. Cambridge: Cambridge University Press, 2022.

Pollock, Griselda. *Differencing the Canon: Feminist Desire and the Writing of Art's Histories*. London: Routledge, 1999.

Povinelli, Elizabeth A. *Geontologies: A Requiem to Late Liberalism*. Durham, NC: Duke University Press, 2016.

Povinelli, Elizabeth A. "Routes/Worlds." *e-flux Journal*, September 2011. https://www.e-flux.com/journal/27/67991/routes-worlds/.

Povinelli, Elizabeth A. "The Will to Be Otherwise / The Effort of Endurance." *South Atlantic Quarterly* 111, no. 3 (2012): 453–75.

Prussin, Labelle. *African Nomadic Architecture: Space, Place, and Gender*. Washington, DC: Smithsonian Institution Press, 1995.

Puar, Jasbir K. *Terrorist Assemblages: Homonationalism in Queer Times*. Durham, NC: Duke University Press, 2017.

Puig de la Bellacasa, Maria. *Matters of Care: Speculative Ethics in More than Human Worlds*. Minneapolis: University of Minnesota Press, 2017.

Purpura, Allyson. "Framing the Ephemeral." In "Ephemeral Arts 1," guest edited by Allyson Purpura. *African Arts* 42, no. 3 (Autumn 2009): 11–15.

Rael, Ronald. *Borderwall as Architecture: A Manifesto for the U.S.-Mexico Boundary*. Oakland: University of California Press, 2017.

Ramirez, Enrique. "Airs of Modernity, 1881–1914." PhD diss., Princeton University, 2013.

Rao, Anupama. *The Caste Question: Dalits and the Politics of Modern India*. Berkeley: University of California Press, 2009.

Rao, Anupama, and Steven Pierce. "Discipline and the Other Body: Humanitarianism, Violence, and the Colonial Exception." In *Discipline and the Other Body: Correction, Corporeality, Colonialism*, edited by Steven Pierce and Anupama Rao, 1–35. Durham, NC: Duke University Press, 2006.

Rawes, Peg, Stephen Loo, and Timothy Mathews, eds. *Poetic Biopolitics: Practices of Relation in Architecture and the Arts*. London: I. B. Tauris, 2016.

Rawlence, Ben. *City of Thorns: Nine Lives in the World's Largest Refugee Camp*. New York: Picador, 2016.

Redfield, Peter. "Bioexpectations: Life Technologies as Humanitarian Goods." *Public Culture* 24, no. 1 (2012): 157–84.

Redfield, Peter. "Cleaning up the Cold War: Global Humanitarianism and the Infrastructure of Crisis Response." In *Entangled Geographies: Empire and Technopolitics in the Global Cold War*, edited by Gabrielle Hecht, 267–91. Cambridge, MA: MIT Press, 2011.

Redfield, Peter. *Life in Crisis: The Ethical Journey of Doctors Without Borders*. Berkeley: University of California Press, 2013.

Rehman, Nida. "Primary Materials: Reading Lahore's Disobedient Landscape." In "Architecture as a Form of Knowledge," dossier edited by Anooradha Iyer Siddiqi. *Comparative Studies of South Asia, Africa, and the Middle East* 40, no. 3 (2020): 565–83.

Rieff, David. *A Bed for the Night: Humanitarianism in Crisis*. New York: Simon and Schuster, 2002.

Rizvi, Kishwar. "Contingency and Architectural Speculation." *Comparative Studies of South Asia, Africa, and the Middle East* 40, no. 3 (2020): 584–95.

Rodney, Walter. *How Europe Underdeveloped Africa*. London: Bogle-L'Ouverture Publications, 1972.

Roy, Ananya. "Slumdog Cities: Rethinking Subaltern Urbanism." *International Journal of Urban and Regional Research* 35, no. 2 (2011): 223–38.

Roy, Arundhati. "The Pandemic Is a Portal." *Financial Times*, April 3, 2020. https://www.ft.com/content/10d8f5e8-74eb-11ea-95fe-fcd274e920ca.

Roy, Srila. "The Ethical Ambivalence of Resistant Violence: Notes from Postcolonial South Asia." *Feminist Review* (2009): 135–53.

Ruiz, Rafico. *Slow Disturbance: Infrastructural Mediation on the Settler Colonial Resource Frontier.* Durham, NC: Duke University Press, 2021.

Said, Edward. *After the Last Sky: Palestinian Lives*. New York: Columbia University Press, 1999.

Samatar, Ahmed Ismail. "Somalia: Statelessness as Homelessness." In *The African State: Reconsiderations*, edited by Abdi Ismail Samatar and Ahmed Ismail Samatar, 217–51. Portsmouth, NH: Heinemann, 2002.

Samudzi, Zoé. "Camps, Archives, and Ancestors." Presentation in Columbia University seminar "Studies in Contemporary Africa," January 26, 2021.

Samudzi, Zoé. "Capturing German South West Africa: Racial Production, Land Claims, and Belonging in the Afterlife of the Herero and Nama Genocide." PhD diss., University of California, San Francisco, 2021.

Samuel, Kumudini, Claire Slatter, and Vagisha Gunasekara, eds. *Political Economy of Conflict and Violence against Women: Cases from the South*. London: Zed, 2019.

Sandvik, Kristin Bergtora. "The Physicality of Legal Consciousness: Suffering and the Production of Credibility in Refugee Resettlement." In *Humanitarianism and Suffering: The Mobilization of Empathy*, edited by Richard Ashby Wilson and Richard Brown, 223–44. Cambridge: Cambridge University Press, 2009.

Sanyal, Romola. "An Architecture of Displacement: Spatializing Identity and Refugee Space in Beirut and Calcutta." PhD diss., University of California, Berkeley, 2008.

Sanyal, Romola. "Squatting in Camps: Building and Insurgency in Spaces of Refuge." *Urban Studies* 48, no. 5 (2011): 877–90.

Scarry, Elaine. *The Body in Pain: The Making and Unmaking of the World.* New York: Oxford University Press, 1987.

Schlee, Günther, and Abdullahi A. Shongolo. "*Pax Borana*." In *Islam and Ethnicity in Northern Kenya and Southern Ethiopia*, 19–38. Woodbridge, UK: James Currey, 2012.

Sclar, Elliott D. *You Don't Always Get What You Pay For: The Economics of Privatization.* Ithaca, NY: Cornell University Press, 2000.

Scott, Felicity Dale Elliston. *Architecture or Techno-Utopia: Politics after Modernism*. Cambridge, MA: MIT Press, 2007.

Scott, Felicity Dale Elliston. *Outlaw Territories: Environments of Insecurity*. New York: Zone, 2016.

Scott, James C. *The Art of Not Being Governed: An Anarchist History of Upland Southeast Asia*. New Haven, CT: Yale University Press, 2011.

Scott-Smith, Tom. "Beyond the Boxes: Refugee Shelter and the Humanitarian Politics of Life." *American Ethnologist* 46, no. 4 (November 2019): 509–21.

Scott-Smith, Tom. "The Fetishism of Humanitarian Objects and the Management of Malnutrition in Emergencies." *Third World Quarterly* 34, no. 5 (2013): 913–28.

Scott-Smith, Tom. "A Slightly Better Shelter?" In "Little Development Devices / Humanitarian Goods," edited by Stephen J. Collier, Jamie Cross, Peter Redfield, and Alice Street. *Limn* 9 (November 2017): 67–73.

Seethaler-Wari, Shahd, Somayeh Chitchian, and Maja Momić, eds. *Inhabiting Displacement: Architecture and Authorship*. Basel: Birkhäuser, 2022.

Sekulić, Dubravka. "Constructing Non-Alignment: The Case of Construction Enterprise Energoprojekt, 1961–1989, Architecture, Construction Industry and Yugoslavia in the World." PhD diss., ETH Zurich, 2020.

Sen, Uditi. *Citizen Refugee: Forging the Indian Nation after Partition*. Cambridge: Cambridge University Press, 2018.

Shahidul Alam: Truth to Power. Exhibition, Rubin Museum of Art, November 8, 2019–January 3, 2021.

Shankar, Shobana. *An Uneasy Embrace: Africa, India and the Spectre of Race*. London: Hurst, 2021.

Sheik, S. Abdi. *Blood on the Runway: The Wagalla Massacre of 1984*. Nairobi: Northern Publishing House, 2007.

Shire, Warsan. "Home." In *Bless the Daughter Raised by a Voice in Her Head*, 24–25. New York: Random House, 2022.

Shringarpure, Bhakti. "Empire and Ambivalence." *Africa Is a Country*, November 24, 2017. https://africasacountry.com/2017/11/empire-and-ambivalence-ngugi-wa-thiongo-maya-jasanoff-and-joseph-conrad.

Siddiqi, Anooradha Iyer. "Architecture as a Form of Knowledge." *Comparative Studies of South Asia, Africa, and the Middle East* 40, no. 3 (December 2020): 24–34.

Siddiqi, Anooradha Iyer. "Architecture Culture, Humanitarian Expertise: From the Tropics to Shelter, 1953–1993." *Journal of the Society of Architectural Historians* 76, no. 3 (September 2017): 367–84.

Siddiqi, Anooradha Iyer. "Crafting the Archive: Minnette De Silva, Architecture, and History." *Journal of Architecture* 22, no. 8 (2017): 1299–1336.

Siddiqi, Anooradha Iyer. "Dadaab Is a Place on Earth: Land and the Migrant Archive." In *Writing Architectural History: Evidence and Narrative in the Twenty-First Century*, edited by Daniel M. Abramson, Michael Osman, and Zeynep Çelik Alexander for Aggregate Architectural History Collaborative, 227–34. Pittsburgh, PA: University of Pittsburgh Press, 2021.

Siddiqi, Anooradha Iyer. "Dadaab, Kenya: Architecting the Border: The Hut and the Frontier at Work." In "Architecture and Colonialism," *The Funambulist: Politics of Space and Bodies* 10 (March–April 2017): 28–33.

Siddiqi, Anooradha Iyer. "Dadaab (Kenya): L'histoire architecturale d'un territoire non identifé." In *Un Monde de Camps*, edited by Michel Agier, 149–63. Paris: Les Editions de la Découverte, 2014.

Siddiqi, Anooradha Iyer. "Emergency or Development? Architecture as Industrial Humanitarianism." In "Camp Cities," guest edited by Julia Hartmann, Franziska Laue, Pia Lorenz, and Philipp Misselwitz. *Trialog: A Journal for Planning and Building in the Third World*, no. 112–13 (2013): 28–31.

Siddiqi, Anooradha Iyer. "Ephemerality." In "Concept Histories of the Urban," dossier guest edited by Anupama Rao and Casey Primel. *Comparative Studies of South Asia, Africa, and the Middle East* 40, no. 1 (May 2020): 24–34.

Siddiqi, Anooradha Iyer. "Heritage as Restitution: The Dadaab Refugee Camps, Kenya." *Curator: The Museum Journal* 65, no. 3 (July 2022): 673–77.

Siddiqi, Anooradha Iyer. "Humanitarian Homemaker, Emergency Subject: Questions of Housing and Domesticity." In *Architecture and the Housing Question*, edited by Juliana Maxim and Can Bilsel, 39–58. London: Routledge, 2021.

Siddiqi, Anooradha Iyer. "Humanitarianism and Monumentality." In "Camp Cities," guest edited by Julia Hartmann, Franziska Laue, Pia Lorenz, and Philipp Misselwitz. *Trialog: A Journal for Planning and Building in the Third World*, no. 112–13 (2013): 14–18.

Siddiqi, Anooradha Iyer. "In Favor of Seeing Specific Histories." In "A Discussion on the Global and the Universal," dossier edited by Daniel Bertrand Monk, Andrew Herscher, Miriam Ticktin, Anooradha Iyer Siddiqi, Lucia Allais, M. Ijlal Muzaffar, Mark Jarzombek, and Swati Chattopadhyay. *Grey Room* 61 (Fall 2015): 86–91.

Siddiqi, Anooradha Iyer. "On Humanitarian Architecture: A Story of a Border." In "Contemporary Refugee Timespaces," guest edited by Angela Naimou. *Humanity* 8, no. 3 (Winter 2017): 519–21.

Siddiqi, Anooradha Iyer. "Radio Free Refugee Camp: Spaces of Hygiene and Political Speech in Dadaab." Paper presented in "No Small Acts: Spatial Histories of Imprisonment and Resistance," session chaired by Ana María Léon and S. E. Eisterer, Society of Architectural Historians annual meeting, 2021.

Siddiqi, Anooradha Iyer. "Reversals: The University and the Camp." In *Inhabiting Displacement: Architecture and Authorship*, edited by Shahd Seethaler-Wari, Somayeh Chitchian, and Maja Momić, 36–46. Basel: Birkhäuser, 2022.

Siddiqi, Anooradha Iyer. "Scholarship as Mutual Aid." In "Caregiving as Method" dossier, Anooradha Iyer Siddiqi, Can Bilsel, Ana Miljački, and Garnette Cadogan, with Javairia Shahid. In "Care," guest edited by Torsten Lange and Gabrielle Schaad. *gta Papers* 7 (2022): 95–99.

Siddiqi, Anooradha Iyer. "A Shadow Heritage of the Humanitarian Colony: Dadaab's Foreclosure of the Urban Historical." In *Things Don't Really Exist until You Give Them a Name: Unpacking Urban Heritage*, edited by Rachel Lee, Diane Barbé, Anne-Katrin Fenk, and Philipp Misselwitz 148–53. Dar es Salaam: Mkuki na Nyota, 2017.

Siddiqi, Anooradha Iyer. "Shamso Abdullahi Farah." In *The Bloomsbury Global Encyclopedia of Women in Architecture*, edited by Lori Brown and Karen Burns. London: Bloomsbury, forthcoming.

Siddiqi, Anooradha Iyer. "Tracing Insecurities: Notations for an Architectural History of Forced Migration." *The Avery Review* 21 (January 2017): 113–23.

Siddiqi, Anooradha Iyer. "The University and the Camp." In "Contingency," guest edited by Dana Cuff and Will Davis. *Ardeth* 6 (July 2020): 137–51.

Siddiqi, Anooradha Iyer. "Writing With: Togethering, Difference, and Feminist Architectural Histories of Migration." In "Structural Instability," edited by Daniel Barber, Eduardo Rega, and e-flux Architecture. *e-flux Architecture*,

July 28, 2018. https://www.e-flux.com/architecture/structural-instability/208707/writing-with/.

Siddiqi, Anooradha Iyer, and Somayeh Chitchian. "To Shelter in Place for a Time Beyond." In *Making Home(s) in Displacement: Critical Reflections on a Spatial Practice*, edited by Luce Beeckmans, Alessandra Gola, Ashika Singh, and Hilde Heynen, 45–60. Leuven, Belgium: Leuven University Press, 2022.

Siddiqi, Anooradha Iyer, Irit Katz, and Mahmoud Keshavarz. "Emplacing Displacement." In *Design, Displacement, Migration: Spatial and Material Histories*, edited by Jilly Traganou and Sarah A. Lichtman. London: Routledge, 2023.

Siddiqi, Anooradha Iyer, and Rachel Lee. "On Collaborations: Feminist Architectural Histories of Migration." In "On Collaborations: Feminist Architectural Histories of Migration," edited by Anooradha Iyer Siddiqi and Rachel Lee, for Aggregate Architectural History Collaborative. *Aggregate* (2022). http://we-aggregate.org/piece/on-collaborations-feminist-architectural-histories-of-migration.

Siddiqi, Anooradha Iyer, and Rachel Lee. "On Diffractions: Feminist Architectural Histories of Migration." In "Of Migration," edited by Anooradha Iyer Siddiqi and Rachel Lee. *Canadian Centre for Architecture* (2021–2022). https://www.cca.qc.ca/en/articles/issues/30/of-migration/81045/on-diffractions-feminist-architectural-histories-of-migration.

Siddiqi, Anooradha Iyer, and Rachel Lee. "On Margins: Feminist Architectural Histories of Migration." In "Feminist Architectural Histories of Migration," edited by Anooradha Iyer Siddiqi and Rachel Lee. *ABE Journal: Architecture beyond Europe* 16 (2019). https://doi.org/10.4000/abe.6932.

Siddiqi, Anooradha Iyer, and Alishine Osman. "Traversals: In and Out of the Dadaab Refugee Camps." In "Urban Divides," edited by Meghan McAllister and Mahdi Sabbagh. *Perspecta: The Yale Architectural Journal* 50 (September 2017): 173–91.

Siddiqi, Anooradha Iyer, and Vazira Fazila-Yacoobali Zamindar. "Partitions: Architectures of Statelessness." *e-flux Architecture*, March 2022. https://www.e-flux.com/architecture/positions/454156/partitions-architectures-of-statelessness/.

Simone, Abdoumaliq. "People as Infrastructure: Intersecting Fragments in Johannesburg." *Public Culture* 16, no. 3 (2004): 407–29.

Simms, Brendan, and D. J. B. Trim, eds. *Humanitarian Intervention: A History*. Cambridge: Cambridge University Press, 2011.

Singh, Ashika, Alessandra Gola, Luce Beeckmans, and Hilde Heynen, eds. *Displacement and Domesticity since 1945: Refugees, Migrants, and Expats Making Homes.* Teaching tool, European Architectural History Network conference, 2019.

Slim, Hugo. "Establishment Radicals: An Historical Overview of British NGOs." In *Many Reasons to Intervene: French and British Approaches to Humanitarian Action*, edited by Karl Blanchet and Boris Martin, 27–40. London: Hurst, 2011.

Sliwinski, Sharon. "The Aesthetics of Human Rights." *Culture, Theory and Critique* 50, no. 1 (2009): 25–27.

Sliwinski, Sharon. *Human Rights in Camera*. Chicago: University of Chicago Press, 2011.

Smirl, Lisa. *Spaces of Aid: How Cars, Compounds, and Hotels Shape Humanitarianism*. London: Zed, 2015.

Smith, Linda Tuhiwai. *Decolonizing Methodologies: Research and Indigenous Peoples*. London: Zed, 2021.

Solnit, Rebecca. *A Paradise Built in Hell: The Extraordinary Communities that Arise in Disaster.* New York: Penguin Random House, 2010.

Somer, Kees. *The Functional City: The CIAM and Cornelis van Eesteren, 1928–1960*. Rotterdam: NAi, 2007.

Sommers, Marc. "The Dynamics of Coordination." Occasional Paper 40, Watson Institute for International Studies, 2000.

Spear, Thomas T. "Traditional Myths and Historians' Myths: Variations on the Singwaya Theme of Mijikenda Origins." *History in Africa* 1 (1974): 67–84.

Spivak, Gayatri Chakravorty. "Can the Subaltern Speak?" In *Marxism and the Interpretation of Culture*, edited by Laurence Grossberg and Cary Nelson, 24–28. Urbana: University of Illinois Press, 1988.

Stanek, Łukasz. *Architecture in Global Socialism: Eastern Europe, West Africa, and the Middle East in the Cold War.* Princeton, NJ: Princeton University Press, 2020.

Stevens, Jacob. "Prisons of the Stateless: The Derelictions of UNHCR." *New Left Review* 42 (November/December 2006): 53–68.

Strayer, Robert. *The Making of Mission Communities in East Africa: Anglicans and Africans in Colonial Kenya, 1875–1935*. London: Heinemann, 1978.

Tamale, Sylvia. *Decolonization and Afro-Feminism*. Ottawa: Daraja, 2020.

Tavares, Rui. *O pequeno livro do grande terramoto*. Lisbon: Tinta-da-China, 2005.

Tayob, Huda. "Transnational Practices of Care and Refusal." *e-flux Architecture*, September 2021. https://www.e-flux.com/architecture/coloniality-infrastructure/411251/transnational-practices-of-care-and-refusal/.

Tayob, Huda, Suzi Hall, and Thandi Loewenson. "Race, Space, and Architecture: An Open-Access Curriculum." http://racespacearchitecture.org/openaccesscurriculum.html. Accessed March 16, 2023.

Terry, Fiona. *Condemned to Repeat? The Paradox of Humanitarian Action*. Ithaca, NY: Cornell University Press, 2002.

Thiong'o, Ngũgĩ wa. "Abdilatif Abdalla and the Voice of Prophecy." In *Abdilatif Abdalla: Poet in Politics*, edited by Rose Marie Beck and Kai Kresse, 11–18. Dar es Salaam: Mkuki na Nyota, 2016.

Thiong'o, Ngũgĩ wa. *Decolonising the Mind: The Politics of Language in African Literature*. Oxford: James Currey, 2006.

Thiong'o, Ngũgĩ wa. "The English Master and the Colonial Bondsman." In *Globalectics: Theory and the Politics of Knowing*, 9–26. New York: Columbia University Press, 2012.

Thomson, Marnie Jane. "Black Boxes of Bureaucracy: Transparency and Opacity in the Resettlement Process of Congolese Refugees." *Political and Legal Anthropology Review* 35, no. 2 (2012): 186–205.

Thomson, Marnie Jane. "'Giving Cases Weight': Congolese Refugees' Tactics for Resettlement Selection." In *Refugee Resettlement: Power, Politics and Humanitarian Governance*, edited by Adèle Garnier, Liliana Lyra Jubilut and Kristin Bergtora Sandvik, 203–22. Oxford: Berghahn, 2018.

Thomson, Marnie Jane. "Mud, Dust, and Marougé: Precarious Construction in a Congolese Refugee Camp." *Architectural Theory Review* 19, no. 3 (2015): 376–92.

Thomson, Marnie Jane. "Stories of Darkness: Congolese Refugees, Humanitarian Governance, and a Neglected Conflict." PhD diss., University of Colorado Boulder, 2016.

Thomson, Marnie Jane. "What Documents Do Not Do: Papering Persecution and Moments of Recognition in a Refugee Camp." *Anthropologica* 60 (2018): 223–35.

Thurston, Anne. *Smallholder Agriculture in Colonial Kenya: The Official Mind and the Swynnerton Plan*. Cambridge: African Studies Centre, 1987.

Ticktin, Miriam. "Building a Feminist Commons in the Time of COVID-19." *Signs: Journal of Women in Culture and Society*. http://signsjournal.org/covid/ticktin/. Accessed January 9, 2022.

Ticktin, Miriam. *Casualties of Care: Immigration and the Politics of Humanitarianism in France*. Berkeley: University of California Press, 2011.

Ticktin, Miriam. "From Redundancy to Recognition: Transnational Humanitarianism and the Production of Nonmoderns." In *Forces of Compassion: Humanitarianism between Ethics and Politics*, edited by Erica Bornstein and Peter Redfield, 175–98. Santa Fe, NM: School for Advanced Research Press, 2011.

Ticktin, Miriam. "Humanitarianism's History of the Singular." In "A Discussion on the Global and the Universal," dossier edited by Daniel Bertrand Monk, Andrew Herscher, Miriam Ticktin, Anooradha Iyer Siddiqi, Lucia Allais, M. Ijlal Muzaffar, Mark Jarzombek, and Swati Chattopadhyay. *Grey Room* 61 (Fall 2015): 81–85.

Trim, D. J. B. "'If a Prince Use Tyrannie towards His People': Interventions on Behalf of Foreign Populations in Early Modern Europe." In *Humanitarian Intervention: A History*, edited by Brendan Simms and D. J. B. Trim, 29–66. Cambridge: Cambridge University Press, 2011.

Trouillot, Michel-Rolph. *Silencing the Past: Power and the Production of History*. Boston: Beacon, 2015.

Tsing, Anna Lowenhaupt. *The Mushroom at the End of the World: On the Possibility of Life in Capitalist Ruins*. Princeton, NJ: Princeton University Press, 2017.

Turton, E. R. "Somali Resistance to Colonial Rule and the Development of Somali Political Activity in Kenya 1893–1960." *Journal of African History* 13, no. 1 (1972): 117–43.

Umbach, Maiken, and Bernd-Rüdiger Hüppauf, eds. *Vernacular Modernism: Heimat, Globalization, and the Built Environment*. Stanford, CA: Stanford University Press, 2005.

Verdirame, Guglielmo. "Human Rights and Refugees: The Case of Kenya." *Journal of Refugee Studies* 121 (1999): 54–77.

Vidal, Claudine, and Jacques Pinel. "MSF 'Satellites': A Strategy Underlying Different Medical Practices." In *Medical Innovations in Humanitarian Situations: The Work of Médecins Sans Frontières*, edited by Jean-Hervé Bradol and Claudine Vidal, 22–38. New York: MSF, 2011.

Walia, Harsha. *Border and Rule: Global Migration, Capitalism, and the Rise of Racist Nationalism*. Chicago: Haymarket, 2021.

Warah, Rasna. *War Crimes: How Warlords, Politicians, Foreign Governments and Aid Agencies Conspired to Create a Failed State in Somalia*. Bloomington, IN: Author House, 2014.

Weitzberg, Keren. "The Unaccountable Census: Colonial Enumeration and Its Implications for the Somali People of Kenya." *Journal of African History* 56, no. 3 (2015): 409–28.

Weitzberg, Keren. *We Do Not Have Borders: Greater Somalia and the Predicaments of Belonging in Kenya*. Athens: Ohio University Press, 2017.

Weizman, Eyal. *Hollow Land: Israel's Architecture of Occupation*. London: Verso, 2007.

Wendel, Delia. "The Materiality of Interpellation: Modern Roofs for Modern Citizens." In "The Ethics of Stability: Rebuilding Rwanda after the 1994 Genocide." PhD diss., Harvard University, 2016.

Wendel, Delia. *Rwanda's Genocide Heritage*. Durham, NC: Duke University Press, 2023.

Wendel, Delia, and Fallon Samuels Aidoo, eds. *Spatializing Politics: Essays on Power and Place*. Cambridge, MA: Harvard University Press, 2015.

West, Cornel. "The New Cultural Politics of Difference." In *Out There: Marginalization and Contemporary Cultures*, edited by Russell Ferguson, Martha Gever, Thi Minh-Ha Trinh, and Cornel West, 19–36. Cambridge, MA: MIT Press, 1990.

Whittaker, Hannah. *Insurgency and Counterinsurgency in Kenya: A Social History of the Shifta Conflict, c. 1963–1968*. Leiden: Brill, 2015.

Whittaker, Hannah. "Legacies of Empire: State Violence and Collective Punishment in Kenya's North Eastern Province, c. 1963–Present." *Journal of Imperial and Commonwealth History* 43, no. 4 (2015): 641–57.

Whittaker, Hannah. "The Socioeconomic Dynamics of the *Shifta* Conflict in Kenya, c. 1963–8." *Journal of African History* 53, no. 3 (2012): 391–408.

Williams, Raymond. *The Long Revolution*. London: Chatto and Windus, 1961.

Williams, Raymond. "Structures of Feeling." In *Marxism and Literature*, 128–35. Oxford: Oxford University Press, 1977.

Willis, Justin. *Mombasa, the Swahili, and the Making of the Mijikenda*. Oxford: Clarendon, 1993.

Wilson, Mabel O. *Negro Building: Black Americans in the World of Fairs and Museums*. Berkeley: University of California Press, 2020.

Wilson, Mabel O. "Notes on the Virginia Capitol: Nation, Race, and Slavery in Jefferson's America." In *Race and Modern Architecture*, edited by Irene Cheng, Charles L. Davis II, and Mabel O. Wilson, 23–42. Pittsburgh, PA: University of Pittsburgh Press, 2020.

Wilson, Mabel O. "Provisional Demos: The Spatial Agency of Tent Cities." In *Design, Displacement, Migration: Spatial and Material Histories*, edited by Jilly Traganou and Sarah A. Lichtman. London: Routledge, 2023.

Wilson, Richard Ashby, and Richard Brown, eds. *Humanitarianism and Suffering: The Mobilization of Empathy*. Cambridge: Cambridge University Press, 2009.

Wynter, Sylvia. "On How We Mistook the Map for the Territory, and Re-imprisoned Ourselves in Our Unbearable Wrongness of Being, of *Désêtre*: Black Studies toward the Human Project." In *Not Only the Master's Tools: African-American Studies in Theory and Practice*, edited by Lewis R. Gordon and Jane Anna Gordon, 107–69. Boulder, CO: Paradigm, 2006.

Zaidi, Sarover. "Homing and Unhoming: Taxonomies of Living." *Chiraghdilli*, August 7, 2020. https://chiraghdilli.com/2020/08/07/homing-and-unhoming-taxonomies-of-living/.

Zamindar, Vazira Fazila-Yacoobali. *The Long Partition and the Making of Modern South Asia: Refugees, Boundaries, Histories*. New York: Columbia University Press, 2010.

Zeleke, Elleni Centime. *Ethiopia in Theory: Revolution and Knowledge Production, 1964–2016*. Leiden: Brill, 2019.

Zeller, Wolfgang, ed. "Special Issue: African Borderlands." *Critical African Studies* 5, no. 1 (March 2013): 1–3.

Zetter, Roger. *Shelter Provision and Settlement Policies for Refugees: A State of the Art Review*. Uppsala: Nordiska Afrikainstitutet, 1995.

Index

Note: Page numbers in *italics* indicate figures.

Abdi, Cawo M., 110
abolition: abolitionist feminist commitment, 48; architectures of, 114; and humanitarianism, 4, 26; and land enclosure, 27; quilombo urbanism and, 121; trade with slave owners, 121, 341n36. *See also* abolitionist settlement; Bombay Africans; land
abolitionist settlement, 341n22; from abolitionist mission to civilizing one, 100, 117–18; from abolition subjects to colonial subjects, 121; cohabitation of rescuer and rescued, 113, 115; farms in, 129; historical predecessor of refugee camps, 251; sedentarization and, 251. *See also* Church Missionary Society; Freretown
Abshir, Deqa, 306, 310
Abshir, Idil, 307
Adam, AbdulFatah, 309–10
Admassu, Emanuel, 316
African myrrh. See *Commiphora africana*
After the Last Sky: Palestinian Lives (Said), 39
Agamben, Giorgio, 76, 307, 308
Agier, Michel, 208
Aidid, Safa, 109
aid workers, 3, 4, 5, 8, 16, 29, 33, 35, 37, 38, 40; prestige of working in Dadaab, 15, 330n22
Akcan, Esra, 5
Akšamija, Azra, 254
Algeria, 127
alien card, 58
al-Shabaab, 280, 281
Anderson, Samuel, 250
anti-slavery movement, 117. *See also* Freretown
aqal. *See* tuqul (aqal, waab)
aquifer. *See* Merti acquifer
architecture, refugee camp: documentation of Dadaab's materiality, 207–9
architectures of immobilization, 309
archives: architects' drawings, importance of, 195, *196–97*, *198*, 199; classification practices, 188; Dagahaley settlement, plan of, *198*; declassification in 2012, 188; Hagadera settlement, plan of, *196–97*; invisibility of humanitarian settlements in, 245; migrant sources, 189; unclassified documents, 188
Arendt, Hannah, 76, 307, 308
Atanasoski, Neda, 90
Atellah, Juliet, 82
autonomy, 102, 279
Azoulay, Ariella Aïsha, 79, 337n35
Azraq camp, 254

Badbaado camp, 269, 270
Bagamoyo, 116
Bajuni community, 205–6; conflict with Kenyan businessmen, 206; double and triple displacement, 206; flight to Mombasa in 1991, 205; settlement at "Mogadishu camp," 206
Banda Aceh, 278
Banerjee, Prathama, 329n11
Ban, Shigeru, 259, 260, 261, 263, 356n32
Baraka, Amiri, 29

Bargash, Sultan of Zanzibar, 117
Barton, Sean, 269
Basel, 260
Bauer, Catherine, 160
Bauman, Emily, 167, 168
belonging: clan, concept of, 330n19; communities of, 15; pastoralists and, 24–25; pastoral migration, land, and borders, 22, 24; Somali history and threat to, 23–24
Benaco camp, 261–63, 357n34, 357nn37–38
Berger, John, 39
Bestemann, Catherine, 75, 124
biopolitics, 144, 162; biopolitical control, 144; limits of biopolitical theories, 144
biopower, 144, 145, 345n13
Blier, Suzanne, 189
Bombay Africans, *116*, 116–17, 341n28
Boran, 15, 23, 124, 340n15
Bordeaux-Mérignac Airport, 263
border-crossing artifacts, 256, 257, 291, 355n19. *See also* inflatable hospital
borderlands, 31, 112; boundary-making, 109; impact on nomads, 128–29. *See also* Somali history
Borders (Adam), 309–10, *313*
border(s), 310, *313*; colonial and humanitarian influence on, 23; eroding, 37, 334n73; kipande and, 57; and migration, 3, 77; nationalism and, 23; refugee camps, 52, 85; refugee status and, 84; state, 78, 83, 90; and unpartitioned land, 77, 337n28. *See also* partition(s) of land
Bouhabib, Hocine, 283
Brauman, Rony, 295
British East Africa Company, 43, 121, 122
Brown, Wendy, 53
building types, 46, 100, 107, 130–38. *See also* makuti; tuqul (aqal, waab)
built environment(s), 166, 187, 206, 217, 255, 259, 295; author's approach to, 34–35, 43–44, 209; historians, 79; role in military histories, 127. *See also* Dadaab built environment; Ifo 2 camp
burial ground (site). *See* grave(s) (tomb)
Burundian Hutu, 207
Cairo, 110, 162, 342n44
Calhoun, Craig, 191
Caminos, Horacio, 163
camp architecture: CARE managers' complaints, 203–4; divided spatial approach, 203; physical planning versus architectural development, 204; UNHCR and donors' expectations, 204
capitalism, 22, 27, 331n38, 347n46; capitalistic approaches, 135; capitalistic practices, 32, 129; capitalist settler state, 147; disaster strategies, 161; Kenya's capitalist orientation, 111; ruins of capitalist development, 143
capitalization of land in Kenya, 112, 114, 121
CARE: camp management, 200–203, 222, 225; compound gate and guardhouse, *91*; cultivation methods, 106, 115; distribution center, *232*, 241; elections, role in, 70, 71; microcredit program, 251, 252; shelters, 156
Carrier, Neil, 307
Casid, Jill, 106
Cassanelli, Lee, 110
Cave Bureau, 316, 318, *318*, 319
cemetery. *See* grave(s) (tomb)
CENDEP. *See* Centre for Development and Environmental Planning (CENDEP)
Centre de Réflexion sur l'Action et les Savoirs Humanitaires (CRASH), 281
Centre for Development and Environmental Planning (CENDEP), 163, 165
Centre for Refugee Studies at Moi University in Eldoret, 162
Cephas, Jay, 117, 138
Château de Penthes, Geneva, 165
Chatterjee, Partha, 124–25
China, 266, 278
Chitchian, Somayeh, 143, 146
Christian humanitarianism and settlements, 113–21
Christian missions, 26
Chuma, James, *116*; role similarity with Hassan, 116, 117
Church Missionary Society, 121, 122; cohabitation of rescuer and rescued, 115
CIAM. *See* Congrès Internationale d'Architecture Moderne (CIAM)

citizenship: acquisition of Kenyan, 57, 59; identification card, 59, 60; by marriage to a Kenyan, 59–60; of mixed-marriage children, 59–60; Somali, 59
Clapham, Christopher, 110
Coast Province, 205, 206
coercive environment: enclosure types, 100; manyatta, 113
coercive settlement. *See* Northern Frontier District (NFD); shifta; villagization
cohabitation(s), 43, 143; Dadaab, in, 14–15; ecological, 145; in emergency, 89; of rescuer and rescued, 115, 116
collaboration(s), 143, 149, 251, 253, 254. *See also* Dagahaley Girls United Center
collective(s): construction workers', 2; refugee construction, 35; women's, 47, 251–52, 253, 254. *See* also Dagahaley Girls United Center
colonial spatial practice(s), 108; building, 27–28; enclosures, 26–27; Northern Frontier, 25–26
colonization: articulations of struggle, 22, 331n38; and land grabs, 23, 33; and migratory worlds, 2; and postcolonial state, 22
Commiphora africana, 9, 81, 173, 220, *220*, 274
commodification: of aid, 250, 255; of design as infrastructure, 257, 263; of humanitarian objects, 257; of process, 264; of signature emergency artifact, 255, 256
Condemned to Repeat? The Paradox of Humanitarian Action (Terry), 296
Congrès Internationale d'Architecture Moderne (CIAM), 165–66, 348n60
Connelly, Maureen, 192, 203, 261, 262, 263, 301
constructed environment(s), 4, 145, 146, 306; in Dadaab, 20, 29, 33, 45, 78, 79, 102
contingent territory, 25, 100; Dadaab as, 111–13; Hassan's farm as example of construction in, 107; land in, 108; Somali history, 109–11
Cooper, Frederick, 115, 121
Corsellis, Tom, 167, 241
CRASH. *See* Centre de Réflexion sur l'Action et les Savoirs Humanitaires (CRASH)
criminalization of the nomadic and the pastoral, 99
critical pedagogy, 145
critical theory, 142, 143, 145, 149
cultivation: architecture of, 106–7; CARE methods, 106, 115; in emergency, 99; the Hassan way, 46, 100, 103–6; in Ifo 2, 149; liberatory settlement and Christian morality, 26, 46, 114–15; and sedentarization, 107
cultural capital, 115
Cuny, Frederick, 163, 164, 166, 167, 177, 254

Dadaab built environment, 3, 5; artifacts of, 17; cohabitations in, 89; communication infrastructure, 207; contradictions in, 17; diversity, reflection of, 209; ecology of domesticity in, 146–47; emergency and development in, 217; ephemerality in, 295–96; impact on representative governance, 8; marketing images of, 215–16; Merti aquifer, enabler of, 17; refugee mothers, contribution to, 39; sedentarization and, 99; sociospatial context of Dadaab, 9–21; tarps, tanks, and tents in, 254–55; in tuqul and makuti, 135; women behind, 297
Dagahaley camp, 99, *136–37*; planning and settlement of, 46, 47; security protocol for MSF staff, 36
Dagahaley Girls United Center, 297, 301
Dainese, Elisa, 250
D'Avignon, Robyn, 25
Davis, Ian, 163, 164, 166
decolonization: of Africa, 23; and perception of borders, 23; process in Kenya, 111, 124
decolonizing, 166; master narratives, 4; minds, 145
Department of Architecture, University of Cambridge, 167
design as infrastructure, 252
detention camps, 251
Deutsche Gesellschaft fur Technische Zusammenarbeit (GTZ), 54

development and emergency: CARE concerns, 201; tensions between, 200–207, 216–17
De Waal, Alex, 129
Dharia, Namita, 27
dispositif, 144, 345n14
disaster, 31, 94, 210, 346n27; management, 165; response to, 266
Dodier, Nicolas, 292
domestication of Africa, 118
domesticity(ies): as core spatial strategy, 146; definition, 160; ecology of, 146, 147; in emergency, 146, 161, 172; forms of, 172; in homemaking, 145, 146, 147, 149; as knowledge, 160; labor, based in, 175–76; and land, 175; migratory living, 172–73; paradoxes of, 173; and shelter, 141, 142–47, 172–77. *See also* Farah, Shamso Abdullahi; homemaking
domestic structuring, 173
Dom-Ino, 256
Dos Santos, Eugénio, 94
doubling, 53, 258; racial architecture of, 86, 89, 92, 308. *See also* partition(s) of the self
Doucet, Isabelle, 189
Doxiadis, Constantinos, 160
Drumtra, Jeff, 203
D'Souza, Radha, 4
Dualeh, M., 210
Dubai, 266
Du Bois, W. E. B., 53, 87, 93, 308
Durban, 266
dwelling(s), 36, 55, 79, 87, 149, 195, 202, 215, 269, 346n24, 361n2; delinked from land, 172; distance from food distribution centers, 67, 68; makeshift, 266; prefabricated, 163, 257, 258, 277; transience in Dadaab, 17; UNHCR design of, 199; "vernacular," 28. *See also* domesticit(y)ies; Farah, Shamso Abdullahi; homemaking; lightweight emergency tent (LWET); makuti; manyatta; NRC shelter(s); shelter: and domesticity; tarp (tarpaulin); tuqul (aqal, waab)
Dymaxion House, 257
earth, 17, 144; and belonging, 25, 175, 307, 316, 317; Google Earth, 2, 214, 310, 314, 316; Merti, *318*; paper and, 82
earthquakes, 93, 94, 256, 259, 283, 286, 291, 359n85
East Africa, 115, 133; first church in, 115–17; history of, 109–12; slave trade, 117–18. *See also* British East Africa Company; tuqul (aqal, waab)
East Timor, 278
École Nationale Supérieure des Beaux-Arts, 291
ecological cohabitations, 145
ecology(ies), 17, 20, 44, 48, 80, 102, 249; ecofeminist approach, 144; ecofeminist architectural histories of migration, 145–146; planetary, 143, 316–319, 317, 318. *See also* Cave Bureau; Dadaab built environment; domesticity(ies)
elections: clan support and, 71, 336n16; in Dadaab refugee camp, 69–71, 84, 85; duties of leaders, 71; echoes of colonial practices, 85; process of and implications of, in Ifo camp, 6–8, 69–71
emancipation: and quilombos, 121
emergency, 2, 4, 8, 44, 75, 80, 81, 84; architecture and, 1, 3, 5, 20, 27, 32, 39, 48, 52; and built environment, 39; domesticities of, 46; environment, 26, 39; humanitarian relief and, 25, 30, 31, 32, 33, 45, 46, 47; intervention and human rights, 45; partitioning of the self, 52, 53; shelter, 1; space and time, impact on, 2, 22; survival in, 39, 43
emergency territory: and development, tensions between, 200–205; establishment of, 190–94, 190–200; production of, 107, 207; selection of, 194. *See also* contingent territory
enclosures: and capitalism, 27; Christian missions, 26; claims to land, 7; coercive settlement, 113, 122–30; and criminalization of itinerancy, 27; Dadaab and "open-air prison," 2, 329n2; and development, 126; identity documents and, 81, 84; villagization (labor camps,

manyatta), 26; liberatory settlement, 113, 114–22; native reserves, 26; problem of, 45; refugee camps and carcerality, 40; sedentarization and, 28; smallholder production, 126
ephemerality, 1; architecture and, 21, 27, 28, 173, 177, 201, 215–16; existential and representational, 21; paper infrastructures and, 82; permanent impermanence, 21, 199, 200, 201, 216, 217, 245; tarp and, 171, 266; wage inequality and, 66, 67
ethic, an, 39–44
ethnic groups, 23, 110, 114; Boran, 15, 23, 124, 340n15; Geluba, 124; Gĩkũyũ, 25, 126, 131, 334n74; Gosha, 75; Maa, 124; Rendille, 23, 124; Sakuye, 124; Samburu, 23, 113, 124, 340n15, 340n20; Somali (*see* Somali)
Everill, Bronwen, 117
expertise, 142, 146, 147, 149–50, 156, 159; The Camp Management Toolkit, 346n34. *See also* humanitarian expertise

family tent, *275*; design iterations, 274–80; signature practice of design, 276. *See also* lightweight emergency tent (LWET)
Fanon, Frantz, 53, 86, 93, 308
Farah, Shamso Abdullahi, 2, 150, *151*, *153*, 253; conversation with, 152–155; domesticity, 159; expertise on emergency shelter, 163, 166, 168, 169, 170; self-help housing, 160; shop, *171*; and worldmaking, 176–77. *See also* domesticity(ies); homemaking; shelter
Fardanesh, Ghassem, 276
farm: Maganai Saddiq Hassan's, 103–6; pedagogy of, 106–7. *See also* shambas (farm plots)
Fassin, Didier, 191, 257
feminist, 7; abolitionist, 48; construction, 138; questions and tuqul, 27; thought, 4, 22. *See also* ecology(ies): ecofeminist architectural histories of migration; biopower
Fichard, Philippe, *264*, *265*
First International Workshop on Improved Shelter Response and Environment for Refugees, *164*, 165–67, 260, 348n56
fixing asymmetry in space: asymmetries and conflicts, aggravation of, 205; Bajuni community, 205–6; documentation of Dadaab's materiality, 207–9; Ifo, Dagahaley, and Hagadera settlements, 207; improvement in living, 207–8; living and cultural spaces, demarcation of, 206; refugees versus host communities in, 207; sociocultural difference, inscription of, 208; Somali majority community, material cultures, 207; Somali sections in Ifo, 208; Sudanese constructions in Dagahaley, 208; taar (telegram or cable), use of, 207
fixing encampment in time: aerial photographic material, 211; Dagahaley plans, 211; early architectural plans for Dadaab, 210–11; graphic documentation in Dadaab, 209–10; Hagadera plans, 210; humanitarian activity, promotion, and marketing images, 215–16, *216*; Ifo camp representative plan, 210, *212*, *213*; IRD work, 211; Iwansson's draft sketch, 210; photos by private individuals, 210; satellite photographic material, 211, *214*, 214–15; self-narration on visual media by residents, 210
food distribution, refugee camps: advantage of proximity to, 230–31; CARE sheds, Ifo camp, *232*; distribution process control, 243; donkey carts, use in transportation, 244; food items for trade, 244; Ifo camp center, *232*, *234*, *235*, *236*, *238–39*; refugee arrival, importance of time in, 244–45; refugee selection for, 242–43; storage warehouses, 242
food storage unit, 173, *174*, *233*
form-making, 30, 31, 251
Foucault, Michel, 144, 145
Fragmented II (Deqa Abshir), *303*, 307, 310
Fraiman, Susan, 160
Franklin, Derek, 125
freedom: fighters, refugees perceived as, 191; of migration, 42. *See also* Mau Mau
Frere, Governor Sir Henry Bartle, 117, 118. *See also* Freretown

Freretown: from abolitionist mission to civilizing mission, 117–18; from abolition subjects to colonial subjects, 121; anti-slavery operations, 117; confinement and protection in, 121; cultivation in, 114–15; Dadaab, comparison with, 115; liberation ideology and land, 115, 118, 121; mission versus colonial goals, 121–22, 341n36; rescuer-rescued relationship, 115–17. *See also* villagization
frontier (border), 110, 111. *See also* borderlands; Somalia
Fuller, R. Buckminster, 256–57

garden: Hassan's, 103, "multi-storey," 102. *See also* farm
Garissa, 15, 25, 26, 56, 65, 108, 112, 125, 126, 155, 182, 183, 184, 185, 190, 202, 218, 219, 225, 253, 280, 282, 343n57
Geeldoon, Maxamed Xuseen, 23
Gelubba, 124
gendered space, 252
Geneva, 37, 156, 165, 186, 192, 203, 262
Gĩkũyũ, 344n70; highlands and European settlements, 25; landlessness and Mau Mau, 126; village structures and the makuti, 131
global South, 34, 169, 342n38, 347n43
Goethert, Reinhard, 165
Gosha, 75
governance: representative governance and spatial practice, 8; social and political capital, 71. *See also* elections; vote (voting)
grave(s) (tomb), 341n24; architecture of, 79, 80; burial site (mound), 80; marked, 74, 76, 77, 80, 81, 172; and traversal, 73, 79, 80, 81, 85
Greater Somalia, 23, 109–110, 112, 124
GTZ. *See* Deutsche Gesellschaft für Technische Zusammenarbeit (GTZ)

"Habitat" conference, 164
Hadraawi, 47, 305, 319
Hagadera, 99, 112, 329n12; camp, planning and settlement of, 46, 47
Hamdi, Nabeel, 165
Handbook for Emergencies, 164, 166, 348n54, 348n61
Haraway, Donna, 189
Harrell-Bond, Barbara, 162, 165
Hartman, Saidiya, 80, 181
Hassan, Maganai Saddiq, 2, 46, 75, 102, 103–6, 107, 113, 115, 116, 127
Hecht, Gabrielle, 259
Henni, Samia, 127, 309
Hijra, 269
historiography, 315, 319
Ho, Engseng, 80
homemaking, 4, 321, 346n26; Abshir's perspective, 307; coercion and collaboration in, 149, 150, 172; in emergency, 142, 144, 147, 149, 176, 176–77, 177; expertise in, 170; and graves, 172; shelter versus, 161, 177. *See also* domesticity(ies), Farah, Shamso Abdullahi; insurgent domesticities; worldmaking
hooks, bell, 144, 145, 189
hôpital gonflable. *See* inflatable hospital
Horst, Cindy, 54, 207, 208
hotel (restaurant), 354n4; collaboration between Somali and Sudanese women, 251, 253
Howard, Jim, 269
humanitarian alibi, 30
humanitarian environments, 256
humanitarian expertise, 160–67
humanitarian iconography, 257, 260, 268; as commodity, 255; as signature emergency artifact, 255
humanitarian intervention: international, 30; and partition, 92; and shifta struggle, 123; and sovereignty, 90, 92; against violation of the individual, 92, 339n66
humanitarianism: capitalistic practices and, 32; Christian liberatory, rehabilitative, 26–27; and development, 26; and imperialism, 121–22; and migration, 32; militaristic, 89, 90; and sedentarization, 26
humanitarian knowledge, 150, 162, 163, 166, 168, 169
humanitarian objects: design histories of, 255; commodification of, 257

humanitarian paradox, 30
humanitarian principles of liberation, 115
humanitarians and refugees, 116
humanitarian settlement(s): aid distribution point, Ifo camp, *240*; blocks and sectors, 224–25; CARE documents, 201; CARE food distribution sheds, Ifo camp, *232*; Dagahaley market, *229*; demarcated territory, transformation into, 99; distribution center, Ifo camp, *232*, *234*, *235*, *236*, *238–39*; distribution of amenities and facilities, 225; emergency and development, tensions between, 200–201; expansion plans in 2006, 218–19; food and water distribution, *229*, 230; food ration chart, *233*; Hagadera market, *230*; Ifo camp, water tap stand, *231*; market place, the driving force, 225, *226–27*, *228*; physical planning versus architectural development, 204; planning process, 194; proximity to food distribution center, 230, 231; ration card, Ifo camp, *237*; ration card, importance of, 243–44; rations distribution system, 242, 243; spatial organization, 224–25; storage warehouses, 242; transitional settlements, 192; warehouse, Ifo camp, *233*
humanitarian space, 251; camp, 2, 6; constructed environment and humanitarian spatiality, 33; emergency response and, 32, 333n65; explained, 30; first settlement, 9; Ifo, 2; military humanitarianism, 89–90; realizing, 31
humanitarian spatiality, 250, 260, 265; and architects and planners, 30–31, 348n61; and constructed environment, 33; Dadaab as an iteration of, 33, 181, 199, 245, 250, 260; emergency territory and, 207, 245; end of Cold War and, 31–32; ephemeral architectures and, 297; explained, 30–31; human rights and, 31, 333n61; institutionalization of, 32, 250; and underdevelopment, 32. *See also* inflatable hospital; MSF Logistique; tank(s); tarp (tarpaulin); tent
human rights: discourses and territory, 45; experiments in settlements, 117–18; individual as metric of rights, 92; movement and architects, 36; NGOs, 30; transgression of sovereignty, 29, 92, 339n66
Hunt, Lynn, 93
Hutu, 207 225, 261, 274

Ibrahim, Rhoda, 133
ICRC. *See* International Committee of the Red Cross (ICRC)
identity politics, 111
Ifo camp: aid distribution point, *240*; CARE sheds, *232*; Cawo Aden Yeru, 266, *267*; Cawo Jube, *19*, *73*; distribution point, *62*, *232*, *233*, *235*, *236*, *237*, *238–39*; hotel, Somali and Sudanese women's, *247*, 251, 253; makuti, *130*; market in, 36, *64*, 336n7; NRC's shelter initiative, 158; Oxfam water tank, *270*, *272*; photo of, *97*; planning and settlement of, 46, 47; plans drawn up for, *212*, *213*; provisions shop, *viii–ix*; self-sustenance, constraints for, 252; shelter initiative in, 46; soccer match spectators, *72*; store and shelter, Farah's design, *139*, 150, *151*, *153*, *171*; tuqul, *133*, *174*; UNHCR aerial view of, 11; water tap stand, *62*, *231*; WFP food storage unit, *233*, *174*
Ifo 2 camp: background, 147–48, *148*, 217, 225; collaborative domesticities in, 149; description, 148–49; IKEA donation to, 256; unofficial inhabitation, 149
IFRC. *See* International Federation of Red Cross and Red Crescent Societies (IFRC)
Iheka, Cajetan, 5
Ikanda, Fred, 207
IKEA: donation, 256; shelter, 275
imperialism: and antislavery movement, 117; cultural, 41; history of, in East Africa, 41; through humanitarian settlement, 117; manyatta, and use of, 114; migration, impact on, 23, 128; partitioning of land, 74, 108, 112; revolutions, suppression of, 114
incarceration: carceral means to sedentarization, 46; carceral migration, 40; and migration, 41–42; of nomads and pastoralists, 111, 128, 129; Odowa, 329n2; "open-air prison," Dadaab as, 2; refugee camps and, 129. *See also* enclosures; manyatta; villagization

incentive: inequality in pay, 68, 335n6; scheme, 54, 55; wages, 280; work, 68, 69; workers, 58, 102; workers' frustration, 68
India, 27, 33, 56, 76, 117, 260, 336n18, 341n28, 342n44
inflatable hospital: construction process, 283; as covering local and global territory, 287–88; description, 282–83; as mobile architecture, 291; optics, use for, 286–87; photographs, *284*, 285, 286, *288*, *289*
infrastructure: design as, 252; ephemeral, 297–301; people as, 252; signature, 294, 296; for transport and communication in Dadaab, 17
inhabitation, 4, 138, 268, 274; approaches to, 22, 142; domesticities and, 146, 172, 177, 310; migration and sedentary forms of, 77, 99, 100; of refugees in Dadaab, 17, 76, 100, 122, 149
"Insecurities: Tracing Displacement and Shelter," 268
Institut de Recherche pour le Développement (IRD), 211, 215
insurgent domesticities, 14, 46, 141, 181, 310, 332n38, 345n5; emergency homemakers and, 146; as expertise, 149–50; in Ifo 2, 147–49; study of social differences working group, 345n5
interior, 142, 172, 175, 220; camp, 63, 79, 81, 102; colonization of, 22, 25, 31, 115, 341n25. *See also* United Nations High Commissioner for Refugees (UNHCR): and family tent
interiority, 142, 146, 159
International Committee of the Red Cross (ICRC), 37, 264, *264*, 265, 295
International Federation of Red Cross and Red Crescent Societies (IFRC), 37, 276, 278
International Rescue Committee (IRC), 34, 36, 37, 56, 219
Intertect, 163, 164
intimacy: environments of, 181; labor, 39; provided by tuqul, 27; scholarly, 33,43, 138, 144
IRD. *See* Institut de Recherche pour le Développement (IRD)
Ireland, 53, 336n18
Iwansson, Per, 99, 195, 210, 254, 271

Jain, Kajri, 33
Jansen, Bram, 83
Jordan, 254; al-Za'atari camp in, 251
Journal of Refugee Studies, 165
Jubaland partitioning, 74–75, 336n18

Kambioos, 2, 9
Karanja, Kabage, 316, 361n16
Kashmir, 24
Kat River Settlement, 117
Katz, Irit, 77, 78
Kaur, Ravinder, 274
Keinan, Hashim ("Abdullahi"), 6, 150–55, 347n35, 356n26
Kennedy, Hollyamber, 78, 101
Kennedy, James, 215, 217, 225, 353n60, 353n71
Keshavarz, Mahmoud, 82
Khadiagala, Gilbert M, 111
Khalif, Najib, 338n48, 338n52
khat (narcotic), 70
Kibera, 309
Kikuyu, *123*, 125. *See also* Gĩkũyũ
Kimbimbi, S., 206
kinship(s), 342n36; as an act of domesticity, 160; in camp, 15; contingent, 149; between refugees and hosts, 15, 51; women forging, 251
kipande (kitambulisho): explained, 57, 58, 336n8; implications of, 58, 60; importance of, 81, 82–83, *83*; and mobility, 25; movement pass, *58*; paper infrastructure, 82, *83*; under UNHCR purview, 82–83
Kismayo, 54, 192, 205, 206
Kiswahili, xvi, 15, 82, 89, 115
kitambulisho. *See* kipande (kitambulisho)
Klein, Naomi, 161
knowledge, desubjugation of, 144
Kobe, 259–61
Koenigsberger, Otto, 160, 163, 167
Kouchner, Bernard, 291, 295, 360n89
Krapf, Reverend Johann Ludwig, 115, 253, 254, 341n24, 341n36

Lake Nyasa, 115, 116
land: abolitionist cultivation of, 46; capitalization, 114; cultivation and cultural capital, 115; demarcation, 109; as sedimenting forms of difference, 101, 343n54
landscape: of the built environment, 79; between camps, 66, 220–22 *221*; of communication hardware, 207–8; of Dadaab, 17, 27, 28, 29, 54, 143, 188, 189, 204, 215, 255, 280, 310; Dagahaley, Hassan's impact on, 46, 75, 100, 105; makuti, 131; of migrations, 51, 206; of tarps, tents, and camps, 32, 47
Lange, Unni, 158
Larkin, Brian, 255
La Sarraz, 165
Le Corbusier, 256, 282
Lee, Rachel, 145, 167
liberalism, 90
liberal state, 143
liberatory settlement. *See* Freretown
lightweight emergency tent (LWET), 276, 279. *See also* family tent
Lisbon earthquake of 1775, 93–94, 256
living off and on land: critical heritage, creation of, 102; and ecological problems, 101; emergencies and, 108; Hassan's farm, pedagogy of, 107; scarcity of resources, 101
Livingstone, David, 116
logistics system. *See* MSF Logistique
Lolachi, Manoucher, 278
Lopez, Sarah, 5, 79
Lorde, Audre, 42, 335nn92–93
Lowe, Lisa, 121
LWET. *See* lightweight emergency tent (LWET)

Maa, 124
Maasai, 13
Mackinnon Road, 118
Mahmood, Saba, 4
Makerere University in Kampala, 162
Mäki, Elsa MH, 316, *317*, 319
makuti: adapted to the modern and sedentary, 135; appearance, *130*; construction of, 46, 131; contingency and enclosure, 131; Native Hut Tax, 131, 135; traditional dwelling, 27; tuqul, comparison with, 27, 135
Malawi, 165
Malkki, Liisa, 273
Mamdani, Mahmood, 85
manyatta, 113–14, 122, *123*, 131, 340n20. *See also* enclosures; incarceration; villagization
Mapela, Jean-Pierre, 280, 281, 282, 292, 294, 301
market(s): bomb explosion in, 69; at Dadaab, 15–17; Dadaab town and camp markets, comparison, 36, 55, 64; description of, 63, *63*; labor in, 69
Martin, Reinhold, 273
MASH. *See* mobile army surgical hospital (MASH)
matatus, 66, 336n9
material culture(s), 44, 159, 207, 259
Materia Medica Minimalis, 292
Mau Mau: detention of, 114, 122, 123, 126, 309; Gĩkũyũ country, 126; Land and Freedom Army, 125; Land and Freedom movement, 26, 111, 123, 340n15. *See also* manyatta
Mbembe, Achille, 87, 93
McCallister, Meghan, 53
McKittrick, Katherine, 7
Médecins Sans Frontières (Doctors Without Borders) (MSF), 38, 262, 280, 295, 357n38; architecture of logistics (*see* MSF Logistique); staff security, 222
Mendoza, Elis, 167
Mérignac, 37, 282, 292, 294
Merti aquifer, *18*, 20, *318*, 319; compromised, 17, 319; Dadaab built environment, support for, 17, 24, 25, 144; freshwater yield, 17; pastoralists and, 24–25
Mezzadra, Sandro, 77
microcredit program, women's partnership and, 251
migration, 310, *314*; versus colonialism, 108; foreclosure of, 43, 128, 129; histories and critical theory, 143; and nation-state, 108, 128; open, 76–77, 129; sedentarization, 99, 100; and space and time, 145. *See also* criminalization of the nomadic and the pastoral

Migrations (Adam), 309–10, *314*
migration(s), feminist architectural, 145
Mijikenda, 115, 131, 135
miraa. *See* khat (narcotic)
Mire, Sada, 21, 34
Mishamo camp, 273
mission(s): and land capitalization, 114; liberatory settlement, 114–122; for maintenance of order, 90; and rehabilitation of freed slaves, 26; religious/Christian missions, 26, 114, 115; villagization, contrast with, 122; visits, 36. *See also* Bombay Africans; Freretown; Rabai mission; Sitrep No. 7
mobile architectures, 28, 37, 47, 55, 173, 242, 250, 256, 258, 291, 294. *See also* food storage unit; inflatable hospital; shelter: single-family; tuqul (aqal, waab)
mobile army surgical hospital (MASH), 291
mobility: between camps, 65–66; Freretown, in, 121; kipande document and, 82; and manyatta, 114, *123*, 131; restrictions to, 112, 128; security and, 66–67. *See also* incarceration; villagization
Mogadishu, 269
Moi, Daniel Arap, 128, 206
Mombasa, 112, 114, 116, 121, 131, 182, 183, 184, 185, 187, 192, 205, 205, 206, 218
Momić, Maja, 146
Mora-Castro, D., 210
moral economy: for domestication of Africa, 118; Freretown as prelude to, 122; and infrastructure, 277; of migration, 100; modern humanitarian, 86
mother(s), 38, 39, 46, 142, 147, 150, 162, 175, 222, 231, 251, 268
MSF. *See* Médecins Sans Frontières (Doctors Without Borders) (MSF)
MSF Logistique, 36, 37, 38; fleet management, as design innovation, 294; hôpital gonflable (inflatable hospital), *281*, 282–92, *284*, *285*, *286*, *288–89*, 290, 291; humanitarian orientation, 280; medical kit, 292; signature practice of, 262, 295; warehouses of, 295–97
"multi-storey gardens," 102
Mursan, Habiba Abdurahman, 297–301
Musée d'Art Moderne, 291
Museum of Modern Art (MoMA), 268
Mutegi, Stella, 316
Muzaffar, Ijlal, 161
mythico-history, 273

Nagoya, 260
Naimou, Angela, 143
Nairobi, 199, 280; checkpoints, 57; highway connection to Dadaab, 218; International Technical Advisers, Ltd., 195; Native Hut Tax, 131; Sitrep No. 7, 186; University of Nairobi, 309; Wilson Airport, 56, *219*
nationalism, Somali, 110
Ndaliko, Chérie Rivers, 250
Neumann, Wolfgang, 165, 173, 192, 199, 260, 276
NFD. *See* Northern Frontier District (NFD)
Ngara District, 261, 262
Nielsen, Brett, 77
Nile River, 116
Ningbo, 278
nomadism: confinement of nomads, 26; criminalization of, 27; and tuqul, 20
Northern Frontier District (NFD): complex demographics of, 124; Kikuyu and, 123, 125; plebiscite in, 124, 342n44; secession history, 124–25; state of emergency, 125; state sovereignty in opposition to self-determination, 124
Norway, 159, 165, 170, 173
Norwegian Refugee Council (NRC), 298, 299
NRC. *See* Norwegian Refugee Council (NRC)
NRC shelter(s): architectural expertise, 156, 157; initiative in Dadaab, 68, 150, 156–58; issues related to, 158–59
Nyerere, Julius, 126

OAU. *See* Organisation of African Unity (OAU)
Obarrio, Juan, 316
Okoye, Ikem Stanley, 25
Oliver, Kelly, 93
Omani: chiefs and treaties with British Navy, 117; farmers, 121

Ophir, Adi, 144, 279
Organisation of African Unity (OAU), 14, 109, 110, 191, 193 350n9
Origins (Adam), 309–10, *311*
Osayimwese, Itohan, 316
Osman, Alishine Hussein, 2, 40, 45, 53, 75, 76, 78, 79, 80, 81, 82, 84, 85, 86, 88, 157, 158, 166, 168, 169, 170, 173, 308; about, 54; arrival in Dadaab, 54, 56; on building tuqul, 68; on citizenship, 58–61; on distribution of rations, 61, *62*; education and citizenship in the United States, 56–57; on elections, 69–71; on governance and social and political capital, 71; on incentive work, 69; on inequality in wages, 68; on kipande and mobility, 58–61, 65–66, *67*; life in Ifo and education, 54, 56, 57; on refugee card, 61, *62*; security, 66–67; on telecommunications in the camp, 72; on water distribution, 63, *64*
othering: race, 86; racial act of doubling, 87–89, 338n59
otherness, northeast, 24
"otherwise, an," 145, 345n12
otherwise, ethically, 144
Owuor, Yvonne Adhiambo, 51
Oxfam water tank: designed for adaptation, 268–69, 357n48; domination of space, 271; in Ifo camp, 270, 272; origin of, 269–71; signature design, 269; synecdochal role, 271, 273–74
Oxford Brookes University. *See* Oxford Polytechnic (Oxford Brookes University)
Oxford Polytechnic (Oxford Brookes University), 163, 165
Oxford Refugee Studies Centre (Oxford Refugee Studies Programme), 162, 165, 241
Ozaki, Ana G., 121

Pakistan, 76, 79, 165, 195, 264, 276, 277, 283
Palais des Nations, 165
Palestine, 28, 39, 53, 74, 78
Pandolfi, Mariella, 191, 257
Paper Arbor, 260
Paris, 38, 291
Parker, Jean "Jinx," 163
partitioning: capitalism and mobility, 100; enclosure of common land, 99–100; settlement and unsettlement, 100
partitions, 308, 310, *312*, 315; architecture and, 78–79; borders and, 77–78; cemetery and the breakdown of, 79; division of land in Dadaab, 78; indivisibility of land, 78–81; open migration and, 76–77; paper infrastructures of, 81–84; reflected and enacted, 92; in scholarship, 75–76. *See also* partition(s) of land; partition(s) of the self; partition thinking
Partitions (Adam), 309–10, *312*
partition(s) of land: and architecture of migration, 53; India-Pakistan, 78, 79, 308; Jubaland partitioning, 74–75; migration, a form of inhabitation, 76–77; the refugee and the camp, 76; underlying principle in refugee camps, 74
partition(s) of the self: Black self, 92–93; community-based division, 84–85; and elections, 85; as experienced versus as recognized, 88; external perception, influence on, 86–87; and individuation, 93; influence of partition of communities on, 86; Lisbon earthquake of 1775, 93–94; need for modern subjecthood, 87; and partition of land, 94; racial act of doubling, othering, 87; racialization in architecture, 86–87; racinated, 93; racination in, 86; refugee recognition process, 86–87; refugee status and, 88; situated practice, disaster response, 94
partition thinking: afterlife of partitions, 94–95; architecture of a tomb, 79; cohabitation forms in emergency, 89; conceptual and material construct, 51; ethnic community as structural unit, 85–86; forms of, 52–53; humanitarian "incentive" scheme, 54–55; kipande, importance of, 81, 82–83, *83*; liberation from, 53; people's power and political authority, 84–85; practices of traversals in, 84; principle of originary partition, 78; in refugee camps, 51; in refugee recognition, 86; reinscribing practice, 78; safety concerns, 66–68, *67*; between state and camp, 55

Peace of Westphalia, 92
Pequena África, Rio de Janeiro, 121
Perroud, Gilles, 294, 295
Pessac: workers' housing in, 282
Pierce, Steven, 86
Pinel, Jacques, 263, 292, 295, 301
planetary framework, 143, 316
pneumatic(s), 291; architecture, 292; rolls, 283
Pollock, Griselda, 44
Popular Mechanics, 291
Povinelli, Elizabeth, 144
prefabrication, 157, 256, 257, 262
prisons, Dadaab settlements as, 2. *See also* incarceration
Pritzker Architecture Prize, 260
Puar, Jasbir K., 90
Puig de la Bellacasa, Maria, 189
Pumzika café, 89, 90, *91*, 255
Purpura, Allyson, 20

Qingdao Gyoha Plastics, 266
Quilombos. *See* Freretown
Quonset hut, 276

Rabai mission, 26, 115–17, 341n25
race: definition, 86; othering, 86, 338n59; and religious or ideological differences, 90; terrorist, 90
racialization: in architecture, 87; in emergency, 87
Rage, Isnina Ali, 2, 5–8; Chairlady of Ifo camp, 5; in conversation with, 6–7; on election process, 6–7; refugee camp representative governance, 7–8; women's role, revelations on, 7–8
Rao, Anupama, 86, 125
rations: distribution points, 63; food distribution and power dynamics, 61–63; ration card, 81–82
Rebmann, Johannes, 115
recognition: establishing to gain trust, 40; of nationalism for colonized Africans, 110; partition(s) of the self, 53, 86–87, 308; in a refugee context, 52; of refugee in partition thinking, 86; refugee status, process for, 84–85, 86–87; UNHCR and refugees, 84
Red Cross, 257, 292
Redding, Stephen, 200
Redfield, Peter, 263, 275, 280, 292
refugee: changing perceptions of, 291; fugitive, 143; and migrant, 3; models of, 76; mother, 142, 150, 162, 231; territory, 55
"Refugee Camp in the Heart of the City," 287, *287*
refugee camps: architecture for social control, 194–95; asymmetries and conflicts, aggravation of, 205; critical heritage, site of, 187; curfew rules, 220, *221*, 222; Dagahaley and Hagadera settlements, 195; definition, 1; design and construction, 188, 189, 199; East African context, 23–24; enduring architecture in, 204–5; expansion plans in 2006 in Dadaab, 209–10; fixing asymmetry in space, 205–9; graphic documentation in Dadaab, 209–10; "ground view," 189; humanitarian settlements in Dadaab, 22; living and cultural spaces, demarcation of, 206; long-term planning process, 194–95; main and secondary roads, 220; management evolution into governance, 201; official visitors' flights to Dadaab, *219*, 219–20; overview map, *10*, *11*, *12*, *13*; paradoxes of, 2; primary sources versus "official" archives, 188; security for UNHCR personnel, 222; settlement, strategy for, 194; site selection, 192–93; taar (telegram or cable), use of, 207; tuqul constructions, early weeks, 194; UNHCR first settlement, 193–94; UNHCR maps, *193*; UNHCR team of 1991, 192–93; vegetation as area demarcation, 220, *221*
refugees, perspectives on, 191
refugee status: acquisition of ration card, 61, *62*; benefits of, 60; eligibility and intelligibility, 88; eligibility criteria, 88–89; inequality in employment, 68–69; international instruments relating to, 191; and partition thinking, 86; process for recognition, 86–87; refugee card, 60–61; refugee rations, 62; registration benefits, 61; UNHCR role in determination of, 84
Rehman, Nida, 79

Rendille, 23, 124
Ripon, Bishop of, 118
Rizvi, Kishwar, 79
Rockson, Garage, 294
Rodney, Walter, 28, 32, 53, 127
Roy, Arundhati, 147
Royal Geographical Society, 117
Ruiz, Rafico, 204
Rusumo Bridge, 261
Rwanda, 34, 167, 260, 261, 261, 262

Sabbagh, Mahdi, 53
"SAFE: Design Takes on Risk," 268
Said, Edward, 39
Sakuye, 124
Samburu, 23, 113, 134
Schellenberg, Werner, 195, 199, 210–11
Scott-Smith, Tom, 275
sedentarization, 25–28, 309, 315; colonial, postcolonial, and humanitarian use of territory, 25–26; colonial approaches in East Africa, 99; kipande passes and mobility, 25; labor camps, 26; land emergency and, 48; makuti hut versus tuqul, 27; manyatta or village, 26; migratory worlds and, 2; obscured by humanitarian activities, 123; of pastoralists, 26–27; villagization, 26
Seethaler-Wari, Shahd, 146
self-help, 252
self-help housing, 160–61; using indigenous knowledge, 164
Sen, Uditi, 76
settlement: coercive, 113, 122–130; liberatory, 113, 114–122; versus migration, 100; settler colonial empire, similarities and contrasts with, 115
Seventh Man, A (Berger), 39
shambas (farm plots): Dagahaley camp, similarity to, 115; in Freretown, 118; visits to, 102
shelter, *148*, 258; aim of, 141; CARE, 156; and critical theory, 144; and domesticity, 141, 142–47, 160, 161, 162; emergency, 165; history of, 142; and land, 175; methodology for domesticity, 141; NRC in Dadaab, 156–59; NRC's initiative and Osman's position, 68; open-air prison, 2; single-family, 173. *See also* domesticity(ies); homemaking; makuti; tuqul (aqal, waab)
Shelter Design Catalogue (UNHCR), 278
shifta, 309; criminalized, 124; detentions village, 113; etymology and meaning, 124; incarceration of, 113; Mau Mau, historical parallel to, 123, 125, 126; mobility, 127–28; pastoralists and Somalis, term used for, 124; villagization and, 125, 126, 127, 128; Wagalla Massacre of 1984, 123
Shringarpure, Bhakti, 309, 361n10
Siedlungen, 148
signature: emergency artifact, 255; form-making, 251
signature practice(s), 47, 249, 268, 276, 279, 295, 296, 297, 301, 315; spectrum of, 259–66; systems and, 257–59, 356nn27–28. *See also* family tent; inflatable hospital; MSF Logistique; Oxfam water tank; tank(s); tarp (tarpaulin)
signifier: aesthetic, 255; of ephemerality, 258; of nation-state, 170; Oxfam water tank as, 271–73; tents as, 173. *See also* symbol
SIGUS. *See* Special Interest Group in Urban Settlements (SIGUS)
Simone, AbdouMaliq, 252
Sitrep No. 7, *179*, 182–85, 190; architect appointment information, 187; archival fragility of, 186–87; founding document, 187
Sliwinski, Sharon, 93–94
Smirl, Lisa, 255
Smith, Linda Tuhiwai, 41
Somali, 9, 15, 36, 89; chiefs and treaties with British Navy, 117, 121, 205; demographics in Dadaab camp, 14–15, 52, 75, 84, 103, 124, 129, 208–9, 225; Hadraawi (poet), 47, 305, 319; migration, history of, 23; networks, 16, 110, 207; routes to Dadaab, 205, 209, 217, 218–22. *See also* Abshir, Deqa; belonging; citizenship; emergency territory; fixing symmetry in space; Hassan, Maganai Saddiq; Jubaland partitioning; Mursan, Habiba Abdurahman; Osman, Alishine Hussein; shifta; Sitrep No. 7; tuqul (aqal, waab); United Nations High Commissioner for Refugees (UNHCR)

Somalia. *See* Greater Somalia; Somali; Somali history
Somali Bantu, 102, 103
Somali history, 22–24, 45, 74–75, 84, 109–12; frontier/borderlands, politics of, 9, 26, 74, 90, 92, 108, 110–12, 124, 128, 343n70. *See also* Jubaland partitioning
Soomaliweyn, 309
Soviet Union, 31
spatial history, 123
spatial politics, 3, 259, 287; architecture and, 27; in the northeast, 24, 122–24; social capital and, 71; tuqul and gendered, 135
spatial practice, 30, 33, 204, 250, 251, 301; humanitarian, 32, 251; humanitarian architecture as, 134–35, 141, 250, 251; representative governance and, 8; of sedentarization, 99, 107, 108; as shelter, 146, 167, 250. *See also* colonial spatial practice
spatial resistance, 292
spatial violence, 43, 127, 316; architecture, 316; colonial practice of dislocation, 127; land and, 101
Special Interest Group in Urban Settlements (SIGUS), 162–63, 165
Sphere Project consortium, 167
Stanićić, Aleksandar, 250
Strayer, Robert, 118
Structures Gonflables, 290–91, 291–92. *See also* inflatable hospital
subaltern and refugee urbanism, 20
subjugated knowledges, 144, 145
subsistence farming, 102–3
Susi, Abdullah, 116, *116*, 117, 253, 254
Swahili: caravans, 115; coast, 116
Swynnerton Plan, 126
symbol: tent as, 173; tuqul as, 135, 307

taar (telegram or cable), 207
tahriib, definition, 23
Tamale, Sylvia, 4
tank(s), 249, 254, 257, 265; water, 195, 199, 255, 282. *See also* Oxfam water tank
Tanzania, 261, 273
tarp (tarpaulin), 249, 254, 257, 265; description, 266; design, 268; used for dwellings, 245; use of in burial, 266
Tata, J. R. D., 163
Taylor, Martin L., 212
tent, 27, 56, 242, 259, 260, 265, 356n31–32; as symbol, 173. *See also* family tent
territory: British imperial territory, 25; circumscription into, 22; co-constructed territory, 5; colonial and postcolonial practices, 45, 52, 74; colonial negotiations over, 24; construction of emergency territory, 25, 45; Dadaab as ghost space, 26, 46; humanitarian intervention in sovereignty, 29, 31; insecurity around constructions of, 125; land as, 52; pastoralists, concept of, 52; political territory, 24; production and reproduction of, 79; sovereign territory and human rights, 92, 339n66; territorial constructions and sense of belonging, 23; territorial delineations, 85; territorialization of British East Africa, 118; traversal of, 78, 79
Terry, Fiona, 296
Thailand, 291
theory, 5, 6, 21, 44, 54, 80, 257, 305, 333nn60–61; architecture of migration as, 44; critical, 142, 143, 144, 149; Dadaab, in, 33–39, 44, 45, 145, 146, 306; of domesticity, 141, 146, 147, 172, 177, 315; of enclosure, 115; feminist, 37, 42, 160; human rights, 92, 339n66; legal, 20; refugee camp and limitations of, 53; of shelter, 46, 149, 177
Thiong'o, Ngũgĩ wa, 127
Thomson, Marnie, 207
Ticktin, Miriam, 92
tomb. *See* grave(s) (tomb)
Toyota Land Cruiser, 263, *293*; fleet management, 294
traversals: across camp boundaries, 172; across partitions in Dadaab, 55; architecture as representation of traversal, 73; a case for discussion of, 54; collaborative knowledge of, 54; Ifo to other camps,

65–66; Ifo to UNHCR, 66; international visitor and refugee, 66–68, *67*; migration as knowledge of, 85. *See also* grave(s) (tomb)
Trim, D. J. B., 92
Tropical Architecture School, 163
Trouillot, Michel-Rolph, 6, 8, 43
Tsing, Anna, 143
tuqul (aqal, waab), 169, 173–74, *174*; appearance, *132*, *133*, *134*, 173–74, *174*; construction of, 46, 132–35; contingency and enclosure, 131; contrast to makuti hut, 27; Dadaab, architectural symbol of, 135; Dagahaley camp periphery, *136–137*; description of, 19; first shelters, 68; gendered architecture, 27; knowledge and cultural practice, 21, 27; makuti, comparison with, 135; and mobility, 133; modernization and sedentarization, resistance to, 135–36; racialized architectural form, 86; recalcitrant architecture, 331n29; significance in Dadaab, 19–20; as symbol, 135, 307; women, role of, 131–34
Turkey, 260
Turner, John F. C., 160, 163
Tutsi, 261
Tyrwhitt, Jacqueline, 160

Uganda Railway, 118
underdevelopment, 28–33, 308; development and, 28–29; humanitarian culture, post–World War II, 29–30; role of nongovernmental activity, 30; of self, 53
United Nations Children's Fund (UNICEF), 185, 203
United Nations Disaster Relief Office (UNDRO), 163, 166
United Nations High Commissioner for Refugees (UNHCR): camp architecture, 204; construction processes, systematization of, 258; distribution area procedures, 241; emergency territory, establishment of, 190–200, 245; and family tent, 274–276, *275*; first settlement, 193–194; ideal residential module, 199; issuance of passes, 84; kipande, 82; largest hosting operation, 2, 329n1; LWET design, 277–278; organization of compound, 222, *223*, *224*; Paper Emergency Shelters, *261*; planned maps, *193*; protection of refugee rights, role in, 83; quasi-sovereignty over Dadaab, 86; refugee status, role in determination of, 84; security for personnel, 222; *Shelter Design Catalogue*, 2016 family tent model, 278–80; team of 1991, 192–93; from traversals to Ifo, 66
United States, 31, 33, 42, 54, 56, 57, 90, 165, 170, 203, 286
Universal Declaration of Rights, 92
University College London, 163
University of the Witwatersrand, Johannesburg, 162
Urban Settlement Design Program, 162
Utopie, 290, 291–92

Verdirame, Giulielmo, 206
villagization: architecture of detention and correction, 127; barbed-wire fencing, 127–28; Dadaab, similarities with, 122; detention, tool for, 122; Freretown, similarities with, 122; manyattas, 122, *123*; "multi-storey gardens" in Dagahaley, similarities with, 122; punitive measures under guise of "development," 127; purpose of, 122; sedentarization prioritized over pastoral subsistence, 126; of shifta, 125; and underdevelopment, 126. *See also* manyatta
Vindiciae contra tyrannos, 92
VITRA (furniture company), 260
vote (voting): mechanism of democracy, 8; plebiscite in the northeast, 24, 111; against communism, 191. *See also* elections

waab. *See* tuqul (aqal, waab)
Wähning, Sabine, 165, 192, 199, 210, 253
war: civil war, Somalia, 56, 109, 191, 192; Cold War dynamics, 90, 111, 162, 163, 166, 271; emergency response to, 315; humanitarian settlements, 22; Ogaden War, 110; shifta, 124, 126, 129, 309, 340n15; World War I, 24, 74, 102, 256; World War II, 29, 191, 291

Warah, Rasna, 22
warehouses, *230*, 233, 282, 292; MSF Logistique's, *286*, 294, 296, *296*
water distribution: Dagahaley, 2, 9, 46; Sector A, Ifo, 64, *64*, 65
water pipeline, *272*
Weissmann, Ernest, 160
Weitzberg, Keren, 24, 110, 124, 125
Weizman, Eyal, 77
Wellington, Mark, 117
Wendel, Delia, 34
WFP. *See* World Food Programme (WFP)
Whittaker, Hannah, 124, 127
Wilson, Mabel O., 27, 87
women's cooperatives, 297–301
Women's Refugee Commission (WRC), 34, 35, 36, 56, 89, 210, 231, 280, 291
World Design Expo, 260
World Food Programme (WFP), 36, 56, 61, *91*, 106, 107, 173, *174*, 185, *233*, 242, 244, 255
World Health Organization, 39, 295
worldmaking, 4, 254, 274, 306. *See* domesticity(ies); homemaking
World War I, 256
WRC. *See* Women's Refugee Commission (WRC)
Wynter, Sylvia, 29, 32

Yeru, Cawo Aden, 266–*67*
Young, Bethany, 35, 40, 102, 150, 192, 231, 253, 297
Yugoslavia, 165

Zamindar, Vazira, 75, 76, 77
Zarins, Jake, 158
Zetter, Roger, 165